PELICAN BOOKS

BRITAIN AND HER ARMY

Correlli Barnett, military historian, was born in London in 1927. He was educated at Trinity School and Exeter College, Oxford, where he received a second-class honours degree in modern history. From 1945 to 1948 he served in the Army. He spent eleven years from 1952 in public relations, first in industry, then in advertising. For his scripts in the BBC television *Great War* series, he won the 1964 Screen Writers' Guild Award for the best British television documentary script. Among his previous books are *The Desert Generals* (1960) and *The Swordbearers* (1963), which both won high praise, and which were translated into five languages. He is a Fellow of the Royal Society of Literature.

CORRELLI BARNETT

Britain and Her Army
1509-1970

A MILITARY, POLITICAL AND SOCIAL SURVEY

PENGUIN BOOKS

Penguin Books Ltd, Harmondsworth, Middlesex, England
Penguin Books Australia Ltd, Ringwood, Victoria, Australia

First published by Allen Lane The Penguin Press 1970
Published in Pelican Books 1974
Copyright © Correlli Barnett, 1970

Made and printed in Great Britain by
Richard Clay (The Chaucer Press) Ltd,
Bungay, Suffolk
Set in Monotype Baskerville

To the memory of
Eric O'Gowan (Dorman-Smith)

Other books by Correlli Barnett

The Desert Generals (1960)

The Swordbearers (1963)

Contents

List of Maps
and Line Illustrations

LINE ILLUSTRATIONS

List of Plates

Acknowledgements

A historical march as long as this is a hazardous undertaking; and the bibliography records my debt to the work of other historians on particular periods or aspects of military history.

My grateful thanks are due to Professor G. R. Elton for his advice on military and constitutional questions under the Tudors, and to Dr Greig Barr for his kindness in reading and criticizing that section of the typescript which deals with the Stuarts and the Commonwealth.

My particular gratitude is due to two outstanding authorities on the history of the British army who were kind enough to read and comment upon the entire typescript, and save me thereby from many errors and omissions: the late Sir Basil Liddell Hart and Mr D. W. King.

I wish to express my appreciation of the courtesy and helpfulness of the Director of Public Relations (Army) and the staffs of the Central Library, Ministry of Defence, the Royal United Service Institution Library, the London Library, the University of East Anglia Library and the Norwich City Library.

I would also like to thank Mrs Robyn Wallis for her resourcefulness in finding the illustrations.

And finally I would like to thank my wife, not only for reading and criticizing the draft narrative but also for her advice, patience and support throughout the preparation of the book.

Introduction

The importance of war and military institutions has been generally neglected in British historical writing, whose tone has been set by the Whig and liberal emphasis on peaceful constitutional progress. In this liberal view war appears as an aberration, an interruption of a 'natural' condition of peace: almost as a form of delinquency unworthy of intellectual attention. The liberal, pacifistic view of history can only be maintained by resolute aversion of the gaze from the facts. For conflict between tribal or social groups and nations constitutes the essential human condition in the absence of a world-state with a monopoly of force. The relations between nation states have always been those of a struggle for advantage and domination, where friendships may indeed burgeon while interests temporarily coincide, but then again languish when those interests diverge. Peace and war in history flow continually in and out of each other, alternative aspects of the single phenomenon of the struggle for power. It is false and unrealistic therefore to divide policy between hard-and-fast categories of 'peace' and 'war'. Policy may shade all the way from trade and diplomatic rivalry through indirect conflict and limited war to total war; the distinctions are of degree, not of kind.

In the case of British history itself, Whig and liberal historians have contrasted what they believe to be the orderly evolution of parliamentary institutions and economic progress with the wars and armies and tyrannies of Europe. Even contemporary historians, except Marxists, tend to neglect the roles of force, conflict and war. Yet the course of British history, protected though Britain has been by the sea and the Royal Navy, has been shaped by war and by military institutions. The liberal optimism and pacifism of the nineteenth century themselves were made possible by victory over Napoleon, a victory consummated by a British general and partly by British troops at Waterloo; liberalism was guarded by the largest navy in the world and by a mercenary army more continually in action than any of the armies of the militaristic nations of Europe.

In fact, battles and armies rather than constitutional lawyers or vociferous politicians have often decided the great crises of British history. Bosworth Field established the Tudor monarchy. The quarrel between Charles I and Parliament was settled by war. The monarchy was restored in 1660 by the intervention of soldiers. James II lost his throne and William of Orange gained it because of the attitude taken by the armed forces. The question of military institutions lay at the heart of the constitutional struggles of the seventeenth century. The Hanoverians were preserved in the eighteenth century from Stuart pretenders by the army. India and Canada were won in war; America lost. The way to Victorian industrial and commercial supremacy was opened on Napoleonic battlefields. In the twentieth century the very survival of the British nation has twice depended on mass armies the British never meant to raise.

The history of the British army, then, is the history of the institution that the British have always been reluctant to accept that they needed. It is their geographical situation as an island nation that has made possible this reluctance. On land the survival of the English has never been threatened by anything more formidable than Scots or Welsh tribes. For continental nations, long frontiers common with other powerful nations made it impossible to deny that national existence depended on the army. The national myths of France and Germany allot a central place to the army. The equivalent place in British myth is given to the navy. The navy can and has assured British survival; but it is only of limited value as an instrument of national policy in Europe or in the interior of any other continent. To wield the balance of power on land, field armies are essential, and therefore throughout British history expeditionary forces have been raised.

British military history is deeply marked by this question of expeditionary forces. Instead of the continuous development of a national army, as on the Continent, there is a succession of sudden expansions to meet particular emergencies, followed by a relapse into peacetime stagnation and national neglect. Further, there is an inherent difference between a continental army and an expeditionary force. A continental army must expect to fight from the first to the last day of a war. In peacetime it must stand ready to defend the national territory at short warning. Its commitment at all times is unlimited. Not so with expeditionary forces, which enjoy the quality of impermanence. They are committed to a particular 'expedition'; that assignment once completed in victory or interrupted by disaster, they can be withdrawn to the safety of the British Isles. The British army has always enjoyed in its continental wars an advantage denied to Europeans; it can legitimately run away.

Because British expeditions going or coming from battle travel by sea, protected by sea-power, another myth about British history has grown up. This 'blue water' view of maritime power insists that small bodies of British troops fighting limited campaigns in distant theatres against detachments of a continental enemy isolated by the Royal Navy have a disproportionately large effect on a war; much larger than direct British intervention in a continental campaign. In pursuit of this dearly-held belief, British troops have died of yellow fever in the Caribbean and dysentery in Mesopotamia. The 'blue water' myth is complementary to the pacifistic myth, because it offers a cheap way of winning great wars; it offers victory over powerful opponents without the need for a large field army. As a bonus, it offers commercial plums like sugar islands or oilfields. No wonder it dies hard. Unfortunately the facts of British involvement with continental wars during the last five centuries do not support the 'blue water' myth. Only when expeditionary forces have been transformed into a field army on the Continent 'for the duration', able and willing to fight major battles against European opponents, has British intervention become decisive. If the British themselves are unwilling or unable to provide a field army for the Continent of Europe, then they have had to find allies who will do the fighting for them; often it has been something of both.

Introduction

The history of the British army, then, is of recurrent need rending aside the anti-military illusions of the nation. It is the history of an institution without steady and continuous growth; rather that of a series of *ad hoc* expansions and reforms tenuously connected by the residual life and organization of the army in peacetime; it is the history of an institution alternately neglected by the nation, or trustingly looked to in moments of fright.

*

The continuous history of the units of the modern British army begins with the army of the Commonwealth and the inclusion of the personnel of one of its regiments in the royal standing forces in 1661. This date is hardly acceptable as a starting-point for a study of British military institutions because the Tudor and early Stuart periods cover the transition from the world of the Middle Ages to that of modern times, an era of great change in military as well as in social and political history. It was in the sixteenth century that certain enduring relationships between military power and English society, as well as enduring strategic patterns, began to evolve. It was then, too, that English and European military institutions began to diverge in response to differing social and political conditions.

A starting point in the continuous process of history must always be arbitrary. This study selects the reign of Henry VIII, when England made a decisive stride from a late medieval to a modern state.

Throughout the narrative, the development of British military institutions within the frame of British society is related to, and compared and contrasted with, developments in Europe. For to confine the narrative strictly to British experience would be artificial, presenting in a false isolation and self-containment what is really only one aspect of a far wider subject. It is the comparisons and contrasts that illuminate British attempts to solve the political and social problems posed by military institutions while also ensuring the protection of national independence, and that equally illuminate the inter-action of strategic need and national attitude.

For this is the history of the army as a British institution rather than a chronicle of regimental battle-honours of the traditional kind; it is a study of the influence of war on modern British history.

I

The Rise of
the Nation State
1509–1603

1
Henry VIII
and the New Arts
of War

WHEN Henry VIII came to the throne in 1509 England had not fought a campaign in Europe since the inglorious conclusion of the Hundred Years' War in 1453. At home there had been almost unbroken peace since Henry's father, Henry VII, had ended the Wars of the Roses by his victory at Bosworth Field in 1485, and founded the Tudor dynasty. Troops had only been needed to defeat the pretender Lambert Simnel at Stoke Field in 1497, to police Ireland (a perennial task) and the Scottish border, and for a trip to Boulogne in 1492. In this unwonted tranquillity, English military ideas had failed to progress beyond those of Agincourt: the longbow rather than the handgun, the bill (a kind of halberd wielded like a two-handed axe) rather than the newer pike, infantry rather than cavalry.

Medieval English military institutions, on the other hand, had been deliberately demolished by Henry VIII's father in his determination to impose the authority of the crown on the great nobles. He forbade private armies of retainers, except under special royal licence in the case of a few trusted magnates. No new royal military organization had replaced this abolished medieval source of troops. Unlike European monarchs, Henry VII had not needed a royal army to suppress by force his overmighty subjects and reunite his kingdom. For the traditional powers and authority of the English monarchy were much stronger than those handed down by struggling medieval European kingships. Englishmen – even jealous nobles – stood more in awe of the Crown and the law than Europeans, whose great vassals exercised almost independent rule over their own lands. English society itself was more closely knit and loyal, less divided by caste and localism. Nor, since Henry VII's foreign policy had been cautious and pennywise, had there been need for large expeditionary forces.

Thus by 1509 the English late-medieval military system had disappeared without replacement – except by a royal bodyguard of 200 men, created by Henry VIII's father in the first year of his reign. 'The Yeomen of the Guard [of our body] of our Lord the King' were formed some eight years after the French monarchy's first regular *gardes du corps*; the Yeomen of the Guard survive to the present day, the oldest military body in the world.

Yet in Europe military institutions and techniques were in the course of immense change, experiment and innovation, forced on by the first great European conflict between nation states. Modern professional armies were being evolved out of the late-medieval host, a development with far-reaching social, political and technical implications. In the reign of Henry VIII – as in the next four centuries – it was European war and European military ideas that provided the setting and the stimulus for English developments.

The first modern war, the Great Italian Wars, had begun in 1494, when the Valois King Charles VIII of France invaded Italy. Charles was opposed by the Habsburg Holy Roman Emperor, titular sovereign over northern Italy, and by Ferdinand of Aragon, whose dominions included Sicily and many small Italian states. Repeated defeats and disasters failed to discourage French ambition. The struggle lasted – with brief pauses for breath – until 1559.

The Great Italian Wars involved most of the martial races of Europe: the French; Germans from the Holy Roman Empire; Spaniards; Italians; Swiss mountaineers eager to make money as mercenaries and extend their territory; even Albanian light horse-men in Venetian employ. All over southern Europe soldiers were swaggering, their clothes not yet uniform, but of all colours and cut, their loyalties identified only by the great banners floating overhead; soldiers marching to the slow beat of the drum, the grinding of innumerable supply carts, the clink of harness. Different ideas of war, different tactics and weapons, were tried out in the rolling smoke of Italian battlefields.*

The army led into Italy by Charles VIII in 1494 was quite unlike the French army which English arrows and bills had defeated at Agincourt in 1415. The dense masses of impetuous, undisciplined feudal chivalry had disappeared. The heavy cavalry now consisted of well-drilled, paid, long-service *gendarmes* ('men-at-arms'), organized into *compagnies d'ordonnance* of a hundred men. Although they still wore armour, their weapon was still the lance,

Europe in the Tudor Era

and they were still recruited from the *noblesse*, they were 'professional' cavalry capable of tactical manoeuvre. The French were strong in artillery. Guns, organized and directed by the brothers Bureau, had blasted the English out of their French strongholds before 1453. Guns had defeated the old English bow-and-bill tactics at Formigny in 1450. The work of the Bureau brothers had been completed by Jacques de Genouilhac, Grand Master of the Ordnance. In 1494 the Italians gaped as the great bronze guns of

* The summaries of sixteenth-century warfare are based on Sir Charles Oman's *Warfare in the Sixteenth Century*.

the French Royal Train passed along their roads – 140 fifty-pounders and 200 bombards (of various calibres from two- to sixteen-pounders) with their supply waggons, gunners, carpenters and powder-makers. Eight thousand horses drew this vast array to battle.

Only in infantry were the French weak. Attempts by Charles VIII's predecessor to raise a national militia force, *les franc-archers*, had failed. War was becoming too professional for peasants called suddenly from their fields. In 1479 the French had lost the battle of Guinegatte because the *franc-archers* gave way. So Charles turned to infantry of proven quality, albeit foreigners: the Swiss. The Swiss were hardy and ruthless; they fought in solid blocks of pikemen, well-drilled, fast-moving, bristling with sharp steel at the end of sixteen feet of pikestave; and they had yet to meet their match. When the Swiss cantons did not need their troops for national purposes, they hired them to the highest bidder. The Swiss were military trade-unionists, prone to lightning strikes over some small grievance about conditions of service, and certain to march home even in the middle of a crisis if their money was not promptly paid: 'no money, no Swiss' ran the saying. Eight thousand of them marched with Charles VIII, together with 2,000 German mercenary pikemen, called *Landsknechte* (a term whose origins and meaning are obscure).

Frenchmen provided the infantry missile-power: 3,000 archers from Brittany and 6,000 cross-bowmen, but only 3,000 arquebusiers. The arquebus was a primitive musket, fired by a length of burning match, or fuse, lowered on to a priming pan by a trigger. It fired a light ball some 200 hundred yards. Being inaccurate – like all infantry fire-arms until the nineteenth-century rifle – it was fired in volleys at close range. Though its match and powder were as susceptible to wet weather as the strings of the bows, its efficiency was not dependent – as was the longbow – on the health and vigour of its owner. The French had been slow to adopt the arquebus, and in 1494 there was only one arquebusier to every six infantrymen in the French army.

The battles in Italy pitted this French army of artillery, pikemen and *gendarmes* against other styles of warfare.

On 6 July 1495, the French, now reduced to 7,000 infantry and 900 *gendarmes*, were intercepted at Fornovo by an Italian army 14,000 strong. This battle marked the end of the traditional Italian *condottieri*, mercenaries who had changed war into a private enterprise business, a carefully bloodless manoeuvring for mutual profit. The *condottieri* cavalry, unused to real fighting, were crushed by the French *gendarmes*, while the Swiss pikeman smashed through the Italian infantry, which included German mercenaries. The battle was over in a quarter of an hour.

In 1503 at Cerignola, the French pikemen and *gendarmes* met their first check at the hands of Gonsalvo de Cordoba's Spaniards, who also had their own national military pattern. A Spanish army was weak in heavy cavalry, strong in infantry, which the Spaniards were the first to equip with the fire-arm – the arquebus – as its principal weapon. For close-quarters fighting they relied on sword and buckler, which they considered more handy than the pike. From their wars with the Moors the Spaniards had developed the *genitores*, light cavalry unarmoured except for a helmet and mailed shirt, and armed with throwing javelins – excellent for harassing or pursuit, but useless in face of heavy cavalry. At Cerignola the Spaniards dug a ditch along their front, topped it with stakes from a vineyard, and posted their arquebusiers behind this field fortification, with the *genitores* in reserve out of reach of the French *gendarmes*. The French, confident in the impact of their *gendarmes* and pikemen, attacked headlong with their entire army in echelon led by the heavy cavalry, only to pile up in confusion in the Spaniards' ditch. The Spanish arquebusiers poured fire into the packed French ranks until finally they withdrew in disorder, pursued by the *genitores*.

Although the Swiss pikes were to win one more great victory at Novara in 1513, Cerignola was a warning of the potency of fire-power. At Bicocca in 1522 the lesson was repeated in a major battle which ended the long Swiss supremacy, and permanently dented their self-confidence. Characteristically it was the 16,000 Swiss pikemen in the French army who themselves brought on the battle of Bicocca. While the French commander, de Lautrec, wished to pursue a cautious strategy of manoeuvre, representatives of the Swiss forced him to attack, threatening that otherwise they would go home.

Facing them was a smaller force, part imperial troops of the Holy Roman Empire and part Spaniards from Sicily, under command of a veteran Italian *condottiere*, Prosper Colonna. Colonna also constructed a field fortification along his front, deepening a sunken road and using the spoil to raise an existing bank. Behind this he posted his Spanish arquebusiers four deep, while guns swept the approach and the road itself. The Swiss pikemen refused to wait for supporting artillery, and marched straight at Colonna's line in the overweening confidence born of nearly two centuries of victory. But Colonna's guns tore gaps in their two dense columns. When they reached the sunken road, they were brought to a halt, surprised and uncertain, before plunging down into it to get to 'push of pike' with the enemy. However, the heads of their columns were brought down in bloody heaps by four volleys from the Spanish arquebusiers. The Swiss tried to rally and climb out of the trap to close with their enemy, but they were finally stopped and turned back by Colonna's own pikemen.

Bicocca proved the power of the fire-arm over pikes, and even the Swiss gradually mixed arquebusiers into their pike formations.

The late fifteenth and early sixteenth centuries were thus a time of experiment in tactics and armament, of differing national methods of fighting. The troops themselves were mostly professional mercenaries rather than militia or feudal vassals or even noble retainers. They were all trained not merely in the use of their own personal weapons, but in action as a body; they were drilled in rudimentary evolutions. Although states recruited largely from their own peoples, specialized troops were usually foreign mercenaries: the French hired Swiss pikes, the Spaniards Italian heavy cavalry, and everybody German *Landsknechte*, as a kind of cheaper, ersatz Swiss. Although the Swiss would never fight each other, mercenaries would appear first in one army and then another, according to the terms offered. After 1515, when the Swiss and French signed a 'Perpetual Peace', the French enjoyed a virtual monopoly of Swiss troops.

Another characteristic fundamental to all European armies in the Great Italian Wars was that although their composition might alter, the armies as a whole were hired 'for the duration'. They were not like militia, called out for a brief emergency and then dismissed. The 'duration' had already lasted fifteen years when Henry VIII came to the English throne, and in fact it eventually proved to last some sixty years, interrupted by brief intervals of peace. Thus continental nations found themselves maintaining permanent armies because they were fighting a permanent war.

These armies were appallingly expensive to the states of the time. Wastage was high since both diet and hygiene were poor, and the ravages of disease added to slaughter in battle. Fresh men were constantly needed. The sixteenth-century administrative systems could not control the corruption and inefficiency among their agents. Cost was further increased by the progress of technology, for the peasant with his home-made bow was no longer good enough, whatever King Henry VIII and his countrymen might think in their innocence. Expensive fire-arms were essential – and the industries to make them. Cannon had rendered medieval castles and town walls almost useless. One by one the famous strong places of Italy had fallen to the French bronze guns.

The engineer was soon challenging the gunner and the gun-founder in turn, however. A new system of fortification appeared, low of silhouette, sloped rather than vertical, solid masonry and earth: poor marks for the gunner and invulnerable to his fire. The cost of re-fortifying the important strategic centres and frontiers of Europe was another heavy charge on shaky exchequers. The inevitable price of military ambition, or even defensive survival, was bankruptcy. It was paid even by the greatest of monarchies, like France and the Holy Roman Empire.

Such were the facts of military and therefore political power in Europe in the early sixteenth century, when under a young king full of lusty vigour, martial as well as amorous, England attempted a major re-entry into European affairs.

Henry VIII's motive was no cool calculation of English interest, but rather a wave of bellicose fervour that seized the King himself and his court. France was the ancient enemy; the King was married to Catherine of Aragon; and so England joined the war on the side of Spain, the Pope and the Holy Roman Empire.

In preparing for war, Henry enjoyed the advantage of the full treasury bequeathed by his careful father, but he had no armed force beyond the Yeomen of the Guard and a few 'gentlemen-pensioners', heavy cavalry modelled on the French *gendarmes*. Henry and his government faced what was to be the perennial English problem: how to intervene effectively in a continental war without a large battle-worthy army; the eternal task of improvising an expeditionary force.

The old feudal levy in its later bastard form of noble retainers had been virtually extinguished by Henry VII, thus removing one of the two traditional English methods of raising a field army. The alternative was the national levy or militia, a descendant of the Anglo-Saxon fyrd, and based on the accepted principle of every man's obligation to defend the national territory in war or civil emergency. The county militia was not, however, intended to produce an expeditionary force. Only volunteers, willing or otherwise, could be sent abroad. Often the militia was reluctant even to quit its own county. Nor was it an obedient military instrument. Continental monarchs might find their mercenaries awkward and even mutinous over money and conditions; the English militia could be awkward in other ways. It was a cross-section of county and town society, from the lords and gentry who mustered and led it to the peasants and yeomen who left their fields and cottages with longbow and bill. Its enthusiasm could be enlisted for national purposes, but not necessarily for policies interesting to the monarch alone. Under the Tudors English loyalty to the Crown was very great – Crown and nation were identified – yet that loyalty had to be won by a combination of authority and careful handling.

From the purely military point of view, the increasing sophistication and professionalism of war lowered the value of the shire levies. The occasional jolly day at the musters or butts was no substitute for thorough tactical drill or experience won in arduous marches and bloody battles. The advent of fire-arms had widened the gulf between the professional and the militiamen, because the handling of arquebuses and volley-firing involved standardized uniform movements not required by archery. Moreover, the militia could not be kept in the field for a long campaign, because farms, estates and shops urgently called them home.

War faced Henry's government with two different strategic problems: the dispatch of a field army to France, and the defence of the northern frontier against the Scots, who were allies of France and always ready to take advantage of English difficulties. The Scots problem was solved by the traditional militia system. In 1512 Henry sent the Earl of Surrey a Commission of Array, '*De arraiendo et monstrum faciendo contra Scotos*', authorizing him to raise the shire militia of Yorkshire, Northumberland, Cumberland, Westmorland and Lancashire. Commissions of Array, begun by Edward I, were the standard method of raising a field force from the militia. Although in the fifteenth century noblemen had sometimes raised personal retainers under these Commissions, since Henry VII's reforms the recipient of a Commission of Array, though usually a prominent peer, acted only as a direct servant of the state.

A Commission of Array could not, however, produce an expeditionary force for France. Standing troops included only the King's household troops, a garrison tied down in Ireland and the garrison of Calais. A field army had to be improvised. Volunteers for foreign service were sought, either recruited by county nobility and gentry, or by anyone prepared to style himself 'captain' and recruit his own company of fifty to a hundred men. In 1513 Henry took 24,000 English troops to northern France, mostly bowmen or billmen of the traditional medieval kind, with light cavalry consisting of mounted archers and 'prickers' from the Scottish border. In a smaller and fruitless expedition to the French Biscay coast in the previous year, 500 'Almaynes' – German *Landsknecht* pikemen – had had to be hired. England being almost totally deficient in modern troops – pikemen, armoured heavy cavalry, arquebusiers – continental mercenaries were now engaged once more. Six thousand *Landsknechte* joined Henry in France, together with a number of Burgundian *gendarmes* to supplement the English semi-armoured horse called 'demi-lances'.

The campaign was successful enough. The English army marched inland, laid siege to and captured Thérouanne and Tournai, and fought its one battle of the war at Guinegatte, on 16 August 1513. It was hardly a battle, rather a cavalry skirmish. The French cavalry pressed too close to the English main body, tried to extricate itself, was charged as it withdrew, and fled in panic, losing forty dead and some distinguished prisoners, including the aged Bayard. From the speed of the French retreat the action became known as 'the Battle of the Spurs'. Henry himself had a brisk gallop and returned happy with a well-publicized victory. In 1515 he made an advantageous peace by which France ceded him Thérouanne and Tournai and agreed to pay him an increased pension. Henry shrewdly got out of the war ahead of his allies, the Emperor and Ferdinand of Aragon, who were trying to make peace behind *his* back.

Although Henry could feel pleased with his first military venture, nevertheless his army had not been put to the test of a major battle. He had only marched against a French army of observation half his own strength, while the French main body was far away in the decisive theatre of war, Italy. Here, two months earlier, the French had been defeated in a major battle at Novara, losing half their infantry. Henry's invasion exemplified a pattern of thought and result long to be repeated in British military history: transient intervention by an army unfit to encounter and defeat a continental power's main body, while that main body was elsewhere; and intervention therefore without effect on the issue of the war.

While Henry was winning the Battle of the Spurs, the Earl of Surrey was dealing with James IV of Scotland. Surrey's army, concentrated at Newcastle, had been raised by medieval methods and a medieval force was the result. Except for Surrey's own 500 licensed retainers, there were no professional soldiers, and of Surrey's retainers only one was a man-at-arms (heavy cavalryman). The army was a cross-section of northern society, armed with bows and bills – comprising peasants, yeomen, townsmen, gentry and lords, all foot soldiers as at Agincourt a hundred years before. The cavalry consisted of 'prickers', irregulars recruited from the border.

Surrey found James IV in a strong position on a ridge at Flodden, a few miles south of the Scottish border. He had no choice but to fight, because his improvised supply arrangements were likely to leave his men without food in a few days, and, worst of all in an age where no man drank water if he could help it, the beer had given out. Although the army could not manoeuvre tactically, it could march, so Surrey boldly marched round the Scots and attacked from the rear.

The Scottish infantry had been equipped with specially imported pikes, but they lacked the drill and discipline which made the Swiss and Germans so formidable. In the hands of raw levies in a close-quarters brawl the pike proved less effective than the handier English bill. The English archers played little part; it was the billmen who hewed the Scots down, killing some 5,000 men, with particularly heavy casualties among the ancient noble families of Scotland. James IV himself was killed, and was succeeded by a child, James V. Victory had made the Scottish border safe from serious invasion for the remainder of Henry's reign.

There was nothing in this war of 1513 to suggest to Henry VIII that he should hire a semi-permanent army on the continental model. The traditional shire levies had won a splendid victory over the Scots, while an expeditionary force made up of English volunteers and foreign mercenaries had beaten the French. Time enough to raise another expeditionary force when war was once more in the offing. Since the treasure inherited from his father had been swallowed up by even this brief war, there was even less incentive for an island monarchy, unwilling to ask Parliament for taxes, to keep an army standing in peacetime. Yet expeditionary forces were to be required twice more during the reign, when Henry's foreign policy again involved the country in the Valois – Habsburg struggle.

The lines of this struggle became more starkly drawn after 1519, when Charles V succeeded to both the Habsburg thrones of Spain and the Holy Roman Empire. The French monarchy, in the person now of the young and vainglorious François I, faced a united enemy on all her frontiers, from Spain to the Spanish Netherlands. The Emperor Charles V was the most powerful monarch in Europe, potentially able to unite the continent; and yet there were weaknesses in his position. The French enjoyed the strategic advantage of interior lines, while Charles V was weakened and distracted at critical moments by the menace of Turkish expansion in the Balkans and in the Mediterranean; and, being a Catholic monarch, by the divisive effect of the Protestant Reformation in his German territories. The struggle between France and the Habsburg Empire oscillated indecisively for years. Although great battles brought temporary advantages, perhaps a short period of peace, the war broke out again and again as the French monarchy pursued its ambition to dominate Italy, unscrupulously but effectively choosing moments when Charles V was distracted by other troubles. The struggle outlasted Henry VIII, Edward VI and Queen Mary, and finally ended, virtually a draw, with the Peace of Cateau-Cambrésis in 1559.

The English intervention of 1522–3 was the work of Wolsey. He owed his place as the King's chief minister to his efficiency as almoner in organizing the expeditionary force of 1513. In 1522 he hoped to exploit the French–Habsburg war to make England the arbiter of Europe. Wolsey pursued a tortuous policy, siding first with the Emperor Charles V and then with the French. He failed, and his failure proved that England did not possess the national or military strength to support Wolsey's pretensions. England was not a great power, for her population was barely four millions compared with France's twelve, and at no time could she place a great army in the field 'for the duration'.

In 1523 another English expedition was sent to northern France, this time under command of the Earl of Surrey. Only 10,000 English volunteers were raised – still all bows or bills – and once again the English looked to their allies to supply specialist mercenary troops such as German pikemen and *gendarmes*. However, the anticipated numbers were not forthcoming. Surrey led his army in a wide sweep to Montdidier, taking various towns *en route* and laying waste and plundering the countryside. But winter came early; frostbite and hunger compelled the army to retreat, and it eventually disintegrated with nothing but frost-bitten limbs to show for its efforts. Far from playing a major role in the European war, the English had merely covered Charles V's Netherlands provinces for him while the decisive campaign was being fought, as before, in Italy. There in 1522 the French had lost the battle of

Bicocca (see p. 7) and in 1525 they were decisively beaten at the battle of Pavia, not least because of their weakness in arquebusiers. The French King, François I, was taken prisoner amid the wreck of his army, and a temporary peace followed.

For England the only result of the 1523 expedition was its cost to an empty exchequer, and Wolsey was forced to try to extract additional taxes from an unwilling and acrimonious Parliament.

In 1528 Wolsey went to war again; this time the pattern of illusion and failure was unmistakable. England was now on the French side against Charles V. There was no enthusiasm at all in the country, and therefore no army. Wolsey's diplomacy, however subtle, thus carried no weight. When Charles V once more defeated the French in Italy, at Landriano in 1529, the Empire and France signed the Peace of Cambrai without even consulting Cardinal Wolsey. This failure was the beginning of Wolsey's downfall.

The last continental raid of the reign was in 1542–5, with the ageing but still ambitious Henry in command. The expeditionary force illustrated the gradual progress of change in English military thought and organization during the reign. As in 1513 the English main body still consisted mostly of bows and bills, and Henry relied once more on his ally (again Charles V) for pikemen, heavy cavalry and arquebusiers. Despite the king's personal interest in fire-arms, especially after their success in the battle of Pavia, the English still had few. One assembly of foot comprised 801 archers, 1,073 bills, 380 pikes, but only 181 'hackbuts'.* The Duke of Suffolk's force included 100 horse, 100 archers and 300 bills, but no 'shot' at all. Even as late as this (1544) an English army of over 28,000 seems to have included fewer than 2,000 arquebusiers and 200 heavy cavalry.

A grandiose plan was made, by which Henry was to march on Paris from the Channel and Charles V from Champagne, but both monarchs ended up besieging strongpoints far from Paris and near their own starting-points. Henry merely captured Boulogne, which the French ceded for eight years at the Peace of Ardres in 1546 along with a pension.

---

*English 'hackbut', French '*arquebus*', from German '*Hackenbuchse*', or 'hook-gun'.

This, the last of Henry's expeditions, had exerted as little influence on European affairs as the others. Unlike the total failure of 1522, there were trophies to give the illusion of success, but the French pension and the temporary prize of Boulogne had cost well over £2,000,000, and the treasury was empty. This brief excursion into war cast a long shadow on English political and social life in the mid-sixteenth century, for to meet the gigantic bill Henry VIII not only unloaded on the market great quantities of lands seized from the monasteries, but also debased the coinage, with all the insidious and socially disruptive effects of sudden inflation.

Technically backward though the native English troops were, Henry VIII's expeditionary armies had not differed in basic composition from those of other European monarchs. Like them he employed a nucleus of national troops, recruited by lords and gentry or professional captains; like them he hired foreign mercenaries on a large scale. Continental armies, however, were beginning their long evolution into permanent institutions, the essential props of absolute monarchies and the unifying force in countries with strong traditions of feudal separatism. There was no such development in England, although (or perhaps partly because) Henry VIII was a strong king on a strong throne. For whereas the continentals were fighting a long war, England only furnished expeditions. Of Henry VIII's thirty-eight years on the throne English armies were in the field for no more than six and between expeditions they were disbanded. During the same period France, for example, was almost continuously at war, often defending her own homeland against serious attack. By 1559, when the Great Italian Wars ended, France, Spain and the Habsburg Empire had had to keep armies in being for some sixty years; armies that had inevitably acquired an almost permanent character. Inevitably, also, these continual wars spurred on developments in tactics and organization which England copied only belatedly.

The power and importance of infantry fire-arms were growing. After Bicocca (1522) and Pavia (1525) the French and Swiss followed the Spanish and Imperialist example by increasing the proportion of arquebusiers to pikemen or archers. Although the French retained their heavy cavalry, the *gendarmes*, the advent of fire-arms led to a reduction of their numbers. The Spanish army, still supreme in disciplined infantry fire-power, did not feel the need for numerous cavalry. Their army in Italy in 1526 included only some 5,000 horse in a total strength of 67,000. In all armies, arquebusiers and pikemen were combined in mixed formations as a defence against cavalry.

The most significant development however during the Great Italian Wars was in military organization. In the early sixteenth century the only permanent unit of an army was the company of fifty to 200 men, under a captain. The company had evolved in the late medieval wars as the unit for recruitment, pay, discipline and tactics. On the march or in battle an army was traditionally marshalled into three great masses: the van or 'vaward', the main battle and the rearward, each perhaps of several thousand men. Between these masses and the company no intermediate formation existed. The need to have larger units grouping several companies and intermediate levels of command between army commander and captain was perceived as early as 1505 by the Spaniards. King Ferdinand appointed twenty officers called '*coloneles*' to take command of several companies. Their name derived from '*cabo de colunela*' – the head of a column, and their command (about 1,000 men) was entitled a 'colonelcy'.

In 1534 François I of France attempted unsuccessfully to create large permanent units in the French army. In the Roman tradition then so culturally fashionable he called his new units 'legions' – 6,000 men strong, named and recruited from seven provinces. A legion was divided into six '*bandes*' of 1,000 men, officered by a captain, two lieutenants, two ensigns and ten '*centuriers*' (centurions). The commanding officer received the Spanish name of colonel. The legions' demise was due not to their organization but to the fact that they were really a militia, an attempt to revive the *franc-archers*, and levied parish by parish. A French army historian wrote that the legions 'distinguished themselves only by their insubordination'. They swiftly disappeared. Instead of demanding useless men, the French kings demanded good money from local authorities, and, in the words of a contemporary marshal of France, 'from this money one made brave men and valiant captains'. More permanent were the *bandes* of veteran soldiers drawn from particular provinces and varying in numbers from 100 to 2,000 men.

Although both the words 'regiment' and 'colonel' were current in Europe by 1559, they did not yet denote fixed units and permanent ranks; they were functional terms applied to temporary groupings of several companies. In twentieth-century terms a mid-sixteenth-century 'regiment' was a battle group or task force, and the colonel equivalent to a force commander.

The Spaniards were the first to establish permanent tactical units larger than the company. Instead of the 'colonelcies' of 1505, new units were formed from 1534 called '*tercios*', after the old three-part division of a medieval host. Originally three *tercios* were formed, in Lombardy, Naples and Sicily, each of 3,000 men, stronger in arquebusiers than pikemen and complete with a staff of nineteen and three officers to each company of 258 men. Such was Spanish piety that, whereas there were only three surgeons to a *tercio*, there were thirteen chaplains.

In Henry VIII's final invasion of France, ten years after the introduction of the *tercio*, there was still little sign of regimental organization. As before, the English army was divided for action into vaward, main battle and rearward, and although the new word 'regiment' was applied to them, it really meant nothing. There was no intermediate organization between these main bodies and the independent companies of about 100 men. Some faint beginning of true regimental organization can be seen in the large companies (up to 450 men) mentioned in the 1544 muster-roll of the Boulogne garrison. Between the captain and the field officer, moreover, were sometimes to be found 'grand captains' appointed to temporary seniority over the others. With no continuity between the army of one expedition and another, however, organization inevitably developed only haltingly.

A discrepancy was already visible between the military system that the English government and people felt to be acceptable and adequate, and the requirements of real military effectiveness. However, after 1523 Wolsey was more concerned with diplomacy than military organization, and in any case he was no innovator. Later in Henry VIII's reign, Thomas Cromwell's transformation of the English state from medievalism to modernity was based not on the continental mould of absolute monarchy, but on a partnership in Parliament between Crown and a cohesive society. In this internal revolution of the 1530s there was no need for a permanent army to support the Crown, although curiously enough a sketch for a standing army was found among Cromwell's papers.* Because of the long crisis of the King's divorce and the growing danger of a Catholic league against schismatic England, strategy during Cromwell's secretaryship was defensive. Though Cromwell radically reshaped the state machine he had no reason therefore to direct his powerful will towards the problems of raising field armies for foreign service.

Such permanent military institutions that evolved in Henry VIII's time owed their existence to needs of home defence, together with the King's personal interest in guns, those modern symbols of power with their 'exceeding great noyse and marvellous rore'. Henry VIII's navy, with its new ships firing heavy ordnance broadside, was defensive in intention, and in fact fought an indecisive battle with the French in 1545 for command of the Channel. For an island people the navy, not the army, was the shield. While continental nations were establishing rudimentary state departments to control the army therefore, Henry established a Navy Board under a Comptroller to administer the navy, its ships and dockyards. Yet even the navy was not yet a permanent force, for just as mercenaries were laid off at the end of a war, so ships were laid up; just as armies were hastily raised for a new war, so the King's ships were joined at need by armed merchant vessels.

Behind the navy Henry built a second line of defence: a chain of modern forts along the south coast from the Medway to Cornwall, of which those at Sandgate, Deal and Walmer commanded the narrow seas. They were modern-style fortifications, low-lying gun platforms. Like the new ships and expeditionary forces, they demanded heavy cannon. The first permanent military department and military administrative officer of state – the Ordnance Department and the Master of the Ordnance – were therefore

---

*I am indebted to Professor G. R. Elton for pointing this out. The sketch plan appears not to have been drawn up by Cromwell himself.

created to deal with artillery. The Master was a person of distinction, usually a peer, and his department produced guns designed for both navy and army, only the mountings differing. At first the guns were largely made abroad. Hans Poppenruyter, the master founder at Malines, made some 140 guns of all calibres for the English after 1510, including twelve heavy cannon, piously called the Twelve Apostles, and used against Thérouanne and Tournai in 1513. This was still a very small train by continental standards. Henry set up permanent gun-foundries in England run by John and Robert Owen and by European experts which first produced bronze cannon, and after 1543 the cheaper iron cannon.

The King also supported the Guild of St George, established in the City of London in 1537 'to be overseers of the science of artillerie, that is to witt, long bowes, cross bowes and hand gonnes'. That such responsibility for military matters should be allotted to a City livery company shows that the modern distinction between 'official' and 'unofficial' institutions did not obtain in the sixteenth century. The Guild of St George has survived to the present day as the Honourable Artillery Company, which is still not part of the regular army, but of that modern militia, the Territorials.

When he died in 1547 Henry VIII left England a formidable power at sea, with the navy organized under its own department of state and with adequate armaments industries and improved artillery under another permanent department of state. Both troops and their administration, however, were still backward compared with the professionalized and increasingly long-standing armies of the Continent. The permanent guards and garrisons in Henry's new forts and in towns of strategic importance were the only standing land force in peacetime, apart from a handful of the Yeomen of the Guard and gentlemen-pensioners. Some garrisons, however, were large; Berwick, for instance, guarding the Scottish frontier, held 500 men. Nevertheless in 1547 English land forces did not begin to compare in number with those of continental monarchies. There was as yet no need for them to do so. Geography, together with the happy involvement of the great European powers with each other, still enabled the English to regard war as a peripheral and occasional activity.

2

The
Elizabethan
Militia

BETWEEN the death of Henry VIII and the accession of Elizabeth
(1558), domestic turmoil badly shook the Tudor monarchy.
During the reigns of the minor Edward VI, when the country
was ruled by Protectors, and then of Mary, the partnership
between monarchy and people and the identification of patriotism
with loyalty to the Crown almost disappeared. To civil troubles
were added the penury of the state resulting from Henry's wars
and the social unrest caused by his debasement of the coinage.
Religious fanaticism further divided the nation, for Cromwell's
political revolution, which had made the Crown-in-Parliament the
supreme authority over the Church, was now rapidly changing
into a doctrinal revolution as extreme Protestantism spread from
the Continent. For the first time since the Wars of the Roses the
size and loyalty of the armed forces available to the Crown became
critical factors in home politics.

The Duke of Somerset's rule as Protector opened with an invasion of Scotland – to 'persuade' the Scots into uniting the two
kingdoms by a marriage between Edward VI and Mary Queen of
Scots. The 'persuasion' took the form of the battle of Pinkie,
which, though a decisive English victory, was not followed up
politically and therefore is mainly interesting as an illustration of
English military institutions in the mid sixteenth century. Somerset's army was strong in artillery thanks to Henry VIII's reforms,
but of some 12,000 infantry only 600 were arquebusiers. The rest
were bows and bills. The decisive striking force consisted of professionals: 500 'bulleners' (heavy cavalry from the garrison of
Boulogne), the gentlemen-pensioners of the royal guard, and

foreign-commanded mercenary *gendarmes* and mounted arque-busiers. An English naval squadron lay off the coast on the army's flank.

Though superior numerically by about 7,000, the Scots had little cavalry, and their infantry were mostly native pikes and High-landers. They were outfought and destroyed largely by cavalry and by gunfire – including that of the fleet. Pinkie was further proof that levies could no longer stand against professionals. For the first time the new cavalry tactics evolved by the German *Reiter* were used on British soil: the *caracole*, by which the horsemen rode up to the enemy in successive waves, fired their pistols and retired to the rear to re-load.

Two years later Somerset had to face a major internal threat. The proposed new prayer book produced a religious explosion culminating in a revolt in Cornwall, while economic troubles burst out in widespread rioting and a rebellion in Norfolk led by Jack Ket. The Cornishmen reached Exeter, and Ket camped on Mouse-hold Heath outside Norwich. The Crown's traditional instru-ment against civil unrest was the *posse comitatus* led by the nobility and gentry. But what if the shire levies shared the grievances of the rebels, or were reluctant to fight their own people? Luckily Somerset still retained some foreign mercenaries. While Italian arquebusiers under a Spanish captain broke the Cornishmen, Italians and German *Landsknechte* slaughtered Ket's followers.

The dependence of the Crown on popular goodwill, and its helplessness without a professional army when that goodwill was lacking, were demonstrated both under Northumberland (Somer-set's successor as Protector), and under Queen Mary. In 1553 the disputed succession between Mary and Northumberland's daughter-in-law, 'Queen Jane' (Lady Jane Grey), led to fighting in which the men of Northumberland's army either sided with Mary or simply melted away, leaving him helpless. Yet Mary was only backed by county levies. Even a small force of professional mercen-aries could have saved the throne for 'Queen Jane'.

Next year Queen Mary herself was in similar danger. Sir Thomas Wyatt raised a rebel force in Kent and marched on London, protesting both on religious and patriotic grounds at the

Queen's approaching marriage with King Philip II of Spain. Again the Crown could field only civilian levies comparable with Wyatt's own forces; again they sided with the rebels or melted away. When the Yeomen of the Guard fled, the capital lay open. But though lacking a professional army, Mary could still rely on the deep-seated loyalty to the Crown. Public feeling swung from Wyatt, and his own following began to melt away in their turn. The rebellion fizzled out in an almost bloodless brawl along Fleet Street.

Mary's reign was marked militarily by a disaster that liquidated the past and by a major reform.

In 1558, the last year of her reign, 25,000 Frenchmen under the Duke of Guise attacked Calais – with Guisnes and Hammes the last remnant of England's medieval military conquests. French guns demolished the fourteenth-century castle's bastions, and their infantry swarmed through the breach. Thirteen days later Guisnes and Hammes surrendered, and the English were out of Europe at last.

The reform, by Act of Parliament in the last year of Philip and Mary, was of the only standing arrangements for land forces – the obligation to serve in the county militia, together with the methods of raising and commanding it. Hitherto the militia system had been based on the Statute of Winchester (Edward I, 1285) under which the Commissions of Array were issued. This statute was now repealed, while the military responsibilities of the sheriff were abolished and military obligations re-defined. All men between sixteen and sixty were liable to serve. For the provision of horses and equipment, the nation was divided into ten classes, from men worth £5–£10 a year (obliged to supply a coat of plated armour, a bill or halberd, longbow and a 'pot' helmet), to men worth £1,000 a year and over (each to supply sixteen horses, eighty suits of light armour, forty pikes, thirty bows, twenty bills or halberds, twenty arquebuses and fifty 'pots').

A new county authority was set up to supervise and command the militia – the Lords-Lieutenant. Henry VIII had already appointed certain nobles to be crown lieutenants for specific regions in emergencies. Protector Somerset made similar appointments during the revolts of 1549. Lord Russell, for example, was appointed 'Governor of the West' and 'King's Lieutenant', and it was under his authority that the Italian arquebusiers dealt with the Cornish revolt. These temporary functions grew naturally out of the 'Commissions of Array' system and were recognized by Parliament after 1549. Philip and Mary's new statute now formally established the title and authority of Lords-Lieutenant, thus enlisting the natural leadership of the social hierarchy. Lest the Lord-Lieutenancy should develop into another kind of independent aristocratic authority dangerous to the Crown, however, the office was not permanent, but was only temporarily filled in emergencies. A second act of Philip and Mary, 'An Acte for the taking of Musters', aimed at eradicating some of the major functional shortcomings and abuses of the militia.

These reforms completed the foundations of English military institutions as they existed before the rise of a standing army.

Until the national danger in Elizabeth's reign, Tudor England had been able to regard war as a distant activity which she could join, or abandon as she chose. In the time of the Cromwellian reconstruction under Henry VIII, it is true, there had been fears of a continental coalition against the royal heretic which had led to the construction of a fleet and the coastal forts. Nevertheless, the danger had never materialized, most of all because the great war between France and the Habsburg Empire left Catholic powers little leisure to concentrate against England. In 1559, however, the year after Elizabeth's accession, the Great Italian Wars – the struggle between France and the Habsburgs – ended with the Peace of Cateau-Cambrésis.

With the death of Charles V in 1558, the Habsburg Empire had once more split. His brother Ferdinand inherited his central European lands and the title of Holy Roman Emperor, and was to be fully occupied by the problems of the Turkish advance in Hungary. Charles V's son, Philip, inherited the Spanish crown, the Spanish empire in Central and South America, and the Spanish Netherlands (modern Holland, Belgium, and the Flanders province of France). In the *tercios*, Philip II of Spain had the finest infantry in the world, disciplined, courageous and experienced.

The treasure of the New World flowed to his ports in the great carracks of his fleet. He was an absolute monarch, and he ruled over the greatest power in the world. Gripped by a narrow but intense piety, he was ready to use his power not only to further the material interest of Spain, but also those of the Catholic religion against heretics.

For in the second half of the sixteenth century the struggle for power became complicated and intensified by the religious struggle. Old allies, like England and Spain, were gradually to become enemies as the gulf between their superstitions widened, while a new and enduring quarrel, both religious and national, was to spring up between the Dutch and their Spanish overlords. The French wars of external conquest in Italy had hardly ended in failure when the religious question divided France herself. Until almost the end of the century France was paralysed by the strife between Huguenots and Catholics. Gradually all the quarrels and power conflicts of Europe were polarized by the single struggle between the Protestant Reformation and the Catholic Counter-Reformation. As the outlines of this struggle became clear, Elizabeth's England stood forth as Protestantism's ultimate hope and stronghold against Spain. No longer could England go to the wars as and when she wished; war with slow and stealthy steps came to her.

The political and military history of Elizabeth's reign falls into three parts. Until 1569 ostensible friendship with Spain continued, though becoming less and less convincing as tension mounted. From 1569 to 1585 there was a 'cold' war full of devious malice and unofficial acts of violence. Finally, from 1585 until the end of the reign England fought a great war both on land and sea. Many of Britain's permanent strategic problems and dilemmas of modern times now made their first appearance. There were the alternative grand strategies of seeking a decision on the Continent of Europe or through distant maritime expeditions; there were the technical problems of joint command and army–navy co-operation; of how to raise and sustain a field army for foreign service under a military system designed to meet limited emergencies at home. And the first of England's colonial wars was in progress in Ireland at the

very period when she was both fighting a continental campaign
and mounting combined operations against Spain itself. So long and
diversified a war threw an unprecedented strain upon the governmental institutions of the time; above all a financial strain, for the
device of a national debt had not been invented. Financial strin-
gency had wide constitutional repercussions, for the unpopularity
of war taxation coupled with Puritan fervour began to change
Crown and Commons from partners into rivals.

The war with Spain was also the source of the most seductive
and enduring of English myths: the myth of sea-power. The successful exploits of Drake, Raleigh and Hawkins were remembered
long after their equally numerous failures had been forgotten.
The glamour and glory of their brief triumphs were to stir the
hearts of Englishmen and distort their strategic judgement for
centuries, while the muddy campaigns in the Low Countries, in
which English, Dutch and German troops held the Spanish army
at bay, shrank to no more than a sentimental anecdote about the
death of Sir Philip Sidney. For it was the Elizabethan sea-dogs
who created the fallacious and perpetual English belief that the
navy could enable England always to win great continental wars
cheaply and painlessly, even profitably. What the proponents of
this maritime strategy forgot was that its success depended on some
other power, an ally – in the sixteenth century, the Dutch – doing
the real fighting, on land and against the enemy's main strength,
his army.

By 1569 Anglo-Spanish friendship had become a façade. The
religious quarrel was deepening, while Spanish and English trading
interests clashed as Hawkins ran contraband negroes into Spanish
America in defiance of Philip II's monopoly. Dramatic, alarming
events, generating hatred and fear, now destroyed all pretence of
Anglo-Spanish amity, and a period of undeclared, indirect and
covert war began. The Viceroy of New Spain, for instance, broke
a local agreement with Hawkins and Drake and treacherously
attacked these 'pirates'. Hawkins and Drake returned to England
with their lives and a lurid story of Spanish perfidy. Spanish
perfidy, in the shape of the inept Spanish ambassador in London,
was at work in England too, stirring up English Catholics in

support of Mary Queen of Scots, the Catholic candidate for Elizabeth's throne, now prisoner in England. The year 1569 produced a plot – the Ridolphi plot, so-called after a Florentine businessman who was a Spanish secret agent – and a rebellion of great peers in northern England, a death throe of the feudal past just as England's first power struggle of modern times began. The Privy Council dealt with the plot, and the militia, under the Lords-Lieutenant, with the rising of the north. Next year the lines of the eventual war between England and Spain were drawn more clearly. Pope Pius V excommunicated Elizabeth, declared her deposed, and called on true sons of the Church (Philip II, for example) to turn his words into fact. A Spanish fleet sailing up the Channel later in the year made the threat seem vividly immediate, but the Spaniards passed on peacefully to the Spanish Netherlands.

It was not Drake's raid on the Spanish Main in 1572–3, nor his round-the-world voyage of commerce-raiding in 1577–80 which drove Spain on towards open war, but the revolt by the Protestant Dutch in the northern provinces of the Spanish Netherlands in 1572. The Spanish reaction to the Dutch revolt was savage, and the Dutch looked to their fellow-Protestants in England for help. Although the Dutch war shattered her careful, cautious and subtle foreign policy, Elizabeth could hardly refuse some assistance. She could, however, refuse to commit England to a great war for which she was not ready. English help was therefore limited to money and volunteers, some of whom were fighting with the Dutch as early as 1572.

However, the struggle in the Netherlands grew fiercer. English sympathy for the Dutch was roused, and the 'hawks' of Elizabeth's court pressed for war with Spain. Like the United States in 1916–17 and 1940–41, England drew reluctantly nearer and nearer to open conflict. The flamboyant exploits of Drake and his fellows dramatized and aggravated the deepening struggle – dramatized it not only for the English, but for Philip of Spain and for onlooking Europe.

In 1584 the leader of the Dutch revolt, William of Orange, was assassinated, and the new Spanish Viceroy in the Netherlands, Alexander of Parma, a brilliant soldier leading the finest army in

Europe, began inexorably crumbling Dutch resistance. The fate of the Dutch independence and of Protestantism, the domination of Flanders and the Narrow Seas now turned solely on England. Next year the Earl of Leicester took an expeditionary force to the Netherlands – the inevitable hastily assembled force of untrained, ill-equipped men – and eighteen years of war began for England.

Throughout these years, the decisive theatre of operations was the Low Countries. The Dutch, with their English allies and German mercenaries, faced the main army of Spain, whose *tercios* – the most experienced and most formidable troops in Europe – were led by such great soldiers as Alexander of Parma and Don John of Austria. The Dutch had no English Channel to protect them, but only narrow canals, and fields and fortresses held by resolute men. This was the vital theatre, for had the Dutch Provinces been re-conquered, the Protestant cause on the continent of Europe would have been militarily lost; England would have had no foothold left and would have been alone in the face of the whole power of Spain.

Since the long struggle in the Low Countries was dependent on English money and men, it was clear to Philip II that both religion and grand strategy alike pointed towards a Spanish invasion of England and the replacement of Queen Elizabeth by a Catholic monarch. He began to prepare a great Armada of ships and troops in Spanish ports. It was to pass up the Channel, brushing aside the English fleet, and then break the Dutch blockade of the Flanders coast. There it would take on board 3,000 of Parma's troops to add to the 14,000 already with it, and ferry them all to England, where they would swiftly disperse the amateurs of the English militia.

The Spanish plan was delayed a full year by a brilliant raid by Drake on Spanish home ports in 1587 – an effective and econo-mical use of sea-power, crippling the enemy fleet before it had even sailed. During the year's delay, Spain's most accomplished admiral and the force-commander-designate, the Marquis of Santa Cruz, died. He was replaced by the Duke of Medina Sidonia, who possessed neither Santa Cruz's experience nor force of leadership. Thus Drake's raid may well have had decisive consequences. On the other hand, Drake's famous and financially profitable raids on Cartagena, San Domingo and Saint Augustine in Florida in 1585–6, the 'Descent on the Indies', were strategically meaningless, though excellent material for legend. The use of sea-power for commerce-raiding could do no more than interrupt, not stop, the flow of treasure from Spanish America to Spain. Though many attempts were made to intercept and capture the Spanish treasure fleets, none succeeded. In addition, the Spaniards re-organized their defences in the Caribbean, and later English attempts to repeat the raids of 1585–6 failed miserably with severe losses of men and ships.

In 1588 the largest fleet ever assembled by Spain, then the world's greatest sea-power, sailed for the Channel: two squadrons each of ten tall gilded galleons and four armed merchant ships from the West Indies trade, a squadron of fast manoeuvrable galleasses (hybrids between oared-galleys and sailing ships), four squadrons of ten heavily armed merchantmen, four Portuguese galleys, a flotilla and twenty-three unwieldy supply ships. On 29 July, the *Golden Hind* reported that the Armada was near the Scillies, and the English fleet – fourteen of the Queen's fighting galleons and forty armed merchant ships – left Plymouth. The English gained the weather gauge and pursued the Armada on its slow way up the Channel, great banners streaming from mastheads above drifting clouds of gunsmoke as the two fleets bombarded each other at long range. The Armada passed through the Straits of Dover unscathed and anchored off the coast at Gravelines.

The English – including even the Lord High Admiral – had been convinced that the Armada had intended to land its men direct on the south coast of England.[1] Its failure to do so was hailed as a decisive victory – the Lord High Admiral knighted Hawkins and Frobisher – although in fact the Spaniards had successfully carried out the first part of their plan, to rendezvous with Parma's army. The gunfire from the English broadsides had not damaged the Spanish fleet, while English flexibility of manoeuvre had been matched by excellent Spanish seamanship which had kept the Armada in a tight and invulnerable formation.

However, the Spaniards were now short of ammunition, and, unlike the English, could not replenish. Their heavy ships could not enter the shallow Flanders ports, but had to anchor in an open roadstead. The English now broke up the Armada by the traditional device of fireships sent in at night. Only then, against a scattered fleet almost out of ammunition, was their gunfire effective. The Armada sailed homewards in disorder round the British Isles, losing a third of its strength on the way.

For the English it was a swift and splendid deliverance from invasion. As later in 1804–5 and 1940, the danger was averted in a single dramatic moment by a single clear-cut battle. This defeat of the Spanish Armada marked the birth of a peculiarly English kind of legend, for other nations, with land frontiers, were always to know that deliverance from invasion rarely came through such single, sudden victories, but through many hard and tedious campaigns.

Other legends grew up around the central legend of the Spanish Armada: the legends of the superiority of English ships and seamen (false),[2] of the decisive effect of the new English broadside cannonade (false);[3] but above all the romantic legend of heroic leadership at sea winning a war in one gallant encounter. For three centuries all these myths were to be woven into a glowing tapestry of the triumph of sea-power, and in that glow, the humble, often squalid service of the army alongside the Dutch over years, not days, was to be too easily forgotten.

For while the English sailors had saved England from invasion, the real issue of the war turned on the campaigns in the Netherlands. Parma himself recognized this. In 1588 he was gradually and inexorably reconquering Spain's lost territories. To Parma, Philip II's invasion plans were a dangerous diversion of strength from the main theatre to a secondary purpose. Parma was right, because while he and his 3,000 veterans waited for Medina Sidonia, the Dutch were given a decisive respite, and an ultimate Spanish victory was never to seem quite so certain again. Many years of dreary campaigning lay ahead in the Low Countries before Spain admitted failure, and all this time a now almost forgotten English army fought and endured. Again as with Trafalgar in

1805 and the Battle of Britain in 1940, the defeat of the Armada in 1588 hardly marked more than the start of the heaviest struggle.

For this land war England still had no military institutions permanent and professionalized like, say, the Church or the Law. There was nothing but the militia – English society (mostly of course rural county society) with a weapon in its hand. The navy, on the other hand, had acquired a kind of permanence under the Navy Board because its equipment and installations – ships and dockyards – were permanent. However, most of its officers and crews were commissioned in wartime and released in time of peace. The Queen's ships that were kept in commission in peacetime traded like any merchant vessel. Hard-and-fast twentieth-century distinctions were non-existent in a time of transition like the sixteenth century.

In the years 1585–1603 the English militia system had to meet two distinct requirements, as in the reign of Henry VIII; it had to prepare to defend the country should the Spaniards land, and it had to provide the reservoir from which expeditionary forces could be drawn for overseas. However, this time the scale and weight of the demands made upon it were unprecedented. How far was the militia successful in meeting these requirements? The answer to this question shows Tudor military institutions stretched to the limit.

The keys to the system were the county Lords-Lieutenant, paid not in money, but, like other Tudor local administrators, in honours and prestige. England was an overwhelmingly rural nation, and her culture was not centred on great cities, as in Europe. Serfdom had already disappeared from the English countryside, and there was no rigid caste system separating social classes or dividing the town bourgeoisie from the country gentry, as on the Continent. English noblemen could and did enter commerce, and successfully, a thing forbidden to their French equivalents. The newly rich merchant, on the other hand, could buy land and become a gentleman. Elizabethan England was in social flux, some men (and families) rising and some falling. Perhaps for this reason stress was laid on the distinction of rank; yet this was a distinction of degree, rather than the absolute barrier of a distinction of kind. The society of an English shire was therefore homogeneous despite its differing social levels. The Lord-Lieutenant and his deputies and the Commissioners of Musters were thus the natural leaders of their county, dealing with the Queen's business collectively, and lending it the weight of their own authority.

Until after 1588 the Lords-Lieutenant were still not appointed regularly or permanently, but only to deal with specific troubles or dangers. Their commissions speak of such things as the 'notorious trouble made in the North part of the Realm', or 'the doubtful proceedings of the French' or 'the great preparations made by the King of Spain in respect of some unkindness that hath passed between us'.[4] The first qualification for a Lord-Lieutenant was royal confidence in his loyalty; in the opening words of his commission: 'Know ye that for the great and singular trust and confidence we have in your approved fidelity, wisdom and circumspection, we have assigned ... you to be our lieutenant ....'.[5] The relationship between the Queen's Council and the Lieutenants was close; Lieutenants were chosen with care, and most of them were either Privy Councillors or friends of prominent members of the Council. The Council would hear to the Lieutenants on local matters, though not always, for sometimes the Council knew better. On 29 March 1571, for instance, the Privy Council rejected a Lieutenant's recommendation of a captain's commission for a Mr George Turberville, pointing out that he 'hath been always from his youth and still is given to his books and study and never exercised in matters of war'.[6]

Though the authority of the Tudor monarchy rested not on a royal army, but on consent and loyalty, the royal leadership as exercised through the Council was strong and clear. Disputes between Lieutenants were swiftly dealt with. Resistance to their authority by any body, however privileged, was sternly rebuked. The town of Launceston, for instance, stood on its ancient charter and refused to join the musters. The Council's reaction summarizes the Elizabethan notion of duty underlying the whole militia system:

... now learn that you, the Mayor and townsmen of Launceston, contrary to this order and otherwise heretofore you have been accustomed, have of late refused and do refuse to join with the rest of the county in the said musters, pretending an exemption and privilege by your Charter, which pretence of yours cannot be otherwise understood than a backwardness and slackness in Her Majesty's service; when in such a case as this is, for the common safety of the realm and the defence of that county whereof you yourselves are a part, you stand so curiously upon the privilege of your Charter. You shall therefore understand that it is your part to join with the rest of the county in this public service, which you may do well enough without prejudice to your liberty ... And moreover, you shall do well to be advised touching the curious standing upon your Charter, lest you cause the same to be called in question and contending for some part to lose all.[7]

The responsibility of Lord-Lieutenant covered the complete range of military activities, from mustering and training to leading the men in action if there was fighting in England. He also had the disagreeable task of levying men for service overseas. He was responsible for morale and public order, and could arrest and punish people who spread rumours or caused alarms and commotions. The Lord-Lieutenant often had other functions within the general Tudor system of unpaid local government, such as that of ecclesiastical or grain commissioner, for instance, or commissioner for public loans.

To help in these duties, the Lord-Lieutenant called on the Justices of the Peace and others of his fellow-gentlemen to act as his deputies (up to five or six, often with one to a large town) or as Commissioners of Musters. A deputy's work was hard, especially if the Lord-Lieutenant were absent:

If aught were well done, the Lieutenant had the praise and thanks, although all the charge and travail is borne by us, but if any business has ill success the blame is laid upon us.[8]

Thus Sir Matthew Arundel to Sir Robert Cecil. However, on their side the Lieutenants sometimes found their friends and neighbours in the county slow to help in times of peace, when hunting and estate business seemed more compelling than preparation for war:

This present day Mr Lieutenant hath mustered at Windsor without the help of any Justice or gentleman of estimation other than the Mayor. I assure your Honour me thinketh it is a thing much out of order that they should not be as ready to serve the Queen's Majesty as they be to seek their own gain.[9]

At the summer musters to which all men between sixteen and sixty were summoned, the county levies were assembled, counted, divided into companies of 100 men under a captain (a gentlemen of the county). Two paid officers appointed by the Lord-Lieutenant – the Muster-Master and the Provost Marshal – carried out the detailed work of the musters. Men fit for service or for manual labour were picked and given some sort of training. Every county had its muster book in which was entered a record of the men, equipment and state of training in every hundred. The Privy Council periodically scrutinized these muster books, which in effect constituted the 'order of battle' of the militia.

Though proudly and patriotically English, Elizabeth's subjects disliked the summer musters intensely, with its waste of time needed for other pursuits, and, as the art of war progressed, its tedious drill with fire-arm or pike. No penalties could prevent a vast deal of shirking. Training was intermittent in the extreme – a few days at a time during the year. The men selected for training were known, not very accurately, as 'trained bands'.

From 1583 to the great invasion scare of 1588 preparations for the defence of the realm became more urgent and thorough. According to their vulnerability to invasion, counties were classified into five groups or degrees, with differing standards of equipment and readiness. Naturally, in an age where men thought it just that those nearest danger should bear the greatest brunt, the coastal shires carried the heaviest burden, and their inhabitants were forbidden to leave. In 1587, as the Armada made ready in Spanish ports, the English pressed on with laying out beach defences, arranging concentration points for levies and assembling warlike stores. The Lords-Lieutenant checked their stores of powder and shot. In October the Privy Council asked every county for a report on their preparations and readiness. The English were apparently taking the approaching crisis with their customary stolidity, for by April the Privy Council had had only fourteen replies, and dispatched blistering letters to the defaulters saying that Her Majesty found it 'very strange and doth not a little marvel at their negligence'.[10]

To give the Lords-Lieutenant and their amateur staff some professional advice and guidance, veteran professional soldiers from the Low Countries like Sir John Norris were sent on tours of inspection. Despite local difficulties and complaints, the nation generally seemed satisfied enough with its warlike preparations – a satisfaction that was to be repeated in the Napoleonic era and later. Their satisfaction was not shared by Sir John Norris as he cast his experienced eye over the rustic levies and their gentlemanly commanders; in his own words, he wondered that he could see no man in the kingdom afeared but himself.

The government reckoned that they would have about 130,000 men in the county levies to oppose a Spanish landing. An 'order of battle' of 1591 indicates that, impressive though this total might sound, comparatively few reached even the standard of readiness that afeared Sir John Norris. The list showed only 42,000 trained and 'furnished', and another 55,000 untrained, although mustered and armed.

The equipment of the levies was varied but inadequate and partly obsolescent; it included bows, pikes, bills, muskets (matchlocks heavier than the arquebus), and calivers (a 'calibre', midway between the arquebus and the musket). In 1590, in the 3,000 men of the trained bands of Essex there were nearly twice as many bowmen as musketeers, four-fifths as many bowmen as calivermen. Nevertheless there had been general improvement in the speed of adoption of fire-arms since the beginning of the reign. The decline of the archers was often regretted, many recalling that, in the military jargon of the time, the English archer under the Plantagenets could nail a French varlet's breeches to his bum with a single arrow.

When the Armada was reported at sea, preparations reached their peak. The Privy Council ordered the Lords-Lieutenant of Dorset, Devon and Cornwall to divide their forces into three groups: one on the coast, another in reserve for an encounter battle with the Spanish *tercios* and the third 'to be sorted with weapons ... reduced into bands' to move at an hour's notice to join the main field army at Tilbury. Immediate protests by the Lords-Lieutenant against sending men out of their own county illustrated another weak point of the militia system – its intensely local character.

The dispersal of the Armada, however, meant that in this first great English war of the modern era, the English military system for defence of the national territory was never put to the test. The gallant nobility and gentry of the shires, bravely mounted and armoured at the musters, the freeholders, tenants and tradesmen in pot or morion, could remain assured they constituted an army fit to face and beat the Spaniards. Unlike the unlucky *franc-archers* and *légions* of France, they never had to fight a desperate battle against really well-trained and experienced troops; their inadequacy, so clearly perceived by Sir John Norris, was never demonstrated.

Here then is the great difficulty of the English militia system. As an institution it was admirable. Instead of professional troops, a specialized body divorced from the life of the nation and possibly an obedient weapon in the hand of a tyrant, it was English society itself, the outward expression of the duty of all men to share in the defence of their country. It was cheap, for only the Muster-Master in each county was a paid crown officer; like the remainder of Tudor local government, everything else was done by the unpaid nobility and gentry, whose social authority was utilized for military purposes.

Yet, unfortunately, as a military instrument the militia was useless except against similar levies, such as rebels or Scots. Luckily for the English, their mistaken faith in the system was never put to the test because of geography. But the result was that long after most continental nations had abandoned levies or militia as a first-line national army, the English remained faithful to the militia. A tradition of amateurism became more and more deeply ingrained.

In the emerging professional armies of the Continent, while the nobility and gentry certainly provided (because of the feudal traditions and privileges of their class) the bulk of the officers, they were in general qualified to command troops by reason of their *professional* status and experience. Under the English system the nobility and gentry commanded simply because of their *social* position; the hierarchy of the county became the hierarchy of command.

However, the militia constituted not merely the home army; it formed the pool of reservists from which expeditionary forces, *real* armies, were levied and assembled. These armies had to match their skill, equipment and organization against the current standards of European war. They were the nearest thing that the Tudor military system produced to the increasingly permanent armies of the Continent.

3

Elizabethan
Expeditionary
Forces

SINCE the end of the Great Italian Wars in 1559, there had been fresh innovations in military tactics and equipment in Europe. In particular the proportion of horse to foot rose. The Civil Wars in France (1562–98) between Huguenots and Catholics were dominated by cavalry. At Jarnac (March 1569) and Moncontour (October 1569) the Huguenots were beaten because the cavalry encounters were decisive. At Coutras in 1587 however, the Huguenots won because their cavalry, in a new deep order, smashed the royalist cavalry charging as of old in two ranks.

The French Catholics enjoyed advantages similar to the Parliamentarians in the English Civil War: they controlled the capital, the government and the machinery of state. The nucleus of the French royal army was Catholic and the Catholics could count on help from the Spanish army in the Low Countries, as well as from hired German *Landsknechte* and *Reiter*. Swiss pikemen continued to fight for them under the old contract of 'Perpetual Peace'. The Wars of Religion produced no great strategic thinkers; as in the English Civil War, local struggles more or less unrelated to each other were fought out all over the country, while the main armies marched to and fro without much plan or effect. The memory of their pillage and destruction, however, made the French later ready to accept an absolute monarchy and a royal army as the price of order and firm government.

When the Wars of Religion opened, the regiment, already an accepted *ad hoc* battle grouping of companies or 'bands', was emerging in France as a permanent organization. The first three French regiments, of Picardie, Champagne and Piedmont, were formed from old royal bands, and by 1567 had been formally recognized. On the Huguenot side the regiment of Navarre (after Henry of Navarre) was formed in 1573. From these four regiments dates the continuous regimental history of the old French royal army.

In the war in the Netherlands, the Spanish army, the first to introduce tactical formations larger than a company, kept their

Mortars, 1575. The coming of artillery doomed the high-walled medieval castle and town. Military engineers developed a new kind of fortification, low in silhouette, to resist bombardment.

tercios of 3,000 men. Their disciplined skill as musketeers, their courage and ruthlessness, made the veteran Spanish infantry the most formidable and dreaded in Europe. Against them the Dutch Protestants could field at first only levies and unreliable mercenaries, and, after 1572, unofficial English volunteers. While the Dutch were unable to hold the open plains of the southern Netherlands (modern Belgium), they could hold out amid the water-seamed countryside of what is now Holland. The modern division of the Low Countries was therefore decided not by race and religion, but by the balance of war. Dutch towns became masterpieces of modern fortification: elaborate, intricate patterns of bastions and ravelines, demilunes, scarps and counterscarps, all surrounded by water. The Spaniards could not deploy their superior strength and skill, and the war became an affair of interminable sieges and small-scale skirmishes on high roads or dykes.

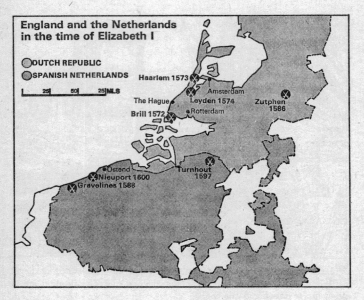

England and the Netherlands in the time of Elizabeth I

○ DUTCH REPUBLIC
● SPANISH NETHERLANDS

Haarlem 1573
Amsterdam
The Hague
Leyden 1574
Zutphen 1586
Brill 1572
Rotterdam
Ostend
Nieuport 1600
Turnhout 1597
Gravelines 1588

This was the war that Leicester's 'official' expeditionary force joined in 1585; and its demands for money, men and organization grew until the force was taken into Dutch service in 1594. At the same time, in Ireland, the Elizabethan government was holding down a colony inhabited by turbulent savages led by bellicose tribal chiefs. From time to time the Irish stopped their inter-tribal strife and turned on the small English garrison and its relatively civilized area (the Pale). Between 1559 and 1566 came the rebellion of Shane O'Neill; more troubles in 1569–72, another rebellion in 1579–83; and finally a really dangerous revolt under the Earl of Tyrone between 1594 and 1603 demanding a full-scale military effort.

In addition there were the sea-borne expeditions to Lisbon in 1589, Cadiz in 1596 and to the Azores in 1597; and expeditionary forces to help the French Huguenots after 1591. All this vast and widely-extended effort fell on the militia system and what new measures and organizations the Tudor government could improvise.*

Legally, units of the militia – like the pre-1914 Territorial Army – could not be required to serve overseas but only as individual volunteers. The militia and Lords-Lieutenant provided the organization of recruitment. The Crown ordered Lords-Lieutenant or Commissioners of Musters to provide so many men from a county. For the expedition to Normandy in 1591, for example, 3,400 men were demanded from twenty counties graded according to size, from 500 for Yorkshire to 50 for Surrey. In five months in Normandy sickness alone reduced these 3,400 men to 800. The ordinary people of Elizabethan England did not therefore spring to volunteer like their descendants of 1914. It was appallingly difficult to get recruits especially when requirements rose to 5,000 men a year. Volunteer officers or troopers were another matter; sons of nobility and gentry waiting for their inheritance were eager for the excitement, swagger and extravagant living associated with a campaign.

For the rank-and-file of the infantry compulsion was needed. It was applied by the Lords-Lieutenant and Commissioners of Musters, sometimes by sheriffs and Justices of the Peace, and sometimes by professional captains sent down to recruit – and applied to those least able to resist it: unemployed 'masterless men'. Vagabonds had been ripe war material since the campaigns of Edward I, and now they formed the main source of recruits for Elizabethan expeditionary forces. In the Privy Council's words they were 'such men as are fittest'. Captain Barnaby Rich has left a moving account of the recruiting process:

The Prince or Council, sendeth down their warrant to certain Commissioners, of every such shire when they mind to have such a number of

---

* C. G. Cruickshank, *Elizabeth's Army*, second edition, is the standard modern work on the Elizabethan military system.

soldiers levied and appointed; the Commissioner he sendeth his precept
to the High Constable of every Hundred; the High Constable of every
Hundred, he giveth knowledge to every petty Constable of every parish
within his circuit that upon such a day, he must bring two or three able
and sufficient men, to serve the prince, before such Commissions, to such
a place; the petty Constable when he perceiveth that wars are at hand,
foreseeing the toils, the infinite perils and troublesome travails that is
incident to soldiers, is loth that any honest man should hazard himself
amongst so many dangers, wherefore if within his office there hap to
remain any idle fellow, some drunkard, or seditious quarreller, a privy
picker or such a one as hath some skill in stealing of a goose, these shall
be presented to the service of the Prince.[1]

Such raw material might not be as unpromising as it appeared,
for a resourceful rogue might well make a good soldier. But men
produced by impressment or downright corruption might also be
totally useless militarily. The Justices of the Peace, for example,
could be bribed to give exemptions; one M.P. wrote that for half
a dozen chickens they would break half a dozen statutes. The rich
but timid could provide substitutes; yet another form of corruption guaranteeing the Queen useless recruits. Falstaff describes it
in a famous passage (though the play is *Henry IV*, Shakespeare is
plainly writing about his own era):

I have misused the King's press damnably. I have got, in exchange of
a hundred and fifty soldiers, three hundred and odd pounds. I press me
none but good householders, yeoman's sons . . . as had as lief hear the
devil as a drum . . . I press'd me none but such toasts-and-butter, with
hearts in their bellies . . . and they have bought out their services; and
now my whole charge consists of . . . slaves as ragged as Lazarus . . .
discarded unjust serving-men . . . revolted tapsters, and ostlers trade-
fall'n; the cankers of a calm world and a long peace. . . . A mad fellow
met me on the way, and told me I had unloaded all the gibbets and
press'd the dead bodies. No eye hath seen such scarecrows. . . . There's
not a shirt and a half in all my company.[2]

Once levied, these cankers of a calm world and a long peace
had to be got to the ports and overseas. At first no administrative
machinery existed for this. For their journey to the port and
lodgings recruits were given 8*d.* a day 'conduct' money advanced

by the county authority making the levy and recovered later from the Crown. They also had 'coat' money for their 'uniform' (not yet so called). Although parties of recruits were escorted either by the levying authority or an appointed leader, unless closely watched they faded away swiftly *en route*, sometimes after bribing their leader. The Council therefore instituted a system of indentures, lists giving name, equipment and parish, one copy for the Privy Council and the other for the escort.

If further delays occurred at the port (want of ships or adverse winds), recruits either succumbed to disease because of crowded conditions, or took their last opportunity to desert. It is indeed a wonder that Elizabethan England, despite these difficulties, managed to send overseas well over 80,000 men to all the various theatres and expeditions, a tribute perhaps to the number of genuine volunteers generally disregarded in contemporary accounts.

Transports were hired by the Crown from private owners, who combined movement of troops with normal trade because of the low hiring rates, rendering the voyage often circuitous. As the war went on, the Crown improved its arrangements and special representatives with powers of requisition were appointed to supervise groups of ports.

Thus, after long and sometimes exceedingly uncomfortable voyages, the troops, whether as an expedition or as drafts, reached the theatre of operations.

So far as organization, discipline and supply of an army in the field were concerned, virtually no regular institutions or system existed when the Elizabethan crisis opened. A semi-regular military hierarchy, with recognized ranks and spheres of responsibility, only emerged gradually from temporary appointments and *ad hoc* arrangements for particular expeditions.

In 1585 Leicester was styled 'Lieutenant and Captain-General' in the Netherlands, 'Lieutenant' being used in a sense similar to 'Lord-Lieutenant', in that he was to be the Queen's deputy. In fact he combined the duties of commander-in-chief and statesman, handling political relations with the Dutch, and even becoming involved in the modification of their constitution. Such independence and power in the hands of a man like Leicester had its dangers;

his successor in 1589, Sir Francis Vere, was limited to military command in the field, with the titles of 'Sergeant-major General' and 'Colonel-general'; and even the governors of garrison towns were independent of him. Yet another delegation of royal authority gradually ended during the reign was the power of commanders-in-chief to award knighthoods in the field.

In an age of slow and unreliable communications, a commander-in-chief necessarily had to take decisions on his own which might or might not accord with the government's wishes. The government therefore tried to control more distant expeditions by giving a detailed directive to the force commander. In the case of Essex's expedition to Spain and the Azores in 1597, the Privy Council appointed a Council of War to advise, or indeed control, Essex. If there was disagreement, Essex's decisions were to stand only if supported by three of the five members.

Under the commander-in-chief, the senior commanders or operational 'staff' appointments were the generals (often called 'colonel-generals', as literally they were) of infantry and cavalry, Master of the Ordnance and Master-Gunner, Forage-Master, Carriage-Master and Trench-Master. Posting the army for battle was the task of the Sergeant Major-General, while its organization and routing on the march that of the High-Marshal, who was also in charge of justice and discipline, and of camp lay-out and preparation.

Beneath the field-officers were the colonels. The first Tudor force to use the word correctly was the volunteer army sent to the Netherlands in 1572 under Sir Humphrey Gilbert; a colonel then commanded a 'regiment' (also the first correct use) of ten companies. The regiment became gradually stabilized as a tactical formation. The French expedition of 1590 was organized in regiments of 900; while at Cadiz six years later regiments were of 750 men.

The regiment being merely a tactical formation, the colonel's duties too were tactical only. Essex's instructions to his colonels made this clear: they were to be in the vanguard in attack, with the rearguard during retreat, to camp in the middle of their regiment and inspect their troops each week. Their sole administrative duty was justice, and they presided over the marshal's court for their own regiment. Colonels were assisted by lieutenant-colonels.

The basic administrative unit of the army was still the company (late 'band') of about a hundred men, and the officer below field rank in sole charge of administration, the captain. The captain was the key to the efficiency and economy of the army – to the entire Elizabethan system of an army in the field. In the words of Professor Neale:

He stood between the Queen's officials and his men, in some respects the exploiter of their labour, in others their representative and defender. He was to a certain extent responsible for arming, clothing and feeding them, all of which were expenses covered by their pay; if provision was made by royal officials – which was not necessarily the case – the sums expended were charged against the company and settled between the treasurer-at-war and the captain when payment was made. He was also responsible, so far as the supply of men allowed, for maintaining his company at full strength; his clerk kept muster rolls to record changes in numbers, and accounts to show how the company stood with the treasurer.[3]

In many respects the military company was still a true private-enterprise commercial 'company', and the captain partly an entrepreneur. In this era of transition from mercenary to standing armies, the mixture of private enterprise and public service was common to all armies in Europe.

The captains were therefore not simply junior officers in a military organization, but semi-independent and all-too-often fraudulent contractors. At first the captains did in fact raise their own companies of volunteers, but although later the Privy Council either appointed or approved captains, the standard of honesty did not noticeably improve.

In three major respects the captains held the key to the army's efficiency and their own enrichment: pay, men and supplies.

The troops were only paid every six months and meanwhile received advances called 'imprests'. The money was paid as a lump sum to the captains, according to the numbers on their muster rolls. Here was a loophole for peculation, particularly by dishonest use of the so-called 'dead-pays'. 'Dead-pays' were in the first instance a purely legal method by which pensions were paid to

Sixteenth-century warfare – a soldiers' camp, from Holinshed's *Chronicles*, 1577. Standing professional armies, organized into regiments and with primitive supply and medical services, were then evolving in Europe.

men no longer on active service. They were also an equally legal method, standard in the Netherlands after 1585, by which the captain was allowed a hundred men's pay for every ninety-five actually in the company, supposedly to permit increased pay both for the captain and for 'gentleman volunteers', and so raise the standard of men. Primarily, however, 'dead-pays' meant the system by which captains put in their own pocket pay for men truly dead or no longer with the company but whose names were still on the muster roll. Since the captains also controlled the issue of food, clothing and other supplies, the muster roll was the key to the system; and therefore the sole governmental administrative control over the army was the muster itself.

By regulation, the men of each company were to be mustered and counted once a month against the company roll; the muster-master then made up his six-monthly records. The muster system, however, was a failure.

The muster office was the key to the efficient management of the army ... Accurate muster returns would have paved the way for immense savings through stoppages on the pay of absentees and corresponding savings in the supply of food and clothing. They would have compelled men to keep arms and equipment in a satisfactory condition. Above all, they would have exposed the magnitude of the captains' deceptions. ... But a corrupt and inefficient muster office was the captains' passport to wealth: and they were clever enough to ensure that it remained so.[4]

In the sixteenth century Victorian standards of honesty were not expected in public servants, in England or anywhere else, and every office had its perquisites. If the captains were crooked, so were the chief pay officials, the treasurer-at-war and his staff. Sir George Carew during his tenure of the post is thought to have pocketed £150,000. Later the army in the Netherlands was paid through merchants.

Supply raised similar problems of organization, supervision and corruption. At first, the victualling of the armies was entirely in the hands of competing private merchants, who took advantage of the army's need to charge high prices for often defective goods. In 1588 there was a mutiny at Ostend partly because of poor rations, partly because of lack of pay. Gradually the government had to take over victualling and create its own administrative machine, although the actual supply remained in the hands of merchants. The Privy Council entrusted the supply of food to the troops in Ireland to a single merchant under stringent contract conditions. Between 1598 and 1601, when Tyrone's rebellion was raging, no fewer than fifteen contracts were made, worth over £100,000. In the Netherlands a 'victualling commissioner' was appointed, and in 1588 the first new-style contract, laying down prices and general stipulations, was signed for a vital commodity, beer, of which half a gallon per man was issued daily. (In Ireland's damp climate, the ration was a quart a day, with half a pint of sack, and every other day, half a pint of whisky.) Victualling contracts specified quantities and a fixed delivery date; the merchants were paid an instalment on signature, and the rest on delivery. Government responsibility was further extended when the Crown assumed the financial risks and set up its own food warehouse on Walcheren for the troops in Holland. Even so, there was room for robbery when the rations reached the captains.

Clothing was issued to expeditionary forces twice a year and was supplied by merchants under contract on a cost-per-head basis. The supervising government office was the Wardrobe, whose distant and inefficient control could not ensure that the goods supplied were of the specification demanded. Finance was in the hands of the Treasurer-at-War, the ingenious Sir George Carew, and actual issue in the hands of the captains; hence clothing proved another huge leak of government money. There were no uniforms as such; Lords-Lieutenant sometimes chose a county colour, and the government's ideas varied from time to time and theatre to theatre. In 1574 infantry coats were to be 'color bleu, Gasconie fashion'; in 1584 troops in Ireland were to be dressed 'in motley, or other sad green colour', an early form of camouflage or khaki (clearly 'motley' was not clown's garb, but probably a tweedy mixture).

The supply of munitions (armour, weapons, powder, etc.) in the field was the responsibility of the expedition's master of the ordnance. The government department responsible for supply both at home and abroad was the Ordnance Office. Under the Master

48

of the Ordnance this office was really the only 'standing' part of the military system, and included a lieutenant, a surveyor, keepers and clerks of the great and small storehouses, clerks of deliveries, and, of course, the master gunner. Beneath them developed a considerable staff: carpenter, joiner, cooper, smith, bowyer, fletcher, grinder, two 'furbishers', two testers of gunpowder and saltpetre, a carter, a messenger, six book-keepers and twenty labourers. The ordnance office was thus a large and complex department of state, as it needed to be to meet its wide responsibilities, ranging from the production and care of artillery, small-arms, personal equipment, to 'trench stores'. A corrupt master-general, like the Earl of Warwick, found abundant opportunity for fraud, but later, when Essex was master-general, accounting, book-keeping and issuing methods were tightened up. No one, however, could prevent the soldiers themselves selling their arms and equipment, though the offence carried the death penalty under royal proclamation in 1590.

Taken as a whole, the organization – or organizations – evolved and improved under Elizabeth must be regarded as successful achievements in the face of difficulties which no sixteenth-century government could altogether surmount – the negligence and corruption at all levels, the novelty both in kind and scale of the national effort required, the variety of and distance between the theatres of war. No army was paid or fed as regularly as the English; and if the English occasionally mutinied, so did the renowned Spanish *tercios* when they received no pay. Accusations of Elizabeth's parsimony and neglect of her soldiers have been proved by detailed research to be false. They are also unreasonable. War is always a prodigiously expensive business. It was so in the sixteenth century and even the treasure of South America could not prevent Spain going bankrupt. War was also a bottomless sink of financial corruption. Firm control at source by the Queen and her Council was probably the only effective method of restricting the fortunes which men could make at the public expense. The augmented wartime income of the Crown was only £300,000 a year, while the contract cost (greatly exceeded) of maintaining 7,600 men in the Netherlands alone was £126,000 a year, and Tyrone's rebellion in Ireland cost almost £2,000,000. Even with some £2,000,000 raised in extra taxation agreed by the Queen's faithful Parliament, the cost of all the wars could not be met out of current income. Debt – financial weakness – was the dry rot of a strong monarchy in the face of the gradually waxing power and confidence of the House of Commons. Strict control over war expenditure was essential, not 'parsimony'. If, at the far end of a chain of greedy and un-scrupulous middle-men, the soldier went short of supplies the Queen had paid for, it was hardly Elizabeth's fault. She kept her armies in the field and she never went bankrupt.

Indeed, care of the soldier improved somewhat. To reduce the very heavy toll of disease overseas, hospitals were established at home and in Ireland, and improved medical services organized in the field. A hospital for maimed soldiers was set up at Buckingham, and Parliament instituted and increased disablement pensions paid from a parish levy.

However, administration, good or bad, is only a means to main-tain a fighting force. It is as a fighting force that an army – a military system – must be judged. Administration can be expanded or improvised, and was; the creation of a trained army without a nucleus of trained and experienced men and an organizational framework is less easy. The English force in the Netherlands eventu-ally taken over by the United Provinces in 1594 consisted of hard and steady troops, better than most in Dutch service. Yet they were separated by nine years of heavy loss and painful experience from the mixture of levies and gallant gentlemen under Leicester in 1585 and by more than twenty years from the volunteers of 1572. The English militia system failed to produce either an effec-tive home defence force or immediately battleworthy expeditionary forces. It would be unfair to blame Elizabeth or her government. So long as war appeared to the English as an occasional emergency rather than a semi-permanent aspect of national life, the solution – a professional army – was in practice impossible, obvious though it may seem in retrospect.

The strategic direction of the war is more open to criticism, although the temptation for a hard-pressed government to engage in glamorous but strategically irrelevant enterprises is understandable.

The struggle between Catholic and Protestant was not only fought out in the Netherlands, but in France in the Civil Wars of Religion. Although Spanish troops from the Netherlands were lent to the French Catholics, the two theatres of war remained virtually unconnected, however, until 1590. In that year Henry of Navarre, the Huguenot leader, won a crushing victory at Ivry in a cavalry battle, and Paris lay open to him. Philip II of Spain reacted to this by repeating his mistake of the Armada year, 1588. He ordered Parma to march south from the Netherlands to fight the Huguenots in France. After the Armada pause, Parma and his veterans had resumed their relentless reconquest of the Netherlands. Now his sovereign gave the enemy another respite. For nearly two years half Parma's army was absent from the decisive theatre. But the English, instead of reinforcing the Low Countries, where a proper supply organization now existed and the troops had settled down into an experienced army, improvised two fresh expeditions, to Brittany and Normandy. The Brittany operations dragged on until 1595, with no prospect of affecting the war. The Normandy expedition was commanded not by a soldier but by the Queen's favourite, Essex. Disease swiftly reduced its raw levies from 3,600 to 800.

These expeditions, based on the lure of sea-power, set a pattern of English war-making that was to be repeated in almost all England's great continental struggles. Even more tempting to the Queen's government was the idea, passionately supported by men such as Drake, that Spain could be easily and decisively crippled, and profitably, by seaborne expeditions to her coast and her American empire. These expeditions not only starved the Netherlands army of fresh drafts, but also milked it of trained troops, despite the English commander's protests – a foretaste of the Great War arguments between the supporters of the Western Front and the protagonists of a Balkan or Middle Eastern strategy.

The great expedition to Portugal in 1589 was a total failure, partly owing to the hesitant leadership of Drake and needless delays in the operations; partly because of the unsolved and novel problems of naval and military co-operation. The problem became more acute when Drake and Norris (the army commander) were separated. In 1596 came the grand expedition to Cadiz, led by a galaxy of Elizabethan military and naval talent: Essex, Howard, Vere and Raleigh. As a combined operation, the venture was a brilliant success. Cadiz was taken and held for a fortnight. Such daring and its dramatic results dazzled the Elizabethans. Together with Drake's 'singeing of the Spanish king's beard' in 1587 and the equally dramatic success against the Armada, it has dazzled English statesmen, historians and sailors ever since. It apparently established, and justified, a peculiarly English way of making war: swift and spectacular in results, low in casualties – very different from the slow, muddy progress of the Dutch from one siege to another.

Nevertheless, the temporary capture of Cadiz was an empty success. Neither the naval nor the land forces available were enough to hold it as a permanent front on Spanish soil, as Wellington held Portugal after 1808. They could do no more than destroy one Spanish town and port, and even that was not entirely accomplished. How could this venture – even if repeated every year – affect Spain's ability and willingness to fight in the Netherlands and France?

In 1597 the English tried to repeat their success, this time against the Azores and the Spanish treasure fleet. It was an utter failure, and while the English fleet was straggling home another Spanish Armada was sailing unopposed to England. Not English sea-power but a north-east gale turned this Armada homewards.

Meanwhile English naval strength, instead of blockading the Spanish Netherlands, was even more widely dispersed in quest of even more glittering prizes – the plundering of the Spanish Empire and treasure fleets. In 1595 Drake and Hawkins led a strong expedition to the Caribbean. They found Spanish defences improved and well-organized; plunder was scarce; Drake died; the fleet came home with little to show. Privateering might make merchants money, but the English with the ships of the era could not cut Spain's sea communications. With the failure of the 1597 expedition to the Azores, the splendid age of Elizabethan sea-power, so rich in legend, so sparse in solid results, ended. It was left to Maurice of Nassau in the Netherlands and his English troops under

Francis Vere to continue their unglamorous but relentless pressure on the Spanish army. It was this pressure which convinced Philip II before he died in 1598 that he could never reconquer the United Provinces, and which eventually led to Spanish acknowledgement of Dutch independence in 1609.

It was after the English regiments in the Netherlands had passed into the direct Dutch service that they fought their two heaviest battles, Turnhout and Nieuport, in both of which they distinguished themselves. An Italian diplomat in the Netherlands wrote of the English troops, 'Best beloved by the natives; brave, patient veterans'.

Turnhout (24 January 1597) was the sequel to a Dutch raid on a Spanish force covering Antwerp. The attacking force, under Maurice of Nassau, comprised fifty companies of foot, including the English regiments of Francis Vere and Dockwray and sixteen 'cornets' of horse, including the units of Horace Vere, Parker and Sidney (800 horsemen). A third of the entire force was English. Eight companies of Scots in Dutch service were also present.

The Spanish commander, the Count of Varas, beat a hasty retreat on hearing of Maurice's approach. He was caught on the move, in column of route, on a stretch of raised moorland amid inundated countryside. Fearing that the Spaniards might pass this open moor into the relative safety of marshland before he could deploy his whole force, Maurice sent in his cavalry with 300 arquebusiers under Francis Vere. The Spanish cavalry was broken, and while a German and Dutch force attacked the head of the Spanish army, the English attacked the rear. At a cost of perhaps fifty men, Maurice of Nassau destroyed Varas' army, with the loss of 2,000 dead and 500 prisoners; it was a spectacularly successful example of surprise and boldness.

The English troops were organized and trained according to Maurice of Nassau's innovations in fighting tactics. Since the Netherlands terrain limited the role of cavalry, Maurice's improvements largely concerned the infantry. He wanted greater manoeuvrability and flexibility than was possible with the large tactical units of the later sixteenth century, like the Spanish *tercio*, which even though reduced by half in 1584 was still a dense, deep mass of 1,500 men. Under the Dutch the regiment shrank to some 800 men, consisting of ten or twelve companies, half pikemen and half 'shot'. Instead of deep, close order, the front was extended: pikemen at three-foot intervals; musketeers on the flanks, firing in rotation, and seeking shelter in the pikes during close fighting. Orders and manoeuvres were laid down in detail in drill books and hammered into the soldiers by rigorous discipline. Like Caesar's troops, Maurice of Nassau's were accustomed to dig themselves in.

On 2 July 1600, English troops under the Vere brothers bore the main brunt of one of the few general actions fought during the Netherlands war. It took place on the beach and dunes just north of Nieuport. The States General had decided on a risky advance down the coast to try to capture the ports of Dunkirk and Nieuport, whence corsairs raided Dutch shipping. There was a more ambitious strategic intention to render the Spanish position in what is now modern Belgium untenable by capturing the entire Flanders coast. Maurice of Nassau, though unwilling to command in a campaign that he considered hazardous, eventually agreed. His fears were justified when Archduke Albert (who had inherited the Spanish Netherlands on the death of Philip II) swiftly collected an army. The prospect of fighting heretics ended a pay mutiny among most of his Spanish troops, for the *tercios* were a curious transitional blend between the true mercenary and national troops moved by national or religious loyalty.

Concentrating and moving rapidly, Archduke Albert reached the coast between Maurice of Nassau and his base in the United Provinces, cutting his communications and so forcing him to fight. Behind him was the hostile port of Nieuport. Though tidal, the river Yser could not accommodate transports for more than a portion of his army, so victory alone could save him.

Both armies deployed on a wide stretch of sand uncovered by low tide, and in the sand-hills beyond. Before the main action could be joined, the tide and fire from Dutch ships forced the Spaniards to side-step into the sand-hills, with their cavalry beyond on a 'green road'. The Dutch army did likewise. The front between the sea and wet farmland was narrow, and so both armies were deployed in great depth. The Dutch van was commanded by Sir Francis Vere, and of its forty-one companies (4,000 men) twenty-four were English. In succession, Archduke Albert attacked Vere with his van, his main battle and finally his rearward. Only then did the stubborn, outnumbered and unsupported English begin to give ground and the Spaniards followed hesitantly, themselves exhausted and disorganized. Maurice's cavalry reserve, including English horse, charged and routed them. The English infantry moved forward again; Maurice ordered a general advance and the Spaniards dissolved. Nearly half the Spanish army was destroyed and 2,500 to 4,000 were killed. Shattered in the general wreck was an Irish Catholic regiment under Colonel Bostock, himself among the dead.

Nieuport was an unusual battle for the period, because it was decided not by cavalry action, but by the infantry fight. In that fight, English troops, experienced, well-trained professionals, had smashed the most highly-reputed troops in Europe.

In Ireland, the English had been fighting a very different kind of campaign with equal skill. Tyrone's rebellion was the first of modern English colonial wars. The enemy enjoyed all the qualities and advantages of insurgents: mobility, knowledge of the country, ability to melt into the population. English armies sweated through the bogs of Ireland pursuing the elusive Irish, while raiding parties cut their own communications behind them. Ireland became a grave of military reputations, including the most brilliant of all, that of the Earl of Essex, Elizabeth's young favourite. Ireland was not popular with the English soldiers: those who could, deserted before they embarked, while their officers found numerous excuses for returning to England on important private business.

In Charles Blount, later Lord Mountjoy, Elizabeth found the equal in colonial war of the Veres in continental campaigning. He landed in Ireland in January 1600. In three years the rebellion, smouldering since 1593, was stamped out. The methods employed by Mountjoy have never been bettered; indeed their pattern has been repeated by European troops all over the world to this day. He took hostages, he burned villages and destroyed crops in country harbouring the rebels, gradually starving them and depriving them of shelter. He harried them with light flying columns which were their equal in mobility. His mobile operations pivotted on a mesh of fortified towns and new forts which the rebels could not take. Whenever the Irish stopped to fight, he smashed them. Although the total of English troops in Ireland rose nominally to 14,000 foot and 1,200 horse, garrisons and protection of communications swallowed most of them, and the normal field force probably did not exceed some 3,500 men.

In 1601 Mountjoy faced a new and more formidable adversary in the Spaniards. Without interference from the English fleet, a Spanish squadron sailed from Lisbon to Kinsale and disembarked some 3,800 veteran troops to assist the Irish. In little more than a month Mountjoy had concentrated some 7,000 men round Kinsale and begun a siege. Gradually, even reluctantly, Tyrone and his Irish marched to relieve Kinsale and join with the Spanish force. Spanish sallies were repulsed, and on Christmas Eve, 1601, masking the Spanish garrison of Kinsale, Mountjoy gave battle to Tyrone. At first the Irish fought steadily, but once the English cavalry had broken their horse, the Irish army gave way and dissolved into headlong flight, each man to his own cabin. In January 1602, the Spaniards surrendered Kinsale. The rest of Mountjoy's Irish campaign consisted of pursuit and pacification. Tyrone himself made his submission a few days after the death of Queen Elizabeth.

II

Military Power and Constitutional Struggle 1603–1714

4
King, Parliament
and
Military Power

WHEN Elizabeth died, the war between England and Spain was still dragging on without prospect of victory for either side, and one of James I's earliest decisions was to end it. Peace was not only a realistic stroke of policy, but accorded with the donnish, pacifistic character of the new king. The Dutch and the Spaniards fought on till 1609.

The English military structure – so painfully improvised, expanded and reformed under Elizabeth – was now dismantled, like one of the twentieth-century wartime ministries. No 'army' except the guards and garrisons of forts and towns remained. Even the militia acts of Philip and Mary were repealed, and the militia system reverted to the Statute of Winchester of Edward I. The gulf between a militia and professional soldiers, already apparent a hundred years before and now so much wider, still went generally unperceived in England. The militia indeed became decadent even by its own standards. The occasional drill days were treated, as one colonel wrote in 1639, as 'matters of disport and things of no moment'. The same colonel draws a vivid picture of the severities of the training:

As trainings are now used, we shall, I am sure, never be able to make one good soldier; for our custom and use is, nowadays, to cause our companies to meet on a certain day, and by that time the arms be all viewed, and the muster master hath had his pay (which is the chiefest thing many times he looks after) it draws towards dinner time; and, indeed, officers love their bellies so well that they are loath to take too much pains about disciplining of their soldiers. Wherefore, after a little careless hurrying over of their postures ... they make them charge their

...kets, and so prepare to give their captain a brave volley of shot at his entrance into his inn; where after having solaced themselves for a while after this brave service every man repairs home.[1]

Even such training was limited to one day a month in summer. Only the London trained bands, fixed at 6,000 men in 1614, took their work seriously; while some private military societies in London also met for instruction by professional soldiers.

Although the Elizabethan military machine was allowed to disintegrate, there was a senior government body responsible for defence which did its best to preserve and improve at least the paper organization and the equipment of the militia. This was the Council of War, composed of eminent soldiers and state servants. It did what it could to combat public indifference, ordering Lords-Lieutenant 'to make a general muster of the trained horse and foot in their several counties, and to see to the sufficiency of the men, horses, and arms, and that all be complete according to the most modern form'.[2] It planned improved training with tours of inspection by veterans from the Netherlands. In 1631 a team of technicians travelled the country to put arms, armour and equipment in order, and ensure 'that expert workmen may be secured so as to render the supply of arms and armour independent of foreigners'.[3] A programme for standardization of design was laid down. Charles I and his government hoped for an 'Exact' or 'Perfect' militia. Intentions were good; some attempt to carry them out was made; but resuscitating the militia in peacetime was like trying to revive a dead carcass.

Under the first two Stuarts, then, England possessed no military power; and undoubtedly this was the conscious and unconscious will of the nation. The only logical foreign policy, therefore, was one of total isolationism. In the European situation of the time this was impossible, even had it been desirable, for in 1618 the wars of religion of the previous century burst out again in the heart of Europe with increased hatred and fanaticism.

The election of Archduke Ferdinand, a Catholic and Habsburg, as King of Bohemia was rejected by the Protestant Bohemians. They deposed him and elected the Elector Palatine, Frederick V. This challenge to the unity of the Holy Roman Empire and the imperial authority was met by force. In the first great battle of the war, the White Mountain in Bohemia in 1620, the Bohemian army under King Frederick was routed and the Emperor Ferdinand swiftly reconquered Bohemia for Catholicism and the Empire. Yet the decisiveness of the victory was deceptive, for it was only the beginning of the Thirty Years' War. Since the Habsburg successes in Germany in the 1620s threatened both princely liberties within the Empire and the Protestant faith, Protestant princes rallied to Frederick. Gradually the war increased in scope and brutality until all Germany was laid waste by pillage and destruction, leaving a scar on German minds ineffaceable for centuries. Meanwhile Spain was again attacking the Dutch in the Low Countries, and the Huguenots rose in France.

Could England stay neutral while the Counter-Reformation set out to reconquer all Europe for the Pope – when the hunted King of Bohemia was James I's own son-in-law?

A pacific King and nation faced the familiar English problem: how to influence events in Europe without incurring the costs and responsibilities of raising the necessary forces. In 1620 the King's military advisers calculated that to regain and defend Frederick's own state, the Palatinate, would demand an army of 25,000 foot and 5,000 horse, costing over £2,000,000 to raise and transport, and £900,000 a year to maintain – horrifying to a hard-up monarch whose authority depended on not asking the House of Commons for money; horrifying too to a House of Commons in whose view war should not merely be cheap, but profitable. So instead of creating an army, James elected to remain neutral and merely send some 2,000 volunteers under Horace Vere to the Palatinate. Vere's force fought well, like so many English expeditions later in history; but, like them it was too small to affect the war. Nor was neutrality so easy in a Europe convulsed by religious war. English opinion, strongly Protestant, called loudly for opposition to Spain and the Holy Roman Empire – though not of course at any sacrifice or cost to the public. A major war in central Europe, people thought, could be influenced and the King's son-in-law restored to his dominions by raids on Spanish America. Not only would this cost nothing; it might even make money. The King, at odds with the Commons, tried to form a European coalition to support his son-in-law. Gradually, inevitably, this continental policy demanded troops. As demands increased, Jacobean England repeated all the mistakes of the Tudors. Men were hastily raised to meet particular emergencies: 6,000 for Holland in 1624, 12,000 for Germany in 1625. They had to be press-ganged, 'for our people do apprehend too much the hardships and miseries of soldiers in these times'.[4] Already England had been forced to raise almost all the 25,000 men originally recommended by the royal military advisers in 1621. But, though equally costly, this was no army: 'Such a rabble of raw and poor rascals have not been lightly seen, and they go so unwillingly that they must rather be driven than led.'[5]

There was no military organization for supplies or anything else. Within a year all but 1,200 of the 12,000 men sent to Germany had died without firing a shot. The desire to avoid sacrifice and expense, to play the great power on the cheap, had involved the English in greater expense for smaller effect than a permanent professional army could have given them.

Under Charles I, this disastrous pattern continued. Once more under the lure of easy success and plunder an English seaborne expedition was sent to Cadiz, this time under the command of Buckingham, the King's favourite. The troops were unpromising: 'The number of lame, impotent and unable men, unfit for actual service, is very great.'[6] The English landing force, once on Spanish soil, was defeated by a warehouse full of wine; in the words of a colonel, 'they became so drunk that in my life I never saw such beastliness'. On their way back to their ships they were routed by the Spaniards.

Two years later, when the tortuous foreign policy of Charles and Buckingham had alienated France too, another maritime expedition was sent to the Isle de Rhé to relieve the Huguenot stronghold of La Rochelle. It returned home in abject failure, having lost 5,000 of its 8,000 men. On the one hand there was this reality of ill-organized, ill-trained, inexperienced men dying in futility; on the other, the soaring fantasies of Charles's and Buckingham's foreign policy. After Buckingham's assassination in 1628, there was even a scheme to ally England with Spain, so that Spanish troops might recover the Palatinate for Charles's brother-in-law, the Elector Palatine. Gradually it all petered out in humiliation; and after 1630 England virtually ceased to have a European policy.

England's external impotence was due partly to the shifting and ill-judged policies of James I and Charles I, but even more to the deepening constitutional quarrel between Parliament and Crown which deprived the latter of any basis for a strong grand strategy. The Commons were only too ready to attack Charles and Buckingham for the ludicrous failure of their enterprises, and yet also argue cogently for a grand, English-led, Protestant coalition against the Habsburgs. In general the war party was harking back in its mind to the Elizabethan legend, thinking of profitable sea-raids on Spain or her empire rather than of large-scale land campaigns in Germany. In any case, they remained reluctant to vote money to support the *King's* policy; and so British intervention remained ineffective. While Europe was ravaged by war, Britain slept in peace. Since the English and Scottish crowns were now worn by the same monarch, men rested tranquilly in their beds as never before in the two countries' history. No wonder the militia thought more of its beer than its drill; no wonder the idea of a professional army entered no one's head. Germany, and the marches of Tilly and Wallenstein, were far away.

However, English and Scottish troops did fight in the great campaigns and decisive battles of the Thirty Years' War, troops as formidable and as well-led as the best continentals – but they fought as mercenaries for the United Provinces, Sweden or France. Throughout this period, therefore, the British did possess standing professional forces – but unrecognized, divorced from the national life.

The English troops in the Netherlands who had passed into the Dutch service in 1593 had continued to fight the Spaniards until the United Provinces and Spain made peace in 1609. The year before, Sir Francis Vere, their old commander, had died in England at the age of forty-seven. In 1605 the English in Dutch service were organized into three regiments. In 1625, when the Dutch were once more at war with the Spaniards for control of the lower Rhine, as one of the theatres of the Thirty Years' War, another regiment of English was formed out of the garrisons of Flushing and Brill.

There were more Scottish soldiers in Europe than English, particularly under the Dutch because of the Calvinist connexion. Scots also marched with King Gustavus-Adolphus of Sweden and shared his two great victories, for the Swedish army included four Scots regiments – Hepburn, Mackay, Stargate and Lumsden – grouped into a brigade under the command of Sir John Hepburn.

Though their contribution to the Thirty Years' War was small compared with that of the Dutch or Swedes, these British volunteers accomplished far more than the 'official' interventions of James I and Charles I. Had the volunteers fought under their own flags as recognized instruments of English and Scottish foreign policy, the two British kingdoms together would have ranked as a considerable power, with corresponding influence on European events; events which were ultimately bound to affect the safety and future of the British Isles. As it was, the volunteers brought their countries no direct benefit, prestige or influence. However, service with foreign armies at least enabled a new generation of British officers to gain knowledge and experience of war during an epoch of rapid change in organization and tactics. Between 1600 and 1640 a generation of able commanders grew up from this standing army in foreign pay: Lord Willoughby, Lord Willoughby de Eresby, Lord George Goring, Skippon, Jacob Astley, Sir Edward Cecil (Lord Wimbledon), the Earl of Essex, Prince Rupert and Prince Maurice, George Monck.

While the English in Dutch service remained faithful to the tactics established by Maurice of Nassau in the late sixteenth century, the Scots of Hepburn's brigade learned the revolutionary methods of Gustavus-Adolphus. Sweden, like the two British kingdoms, was separated by water from the war raging in Germany. With 1,500,000 inhabitants, moreover, she hardly rated as a great power. King Gustavus-Adolphus's reaction to this was simple and straightforward; he wrote to his chief minister, 'We must remove the seat of war to some other quarter than Sweden, for we are nowhere weaker than in Sweden'. He therefore decided to intervene on the mainland of Europe, in Germany. He mobilized and employed Sweden's small human and financial resources with the utmost efficiency, supplementing them by subsidies from France or England and foreign volunteers, allies or mercenaries.

Gustavus-Adolphus was only aged thirty-five when he took his army to Germany, and he had been fighting for seventeen of those years. He had all the qualities of a great leader: originality, will-power and drive, decision, capacity to pick out important factors in the complicated events and situations, ability to lead men or drive them when that was necessary. Although an able general in battle and manoeuvre, his special talent lay in the creation of the military instrument itself and his novel ideas on its use, whereby speed replaced deliberation, movement replaced static warfare, and the fire-arm became the decisive weapon.

Two-thirds of the Swedish infantry were musketeers, no longer stationed on the flanks of the pike companies, but forming separate bodies. They were given 'Swedish feathers' – light stakes tipped with steel, precursors of the bayonet – as some protection against cavalry. A Swedish regiment, just over 800 men, was about half the size of the Spanish *tercio*. It was divided into two half-regiments or '*battaglia*' (Italian, hence 'battalion'). A third of the musketeers were detached for special duties, such as guarding baggage. Musketeers in the main body of the army were organized in a more flexible formation: the '*peloton*', or platoon, of forty-eight men. To increase the width of front the musketeers fought in only six or even three ranks, thus allowing every rank to fire simultaneously if necessary.

Hitherto each rank of musketeers had marched to the rear to re-load after firing, moving round the flanks of their company, a difficult movement which could easily degenerate into flight. Gustavus-Adolphus drilled his men to retire by files through their company. This enabled tactical retirement to be easily controlled by non-commissioned officers, while conversely it permitted an orderly advance. The Swedish battle order allowed three feet between files. All this was in direct contrast to the Spanish-model masses still adopted by the armies of the Holy Roman Empire.

The cavalry also was re-organized and re-equipped to increase their mobility. Cuirassiers carried no armour but helmets and cuirasses. They were armed with two pistols and a sword, much like the German *Reiter*; but unlike the *Reiter* the Swedish cavalry charged in three or four ranks instead of ten or more, and instead of firing their pistols in the *caracole*, they fired one pistol volley at close range, and then charged straight home at the trot with the sword. To support cavalry in a charge, or while rallying after-

wards, Gustavus-Adolphus posted bodies of musketeers between squadrons.

Before Gustavus-Adolphus artillery, although mobile enough for movement to and from a battlefield, had generally been placed in a static gun-line during battle. Gustavus-Adolphus wanted guns as regimental weapons to give tactical fire-support. He experimented with different kinds of light artillery. The famous 'leather-guns' (light metal barrels, bound with leather) were handy, but their life was too short. He therefore introduced two- and four-pounders, each weighing only about five hundredweight, two guns per regiment. They could fire faster than a musket and used grape or canister shot, devastating against the Catholic mass formations. The heavier field artillery was standardized in three weights, twenty-seven, eighteen and twelve hundredweight, firing solid shot, grape and canister. The standard siege guns were of sixty, thirty and fifteen hundredweight, firing solid shot.

As interesting as Gustavus-Adolphus's innovations within each arm was his combination of all arms in action. Musketeers, cavalry and infantry were all mutually supporting. The organization of his supply services also marked a decisive advance in the art of war.

Gustavus-Adolphus's intervention in the war in Germany was occasioned by the growing success of the Imperialists under Wallenstein. Wallenstein was one of the last, and perhaps the greatest, of the mercenaries. His army of 40,000 under his personal command was virtually a private enterprise created to make profit out of war. He had offered the army to the Holy Roman Emperor free of charge, on condition that he had undivided control of it. The profit on 'the business' and the army's maintenance in the field were to come from plunder; another motive was thus added to fanatical religious cruelty and the incidental barbarities of war. Wallenstein's army ground on through the rich and prosperous lands of Germany, leaving behind them a kind of burnt stubble-field. By 1628 it seemed that the Austrians and Catholics might soon reach the Baltic and North Sea coasts. It was to prevent this that Gustavus-Adolphus landed his army in Germany. Two great battles (Leipzig or Breitenfeld, 1631, and Lützen, 1632) achieved his objects.

At Breitenfeld, Gustavus-Adolphus's opponent was not Wallenstein (he had been temporarily dismissed by the Emperor as overpowerful), but the other renowned Catholic commander, Tilly. Two different systems of war collided; the ponderous, slow-moving masses of Catholic cavalry and foot, supported by static batteries on the old Spanish model, and the extended Swedish line of small mixed bodies of troops and mobile guns. It was a crushing victory for flexibility and fire-power. Fleeting opportunities were swiftly exploited by the Swedes before the sluggish Imperialists could move. It was, in the words of General Fuller, 'the first great land battle of the modern age'. Hepburn's Scots brigade played a crucial part in the decisive Swedish tactical moves and assaults, and men personally no better than the poor fellows squandered in King Charles's hasty cutprice expeditions, but fully trained and disciplined, defeated some of the best troops in Europe:

The enemies Battaile standing firm, looking on us at a neere distance, and seeing the other Briggads and ours wheeling about, making front unto them, they were prepared with a firm resolutione to receive us with a salvo of Cannon and Muskets: but our small Ordnance, being twice discharged amongst them, and before we stirred, we charged them with a salvo of muskets, which was repaied, and incontinent our Briggad advancing unto them with push of pike, putting one of their Battailes in disorder, fell on the execution, so that they were put to the route.[7]

This description by a Scottish officer gives a vivid impression of the clash of the two systems. They were a military reflection of the social and psychological differences between Protestantism and the Counter-Reformation: individual intelligence and enterprise against the mass, docile obedience of well-drilled children of the Church under its rigid hierarchy.

In 1632 Gustavus-Adolphus encountered the great Wallenstein, restored to his command for the express purpose of crushing the Swedish King. When after manoeuvring for position their armies eventually clashed near Lützen, Wallenstein awaited Gustavus-Adolphus's attack in a strong defensive position protected by trenches and strong batteries of guns. His troops were deployed in great squares each of 3,000 men, with musketeers at the corners. On each flank was massed cavalry. It was a formidable array for inferior numbers to attack, but in the bitter swaying fight that followed the Imperialist masses proved too clumsy and immobile to exploit their initial repulse of Swedish attacks. Gradually the Swedes, repeatedly advancing in brigades of three battalions in arrowhead formation, disorganized the Imperialists. The Swedish cavalry, charging home with the sword, broke the Imperialist cavalry. A desperate struggle took place for the Imperialist guns;

Gustavus-Adolphus himself was killed; the battle degenerated into a soldier's fight at close quarters. Gradually the Imperialist masses lost their cohesion and withdrew in utter confusion.

It was an expensive victory, but Breitenfeld and Lützen together shattered the Holy Roman Empire's dream of ending the war swiftly by the conquest of all Germany and its restoration to Catholicism. It was time for a compromise peace dictated by military stalemate. However, France, under Cardinal Richelieu, now exploited the situation in order to pursue the French monarchy's old quarrel with the Habsburgs and the power struggle of the Great Italian Wars was resumed. The war was thus to drag on in increasing ferocity and horror until 1648, by which time England and Scotland had fought and decided their own civil war. English and Scots troops continued to serve in the Thirty Years' War after Lützen, for units of both still remained in Dutch service, while Hepburn's Scots passed to the French army, which also included two Irish Catholic regiments.

*

The disorder in France after the Wars of Religion and the renewed claims of the nobility for quasi-independent feudal powers had forced the French crown to fight for its authority. A standing army was the result. An army had indeed been 'standing' in France almost continuously throughout the sixteenth century; an emergency force to meet continuous emergency. Since 1569 there had been permanent regiments of native-born infantry. France's rise to greatness as a modern military power dates, however, from about 1624, during Cardinal Richelieu's administration. The reduction of the power of the French nobles at home and the expansion of France in Europe were twin aspects of a policy of royal glory and supremacy, in which the essential element was a strong army. In 1628 the twelve oldest regiments were given a permanent status. In the event of future peacetime reductions they would not be disbanded, but reduced in numbers of men and companies. This was in fact a period of rapid expansion preparatory to Richelieu's intervention in the Thirty Years' War. By 1635, when France entered the war, she had five field armies numbering 100,000 men, including 18,000 horsemen; an indication of the scale of effort required of a continental power wishing to conduct an active foreign policy. The *arrière-ban*, or feudal peasant levy (very roughly the equivalent to the English militia) was also called out in 1635 and 1639, but it had not kept pace with the progress of tactics and discipline among professional troops. Richelieu himself acknowledged that the *arrière-ban* 'served only to corrupt others and ruin the country'.

However, despite its size and strength, the French army showed the limitations of early-seventeenth-century techniques of state organization. The regiments were still semi-private enterprises under control of their colonels – merchandise, personal property. There was no uniform coat, for each regiment chose its own. The state provided neither fodder, nor victuals, nor hospitals. The soldier provided for himself and his animals out of his pay.

The French government faced problems of discipline, financial control and administration similar to those which Elizabeth's government had failed to solve fifty years earlier. How could the 'private enterprise' of colonels and captains be made compatible with public welfare and service? Richelieu, servant of an absolute monarchy, tackled the fundamental weakness of a system which encouraged peculation. Men were now to be paid not by their captains but by state commissioners, one per regiment. No longer could the captains inflate their muster rolls with dead-pays, or withhold or embezzle the soldier's money. Moreover, through the commissioners' pay lists the King received a true weekly state of his armies' strength.

The French army was thus emerging from a century of foreign and civil wars as the only sure prop of a monarchy which had to fight to maintain its power. And while Richelieu consolidated the King's authority at home, the Thirty Years' War involved France in yet another external struggle which demanded the evolution of large and efficient military institutions. In the British kingdoms, circumstances were very different. The monarchy had enjoyed more than a hundred years of supreme authority. The parliamentary challenge under James I and Charles I was not to be compared with the pretensions of the great French nobility. And instead of constant war and domestic turmoil, only brief expeditions had interrupted Britain's peace and prosperity. Nevertheless, the questions of military power and of authority over it were crucial to the English constitutional struggle.

For a hundred years the strength of the English monarchy had rested not on military force but on law and custom, on the identification of interest of king and nation, all springing from England's medieval evolution of centralized royal government so much earlier than other countries. To this traditional strength of 'King-in-Parliament', both Parliament and Crown now looked in differing ways, each seeing the quarrel in terms of ancient law and right rather than of power struggle. Hence Charles I, despite his belief in absolute monarchy, did not create a military instrument to subdue his unruly subjects, although had he done so, he could, like Cromwell in 1653, have disregarded the Commons and their legalistic manoeuvres.

In France under Louis XIII and Richelieu royal authority rested on the army – in the 1630s and 1640s taxes were even collected by armed force. In Germany, where in some states the assemblies enjoyed greater formal powers than the English Houses of Parliament, the princes could plead the emergency of the Thirty Years' War to make a convincing case for emergency taxation on royal authority and for the raising of standing armies. In England, on the other hand, Charles I endeavoured from 1629 to free himself from the Commons' control over taxation by virtually abandoning any foreign policy, with all its implications in terms of costly armies. However, he could not then plead national emergency to raise an army.

The Commons were well aware of the danger to their position which a royal army would represent. It would outweigh not only their control of taxation but also their own military force, the London trained bands, then the most efficient military instrument in the country. Parliamentary sensitivity to signs that the King was organizing an army expressed itself in the Petition of Right in 1628. The human debris of the Isle de Rhé expedition was billetted about the country, an undisciplined, violent rabble. The government issued commissions to the Lords-Lieutenant that martial law rather than the slow process of common law be employed to control them. But troops in England subject not to common law but solely to military law administered by the King's officers was a danger signal, as was the subjection of civilians to martial law. The troops, demoralized though they were, could be used as a subtle means of royal pressure, by billetting (or threatening to billet) them on persons reluctant to pay forced loans or 'benevolences'. In the Petition of Right, the Commons therefore humbly prayed that:

... your Majesty will be pleased to remove the said soldiers and mariners, and that your people may not be so burdened in time to come; and that the foresaid commissions for proceeding by martial law, may be revoked and annulled; and that hereafter no commissions of like nature may issue forth to any person or persons whatsoever, to be executed, as aforesaid lest by colour of them any of your Majesty's subjects be destroyed or put to death, contrary to the laws and franchises of the land.[8]

This was a direct challenge to the prerogatives of the Crown. However, the country was now at war with both Spain and France, and Charles desperately needed a vote of supply; one lever of power – taxation – held by the Commons forced him to loosen his own grip on the other, military strength. He accepted the Petition of Right. But next year he dissolved Parliament and embarked on eleven years of personal rule.

Yet still the questions of finance and military power remained indissolubly linked – and the key to the constitutional battle. Only by the utmost economy and by various dubious expedients could Charles finance his personal government and thus remain independent of the Commons. No funds were available to pay an army. The Tudor equation having been upset by the ambitions of the Commons and the pretensions and tactlessness of Charles, the Crown's basic weakness was exposed. After 1635 the finance/armed-force issue appeared again over the question of ship money and its legality, particularly in the case of John Hampden. The judgement of twelve to two by the judiciary in the King's favour in the Hampden case was meaningless, because in the face of general reluctance to pay, not to say evasion, and the consequent administrative difficulties the King's attempts to collect ship money in the absence of coercive force were fruitless. The Crown still faced its perennial dilemma: no money, no army ... no army, no money.

Between 1639 and 1642 the relations between King and Parliament degenerated from legal and constitutional disputes into an increasingly open struggle for power. Here Charles's military weakness was a cardinal factor. It put an end to his attempt at personal rule; it was the direct cause of the Commons' triumphs in 1640–41 and of their soaring constitutional claims which at last, in 1642, led to the quarrel being put to the decision of war.

In 1639 the King and Archbishop Laud attempted to impose on the Scots Calvinists a new prayer book based on the English Anglican version. The result of this tactless attempt was rebellion. The Scots signed the National Covenant, binding themselves to protect their bleak religion, raised an army and appointed as Commander-in-Chief Alexander Leslie, an experienced soldier who had served with Gustavus-Adolphus in Germany.

Charles now had to raise an army or see his prestige and authority destroyed. At once the weakness of a king and a country without a permanent professional army was demonstrated. Charles had nothing except the militia system that had served the early Tudors well enough against the Scots. But this was another century, another dynasty. When the northern 'trained bands' were called out, and 20,000 foot and some 1,200 horse assembled at Newcastle, all the military shortcomings of the militia – indiscipline, lack of organization, leadership, equipment, supply, and training – once more became painfully evident. And since the militia was only English society in arms, and English society was not enthusiastic about a war to impose Anglicanism on the Scots on Charles's behalf, the one factor contributing to the (limited) effectiveness of the militia under the Tudors – identification of the royal and national interests – was now lacking.

A force of 5,000 men under the Marquis of Hamilton, together with a fleet, was sent to threaten the Scottish coast; though well armed, this force had no idea how to use its weapons, for Hamilton reported that 'they were so little exercised that out of the 5,000 there were not 200 that could fire a musket'.[9] The main body of some 15,000 men under Charles himself was a sorry spectacle of

A satirical view of the English soldier in Ireland, *c.* 1640, an adept at plunder, both of edibles and of portables. Plundering and free-quarter were traditional compensations for the dangers and hardships of soldiering.

military futility. Sir Edmund Verney described the King's camp:

> Our men are very raw, our arms of all sorts naught, our victuals scarce, and provisions for horses worse ... I daresay that there never was so raw, so unskilful, and so unwilling an army, brought to fight.[10]

Such a force was clearly unfit to fight Leslie's Covenanters, and so it remained defensively on the border. Now at last, far too late, the King set about creating a professional army. Haste forced him to rely on foreign mercenaries, and negotiations were opened with the Spaniards in the Netherlands for some 6,000 infantry and 4,000 horse.

Meanwhile, an English force had bolted in face of a Scots detachment under Leslie, and the 'First Scots War' or 'First Bishops' War' ended inconclusively with a treaty including many concessions to the rebels.

Next year, Charles again attempted to assert his authority over the Scots. Again the militia of many countries was called out to raise an army of 30,000 men. Again English society's lack of interest in their King's Scottish policy was shown by desertions, mutiny and dispersal for plunder. The Commander-in-Chief, the Earl of Northumberland, reported in June 1640 that 'so general a defection in this kingdom hath not been known in the memory of any'.[11] Sir Jacob Astley wrote,

> I have orders ... to send 4,000 or 5,000 men to Newcastle; but, considering there is not such a number yet come, and those that are come have neither colours nor halberds, and want drums ... I am to receive all the arch-knaves in this kingdom, and to arm them at Selby. Before I came to Selby, some 500 of them were brought by Lieutenant-Colonel Ballard, and these beat up the officers ... and broke open the prisons.[12]

Negotiations for mercenaries had failed because the King had no money, not even to keep the mutinous rabble at Newcastle in the field. Having accepted the Petition of Right, the King could not even use military law to maintain discipline. When one of his generals offered to hang offenders, the law and the consequences, the King showed the fatal hesitation and squeamishness which distinguished him so sharply from Cromwell.

On 20 August 1640 the Scots crossed the border, searched for the English, found them at Newburn and scared them away with artillery. Bishop Burnet noted that 'the whole army did run with so much precipitation, that Sir Thomas Fairfax, who had a command in it, did not stick to own that till he passed the Tees, his legs trembled under him'.[13]

This miserable defeat in 'the Second Bishops' War' spelt disaster for Charles and the end of his personal rule. By the Treaty of Ripon he was forced to grant the Scots indemnities of over £400,000, and to allow them to occupy the three most northerly English counties as security. Payment was possible only by summoning Parliament and persuading it to grant subsidies. Indeed, without parliamentary help, Charles could not even pay his own army. Military failure had thus ended the long constitutional stalemate between King and Commons. Without the so-called 'Bishops' Wars' against the Scots, the old pattern might have continued indefinitely: personal rule, a brief occasional Parliament, empty debates, useless legal wrangling over such things as tunnage and poundage and ship money, Commons petitions, royal declarations.

But now power in the state, so evenly balanced during the previous fifteen years, swung heavily towards Parliament. Although money was still a powerful lever – made more so now by the King's desperate plight – the Commons had a new lever in the Scots army, a natural ally of the bishop-hating Commons. Its Commissioners in London were in communication with parliamentary leaders. Against this coalition Charles had nothing but a mutinous rabble markedly out of sympathy with his Anglican religious policy.

Charles's new chief minister, the Earl of Strafford, was an able and ruthless man whose record as President of the Council of the North and Lord Deputy for Ireland marked him as potentially a great servant of an absolute monarch. In Ireland he had expanded the standing army (Ireland had always needed its garrison) by some 8,000 men, and this army, mostly Catholic, was the only possible military force which the King could hope to use. But Strafford was appointed too late. In face of near-bankruptcy, national defeat, invasion, a country seething with indignation and discontent, Strafford had no time to organize. He could see no solution other than to call Parliament, believing that with the traditional Scottish enemy actually on English soil, the Commons might postpone their doctrinal discussions about the nature of God's Word and the face of the Whore of Rome, and forget their grievances against the King. In fact, Strafford believed that the Commons would vote large subsidies and support the King in expelling the Scots.

Strafford was disastrously wrong. The calling of Parliament unloosed a flood of grievances. It was therefore dissolved. Strafford tried to re-organize and carry on absolutist government, looking to the army in Ireland to rescue the King. The rout at Newburn demolished his hopes. Parliament had to be summoned again; the floodgates were opened; and the revolutionary legislation of the Long Parliament from 1640 to 1641 followed.

The Commons' Grand Remonstrance of 1641, dilating on their view of the events of the reign, significantly recalled the use of martial law and

the charging of the kingdom with billetted soldiers in all parts of it, and the concomitant design of German horse that the land might either submit with fear or be enforced with rigour to such arbitrary contributions as should be required of them.[14]

The Remonstrance also emphasized the threat posed by Strafford's Irish army and expressed the current fear that the King might use military force to resolve the constitutional struggle:

They [certain lords and bishops] have attempted to disaffect and discontent His Majesty's army, and to engage it for the maintenance of their wicked and traitorous designs; the keeping up of Bishops in votes and functions, and by force compelling the Parliament to order, limit and dispose their proceedings in such manner as might best concur with the intentions of this dangerous and potent faction.[15]

Here, in a paragraph, is summed up the underlying factor of power beneath all the constitutional argument of the reign. Unfortunately for Charles, the accusations were not accurate, for the army was not loyal, nor an efficient military instrument; it could not do what the Commons suspected. This failure to provide himself in good time with an instrument to impose his will was Charles's ruin. His weakness was finally demonstrated in January 1642, when he himself, finally goaded by his wife into a display of ruthless action, went to the House of Commons with a few soldiers to arrest five recalcitrant members. They had gone into hiding, and the Commons were protected by the pikes and muskets of the London trained bands, the best body of troops in the kingdom. It was the King, not the Parliamentarians, who now had to abandon the capital as both sides prepared to settle their dispute by war.

Force was at last to be employed to settle the constitutional question, but in circumstances disadvantageous to the Crown. During the King's eleven years of personal rule he had controlled the machinery and authority of the state and, with Parliament dissolved, his opponents had been scattered without a focus. Up to 1639, even a small army under the King's command could have permanently established his personal rule. Now it was no longer a question of the head of state, an anointed king, maintaining his authority by force against dispersed pockets of discontent; it was a question of civil war between two factions.

The issue on which the two sides finally split was appropriately enough the militia, and control over it. For as the constitutional argument became increasingly threadbare, the contestants began openly to jockey for such military forces the kingdom had. Parliament claimed that the King had no inherent power over the militia and passed an ordinance asserting their own control and appointing their own county lieutenants with power to put down insurrections and rebellions. Parliament's meaning being thus clear enough, the King and court retired to York and the Queen took ship to the Continent to sell the crown jewels.

Parliament fired after the King yet another of their wordy statements, the Nineteen Propositions, amounting essentially to one – that Parliament should reign in the King's name. When the King rejected this, Parliament appointed a Committee of Safety, commissioned the Earl of Essex to raise and command an army of 10,000 men, and neatly declared that anyone loyal to the King was a traitor. It was war.

5

The Civil War
and the
Commonwealth Army

FOR the first time for nearly 160 years, there was war in England – 160 years during which Europe had been fighting almost continuously. Both Parliament and King needed armies that did not yet exist. In 1642 the King could call only on loyal gentry used to horses and fire-arms; brave, impetuous but inexperienced men. Parliament could call on the one disciplined body of infantry that could be used for a campaign and not just for local action, the London trained bands. Now their diligence on the drill ground, so mocked by their fellow-citizens, was rewarded. Otherwise there was nothing but the militia. This was now put under unprecedented strain, not only because for the first time England faced major war on her own soil instead of a mere threat of invasion, but also because two rival authorities were competing to mobilize it. When the King issued the traditional Commissions of Array to the Lords-Lieutenant, Parliament had already anticipated him with their Militia Ordinance. There were local disputes, even scuffles, between the rival county authorities for control of the arsenals and the county militia generally. Gradually a regional pattern emerged. The King controlled Wales and the west; Parliament the south-east and east, including London. The machinery of government, including the Board of Ordnance and the navy, thus remained in the hands of Parliament. The Midlands and north were disputed zones. The great commercial cities and ports were Parliamentarian.

Both King and Parliament soon lost faith in the militia. Thus at its first decisive test the traditional English military system collapsed. Where possible the King seized militia equipment for new regiments of volunteers, men with his cause at heart, men able to stay in the field. He showered commissions on gentlemen able and willing to raise regiments. Magnates like the Marquis of Newcastle produced fine bodies of troops from their tenants and estate servants. However, the prodigality with which the King issued his commissions led to disorganization, for while new regiments were continually being raised, existing ones withered for lack of replacements. The Royalist army gradually turned into a collection of company-strength regiments.

While in the King's army colonels and captains frequently raised new units at their own expense, the public paid for the Parliamentary forces. However, both systems of raising volunteers were liable to the abuses current in the American Civil War two centuries later. Men could volunteer for one unit, take what bounty was offered, desert, and join another. A man could become a professional volunteer, making a profit out of war without ever undergoing the fatigue of marches or the dangers of battle. Both sides therefore suffered from the lack of organization inherent in a military system without a standing army under its own department of state.

Economically the Royalists were weak. They had no City of London, with its immense financial resources, few ports from which to draw customs dues, few industrial or trading cities. The wealth of the King's supporters was in land, and therefore not easily convertible. The plate and jewels of old families or Oxford colleges were but a temporary stop-gap. Good armies depend on regular pay and supplies; the King could guarantee neither. The Royalist armies were forced to live off the country; they became adept at plunder – hardly a method of endearing the royal cause to the locals.

The King's forces were therefore inferior from all points of view except the martial virtues; in these, however, they were at first superior, from the King himself down to the sturdy tenant in the ranks. Though sometimes fatally weak and hesitant, Charles displayed considerable strategic sense and aptitude for command. His nephew, Prince Rupert, aged only twenty-three, had served in Germany and Holland in the Thirty Years' War, and although at first commanding only the cavalry, he exercised more authority over the army than the old Earl of Lindsey, the titular Commander-in-Chief. The Royalist command organization therefore was – or should have been – relatively simple and compact. Not so with the Parliamentarians, for the two Houses now had to make good their claim to be competent to run the country. The Parliamentary Commander-in-Chief, the Earl of Essex, controlled neither grand strategy nor even all the Parliamentary armies, for he and his fellow-commanders were subjected to a stream of messages and letters from the Westminster politicians.

Both sides were hampered by the intense local spirit of their troops; at critical moments unhappy generals would find that supposedly reliable regiments either refused to move, or had gone home. To offset this localism Parliament encouraged regional associations of counties, of which the Eastern Association was the most famous and successful.

Although there were veterans of the Thirty Years' War on both sides in field commands, the regimental and brigade officers were mostly without military experience. Often they were selected not for ability, but because their social position in some district enabled them to recruit a regiment. Thus the weakness of the Elizabethan militia – military rank dependent not on ability but on social standing – survived the wreck of the militia system, and was perpetuated in the new armies now being raised. The early years of the civil war were therefore characterized by amateurism and by narrow parochialism. This was no war of manoeuvre and battle between two main armies, for both sides had several armies each pursuing some private objective in a different part of the country. Little local wars went on, with sieges of obscure and military unimportant country houses and minor affrays. A host of small garrisons further sapped the strength of the main armies.

Though the passage of the King's or Parliament's soldiers through a district might be vexatious or even unpleasant, the war did not ruin the population or destroy towns, villages and farms as did the Thirty Years' War on the Continent. After two years of war, a yokel on the battlefield of Marston Moor was astounded to be told that King and Parliament were about to fight a battle where he stood: 'What! Have they two fallen out then?' Atrocities were few; the Puritans vented their wrath on Gothic images in churches and by smashing stained glass, while towns were not sacked but subjected to Puritan preaching, perhaps a subtler punishment. Loyalty to King or Parliament did not necessarily inhibit the courtesies of country life. Yet the armies themselves generally fought resolutely and gallantly.

Despite the chaos of local conflicts and the difficulty of forming and retaining armies of any size, there was a broad strategic pattern. If the King was to win, he had to re-conquer London and the south-east, with all their resources, including the machinery of government. His best hope of so doing was to force a decisive battle on the Parliamentarians, trusting to the superior courage and horsemanship of his cavalry to ride down the lower classes in the Parliamentary infantry.

The one major battle of the 1642 campaign was fought when the King attempted to by-pass Essex's army and march into London. The battle took place on 23 October at Edgehill. Both sides displayed little skill, but much bravery and determination. Eventually, however, Essex withdrew, uncovering his communications to London and leaving the King free to advance. The opportunity was missed. By the time the King could re-organize his forces and march on London via Oxford (later his headquarters) Essex had reached the city via St Albans. Reinforced by the London trained bands and well entrenched, Essex confronted Charles at Turnham Green with a numerically superior force. The King retired to Oxford, and the armies went into winter quarters. The King had failed to exploit his first and perhaps unique opportunity to win the war by a stroke on London.

The 1643 campaign opened with the Royalists capturing the south-west, including Bristol, thus finally gaining control of a great seaport and trading city. Charles's planned strategy for this year was the most coherent of the war. Newcastle's Yorkshiremen were to march on London from the north; Sir Ralph Hopton's Cornishmen, after their local victories, would reinforce the King at Oxford; he and Newcastle would then close on London from north and west.

This clear plan quickly disappeared amid the confusions of war and the impact of the unforeseen. The royal armies proved unwilling to march on London while Parliament held places like Hull and Plymouth in their home districts. The campaign therefore degenerated into unrelated marches and counter-marches in the west, the middle west, Yorkshire and Lincolnshire. On balance it was the King's year, for he secured the south-west and Yorkshire, but an outcome to the war was as far away as ever.

Parliament therefore looked for an ally, and found it in the army of the Scots Covenanters. In return for its support, the Parliamentarians signed the Solemn League and Covenant, promising – though undoubtedly without general support – to introduce the Presbyterian system of Church organization throughout England, Ireland and Scotland.

Two years of war had demonstrated the shortcomings in organization, recruitment and supply of both sides' hastily improvised armies. Even Parliament paid its troops late or not at all. In December 1643 Essex reported,

My desire is that if there be no pay like to come to me by the latter end of the week I may know it; I not being able to stay amongst them to hear the crying necessity of the hungry soldiers.[1]

The field armies of both sides were increasingly depleted by the growing number of local garrisons, some merely bases for foraging. The King's army suffered from the number of company-sized units styling themselves regiments, while Parliament's army lacked homogeneity, being raised by county committees. Both sides were fettered by localism. This was an age when most men lived all their lives in one county, perhaps in one 'hundred', anywhere else being 'foreign'. Apart from itinerant merchants or pedlars and the upper classes, the professional soldier was perhaps the only 'mentally mobile' man of the seventeenth century. And professional soldiers were rare indeed. When enthusiasm of amateurs quickly waned, voluntary enlistment was becoming a farce. The Parliamentary governor of Gloucester wrote:

All my best men run away for lack of clothing, and other requisites, and take service in other parts and associations where they may have a better and surer entertainment. For it seems there is such a liberty given that all comers are entertained by every association without enquiry so that they be well mounted or appointed. The consequence is that in some armies it is personally more advantageous to be traitors, cowards, and runagates, than to be faithful, resolute and constant soldiers to any place or service, which state of things tends to the great detriment of the service and discouragement of all gallant and faithful soldiers. ... The desertion of our soldiers to seek new entertainment upon any new levies being heard of, is the true reason, I conceive, why our armies moulder away from great strengths to nothing.[2]

As in the days of Elizabeth's foreign expeditions impressment – conscription – had to be adopted by both sides during 1643. And, as before, the local authorities naturally selected their rogues and misfits as soldiers.

With such a military 'system', armies could be painfully got together only for a single march and battle, after which they dispersed – either to serve separate, regional interests, or merely in order to subsist.

The campaign of 1644 followed this pattern of futility, despite the intervention of a Scottish army under Leven. By mid-summer this army had joined the Yorkshire Parliamentary forces under the Fairfaxes (Ferdinando, Lord Fairfax and his son Sir Thomas) and the army of the Eastern Association under the Earl of Manchester. The combined force besieged Newcastle's Royalists in York. But while Parliament was apparently securing Yorkshire, Prince Rupert won Lancashire for the King and crossed the Pennines. Although Parliamentarians raised their siege to meet him, Rupert slipped past them into York and later emerged reinforced by Newcastle's men to give battle.

The main forces clashed in the Battle of Marston Moor (July 1644), the largest battle of the war so far. Counting Leven's Scots, the Parliamentarians outnumbered the Royalists two to one in infantry, although in cavalry the armies were equal. They were drawn up on the standard pattern as practised on the Continent – infantry in the centre, cavalry on the flanks. The Parliamentary commanders typified the diversity of talent and origin characteristic of the Civil War. The Earl of Manchester, a pious, elegant, Puritan grandee, who for that reason commanded the army of the

The marching Postures of ye Harquebusiers

Mounted arquebusiers under Charles I. By the time of the Civil War, full
armour was rarely worn in the field, and horsemen were usually equipped with
pistol and sword, rather than carbine.

Eastern Association, contrasted sharply with his cavalry commander, Oliver Cromwell, a plain squire, uncultured, violent and ruthless. Sir Thomas Fairfax was in his early thirties: 'Black Tom', a lean, dark, thoughtful commander, both brave and wise. Leven, an old and rugged Scot, had learned his trade under the greatest soldier of the age, Gustavus-Adolphus.

On the Royalist side, Prince Rupert, though only twenty-three, was a veteran of both the Dutch and the Swedish wars, a master of his profession – not at all the mad cavalier of legend. Frankness and generosity, pride and spirit, courage, speed of decision – these were the qualities that earned him the loyalty of his troops and made him so formidable in the field. Lord George Goring was the more typical Cavalier, a veteran of the Dutch Wars, hard-drinking and foul-mouthed, but an able commander and shrewd tactician. Finally there was the Marquis of Newcastle, Royalist leader in the north, a great aristocrat, with all the grand stateliness and generosity that went with his station in the mid seventeenth century. He kept his own elegant court; he wrote his own romantic verses; he did not rise to face the rigours of war until eleven in the morning. The 'Cavaliers and Roundheads' of legend have little foundation in fact, for the commanders of both sides wore their hair long; Rupert's as well as Cromwell's horse wore steel helmets and half-armour.

The troops also presented the contrasts of the war: the psalm-singing yeomen and small squires of the Eastern Association horse and the gallant gentlemen of Rupert's horse opposite them, skilled but lacking discipline; Leven's solemn Calvinist Scots and their Swedish discipline; the sturdy Yorkshiremen of Newcastle's white-coats, peasants and tenants, feudal in their composition and loyalty. The armies faced each other across a ditch in the thundery heat of late afternoon, each regiment distinguished by its banner and dressed according to its own taste: Royalist white-coat infantry, red-coated Parliamentarian infantry of the Eastern Association, their cavalry in buff coats, Rupert's horse in blue. In this era the men wore a field-sign to distinguish one army from another in the heat of battle and at Marston Moor the Parliamentary sign was a white handkerchief in the hat.

As in contemporary continental battles, cavalry action on the

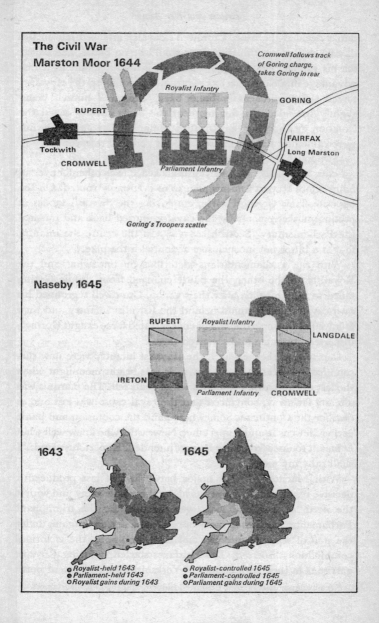

The Civil War
Marston Moor 1644

Cromwell follows track of Goring charge, takes Goring in rear

Royalist Infantry

RUPERT

GORING

Tockwith

FAIRFAX

Long Marston

CROMWELL

Parliament Infantry

Goring's Troopers scatter

Naseby 1645

RUPERT

Royalist Infantry

LANGDALE

IRETON

Parliament Infantry

CROMWELL

1643

1645

○ *Royalist-held 1643*
○ *Parliament-held 1643*
○ *Royalist gains during 1643*

○ *Royalist-controlled 1645*
○ *Parliament-controlled 1645*
○ *Parliament gains during 1645*

flanks decided the issue. Cromwell's cavalry attacked late in the day when Rupert, thinking there would be no battle, had called for his supper. Nevertheless, although initially caught at a disadvantage in a close-quarters sword-and-pistol fight, the Royalists forced the Parliamentary horse back, Cromwell himself being slightly wounded. At this moment the Scots cavalry saved the situation by charging the Royalists in flank. They gave way, but were rallied by Rupert himself and his personal reserve:

'Swounds! Do you run? Follow me!'

Scots, 'Ironsides'* and Royalists hacked at each other for over an hour before Rupert and his men were eventually routed. On the opposite flank Goring's horse, employing the Swedish tactics of posting musketeers among the cavalry, hurled back and pursued the Parliamentary (Scottish) cavalry. In the centre the infantry fought a bitter but inconclusive action with the pike.

With the Parliamentarians victorious on one wing and the Royalists on the other, the battle changed front. While Goring failed to rally his men after their gallop, Cromwell regrouped his own cavalry, led it round behind the Royalist infantry and then followed in Goring's tracks. His concentrated force caught Goring's dispersed horsemen and scattered them.

Deprived of their cavalry, the Royalist infantry were now surrounded and gradually cut down. It was bright moonlight when the last of Newcastle's stubborn white-coats fell. The marquis was already far away, convinced that the royal cause was lost and *en route* for the Continent. Somewhere amid the confusion and panic earlier Newcastle and Rupert met. Newcastle, who knew well what *he* meant to do, asked what Rupert intended. Rupert answered: 'I shall rally my men.'

With Marston Moor a major battle had at last produced a decisive result, for the Royalists had lost a whole army and with it the north of England. Now was the time for the triumphant Parliamentary armies to press on ruthlessly. But once again, under the pull of separate interests and rival ambitions, the victorious combination dispersed. The Fairfaxes started reducing Royalist garrisons in their own county of Yorkshire; the Scots went north

* A nickname used first for Cromwell himself, and then for his troopers.

to besiege Newcastle; and the Eastern Association troops marched back to Lincolnshire. For want of a firm unified direction of the war by someone who understood strategy, the victory of Marston Moor led to no direct or immediate effect. Although the Royalist cause had suffered permanent damage, the third campaign of the war drew to an end without sign of decision. This at last brought home to Parliament that its system of war would not do. In December 1644 a Member of Parliament said:

Our victories, the price of blood invaluable, so gallantly gotten and, what is more pity, so graciously bestowed, seem to have been put in a bag with holes; what we won one time, we lost another. The treasure is exhausted; the country is wasted. A summer's victory has proved a winter's story. Men's hearts have failed them with the observation of these things.[3]

In June, before Marston Moor, Sir William Waller, Parliamentary commander in the west, had put his finger on the essential flaw in the system: recruiting, command, organization and sense of loyalty were all local or regional: 'Till you have an army merely your own,' he told Parliament, 'that you may command, it is impossible to do anything of importance.'[4]

Parliament had toyed with the idea of turning Essex's forces into a new-style army with regular pay and standard organization, and had passed an ordinance to this effect in March. Little had come of it; and now nothing could because Essex's army had been trapped in Cornwall and had had to surrender. The need for a change of method was now not merely desirable; it was urgent.

The system of command and political direction also required reform. The attempt by the House of Commons to run the country and the war had not been successful. Its strict control of its military commanders had not produced happy results. Some of the commanders themselves – like the Earl of Manchester – owed their positions to their social and political standing rather than military ability or experience. The end of 1644 was that moment, well-known in English wars, when half-hearted men and hesitant measures must go. Yet even now the process of reform took from November 1644 till February 1645 and was resisted to the last; the spur was not the 'statesmanship' of the House of Commons, as Trevelyan puts it, but dire necessity. The Self-Denying Ordinance barred from military command all members of either House of Parliament, thus eliminating political or purely aristocratic generals. A new military system was begun by the Ordinance of February 1645, which included a scheme for a 'New Model' army, nationally controlled and commanded and regularly paid.

Two years of war at home had been enough to cause the English to create at one stroke a standing professional army such as continental nations had taken 150 years to develop.

*

While the tactics and discipline of the New Model were an advance on all but the best of earlier units in either army, what made it a 'New Model' was its national basis and standardized organization.* The army was to number 22,000 men – 14,400 foot, and 7,600 cavalry or dragoons (mounted infantry). It was to be supported by taxes levied on those parts of the country that had suffered least from the war. The original intention was that the New Model should be based on the armies of Waller, Essex (reconstituted after the surrender in Cornwall), and Manchester, thus uniting three major Parliamentary forces. But early in 1645 these armies numbered only 600, 3,000 and 3,500 infantry respectively. The shortfall of 7,300 could only be made good by impressment, and desertions followed this. At first therefore the New Model army was far from being a devoted band of crusaders, though Cromwell's men of the Eastern Association formed a solid core. Even in May 1645, when the New Model took the field, it was still under strength. Time passed before religion and victory enabled it to dispense with the press-gang.

The New Model organization was laid down in the report of the Committee of Both Kingdoms to the House of Commons which had recommended the reforms. The infantry were to be divided into twelve regiments each of 1,200 men (a third larger than a Swedish regiment – similar to a Dutch), the cavalry into eleven regiments each of 600 men (twice the size of the Swedish squadron,

* C. H. Firth, *Cromwell's Army*, remains the authority on the New Model.

and three times that of a French regiment), plus 1,000 dragoons.

The previous battles of the Civil War and of the Thirty Years' War had shown cavalry to be the decisive arm. Cromwell had realized after Edgehill why the royalist horse had proved superior; as he later told John Hampden:

Your troopers are most of them old decayed serving-men, and tapsters, and such kind of fellows; and their troopers are gentlemen's sons, younger sons and persons of quality: do you think that the spirits of such base and mean fellows will ever be able to encounter gentlemen, that have honour and courage and resolution in them? ... You must get men of a spirit: and take it not ill what I say – I know you will not – of a spirit that is likely to go on as far as gentlemen will go: or else I am sure you will be beaten still.[5]

Hampden at the time, according to Cromwell, replied that 'He [Cromwell] talked a good notion, but an impracticable one'.

Being better paid, the cavalry on both sides had always attracted a more intelligent, higher class of recruit than the infantry. However, the most formidable of all the Parliamentary cavalry was Cromwell's own of the Eastern Association. Recruited from the yeomen, small squires and farmers of East Anglia, the Eastern Association troopers, though of humbler origin than the Royalists, were equally proud and independent. Moreover, against the cavaliers' gallantry they could set sober and intense religious convictions. They were something new in the history of armies and wars, and they were Cromwell's creation. In September 1643, Cromwell wrote to a colleague:

... a few honest men are better than numbers.... If you choose godly honest men to be captains of Horse, honest men will follow them.... I had rather have a plain russet-coated captain that knows what he fights for, and loves what he knows, than which you call a gentlemen and is nothing else.[6]

Such a kind of soldier is unique in English history. They were the core of English society, modest, independent, intelligent, inspired by unshakeable religious conviction. No more formidable troops ever took the field in any country. Cromwell's Eastern

Association horse was the pattern for the New Model cavalry in organization, equipment and discipline.

The tactics and methods of the Ironsides were essentially those of Gustavus-Adolphus's Swedes, although the New Model cavalry abandoned the Swedish custom of including musketeers in their formation. They also relied on shock action and the sword, using their pistols once only at close range. They charged at a rapid trot, not a gallop; it is possible, though not certain, that the Royalists charged at a faster pace. Shock depended less on speed than the momentum of heavy cavalry advancing in mass, knee to knee. It was essential that the men be packed as tightly as possible; one writer said that 'every left-hand man's right knee must be close locked under his right-hand man's left ham'.[7] If the charge alone, however, failed to break a resolute enemy, the opponents then sat and hacked with their swords. Of the fight at Gainsborough in 1643 Cromwell writes:

... We came up horse to horse, where we disputed it with our swords and pistols a pretty time; all keeping close order, so that one could not break the other. At last they a little shrinking, our men perceiving it pressed it upon them, and immediately routed his whole body.[8]

The New Model troopers were armed with a pistol and a sword. Full armour had long been discarded as too heavy, cumbersome, uncomfortable and anyhow penetrable by a heavy ball. Cromwell's cavalry wore a steel helmet, with nose or face-guard and a 'back-and-breast'; the leather or buff coat also gave some protection against sword cuts.

The essential difference between Ironsides and Royalists lay not in equipment or tactics but in discipline. Clarendon, the Royalist historian of the war, himself a participant, noted:

Though the King's troops prevailed in the charge and routed those they charged, they seldom rallied themselves again in order, nor could they be brought to make a second charge the same day ... whereas the other troops, if they prevailed, or though they were beaten and routed, presently rallied again, and stood in good order till they received new orders.[9]

A regiment of horse was divided into six troops of 100 men. Regimental officers were a colonel and a major (who each also commanded a troop), while a troop included four commissioned officers, captain, lieutenant, cornet and quartermaster, and three non-commissioned officers, known as corporals of horse. The lieutenant commanding the colonel's troop ranked as a junior captain and was entitled 'captain-lieutenant'.

The New Model also included a regiment of 1,000 dragoons (from French '*dragon*' – a kind of short musket). Dragoons were mounted (and therefore highly mobile) infantry designed for scouting and skirmishing, advanced and rear guards, and the seizure and defence of bridges and other important tactical points. Any nag that could carry a man was good enough for them. A dragoon's equipment resembled that of a musketeer rather than a trooper, for he carried a musket instead of a pistol, probably wore a red instead of a buff coat, and lacked the cavalryman's back-and-breast; he also probably wore the musketeer's broad-brimmed hat instead of a 'pot'. His musket, however, was not the musketeer's matchlock, but a firelock; in other words, an early form of flintlock requiring no match or complicated manipulation, a better weapon for use on horseback or for skirmishing on foot. Not counting the dragoons, the proportion of cavalry to infantry in the New Model was one to two; approximately that of all contemporary field armies.

The twelve New Model infantry regiments were each divided into ten companies of unequal size: 200 in the colonel's company (under a captain-lieutenant), 160 in the lieutenant-colonel's, 140 in the major's, and the remainder 100 each. Company officers were a captain, a lieutenant, and an ensign; non-commissioned officers were two sergeants, three corporals and a gentleman-at-arms (storekeeper!). The larger companies had a higher complement of non-commissioned officers.

From the beginning of the century the proportion of musketeers to pikemen had been rising in continental armies; under Gustavus-Adolphus it was two musketeers to every pikeman, and the English New Model followed suit. Nevertheless, for sentimental though illogical reasons the pike enjoyed the higher prestige, as being more ancient and less mechanical. The 16–18 foot pike took some

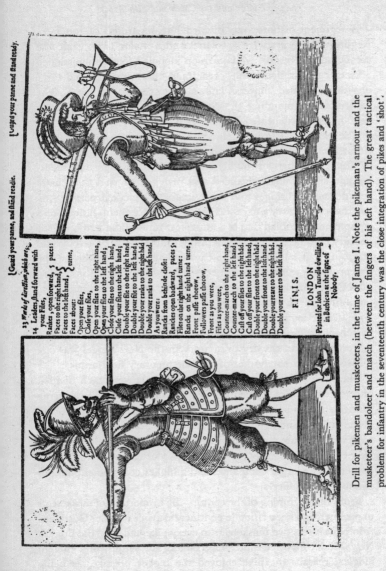

[Guard your panne, and stand readie.]   [ward your panne and stand steady.]

13 *Words of direction, which are,*

14 Leaders, stand forward with your Files,

Ranks, open forward, 5 paces:

Faces to the right hand,
Faces to the left hand, } turne,
Faces about:

Open your files,
Close your files,
Open your files to the right hand,
Open your files to the left hand,
Close your files to the right hand,
Close your files to the left hand,
Double your file to the right hand,
Double your file to the left hand,
Double your ranks to the right hand,
Double your ranks to the left hand.

As you were:
Ranks from behinde close:
Ranckes open backward, paces 5,
Files on the right hand turne:
Ranks on the right hand turne.
Front passe thorow,
Followers passe thorow,
Front as you were,
Files as you were.
Counter-march to the right hand,
Counter-march to the left hand,
Cast off your files to the right hand,
Cast off your files to the left hand,
Double your front to the right hand.
Double your front to the left hand.
Double your reare to the right hand.
Double your reare to the left hand.

FINIS.

LONDON
Printed for Iohn Trundle dwelling
in Barbican at the signe of
Nobody.

Drill for pikemen and musketeers, in the time of James I. Note the pikeman's armour and the musketeer's bandoleer and match (between the fingers of his left hand). The great tactical problem for infantry in the seventeenth century was the close integration of pikes and 'shot'.

handling, and since the pikeman wore even more armour than the trooper (as well as a back-and-breast, he carried 'tassets' or thigh guards), tall, strong men were required. The task of the pikemen was to protect the musketeers against cavalry and overwhelm the hostile infantry 'at push of pike'. They were in fact the backbone of an army. Even in defeat at Marston Moor the Royalist pikemen had stood firm amid the rout.

The musketeers provided the infantry fire-power. Originally the musket had been so heavy that it was supported on a rest, for its superiority over the lighter and now obsolete arquebus lay in its heavier ball and higher penetrating power. The musket now became gradually reduced in length and the clumsy rest was discarded, though it still fired a one-and-a-quarter-ounce ball. The bulk of the infantry had not yet been issued with firelocks, since they were too expensive. The mid-seventeenth-century musketeer was something of an itinerant military Christmas tree lit up for the occasion. On the prospect of action he lit both ends of his match and held them between his fingers. He carried twelve wooden, leather or metal cases containing ready-made charges on a shoulder-belt or bandoleer; the cases rattled loudly with movement or in a wind. There was also a flask of powder, a pouch of shot, a sword, the musket itself, and his 'snapsack' of food, perhaps enough for seven days.

The loading and firing of the musket required complicated manipulations according to standard drill. An army could burn up to five hundredweight of match for every 1,500 men every twenty-four hours; a staggeringly inconvenient rate of consumption. To be caught with matches unlit or extinguished by rain was disastrous. All in all it was never the musketeer's wish to be caught in open ground by cavalry; hence it was that pikes and 'shot' were complementary and, if well-trained, acted as a single body. A musket volley could stop horse and man and carry up to 400 yards, while the pikemen could hold cavalry away from the musketeers as they re-loaded.

The New Model infantry usually fought six deep, but sometimes only three deep to extend their front and allow all three ranks to fire a volley together. When pressed, the musketeers retired into the protection of the wall of pikes, though not behind the pikemen. If cavalry nevertheless broke in, the musketeer could still use the butt end of his musket club-fashion.

Artillery did not play a great role in the Civil War, although the New Model was provided with a powerful train. There were no elaborate modern fortresses as on the Continent, only improvised earthworks. In the field the light guns ('sakers', 'minions' and 'drakes' firing balls of 5–6, 3½ and 3 pounds, respectively) were not decisive, being used principally for a preliminary exchange before battle was really joined.

Parliament was determined that the basis of the New Model system should be regular pay. The Committee of Both Kingdoms had estimated that this would cost nearly £45,000 per month or £585,000 a year. In fact this proved insufficient, and even the New Model was in arrears by 1647. Nevertheless, it was paid far more regularly and promptly than any previous force on either side, and this unquestionably contributed to its success. In 1645 the infantry-man was paid 8*d.* a day, less than a farm labourer – no wonder he had to be press-ganged and was socially, intellectually and educationally inferior to the cavalryman. The dragoon received 1*s.* 6*d.* a day, and the trooper 2*s.* The trooper was of a higher calibre altogether; most were literate and able to supply their own horse. An officer for the first and last time in the history of the British army until the present day could live on his pay; a colonel of horse received 22*s.* a day (plus 12*s.* allowance for six horses), a major 15*s.* 8*d.*, a captain 10*s.* Special acts of courage were rewarded, and commanders received generous grants of land and pensions.

The supply arrangements of the New Model were perhaps the least successful of its innovations. In fact supply was the endemic weakness of seventeenth-century armies, as of their predecessors. The problems of procurement, storage, movement and distribution of food, clothing and fodder were beyond the administrative techniques and machinery of the time. The Swedish and Imperial armies of the Thirty Years' War, campaigning in a country (Germany) devastated by war, had their own commissariat with magazines along the line of march. Even so they lived largely off the country, and a good commissariat was one that could strip it bare and distribute the proceeds in an organized way, rather than leave it to marauding by the soldiery. Although the French army supplied its troops with bread and wine, the men had to buy (or steal) their own food or fodder.

During the Civil War the armies were campaigning at home in comparatively rich country. Although some supplies followed the armies, either in wagons or on the hoof, the troops mostly lived on the country and often went hungry. Subsistence was generally by 'free quarter', which meant that householders had to feed and lodge the troops (the amount and nature of their obligations being theoretically strictly regulated) in return for a ticket to be re-imbursed later. In addition county authorities could be instructed by warrant to collect supplies for an army. 'Free quarter' was not popular. Soldiers could be unwelcome guests even if not actually brutal or licentious:

My house is, and hath been full of soldiers this fortnight, such uncivil drinkers and thirsty souls that a barrel of good beer trembles at the sight of them, and the whole house is nothing but a rendezvous of tobacco and spitting.[10]

'Free quarter' was gradually abolished after the foundation of the New Model and the introduction of regular pay. Instead, basic rations were issued to the troops (paid for by deduction from their pay), or they bought their own food, as in the French army. Only in Cromwell's and Monck's later Scottish campaigns was there a fully organized supply and magazine system, partially seaborne.

The regiment was the largest tactical and administrative unit, although in battle the army was generally divided into a centre and two wings, and so directly above the colonels came the general officers and staff of the army.

Command of the New Model was given to Sir Thomas Fairfax, an able thirty-three-year-old. Second-in-command was Skippon, entitled Major-General of the Army. Below him came the Lieutenant-General of the Horse, Oliver Cromwell, who, although a Member of Parliament, was exempted from the Self-Denying Ordinance because he was campaigning at the time. In 1647, when Skippon was sent to command the force in Ireland, the post of

Lieutenant-General of the Army was created, and Cromwell was appointed to it. The major-general was normally responsible for drawing up the army on the battlefield, while the lieutenant-general was second-in-command or chief of staff.

A general's lieutenant standeth as his second in all powers and authorities whatsoever ... to all general officers of the army he is 'the interpreter of what the general intendeth'.[11]

The artillery and engineers of the New Model were under command of the Lieutenant-General of the Ordnance, Thomas Hammond. (Names of engineers were often foreign, suggesting a lack of experienced English men.) The Comptroller of Artillery was Richard Deane, later a general at sea. Military justice was under a Judge-Advocate and two (provost) Marshal-Generals; supply under a Commissary-General of victuals; transport under a Waggon-master-General; and pay under two Treasurers-at-War assisted by special parliamentary commissioners. Medical officers and chaplains were provided. Unique to the English was a special officer, the Scoutmaster-General, in charge of reconnaissance and intelligence. His subordinates clearly sometimes encountered the usual hazards of the spy, for one Scoutmaster lamented to Cromwell:

I have not a few times sighed that men set to work by me have necessarily sinned, and one or two complained thereof to me, and desired therefore the greater wages, which last never troubled me ...[12]

The New Model was a thoroughly well-found military machine. Its commander-in-chief had full powers in matters of strategy, discipline and promotion and was largely free from political interference. The officers were men of solid social background, neither mean (as their opponents pretended) nor rich and fashionable, but with a sprinkling of men promoted from the ranks, something virtually unknown after the Commonwealth. Promotion was generally by merit, sometimes by seniority, seldom by favouritism. Up to the end of the Protectorate in 1660 the army offered good opportunities of social and financial advancement – in short, was a true profession.

*

The New Model at first took the field in 1645 alongside the other

Parliamentary armies. When the First Civil War ended in 1647 it became *the* standing army of the Parliamentary regime. This was something new in English history: armies there had been, but never before 'the Army'.

When the campaign of 1645 opened the war was still confused and indecisive. Charles was trying to recover his strength, based on a firm hold over the west country. In Scotland the Marquis of Montrose with a small force of Highland tribesmen won several victories for the King by the brilliance of his leadership and strategy, and became a legend. But his force was too small and undisciplined and his operations too far away from the main theatre of war to achieve major results. Nevertheless he gave the King hope. The King's own strategy, fatally haphazard and indecisive, eventually led him to give battle to a superior Parliamentary army at Naseby, Northamptonshire. The attrition of a long war had weakened the ill-organized Royalists and their dispositions were faulty. Charles's army numbered only 4,000 horse and 3,500 foot against 6,500 horse and dragoons and 7,000 foot of the New Model under Fairfax. This time, unlike at Marston Moor, Rupert and Cromwell were not facing each other.

Rupert charged the Parliamentary cavalry commanded by Ireton, who was wounded, and broke them. Again the Cavaliers' fatal indiscipline was their undoing, for Rupert's horse careered wildly off the battlefield and busied itself fruitlessly with the Parliamentary baggage-train. In the centre the infantry clashed in a bloody struggle. On the other flank Cromwell routed the Royalist horse under Sir Marmaduke Langdale, but kept his Ironsides well in hand. While three regiments followed Langdale, the rest wheeled against the flank of the Royalist infantry. The King was about to lead his reserve cavalry to Langdale's assistance when a peer dissuaded him, even turning the King's horse round. The Royalist cavalry thought this a signal for withdrawal – and withdrawal turned into rout. The Parliamentarians closed round the Royalist infantry. When Rupert at last returned, his troopers with their blown horses would not face the grim and triumphant Ironsides; he too hurried from the field.

It was a crushing victory: 5,000 prisoners, the King's entire baggage-train, 8,000 stands of arms, and over a hundred English and Irish prostitutes fell into the hands of the Parliamentarians.

Naseby was the King's ruin. Although a year passed before all the Royalist forces could be hunted down, before the King's last hope was destroyed by the relentless red-coats, the war had really been decided when Parliament reformed its military system. The Royalist historian, Clarendon, acknowledged:

Those under the King's commanders grew insensibly into all the licence, disorder and impiety with which they had reproached the rebels; and they again into a great discipline, diligence and sobriety: which begat courage and resolution in them, and notable dexterity in achievement and enterprises. Insomuch as one side seemed to fight for monarchy with the weapons of confusion, and the other to destroy the King and government with all the principles and regularity of monarchy.[13]

A year and ten days after Naseby, Oxford, the King's capital, surrendered. In Scotland Montrose and his Highlanders were finally subdued by the Presbyterians at Philliphaugh. The King surrendered to the Scots, who at the beginning of 1647 handed him over to Parliament in return for £400,000 arrears of pay. The Civil War was ended.

The tremendous consequences of the war now became apparent. The army had emerged not merely as an obedient and efficient military instrument, like the armies of absolute monarchies abroad, but as a great institution in the state, rivalling, indeed outweighing, Parliament.

The original Ironsides had always been a focus of religious radicalism, their ranks filled by the 'Saints', religious democrats who believed that each man must establish his own relationship with God, that any form of religious authority and hierarchy was wrong – not merely episcopacy and papism, but Presbyterianism as well. Their varied political views were radical, almost revolutionary – universal manhood-suffrage and abolition of King and House of Lords, for instance. Cromwell encouraged recruitment of 'Saints' into his cavalry because their fanaticism and self-discipline made them superb soldiers. The New Model had been built on the

Ironsides, and 'the Army' on the New Model: from general to trooper, these 50,000 formed a corps of religious independent-minded men. Officers and other ranks would meet to discuss the scriptures, pray and sing psalms instead of the more worldly pleasures indulged in by other armies. One of three famous preaching chaplains to the army, Dell, wrote:

The Lord hath poured forth [the spirit of Prayer] *upon* chief Commanders, *but on* very many *of the* inferior Officers, *and* common Troopers: some of *whom, I have by* accident *heard* praying, *with that* faith *and* familiarity *with God, that I have stood* wondring *at the* grace.[14]

God's hand was seen even in a local route march; His intervention decided battles; the army and its soldiers were His instruments, performing His will on the battlefield, in captured cities, or by disfiguring captured whores. As Cromwell himself wrote of Naseby:

I can say this of Naseby, that when I saw the enemy draw up and march in gallant order towards us, and we a company of poor, ignorant men, to seek how to order our battle – the General having commanded me to order all the horse – I could not (riding alone about my business) but smile out to God in praises, in assurance of victory, because God would, by things that are not, bring to naught things that are. Of which I had great assurance; and God did it. O that men would therefore praise the Lord, and declare the wonders that He doth for the children of men![15]

Although the Civil War had begun as a constitutional quarrel, it was sharpened by opposition to Laud's churchmanship, ultimately religion – democracy in religion or 'congregationalism' – became the central issue. In Cromwell's own words, 'Religion was not the thing first contested for, but God brought it to that issue at last, and gave it unto us by redundancy and at last it proved which was most dear to us'.[16]

No army had ever been inspired by such religious fanaticism. The Crusaders had fought *for* the Church: Parma and Alva's terrible veterans had been an army *of* the Church. But the Puritan army of England was its *own* Church, or rather a religious movement in itself. Unlike the other contemporary professional armies, it was not a docile, obedient, politically unthinking instrument. It had strong, though varied, views on society and political organization as well as religion. By 1647 'the Army' had emerged as the most powerful estate of the realm, with ideas very different from those of its titular masters, the members of the two Houses of Parliament.

For the Parliamentary leaders were Presbyterians. By the Solemn League and Covenant with the Scots they had promised to introduce Presbyterian church organization throughout the land. They visualized a settlement with the King and a new constitution on much more conservative lines than did the army. So when the war ended and the King was captured, Parliament and its army split. Parliament found itself in its turn as weak and impotent as had been the King. A debate or a resolution lacked force in face of a cavalry regiment with drawn swords and God's blessing. An army only two years old rapidly became the centre of English life, occupying the places of both King and Parliament. From 1647 to 1660 military power decided the making or unmaking of regimes and constitutions.

*

By their stupidities after the end of the Civil War both King and Parliament contributed to the emergence of the army as the most powerful factor in English life in 1647. With the Civil War over and Charles their prisoner, Parliamentary leaders saw themselves as masters of England and proceeded to violate every interest of the army, religious and material. It began to clamp Presbyterianism on the country and forbade independents to preach. It ordered all independents to be purged from the officer corps. For good measure it outraged the non-religious elements in the army by proposing to disband it without settling its arrears of pay. Yet it still hoped to raise a new army to crush Catholic rebellion in Ireland. The Long Parliament was indeed no advertisement for Parliamentary government.

Parliament's actions consolidated the divergent factions of the army and turned it into an organized political force. The officers, accustomed in wartime to meet in councils of war, began to meet in political council. The rank-and-file appointed 'agitators' (agents) to represent them under 'the Solemn Engagement of the

Army' (5 June 1647). The officers' and soldiers' councils were combined into a 'General Council of the Army', thus giving it a political organization and a directing body.

With victory therefore the Parliamentarians had split into two factions, a development most welcome to the King who saw the chance of playing off Parliament against the army. Since at this stage no one thought of any solution other than the retention of the monarch, though under constitutional restrictions, Charles was the focus of political manoeuvre in as much as he was the source of executive authority in the realm. Army and Parliament proceeded to propose rival plans for a settlement to Charles. Parliament proposed the establishment of Presbyterianism as the national religion for a trial period of three years and a return to the constitutional balance of August 1641; in other words effective Parliamentary controls of the King's executive powers. The army submitted the 'Heads of the Proposals', drafted originally by Commissary-General Ireton. This was a highly intelligent constitutional document and a tribute to the intellectual ability and breadth of vision of the New Model soldiers. Instead of leaving Parliament supreme, the army proposed limitations on Parliament itself – biennial elections and a redistribution of seats. With characteristic tolerance it proposed religious liberty instead of predominance of kirk or church. The King was to be advised by a Council of State.

The year 1647, like the years 1640–41, produced a flood of propositions, remonstrances and other documents. But the King's tortuous answers to Parliament and army concealed dealings with a third party – the Scots. Just as in 1640 Parliament in its military weakness had looked to the Scots army as a counterweight to the King's forces, so in 1647 the King looked to the Scots to offset Parliamentary military power. This shady bargain led to a second civil war in 1648, with Royalist revolts in Wales, Kent and Essex and a Scots invasion. Cromwell defeated the Scots at Preston and Fairfax broke the revolts in Kent and Essex. Meanwhile, however, the Presbyterian Parliamentary leaders had continued to negotiate with Charles, regarding him now as their mainstay against the army's religious and political extremism. This strange alliance, impotent though it was, left the army supported only by a narrow section of popular opinion in the country. When Cromwell and other extreme independents like Ireton decided that Charles was so unreliable that it was better to execute him than negotiate further, this decision split the Puritans yet again, moderate soldiers like Fairfax disowning the regicides and republicans. Cromwell and his associates were now a small minority dependent solely on military power.

Meanwhile the army, in the shape of Colonel Pride and his dragoons, had dealt with Presbyterian members of Parliament, 'purged' the Long Parliament and left a 'Rump' of army sympathizers. The independents of the army and the 'Rump' now set up 'a Commonwealth or Free State' of England, without King or House of Lords.

*

The military history of the Commonwealth was marked by a succession of ruthless triumphs. In 1650–51 Cromwell, now Commander-in-Chief in place of Fairfax, dealt with Charles II's attempt to use the Scots to regain his throne. One Scots army was defeated at Dunbar, while another force, lured into England by Cromwell, was destroyed at Worcester in 1651. In 1649–50 Cromwell broke the Catholic Irish rebellion, capturing their strongholds of Drogheda, Wexford and Clonmel amid scenes of ruthlessness presented as God's work and a just visitation on the Irish. (Cromwell's savagery to the Irish has in fact been exaggerated; in 1641–6 the Royalists had behaved even worse.) The excellence of the supply organization was a feature of the Irish campaign. In the subsequent colonial pacification the Cromwellians successfully repeated Mountjoy's tactics of fifty years earlier.

In 1654 General Monck, a former Royalist officer now commanding the Commonwealth forces in Scotland, pacified the Highlands by a similar system of fortified strongpoints and mobile columns. Many royalists in Scotland found Independent rule preferable to that of the Presbyterians, for the Independents at least stood for religious toleration. The English army even put an end to trials for witchcraft. The three British kingdoms were now united into a single Commonwealth.

Abroad, the name of the Commonwealth resounded with the clang of iron. Cromwell himself had all the qualities of leadership which the Stuarts lacked, and he was assisted and advised by a Council of State of able men trained in war. Soldiers like Monck, Deane and Blake were sent to sea, and the navy became a grimly professional force instead of the rather ramshackle institution under the monarchy. Britain now had both the force and the determination to influence continental politics. In 1652–4 came a trade war against the Dutch, and in 1655–8, another trade war in alliance with France against a now declining Spain. In the battle of the Dunes outside Dunkirk (14 June 1658) Lockhart's red-coats tore to pieces a Spanish and Imperialist army, including a unit under the exiled James, Duke of York; and at the siege of Ypres Morgan's troops showed the French how to storm a fortress.

Although Cromwell's foreign policy did not produce great results, England was respected as she had rarely been since the days of the Plantagenets. The roar of Blake's guns sinking the Spanish fleet at Tenerife and the shout of Lockhart's red-coats attacking on the Dunkirk dunes conveyed an unmistakable diplomatic message.

Numerous though the Commonwealth's military and naval successes were, there is one blot on the record of efficiency and thorough organization – an expedition to capture the Spanish West Indian island of Hispaniola. Even Cromwell was captivated by the Elizabethan legend of Drake and the Spanish Empire. The expedition repeated every mistake and failing of Elizabethan seaborne expeditions and initiated some fresh errors destined to be repeated during the next three centuries. The troops used were hurriedly assembled drafts, not whole seasoned regiments; the officer responsible for the supply organization proved incompetent; crooked contractors reaped another harvest. When the expedition at last reached its destination in 1655, the old problems of joint command arose once more. The land force commander, Venables, and the naval commander, Penn, differed in temperament and did not find co-operation easy. Dysentery and yellow fever swept through the expedition. Though Jamaica was eventually captured, it involved considerable additional effort and a constant drain of reinforcements.

At home political rule by Cromwell and the army was firm and efficient. It found the country in the chaotic aftermath of civil war and swiftly turned it into a great, well-administered state. Yet it had no broad-based national support; it did not reflect the natural structure of English society, nor did it accord with English political habits and loyalties. Gradually support in the country shrank until it was virtually non-existent outside the army. The Civil War had naturally turned the Royalists into opponents, and sequestration of their estates as 'malignants' and an unjust load of taxation (partly to support the army) did nothing to reconcile them. The Presbyterians – moderate Parliamentarians, the original source of opposition to Charles – had been driven into opposition to the army during the 1647 quarrels. The remaining moderates supporting the army's cause – the last of the solid gentry and nobility – had been outraged by the execution of the King, as evidenced by Fairfax's resignation as Commander-in-Chief. Between 1650 and 1653 the remnants of the Puritan movement – the Rump Parliament and the army leaders – also fell out. The army leaders demanded that the Rump remedy certain practical grievances and arrange for its own dissolution. When in 1653 there seemed no prospect of it doing either, Cromwell closed it down with a file of musketeers and some strong language of his own. Now the Puritan cause was represented by the army alone.

For the next five years Cromwell struggled with the insoluble problem of how to return to constitutional government based on the consent of English society *while at the same time* preserving a republic and religious freedom. Various constitutional subterfuges were employed to conceal the fact of military rule. First, a council of officers nominated an assembly of Puritan notables, known as 'Barebone's Parliament' after the renowned Puritan fanatic, Praise-God Barebone. This was followed by a new constitution called the Instrument of Government, under which Cromwell became uncrowned king, styled 'the Lord Protector of the Commonwealth of England'.

Cromwell's promotion to sole executive, although buttressed with a Council of State as support and safeguard, caused a further diminution of Puritan support. Even the army independents and radicals saw the Protectorate as a betrayal of the Commonwealth, of the fundamental principles of the cause. When the first Protectorate Parliament met, the failure of Cromwell's search for a wide basis of consent was demonstrated. A vociferous minority of members set to work to criticize the new constitution and even to undermine the Protector's grip on the army, or reduce the army in size. In 1655 Cromwell dissolved his Parliament. Far from settling down and accepting the Protectorate, the country was restless; there were Royalist plots, Leveller plots, even a rising near Salisbury. As a precaution Cromwell reorganized local government into eleven districts under major-generals, each supported by a mounted *gendarmerie* drawn from loyal militia. Their duties included police surveillance of known enemies of the regime and reporting on and influencing public opinion, together with traditional local government activities previously the prerogatives of the Lords-Lieutenant and county gentry. The major-generals' districts cut across the organic structure of English local life and traditional county loyalties. The largest and most powerful class in the country – the gentry – saw their position of leadership and control over the lower classes and county affairs removed from them and given to soldiers. They did not care that in fact the major-generals were often more efficient and more just in dealing with the lower classes than they themselves had been. The legend that the rule of the major-generals was a cruel tyranny sprang from the gentry's fury at having to concede precedence and power in their county to a professional soldier of perhaps undistinguished origin.

Still Cromwell sought that elusive popular consent which alone could give the Commonwealth some lasting foundation. But historically the English were habituated to monarchy. The Civil War had not been fought to abolish monarchy. Despite all Charles's foolishness and deceit only a small minority had wanted him executed; still fewer wanted a republic. In response to this deep monarchical sentiment, the Lord Protector acted increasingly like a king; his court exchanged its military simplicity for ceremonial trappings. In 1657 his second Parliament proposed, by the Humble Petition and Advice, that he should in fact become king and found a dynasty. Under pressure from his military colleagues Cromwell rejected the throne, but he did accept certain proposals in the Humble Petition and Advice reminiscent of the traditional constitution, such as a (nominated) second chamber and increased powers for the Commons. But again renewed opposition in the Commons forced him to dissolve Parliament.

The Commonwealth rested with increasing nakedness on the power of the army. Yet the army itself was no longer the dedicated body it had been in 1647. A new class of officer, more professional, less religious, had appeared. Senior officers, growing rich by speculation in sequestered Cavalier estates, became divorced from their rank-and-file, whose pay was still often in arrears. Indeed a racket connected with the soldiers' pay brought the interests of officers and men into direct conflict. To cover the difference between pay actually received and pay owed, soldiers were given 'debentures' to be redeemed later from the sale of church and Cavalier estates. Officers bought up these debentures at cut-prices, and a vast traffic grew up whereby they made fortunes and founded landed families out of money owed to their soldiers. The Council of the Army came to represent merely a land-owning minority.

In fact the whole structure of the Commonwealth, and even the solidarity of the army itself, depended on one man, Oliver Cromwell; and on 3 September 1658 he died.

His son Richard, an agreeable country gentleman, was proclaimed Protector. A weak king can at least call on the instinctive habitual loyalty of society and the ingrained habit of obedience to the law. A weak protector can call on nothing. Richard was in the hands of the army leaders. The proclamation of his accession was signed by many army officers, while the Council of State officially informed the Council of Officers that he had succeeded his father. This was formal recognition that the army – some 40,000 men (in the British Isles and abroad), supported by a permanent annual budget – was now a great estate of the realm.

An eight-month tussle ensued between Richard Cromwell and Fleetwood, the Commander-in-Chief, mainly over the question of who should control army appointments. Fleetwood forced Richard to dissolve his Parliament and 'abdicate' as Protector, and the Rump Parliament was recalled in May 1659. This obsolete assembly, reduced by purges to Independents like the army leaders themselves, nevertheless followed the pattern of Commonwealth parliaments and began to display unwelcome indifference to the army's wishes. Once more a general (this time Lambert) took soldiers down to the Commons and dissolved the House.

The Republican regime was reduced to constitutional chaos, for authority now rested openly on the sword, and the sword was no longer wielded by a great man like Cromwell, but by factious and quarrelsome soldiers like Fleetwood. Not only the Royalists, but even the Presbyterian moderates wanted the monarchy back. The City of London had had enough of expensive wars and armies, while even the common people (whom no one really bothered about) were tired of canting, psalm-singing soldiers and the prohibition of all joys and amusement. The Independents had made the fatal mistake of equating dreariness with Godliness.

However, the army leaders possessed the only power of coercion in the kingdom; how, in face of Fleetwood's and Lambert's soldiers, could the nation express its desire to return to the familiar pattern of life?

Once more, a constitutional and national crisis turned on the question of military power. Soldiers had deposed the monarchy and killed a king; soldiers now restored the monarchy.

For an effective military force was needed to tip the political scales. It was provided by General George Monck, the Commander-in-Chief in Scotland, and his army of 10,000 men. Monck himself had been a Royalist officer in the Civil War and had later served in the New Model with distinction in Ireland and Scotland. He was a moderate man who had supported Cromwell as the only alternative to chaos, but who would not serve his feeble son Richard. Monck saw that a return to monarchy was the inevitable, and right, solution. In a highly political situation he acted with political skill and judgement, and yet he was the archetype of the professional soldier, the loyal servant of a properly constituted authority. Monck had trained his army and selected its officers with care; it was efficient and totally loyal to him.

The Republican Council of State (itself a creation of the Rump) appointed Monck Commander-in-Chief of the army in opposition to General Lambert, the former Commander-in-Chief. Monck marched south from Coldstream on the Scottish border, greeted everywhere as a saviour. Would Lambert's army fight its fellow-soldiers under Monck? It would not. The Restoration proceeded swiftly. Monck called a free Parliament which invited the king to return, and on 29 May 1660, King Charles II entered his capital. The Commonwealth adventure was over.

*

The experience of the Commonwealth and Protectorate left a deep scar on British minds and memories so far as a national army was concerned. From 1660 to the present day the history of the army as an institution has been constantly governed by this national aversion to a standing army as a major state institution. In 1660 the division of authority between king, people and military had yet to be finally decided. In Europe, too, it was the outstanding problem of the seventeenth century, each state and nation having its own peculiar and complex problems, each moving towards separate solutions. Did a king's power lie primarily in his role as civilian executive authority in the state, or in his role as personal commander – owner – of the army? Or in both, and in what proportions?

By the end of the seventeenth century different countries were to return different answers. In France the King became sole legislator *and* Commander-in-Chief. In some German states, like Prussia, the bitter experiences of the Thirty Years' War and other conflicts produced standing armies which gave the princes power to break traditional constitutional and civilian checks on royal authority. When army commander and head of state were identical, military power and absolute monarchy could together determine a nation's destiny, and national existence could be made synonymous with the possession of a powerful army. By 1660 France was already on this course, while in Germany the issue between orderly constitutional development and absolute military monarchy was still undecided. In England, however, both absolute monarchy and military power had suffered a major setback. A standing army was a very long way from acceptance as a natural and desirable aspect of the nation's way of life.

6
Armed Force and the Constitution 1660–89

In 1660 the mood of the British people was rather like that of a married couple after a stupendous row: a delusive harmony, an unjustified hope for a trouble-free future.

The constitutional harmony which King Charles II and the Cavalier Parliament hoped to recreate was that of 1640, *after* Charles I had abandoned his extreme absolutist pretensions, but before the House of Commons had virtually usurped the Crown's executive powers. In settling the future relationship of King and Parliament, and their respective functions and authority, the question of the army – of military power – was highly important. Lack of an army had made Charles Parliament's prisoner in 1640; a quarrel over the militia had actually ignited the Civil War; and now, in 1660, there existed a long-service professional army of some 40,000 men. Although this army obeyed General Monck, now the King's Captain-General, it had been raised originally to serve Parliament against the monarchy. Moreover, its pay was in arrears, a factor always inclined to make soldiers restless and reluctant to disband.

The solution of the problem of the army was one of the keys to the Restoration constitutional settlement. That adopted was simple, based on the perennial English assumption that the war or emergency just over would be the last. The army was to be paid off and disbanded. The safety of the kingdom would be entrusted, as for centuries, to the militia – English society with a pike or matchlock in its hand. The proven military uselessness of the militia between 1639 and 1642 carried no weight with those who in 1660 proposed to resurrect it to replace 'the Army'. They were thinking in terms not of military effectiveness, but of social and political advantage. Royal ministers were attracted by the idea of a select mobile militia, similar to that of the Commonwealth major-generals. The suggestion failed simply because it was potentially too effective. The more militarily effective the national armed forces, the greater was thought the danger of tyranny.

The post-Restoration militia system was set up by the Militia Acts of 1661, 1662 and 1663.* That of 1661 was a temporary measure stating that command of all military forces and forts belonged to the King and to neither House of Parliament. However, the 1662 Act (the principal measure) in effect removed all substance from the King's prerogative of command. Instead of his prerogative right to levy money and embody the militia as in past emergencies, the King was empowered to raise only the miserly sum of £70,000 a year for three years to pay such militia forces as might be needed for active service. To reduce the influence of the great county magnates – the King's men – the Act stipulated that Deputy-Lieutenants (drawn from the squirearchy) should join with the Lords-Lieutenant when men and money were to be levied. Men and equipment were to come from three sources: individual contributors, group contributors and parishes; the scale of contribution being graded by income. The Act specified the arms and equipment to be supplied to each militia man, horse and foot.

The paper strength of the Restoration militia differed little from that of Elizabeth's day: 90,000 men, of whom only 6,000 were cavalry. As before, the militia reflected the pattern of English society; in this case, the growing distinction between town and country. Contemporary documents distinguish between 'town bands' and 'private' or 'freehold' bands; the cavalry, in particular, was supplied by the counties, and of course essentially by the gentry.

Immediately after the Restoration, while old Commonwealth men were still restless and rumours of plots and insurrections were rife, the militia again fulfilled the only function it had ever carried out effectively – that of amateur political police and riot force.

* See J. R. Western, *The English Militia in the Eighteenth Century* for an excellent treatment of the whole subject of the late Stuart and Hanoverian militias.

Yet even for this it was soon felt to be inadequate in the face of apparently serious new danger to the state. And this apparent danger produced another, and major, step forward in the history of British military institutions: the retention of regimented bodies of troops in peacetime.

Apart from the small non-regimental units that had always garrisoned coastal forts and fortified towns, it had been intended at the Restoration to retain only the King's bodyguard (which had accompanied him into exile) to guard his palace and person, on the lines of Henry VII's Yeomen of the Guard or Henry VIII's Gentlemen-at-Arms, both of which had now become ceremonial bodies. But in 1661 a fanatical Fifth Monarchist named Venner led an armed rising which seemed to the newly restored King and his supporters more dangerous than mere plots. With many old Cromwellian soldiers still in the country, the militia suddenly seemed a precarious protection for the monarchy. The disbandment of Monck's army was halted, though only two regiments were by then left intact.

In the forenoon of 14 February 1661, the survivors of that splendid army that had been victorious at Naseby, Dunbar, Preston and Worcester, in Ireland and on the dunes of Dunkirk paraded on Tower Hill. When the Lord General's Regiment of Foot and the Lord General's Lifeguard of Horse laid down their arms, it was the end of the brief history of the Commonwealth army. However, the regiments immediately took up their arms again in the royal service, as the Lord General's Regiment of Footguards and the Lord General's Troop of Guards. The first regiment survives to this day in the Coldstream Guards, while the second was later merged into the Lifeguards.

In the same year (1661) the men who had guarded Charles II in exile were formed into two regiments of foot-guards and two troops of horse-guards. In 1665 these foot-guards were amalgamated into one regiment, the First Foot-guards, which survives today as the Grenadier Guards. As the Coldstream embodies the traditions of the New Model, so the Grenadiers can look back to the Royalist foot of the Civil War. Being originally a royal regiment they have precedence over the older Coldstream. The two troops

of horse-guards were named the King's Own, or First, Troop of
Life-guards, and the Duke of York's, or Second, Troop. They survive in the modern Life Guards. The modern Royal Horse Guards
(The Blues), now amalgamated with the Royal Dragoons, have a
somewhat tenuous connexion with Cromwell's horse: in February
1661 a recently disbanded Commonwealth regiment, only created
in 1660, was re-formed as the Earl of Oxford's Regiment of Horse –
another result of Venner's uprising.

An even older regiment traces its history in British employment
back to Venner's revolt, for the government called back to Britain
the Scottish troops in French service. The French regiment *Royal
Écossais* had been raised in 1633 and later absorbed Scottish units
which had fought under Gustavus-Adolphus at Breitenfeld and
Lutzen. Although these troops returned to the French from 1662
until 1678 (apart from 1666–8), they date their seniority in the
British service from 1661 as the First, Royal, or Scots Regiment of
Foot: now the Royal Scots.

Thus at the very moment when the government was disbanding
its army, Venner provided fresh reason for the maintenance of regular military forces. At the same time Charles's Queen, Catherine
of Braganza, brought Tangier to the English Crown as part of her
dowry. This required a garrison as defence against the Moors, so
the 'Tangier Regiment of Foot' was raised and the British army
began its long service in Africa. When Tangier was abandoned in
1684, the regiment was brought home and placed on the English
establishment as 'Our Most Dear Consort the Queen's Regiment
of Foot'. It survived into our own times as the Queen's Royal
Regiment.

In Scotland the Commonwealth regiments were not disbanded
on the Restoration, but in 1662 were taken into Portuguese service;
and Portuguese independence from Spain constitutes the last
monument to the military prowess of the Commonwealth of
England's army.

The Restoration meant that England and Scotland became separate kingdoms again. A separate Scottish military establishment
was formed, and lasted until the final union of the two kingdoms
in 1707; the regiments of this establishment are now represented by

the Royal Scots Greys, the Scots Guards, the King's Own Scottish Borderers and the Royal Highland Fusiliers.

The oldest regiments in the British army therefore trace their continuous history in the service of the British Crown to 1660–61 and to the odd combination of a Fifth Monarchy plot and a Roman Catholic dowry. Some nineteenth- and twentieth-century historians have described the military developments of 1660–61 as a great watershed in the history of British military institutions, maintaining that they mark the foundation of the British standing army. But in fact no definite date for the creation of the army can be fixed. The British standing army, like the British Cabinet system, evolved gradually, unacknowledged as such until long after it existed in fact. By 1660–61 the English aversion to standing armies in peacetime was already strong. Those statesmen who decided to retain the last two regiments of Monck's army and the pre-1660 royal regiments had no intention of creating a standing army; they were merely temporarily reinforcing the guards of his Majesty's person in order to maintain public order. 'Guards and garrisons' there had been in peacetime for centuries. Fifty years later the Mutiny Acts were still proclaiming that a standing army in peacetime without Parliament's consent was illegal; and troops in Britain were still described as 'guards and garrisons'. Although historians with hindsight were to know that the regiments of 1660–61 became permanent, neither Monck, Charles nor Clarendon had any such idea.

Other considerations, too, show the belief that the British army was founded in 1660–61 to be arbitrary and unreal. In 1663 troops in regiments totalled 3,574 men, and the garrisons 4,878. This hardly amounts to 'an army', for the Commonwealth army in 1659 numbered some 40,000, while the French army after the Peace of the Pyrenees in 1659 included forty-eight infantry regiments. Moreover, only one of the regiments of 1660–61 was in fact new, for the regimental histories of Monck's two units can be traced back to the Civil War, as can that of Oxford's horse, while the royal regiments had served the King in exile, and can also claim indirect links with Royalist units of the Civil War. The Scottish regiments which gave birth to the Royal Scots had been in existence for nearly a century before they entered British service. Only the Tangier Regiment was really new, and that was raised for service outside the kingdom.

Looked at through seventeenth-century spectacles, therefore, 1660–61 marks no great watershed, but a limited though important step in the growth of the British army.*

*

The constitutional harmony of the Restoration proved illusory and in fact the country was destined for a further fifty years of bitter political warfare that included another revolution. In this further contest between Crown and Parliament, executive and legislature, the organization and control of military power was again of central importance. Similar contests were taking place in Europe, and their outcome also turned on the linked questions of royal income and royal armies. The absolute monarchy of Louis XIV of France set an example for other monarchs and constituted a warning to parliaments or estates. Although the Treaty of Westphalia in 1648 ended one general war, there was fighting in Europe for most of the century. Wars gave the princes an excuse for raising emergency taxation and maintaining standing armies. Once a prince had been given the right to raise taxes, or even a long-term grant, he was independent of Parliament and could coerce his subjects by means of his army. Englishmen knew of the constitutional struggles abroad, and absorbed their lessons.

A standing army was therefore regarded as the instrument of the King, and consequently dangerous. Apart from guards and garrisons, the militia was the only military force recognized under the constitution because, being English society in arms, it was not unquestioningly obedient to the King. When the constitutional struggle once more became acute, the militia and regular troops were regarded not as militarily complementary, but as totally opposed conceptions. Unfortunately for supporters of the militia, its effectiveness in the defence of the realm continued to fall. It had

---

* It is not intended to record the raising of every regiment, and its subsequent permutations of name, seniority and equipment, but to do so only in connexion with some significant change in the history of the army as a collective institution, or a new development in arms and tactics.

all its old disadvantages: lack of mobility, the difficulty of keeping forces in the field, the widening gap between trained troops and civilian levies, amateur officers. Moreover, after the Restoration, the central government relaxed its grip on the local unpaid administration, an aspect of the abdication of conciliar government in favour of a private landed oligarchy. As a result the militia became even more decrepit. By the 1670s some county militias had not been mustered for four years. During the third Dutch war, the Suffolk militia, on the exposed eastern coastline, found itself short of officers for such cogent reasons as 'death', 'sulking' and 'fear'.[1] As early as 1666, the inefficiency of the militia during the second Dutch war caused the project for a select mobile militia to be revived. Three regiments of horse, an infantry regiment and seventeen independent troops of horse were raised. In 1667 the Dutch raid on Chatham led to the force being raised again and expanded to 12,000 foot and 3,200 horse. A select force could be better trained in formed bodies and it could be kept in being during an emergency, whereas the men of the ordinary militia were urgently needed at home. Unfortunately the government lacked funds to perpetuate the select militia, the only effective element of 'the constitutional force'. Moreover, the very effectiveness of the select militia and the fact that it could be kept together for limited periods aroused fears of a new standing army. The first article in Clarendon's impeachment in 1667 alleged that he 'designed a Standing Army to be raised, and to govern the Kingdom thereby'.[2] The militia ceased to be politically acceptable the moment it became militarily effective.

Control of the militia was a major bone of contention between Charles II and Shaftesbury during the exclusion crisis of 1678–81. Shaftesbury and his party were attempting to exclude the King's brother, James, Duke of York, from the succession because he was a Catholic, and to extract constitutional concessions from the Crown. As often, foreign events and domestic pressures inter-acted. By 1678 the shifts of Charles II's foreign policy had brought him to the brink of war with his old paymaster, Louis XIV. At last the Crown had a policy that Parliament could support. Instead, however, there was peace in Europe (by the Treaty of Nymegen) and civil turmoil at home. Titus Oates's ingenious lies about a Popish Plot frightened English public opinion into a panic that was well exploited by Shaftesbury and the Whigs. Facing possible organized mob violence, the King wished to keep his 10,000 soldiers mobilized, but Parliament demanded their disbandment, and the embodiment instead of 60,000 militia for six weeks. Although the militia were not called out, the newly raised troops were paid off, leaving only the King's guards. By the end of the exclusion crisis in 1681, the Whigs had whipped up anti-Popish and radical feeling almost to the point of revolution. London was so hostile to the King that he summoned his fourth Parliament to meet him in Oxford. However, the King possessed two weapons sufficient to break Shaftesbury and the Whigs: a new French pension making him independent of parliamentary grants, and his guards. These, lining the streets of Oxford, countered Shaftesbury's threat of insurrection by a show of disciplined military power. Charles II's position in the constitutional crisis of 1681 was very different from his father's forty years earlier.

*

Charles II was too intelligent or too easy-going to push his claim too far; his object was rather to defend royal power against parliamentary encroachment than to expand it. He acted more like a clever politician than a haughty monarch in the style of Louis XIV. He did not use his victory of 1681 or his troops to extend his royal power, but to bolster his supporters in the country by, for instance, re-organizing city corporations and purging them of Whigs.

His brother, who succeeded him as James II in 1685, had no political gifts and no desire for them. He was honest, narrow-minded, bigoted and inflexible. He modelled himself on Louis XIV. James was a Roman Catholic, and saw his life's work as the liberation of Roman Catholics from all penal disabilities, and the restoration of Britain to the Church of Rome. A head-on collision between King and Parliament was therefore inevitable. Once more, the questions of military power and its control were among the major points of conflict and, eventually, the key to the outcome of long constitutional struggle under the Stuarts.

The rebellion in 1685 of Monmouth, Charles's bastard son and a Protestant pretender, gave James early justification for increasing the royal forces' strength, for the county militias in the west country proved incapable of dealing with their fellow-rustics under Monmouth, being sympathetic to his cause and reluctant to fight their own people. Royal troops were concentrated as a field force under John Churchill (his first independent command), who was however superseded by the Earl of Feversham, a professedly Protestant Frenchman. Nevertheless the army broke Monmouth's courageous but ill-armed, inexperienced, untrained peasants at Sedgemoor.

On 9 November 1685 Parliament re-assembled. It was as docile and obedient a body as every form of gerrymandering, pressure and corruption could make it. However, in the speech from the throne James proposed such outrageous measures that even this docile Parliament was roused to sharpening opposition that ended in revolution. James referred to the incapacity of the militia even to deal with Monmouth's peasants and told the Commons that he needed 'a good force of well-disciplined troops in constant pay'; worse, he insisted on including Roman Catholics in the army 'if there should be another rebellion to make them necessary to me'.[3] The King's supporters argued that the state of Europe and the necessity for order at home required an army of 10–15,000 men. Sir Winston Churchill, a burgess of Lyme, moved that a supply be granted 'for the army'. 'For the army' – it was a phrase that stuck in parliamentary throats; it acknowledged the inadmissible. In the ensuing debate, the militia and a professional army were again contrasted in black-and-white. To James's critics, a standing army officered by Roman Catholics was the direct prelude to arbitrary rule. In the face of mounting criticism and much to his distaste, James chose to forego the prospect of a parliamentary grant to support the army, and prorogued Parliament.

The King infiltrated Roman Catholics into various public services under cover of a pretended power to dispense with laws that barred non-members of the Church of England. He steadily created an army. In 1685 alone nine new foot regiments, five regiments of horse and two of dragoons were raised. Although the object was to suppress the rebellion, the troops were retained in service afterwards

in defiance of constitutional practice. Many garrison and fortress troops were enregimented. The regiments themselves were
concentrated into a field army for the first time during a peace; an
army permanently encamped at Hounslow, close to the capital.
James II was an able military administrator; he had been an excellent Lord High Admiral; and now, exercising command of the
new army in person, he brought in new training methods, a drill
book and training camps.

In Ireland, where there had been standing forces on a separate
establishment since the Tudors, the Irish army of some 10,000 men
was purged of Protestant officers in favour of Papists. The same
process was also begun in the English army, although it met with
stout resistance. During 1686 and 1687 James discovered that a
professional standing army in England was not necessarily a blindly
obedient instrument of the royal will. For James's army was overwhelmingly Protestant, and overwhelmingly unwilling either to
become Roman Catholics, or serve Roman Catholic policies. Its
sentiments were well-expressed by Colonel Kirk of the Queen's,
who, when sounded about quitting the Church of England,
'regretted to say he was pre-engaged, for when at Tangier he had
promised the Sultan of Marocco [*sic*] that if ever he changed his
religion he would turn Mohammedan'.[4]

Nevertheless, by 1688 James had brought the strength of the
armies in his three kingdoms to over 34,000 men. It might well be
said that if the British royal standing army was in fact founded at
one given time, it was between 1685 and 1688, and that James II
was the army's creator. It was paid for by the simple device of
diverting funds from the militia.

The King resolutely pursued his plan of subverting English
Protestantism from the top, wilfully blind to the more and more
manifest signs of national anger and of the unity of all classes
against him. The birth of a son to James projected the dangers of
Popery and absolute monarchy far into the future, and gave fresh
impetus to those who were plotting his downfall. What was later
to be dignified by the Whigs as 'the Glorious Revolution' now took
the form of grave territorial magnates and leading statesmen conducting discreet negotiations among themselves and with William

of Orange. William's Stuart wife, Mary, would provide the Protestant succession if James could be deposed, while William and his Dutch forces would provide the leadership and force.

The discreet advances being made to William by English notables and the virtually united national opposition to James offered William the opportunity of adding English power to his anti-French coalition. However, not until he had received a formal invitation from English notables, did William commit himself to invading England. He had no wish to emulate Monmouth, and find himself high and dry on public indifference or hostility.

Yet, despite almost unanimous national support for William, the success of his invasion – of the 'Revolution' – depended entirely on the attitude taken by the royal army and the Royal Navy. The Royal Navy was only slightly weaker in strength than the Dutch fleet. Since the troop transports would greatly hinder the Dutch warships, it was possible that James's fleet could prevent the landing. In the face of the direct French danger to the Netherlands, William could take no more than 14,000 troops with him: perhaps half James's available field forces. Even should William then successfully land, he would very probably be exposed to defeat in battle if James's army only remained loyal to its paymaster. The issue of the 'Glorious Revolution' depended on strategic factors.

William sailed on 19 October 1688, but was driven home again by a storm. Then the wind swung round to the east – a 'Protestant' wind. William's armada sailed again on 1 November. In England, the King and the nation that hated him waited alike for news either of William's landfall or of a great sea battle. However, the royal battle-fleet under Dartmouth, in what Ogg has called 'one of the most ambiguous episodes in the history of the Royal Navy' failed either to intercept or fight William's armada.

On 5 November, William landed at Torbay, marched to Exeter and there concentrated his forces. James ordered the main body of his army forward to Salisbury, where the roads to the west forked. Desertions began as soon as the army moved, and undermined the King's confidence. On 24 November James held a council of war. Feversham, the Commander-in-Chief, a Huguenot Frenchman, recommended retreat behind the Thames. Churchill, a devoted Protestant and the ablest soldier in the royal army, urged James to give battle. He was overborne. The decision to retreat was made, an absolutely fatal decision to James, demonstrating uncertainty instead of strong leadership and handing the initiative irrevocably to the outnumbered enemy.

Later that night after the council of war Churchill rode over to William's camp. It was a shattering stroke at the military effectiveness of the royal army. Churchill's desertion was followed by that of other notables: Prince George of Denmark (Princess Anne's husband), Princess Anne herself, and great peers like Danby who seized towns in the north and Midlands in William's name. The mentally blind King at last saw that virtually every man's hand was against him; that his army, so carefully created, would probably fight badly or not at all. It was a moment to test James's mettle as a King; James responded to it by ordering the disbandment of the army and fleeing to the Continent. The military factor had decided the King's fate. The events of the 'Glorious Revolution' are in many ways an episode in military history as much as in political or constitutional history.

*

With William and Mary upon the vacated throne, an attempt was once more made to deal with the fundamental problem of military power and political liberty. James's standing army had badly frightened the nation – far more than had Cromwell's. It had been so plainly designed to coerce. In fact the army had proved a broken sword in James's hands, for the army and its officers had actively helped the Protestant and constitutional cause. However, the negotiators of the Revolution settlement dealt with the problem of military power in terms of James's intentions. There was now the terrifying example of Louis XIV in the full tide of his success. British statesmen wished to be sure that no future British monarch could similarly use an army as the foundation for arbitrary power and absolute monarchy.

There was the simple, traditional solution – no standing army at all in time of peace. Unfortunately this was no time of peace. In March 1689 James II and a small French army landed in

Ireland, almost all of which now lay in the hands of Catholic rebels. Throughout 1688 Europe had been lurching towards general war. The coalition led by William of Orange was preparing again to resist Louis XIV's unslaked ambition. In February 1689 the Dutch declared war on France. More declarations followed; and in May the three British kingdoms entered the struggle behind their new Dutch king. Therefore, far from it being possible to disband James's army, it was necessary to maintain and enlarge it.

The national emergency greatly complicated the constitutional dilemma. It was still the unchallenged prerogative of the king to raise, command and administer armed forces in time of war or danger. William III enjoyed a legitimate opportunity for enhancing royal power that had been denied to James. Throughout the century war had opened the way for European princes to raise both armies and emergency taxation, which were later both kept on in peacetime. Princes thus gradually won political independence from their parliaments. The English Parliament, on the other hand, had already gained one major victory that European estates had lost or were losing: control even over war taxation. However, James had shown how easy it was to maintain a standing army by diverting money from other purposes.

The future constitutional place of military forces and of their royal command in peacetime was laid down in the Declaration of Rights. An initial list of James II's misdemeanours accused him of 'Levying Money for and to the use of the Crowne by Pretence of Prerogative for other time and in other manner than the same was granted by Parlyament'; and 'raising and keeping a Standing Army within this Kingdome in time of Peace without consent of Parlyament and Quartering Soldiers contrary to Law'.[5]

The Declaration went on duly to declare that both these procedures were against the law. The problem of military power in peacetime was thus resolved; under no colour of legality could the crown continue to keep forces on foot unless Parliament willed it.

There remained the question of martial law. Martial law (summary and speedy justice applied to civilians as well as soldiers in time of great national danger) and military law ('King's Regulations' for the internal discipline and justice of the army) had not yet become distinct. There was the fear, expressed as long ago as 1628 in the Petition of Right, that 'martial law' for the disciplining of soldiers might be applied to civilians in place of common law; in other words royal prerogative justice in a new form. Martial law had in fact been technically illegal since the Petition of Right, although sheer functional need had forced military commanders to issue Articles of War and administer summary justice within the forces. In 1689 the place of martial law, in the sense of military law applied to troops, still required constitutional definition.

As often in history, particular events impinged on general problems. There was a mutiny at Ipswich among troops destined for Flanders. The hasty result was the first Mutiny Act. This Act recognized that a special system of justice was necessary for armies, but only in respect of mutiny, sedition or desertion; and it authorized execution as the most severe penalty for these crimes. It further authorized the Crown or its generals to convene courts martial for trying such crimes.

However, the concessions did not extend to the delegation to the Crown of power to promulgate a complete military code, and the Act was given a fixed duration of less than a year. The preamble repeated the Bill (later the Declaration) of Rights on the illegality of standing armies 'within this Kingdom' in time of peace, 'unless it be with the consent of Parliament'; and stated once more that martial law could not be applied to civilians in place of common law. The Act was not to apply to the militia.

It would thus be wrong to exaggerate the importance of this first Mutiny Act, simply because we now know that it was the beginning of a series of such acts up to the present day; acts which now place the governance of the armed forces entirely under annual Parliamentary sanction. The Act neither formally recognized the existence of a standing army, nor did it in any way 'legalize' the army, nor did it establish Parliamentary control over the army. The Act merely legalized within tight limits military justice as it had always existed. It was an emergency and temporary measure. The phrasing 'Whereas, the raising or keeping a standing army within this Kingdom in time of peace unless it be with the consent of Parliament is against law' suggests that a peacetime army was not normally to be expected. Nor was the passing of a fresh mutiny act on the expiry of the present act essential for the legal continuance of the army. Under William and Mary and under Anne there were often gaps of several months between mutiny acts.

The attempt of the Revolution settlement to define the constitutional place of military institutions suffered because it was followed by a quarter of a century of almost continuous war with France. For yet another 'extraordinary' emergency over-rode political choice and led to major developments, both constitutional and administrative.

7

Marlborough's Military System

IN the second half of the seventeenth century France dominated the political life of Europe. A succession of able leaders – Richelieu, Mazarin and then King Louis XIV himself – imposed unity and centralized efficiency on a hitherto disunited country. Fine roads and waterways helped to link all France with Paris. The French state, some twenty millions in population, easily outmatched any other state of Europe.

By the great Condé's victory over the Spaniards at Rocroi in 1643 France had taken the place of Spain as the foremost military power. It was to France henceforward that men looked for example in the organization of armies and the art of war. In this epoch of corruption and incompetence, absolute monarchy was a short-cut to efficiency at the sacrifice of constitutional government. Two great war ministers, Le Tellier and his even more able son Louvois, attacked the chaos and abuse that was common to all seventeenth-century armies except that of the Commonwealth of England.

Food supply, quartering and care of the sick were transferred from the controller-general of finance to the war minister. Intendants and commissaries were given wide powers under the war minister's direction over supply in the field. The war minister became responsible for national fortification. The general staff was re-organized. March organization – daily stages, victualling stops, itineraries – was laid down in detail. Louvois attacked the vicious system by which the royal army was a patchwork of private businesses – regiments – owned by its officers, whose main concern was profit rather than efficiency. Not even a minister of Louis XIV could abolish the system, for it was rooted in French society, and places in the royal bureaucracy were also objects of private trade. Louvois therefore strove to ensure that officers were professionally competent; to control the prices demanded in the sale of commissions, and to subject the transfer of regiments to royal approval.

Because the French army was officered by the *noblesse*, social rank had enjoyed precedence over military rank in the higher commands. Louvois abolished this; instead a hierarchy of rank was set up, and marshals of France actually began to obey their seniors. The way was opened for commoners like Catinat to become marshals. Louvois tried to remedy the abuses of the muster, especially the '*passe-volant*', the man who appeared on muster-day but on no other, passing from unit to unit according to need. A new kind of regularity, uniformity and discipline began to shape the French army. In 1663 Louvois created a new model regiment, the *Regiment du Roi*, and gave it to a first-class disciplinarian, Colonel Martinet, who later became inspector-general of infantry and gave his name to the English language as the synonym for a very strict officer.

The French artillery, which had been, like the English, under a curious half-civilian, half-military regime, was reformed. The war minister took it over from the Grand Master of the Ordnance and in 1677 the Royal Fusiliers (*Fusiliers du Roi*) were formed, composed of six battalions of gunners, labourers and escort troops. In 1693 they became the *Royal-Artillerie*, twenty-three years before the British Royal Artillery was formed.

In 1688 Louvois set up a militia not unlike the select militia that had failed to establish itself in Britain. Each parish was to raise, arm and equip a militiaman, and clothe and pay him for two years' service. Twenty-five thousand men were to be raised, for thirty regiments. On mobilization they were to be treated and disciplined like the members of the regular army; the very thing the British Mutiny Act excluded. Some of the French militia units, especially those containing old veterans, became efficient, and fought well under Catinat in Italy. After 1706, however, the French militia served merely to feed line regiments with men, and was thus a limited form of conscription.

All through the seventeenth century, the French army had been growing in size. In 1688 there were 115 regiments; between 1706 and 1713, 243. This army had been led to victory after victory by a succession of great commanders: Condé, Turenne, Vendôme, Luxembourg.

Most of the troops were now native Frenchmen, although Swiss mercenaries, Catholic Irish ('the Wild Geese'), Scots and other foreigners continued to furnish crack regiments. During the reign of Charles II an English contingent ('The Royal English Regiment') including the future Duke of Marlborough had learned continental war at first hand in the French service under the great Turenne.

Two inventions slowly but greatly changed military tactics in the era of French greatness between 1660 and 1714: the bayonet and the flintlock musket. The matchlock musket was slow-firing, clumsy to operate and vulnerable to wet weather; between shots the matchlock musketeer was nearly helpless against hostile cavalry unless protected by pikemen. The eventual answer was found by turning the musketeer himself into a 'pikeman' by means of a removable spearhead attached to the muzzle of the musket. The 'bayonet' (named after the putative place of invention, Bayonne) is mentioned by the French general de Puysegur as having been first used in 1647, and it was first officially recognized in the French army in 1671. In the British service it was issued to the Tangier Regiment in 1663, to new dragoon regiments at home in 1672, and as a regular issue to grenadiers and fusiliers after 1678.

The early 'plug' bayonets (plugged into the musket muzzle) had the serious fault that once they were fixed, the musket could not be fired. After 1697 the socket bayonet permitted ease of fixing and unfixing and a firm and rigid lock on the musket. By 1705 the pike was obsolete.

The flintlock employed the friction of flint against a frizzen instead of lighted matches to ignite the powder in the priming pan. Wheel-locks worked on the same principle. The German *Reiter* and other troops had been equipped with wheel-locks by 1600, since matches could not be used on horseback. The wheel-lock was wound up like a modern clockwork toy. When the trigger was pressed, the wheel revolved rapidly against a flint, sending a shower of sparks into the powder. However, the wheel-lock was too complicated and expensive for general issue to infantry.

The first flintlocks were known as 'snaphances', from the Dutch 'snap-haan', a snap-cock, a reference to the shape and action of the mechanism that held the flint between two jaws. The later 'fusils' (from the French for a frizzen, or rough surface from which the flint struck sparks) was little different in system. When the trigger was pulled, the arm holding the flint 'pecked' downwards against a curved frizzen. This action at the same time lifted the hinged cover (integral with the frizzen) of the priming pan, thus exposing the powder, and showering sparks into it.

The introduction of the flintlock, 'fusil' or 'firelock' doubled the rate of fire of infantry. By 1700 a well-trained man could fire a shot a minute. The fusil gave its name to the French and English fusilier regiments, who at first were special troops often detailed to guard artillery trains, where the conjunction of open powder barrels and lighted matches was not propitious. Grenadiers too (also specialists in a new weapon, the throwing bomb or 'granade': from pomegranate) were equipped with fusils.

Bandoliers and powder horns were generally replaced by made-up paper cartridges in pouches in the English service between 1692 and 1697.

Flintlocks and cartridges led to improved fire tactics in the wars of Louis XIV. English infantry fought three deep, the first rank kneeling; the French four deep, the first two kneeling, the third stooping. Only gaps of a few paces between battalions interrupted the firing line. In order that fire should be continuous, volleys were given in succession, not by ranks, but by platoons designated to different 'firings'.

As a result of the greater effectiveness of infantry, the proportion of foot to horse rose from one to two in Turenne's early campaigns to three to one before his death. Nevertheless, cavalry, because of mobility and shock, remained the decisive arm. While the French cavalry relied like the old German *Reiter* largely on the fire-power of their pistols, the English cavalry remained true to Cromwell's tactics – the impact of horsemen, knee to knee, at 'a pretty round trot'. Marlborough '... would not allow the horse but three charges of powder and ball to each man for a campaign, and that only for guarding their horses when at grass, and not to be made use of in action'.[1] Marlborough reintroduced breastplates as protection against the French cavalry's pistol-fire.

*

Since 1660 Louis XIV had employed French military power to expand French territory and influence to the general alarm of other European states. In Italy and Germany he threatened the interests of the Habsburg Holy Roman Emperor. In the Netherlands he threatened Spanish territory, and by consequence the territory beyond of the United Netherlands. His advances had been resisted step by step by William of Orange. Now that William was King of England and Scotland, the British too became drawn into the great struggle to limit French expansion. The British and French were to be at war from 1689 to 1713, except for a delusive peace between 1697 and 1701. The first war was called the War of the League of Augsburg, after the name of William's anti-French coalition. The second was the War of the Spanish Succession, fought to prevent a French prince inheriting the Spanish throne, an event which would hand over the Spanish Empire to the control of Louis XIV, and perhaps eventually lead to the union of the French and Spanish crowns. The British also fought to secure their own Protestant succession, because in 1701, on the death of James II, Louis XIV recognized his Roman Catholic son as James III.

Under William III in the first part of the struggle and under Marlborough in the second, Britain became the mainstay of the coalition against France. She became a great military power. Despite this, Britain did not follow the pattern of contemporary France or Prussia and become a militarized monarchy. She succeeded in producing an army that was militarily powerful, but politically insignificant.

This eventual British escape from military monarchy owed much to an acute British awareness of the dangers, yet perhaps more to geography. Geography exerted its eternal effects: the coming war took place abroad, in Spain, in Flanders, in Germany, in Scotland, in Ireland. The danger of invasion was banished, except for a brief scare in 1708, by the naval victory of La Hogue in 1692, and so the forces in England itself remained small. The armies with their military law and discipline and their potential coercive power were all abroad. As in the days of Elizabeth the army was something apart, far off, living among foreign civilians. It came home only in small units, and in order to disband. It was otherwise with continental nations, where the armies were often based in their home countries, and kept on foot through the winter for the next campaign.

In Britain, too, the royal prerogative control over the army weakened between 1689 and 1714 because of the general growth of ministerial responsibility. The ministers ultimately responsible for the army were the two Secretaries of State. When they became less of royal servants and more of ministers answerable to Parliament, the royal control of the army became increasingly shared with Parliament, without formal diminution of the royal prerogative. Then again, while James and William were both military men who took a personal interest in the army, Mary and Anne clearly were more content to leave military affairs to competent advisers.

Even military administration, the Crown's unchallenged constitutional prerogative, came more and more under the scrutiny and control of Parliament. By a tortuous process the personal clerk of the Commander-in-Chief evolved into a kind of junior war minister responsible to, and a member of, Parliament.*

Charles II in exile before 1660 had appointed a military secretary, the Secretary-at-War, a personal clerical assistant such as Monck also employed. After the Restoration the post was dignified with the title 'Secretary to the Forces', but its incumbent had only the status of clerk. All warrants for military affairs had to be signed by either the Lord High Treasurer or by one of the two Secretaries of State. Because of its usefulness, the office gradually extended in powers and scope. In 1683 an able and assiduous bureaucrat, William Blathwayt – a military Pepys – became Secretary to the Forces. He was to occupy the post for some twenty years. This

---

* The account of the late Stuart military administration is based on Colonel Clifford Walton, *History of the British Standing Army, AD 1660 to 1700*, and Major R. E. Scouller, *The Armies of Queen Anne*.

continuity too promoted the rise of the office. A further circumstance bestowed power, for Blathwayt went as personal assistant to William III on his campaigns in Flanders. He was able to supervise the whole confused military system from the vantage point of the King's side. Such was Blathwayt's talent that he even conducted some of the general business of a Secretary of State. Blathwayt's powers hardly diminished when he and William returned to England in 1695. By 1702, under Anne, Blathwayt, together with the Paymaster-General, was presenting the military estimates to the House of Commons by Commons order. Here was emerging the essential constitutional link between royal administration of the army and parliamentary control. The career of Blathwayt had transformed the Secretary to the Forces into a blend of a modern senior civil servant and a junior minister.[2]

Blathwayt's successor was a somewhat lazy politician, Oliver St John. However, because he *was* a politician he lifted the post right out of bureaucracy into minor 'cabinet' rank, although it remained under the Lord Treasurer for warrants and under the Secretaries of State for other policy decisions and instructions. The Secretary to the Forces was now both the government's executive director of military affairs and also the government's Commons spokesman on army matters. St John's successor after 1708, the able Walpole, continued the transition towards a completely ministerial post anchored in the House of Commons. Although technically the Secretary to the Forces was still the Commander-in-Chief's secretary, Marlborough, the Commander-in-Chief, was not even consulted when Grenville was appointed to the post in 1710. Scouller, the most recent historian of the late Stuart military system, considers that the evolution of the post of secretary to the forces is the most important administrative development during the period. Yet the post remained apparently humble and constitutionally obscure. It did not therefore arouse the apprehension that would have been caused by the creation of a great office of state in charge of the army.

The Secretary to the Forces, or Secretary-at-War, was in any case only one of several competitive functionaries within the British military 'system'. Constitutional security against militarization was partly found through division of administrative power. For when the British military machine greatly developed to meet the challenge of war, it did so in ways very different from the clear-cut single channel of administrative command in France, running from absolute monarch down through minister of war.

*

In Britain there was no single great department of state dealing with military affairs, because since the disbandment of the Commonwealth army there had been in theory no army. Instead military affairs were shared out – not at all clearly – between several officers of state, including the Secretary to the Forces.

The sovereign was by his prerogative Commander-in-Chief of the armed forces; they were peculiarly his 'private' royal instrument, and even today there is a 'royal' as opposed to a 'national public service' flavour about the armed forces. However, only the army is a prerogative force, the navy is not. Naval commissions have only been signed by the sovereign instead of by the Admiralty since the time of Edward VII.

Charles II had deputed his executive military responsibilities to Monck as 'Captain-General and Commander-in-Chief of all Forces', and later to Monmouth, though as Captain-General only, since the forces were by then too scanty to merit a Commander-in-Chief. James II and William III exercised their royal command of the army in person. William was more than any man responsible for the successful creation of a British continental field army. Queen Anne left military affairs largely to Marlborough and to her various advisers at home until the period of Marlborough's decline from influence. However, Marlborough, as Captain-General 'for the commissioning, regulating, and keeping in Discipline our Troops and Land Forces', enjoyed notably narrower powers than had Monck, who had enjoyed the scope of Louvois or of a modern Secretary of State for War and Army Council combined. And since Marlborough was abroad during the campaigning season, he could only exercise indirect influence on the central administration of the army.

The Secretary to the Forces, as the instrument of the royal prerogative, gradually came to execute the duties of a war department. His administrative functions and position were never defined. On high questions of policy he was responsible to three separate ministers of the state: the two Secretaries of State for strategic and operational instructions, and the Lord High Treasurer for warrants and financial matters. Since the division of responsibility between Secretaries of State was geographical ('Northern' and 'Southern' Departments), one Secretary might order the concentration of a force at the port of embarkation, and the other its subsequent operations.

The Master-General of the Ordnance ran a bureaucratic empire separate from both the navy and the army, both of which it supplied with guns, all kinds of munitions and war supplies. The Master-General provided the trains of artillery, which were partly crewed by civilians and were wholly under a different system and scale of pay and promotion from the rest of the army.

Nevertheless the Master-General was not a responsible minister of state; the Lord Treasurer (in particular) and the two Secretaries ranked above him. It was the coincidence that Marlborough was himself Master-General and also a close friend of the Lord Treasurer, Godolphin, that did much in practice to unify theoretically unconnected functions.

Some attempt was made to co-ordinate all the various agencies. There were the Lords of the Committee for the Affairs of the Army; a committee of the Privy Council whose sphere of action was hard to define. Other Privy Council committees considered special questions such as particular expeditions.

There was one committee that might have grown into an effective 'army council', probably at the cost of arousing parliamentary suspicion – the Board of General Officers. It was created in 1706, primarily to deal with recruiting abuses. But instead of evolving into a body occupied with larger questions of co-ordination, policy and planning, it moved the other way, and after 1708 became entangled in such questions as the precedence of regiments and the detail, cost and quality of uniforms. This last was a very necessary function, since in fact regimental colonels provided uniforms.

In so far as co-ordination of policy and administration of the land war was achieved, it was less owing to the formal machinery than to personal relationships: the powerful and direct impetus of a well-informed sovereign in the case of William III, and later the close trust between Marlborough, Godolphin and Queen Anne. Even by the end of this great war of some twenty years, no war minister or war department had been created in Britain: sovereign, Commander-in-Chief, Master-General of the Ordnance, Lord Treasurer, Secretaries of State and Secretary to the Forces continued to share responsibility. It was a sharp contrast to the navy under its effective and omnipotent Navy Board. A combination of political suspicion of royal armies and administrative confusion thus ensured that not even a major war could erect the army into a great British national institution.

As there was normally supposed to be no peacetime army and no war department, there was no kind of general staff either; and none emerged during the war. Staffs belonged to armies in the field. Marlborough's staff consisted of a Quartermaster-General (duties akin to a modern Chief of Staff), Provost-Marshal, Chaplain-General, Surgeon-General, Waggon-Master-General, and aides-de-camp who acted as liaison officers. Some other armies had an Ordnance Officer. There were also staff officers responsible not to the Commander-in-Chief but to home government departments, like the Deputy-Judge-Advocates (military justice, and sometimes also musters, as commissaries of musters), who were directly under the Judge-Advocate-General for the exercise of Crown powers under the Mutiny Acts; the Commissaries-General, civilians responsible for supply; the Paymaster who, on behalf of the Treasurer, distributed pay in gross to the regiments; and the Commissary-General of Musters, or Muster-Master-General, who checked abuses of the muster system, also on behalf of the Treasury.

The Commander-in-Chief in the field enjoyed direct access to all those gentry at home who were supposed to supply him with his needs, from orders to money: Lord Treasurer, Board of Ordnance, Secretaries of State, Privy Council, Secretary-at-War and the sovereign. In the end, therefore, all really depended on the qualities of a Commander-in-Chief; upon his capacity to improvise a combined headquarters organization in the field under his personal direction, although not entirely under his personal authority. If a

Marlborough commanded, the 'system' worked. Some later eighteenth-century campaigns were to reveal what happened if there was no Marlborough.

Just as the captains and companies had been the basis of all administration in Elizabeth's army, so were the colonels and regiments in the late Stuart army. In the infantry the regiment (usually of one battalion, so that 'regiment' and 'battalion' were interchangeable terms in a tactical sense) was the largest permanent unit. Except for guards and specially equipped troops like fusiliers, regiments were named after their colonel ('Macartney's', 'Mordaunt's', 'Wade's' etc.), and changed their names when their colonel changed. Order of seniority, based usually on the date of first raising, contained the germ of the eighteenth-century numerical designation of foot regiments. Excepting the Scots units, there were no corps named after counties or regions, although the French army's regiments, for example, were often named after provinces. During the war battalions were coupled in brigades that lasted for the duration, like divisions in the twentieth-century world wars, and achieved a similar sense of identity. By 1700 there were eleven companies, plus one of grenadiers, to a battalion; each company being of one captain, two subalterns, three sergeants, three corporals, two drummers and from a hundred men (war footing) to sixty men (peacetime). In the cavalry the number of squadrons to a regiment varied, and therefore cavalry were counted in squadrons of three troops each rather than in regiments.

Promotion was supposed to go according to merit tempered by seniority. A list of deserving officers was kept at Whitehall. The sovereign was the spring of all promotion, and colonels sent their recommendations to him or the Commander-in-Chief in the field via the Secretary to the Forces (Secretary-at-War). An officer's body was not yet cold before his brother officers were soliciting his post; prospects of promotion lent a peculiar interest to viewing the field after a battle. No string was left unpulled. In 1690 Lieutenant-Colonel Coote wrote asking for the vacant colonelcy of an Inniskilling regiment, on the grounds that he was senior lieutenant-colonel in the army, and because 'the lieutenant-colonel, one Creighton, is an old blockhead', unfit to command.[3]

Purchase of commissions was not peculiar to the army. The buying and selling of public offices was a general feature of the age, abroad as well as in England, and of long history. It was looked on as the modern age would regard the sale of doctors' practices. Even under the Commonwealth, the purchase of commissions and regiments had been usual. However, under the Commonwealth purchase had taken the form of a direct bargain between state and purchaser, rather than that of a purely private transaction. The state had retained the disposition of its regiments and the profit from the sales. After the Restoration, purchase gradually grew into a private racket, injurious to the efficiency of the army. In 1684 the government first tried to regulate transfers and exact a five-per-cent rake-off; then later announced that 'His Majesty was this day pleased to declare that he will not for the future consent to the selling any Military employment'.[4] Purchase outlived this edict by nearly two centuries. The abuse became rather more marked, taking often the form of a bribe for successful recommendation for a promotion. William III forced new officers to take an oath that they had not bought or bribed their commissions, but in 1695 Colonel Hastings of the 13th Foot caused a national scandal by his trafficking. One accusation in the House of Commons at this time put the enduring case against purchase: Hastings 'had taken money for the recommending to commands in his regiments, to the great discouragement of the Officers who were to serve in his Majesty's armies, who ought to be such as deserved their commands, and not such as paid for them'.[5] Although Hastings was cashiered, this did little good. By the Mutiny Act therefore new officers were required to swear:

I, AB, do hereby declare that I have neither directly nor indirectly, by myself or any one for me with my knowledge, given or promised hereafter to give any sum of money, present, gift or reward, to any person whatsoever for obtaining my Commission ...[6]

The prices of commissions varied widely; a colonelcy in the First Foot-guards in 1681 cost £5,100, while £400 would buy an ensigncy in the same regiment in 1698.

The military consequences of a system whereby an officer owned his rank, was a 'share-holder' in his regiment, or, if a colonel, actually owned the regiment, was a decline in professional zeal and discipline. Promotion was divorced from merit; general obedience to the needs of the service was hard to exact from a conglomeration of independent private interests.

However, the purchase system offered the state and the nation such solid financial advantages that it became a rooted institution. If officers could gain their main income privately out of rackets, there was no need to pay them economic salaries; and there was thus a marked saving on the cost of the army, to the great joy of a grudging tax-payer. In the late Stuart period, therefore, another long-lived tradition of the British army became established: that of lack of professionalism among its officers redeemed by the competence of the non-commissioned officers and the fortitude and discipline of the men. Nevertheless the officer did not do quite so badly out of the public purse – half-pay provided him with a pension for life after what might be a very short period of service, especially in the case of regiments raised for a war and disbanded at the end of it. In *this* respect the temporary officer of the early eighteenth century was much better off than his successors of 1914–18 and 1939–45.

All the power that had been so abused by the Elizabethan captain, all his rackets, had thus descended to the Stuart colonel. The colonel raised the regiment, paid it, clothed it, replaced its lost equipment, and made whatever welfare arrangements seemed appropriate for the regiment's wounded and widows. A new racket now developed by which the soldier himself could be robbed of his pay under colour of various legitimate stoppages.

The pay of a soldier (2s. 6d. a day for a trooper, 1s. 6d. for a dragoon, 8d. for the foot: the same as in 1659 despite inflation) was divided into three parts. There was 'subsistence money', at the daily rate of 2s., 1s. 2d. and 6d., out of which the soldier had to feed and accommodate himself and his horse, for the government only occasionally and in the field provided rations. The difference between total pay and subsistence money was called 'the gross off-reckonings'. Until 1684 no deductions were made from these except a shilling in the pound to help support Chelsea Hospital. Gradually, however, all kinds of deductions crept in – for rations in the field, hospitals, medicines, tithes, fees payable by regiments to various bureaucrats like the auditors and the Paymaster-General, even arms and powder until 1697. What was left after these deductions were the 'net off-reckonings' – the soldier's net pay. However, legal stoppages were augmented by various ingenious illegal ones invented by colonels, who withheld even the soldier's subsistence money; sometimes up to half of it. The government on its part delayed paying regiments for years, and finally settled with 'tallies' worth only a fifth of the pay due, or 'debentures' worth even less. As one historian has written:

The whole system of military finance in the seventeenth century was one vast entanglement of fraud. Not only did officers defraud the soldiers, but they defrauded the government also, while the government in turn defrauded both officers and soldiers.[7]

These deductions and frauds, combined with the purchase system, had a profound effect on the standing of the military man in British society. The officer tended to become a corrupt tradesman or a rich playboy instead of a salaried state-servant; the soldier ceased to be a respected person earning a respectable wage. Only five years after the army of the Commonwealth had been disbanded, an observer wrote of the guard at Sandown Castle:

A company of Foot was sent from Dover to help guard the place, pitiful weak fellows, half starved and eaten up with vermin, whom the Governor of Dover cheated of half their pay, and the other half they spent in drink.[8]

Such descriptions became increasingly general. A vicious spiral had begun. Soon soldiering reached the low place in British society it was to occupy until the Great War in 1914, an occupation despised by the middle and working classes as a disgrace hardly less than prison. Not until after 1914 was the British army again generally to receive the rank-and-file of the social standing of Cromwell's troopers.

At the same time, a soldier's life was becoming less attractive to the very kind of roughneck or rogue to which recruitment was reduced. Roystering had traditionally compensated for discomfort, danger and poor pay. The soldier's conception of heaven had been free quarter in some private house, where he could drink his host's beer, smoke his tobacco, make free with his wife, and threaten to knock his teeth down his throat with a sword-hilt if he objected. Free quarter was now illegal, and aroused strong protests. Under William of Orange new continental ideas of discipline reduced roystering. The combination of social misfits with stricter discipline led inevitably to harsher and more frequent punishments: the lash, the wooden horse (two boards at a sharp angle, astride which the victim sat for a given time, perhaps with muskets attached to the ankles to increase the discomfort). Another tradition grew – that of the brutalization of army life.

The decline in the standards of the army after the Restoration had been swift. At the beginning of Charles II's reign recruits had to furnish 'testimonies of courage and fidelity'; at the end men were being hanged to discourage desertion. Old men, men with squints, men deformed – all were accepted. The British troops in the Dutch service who came home in 1685 at the time of Monmouth's rebellion caused astonishment because they were young and fit. Clarendon wrote home from Ireland that Tyrconnel, commanding the army in Ireland, had told him:

God damn me! This Scotch battalion which is newly come into England, has undone us; the King is so pleased with it that he will have all his forces in the same posture. We have here a great many old men, and of different statures; they must all be turned out, for the King would have all his men young and of one size.[9]

Once the wars with France began, recruitment became the fundamental problem of the military system. Recruitment was supposed to be based on voluntary enlistment. Regiments sent round recruiting parties to recruit by 'Beat of Drum', on 'beating orders' from the sovereign or Commander-in-Chief. If the king's (or queen's) shilling could be somehow got into the hands or pockets of some yokel, drunk or sober, an enlistment had been made. Straightforward impressment was normally illegal, although men were impressed for special purposes by royal warrant (such as fifteen drummers for Virginia). However, men were virtually kidnapped; in London the recruits' depot in the Savoy was no better than a prison.

From 1694 impressment became legal in Scotland. In 1701 the English Parliament passed an act authorizing Justices of the Peace to levy able-bodied men without lawful calling, employment or visible means of support. This was the ancient system of conscripting men least able to argue about it. The same act released capital offenders for the forces, and offered insolvent debtors release from prison on enlistment or on finding a substitute.

This measure failed to produce the men. In 1704 the House of Commons approached open conscription when it resolved:

That a Power be given for one year to levy men in the respective counties of the Kingdom for increase of the marine companies, and for recruiting the land forces.[10]

However, the bill brought in was gradually whittled down until only the unemployed remained subject to call-up, while harvest workers and others were exempted, an early example of reserved occupations.

In 1707 the Recruiting Bill proposed a compulsory levy on parishes and counties of 16,000 men. This was rejected by the Commons. The Act, as passed, merely tightened up means of pressing the out-of-work and the penalties for slackness or obstruction. In the absence of general conscription, the burden of service continued to fall on a fraction of the population. In March 1708 only 868 men had been recruited (of whom thirty-seven were volunteers) out of 18,657 men needed for all theatres. The Recruiting Act was therefore re-shaped – but without conscription. For the first time short-term enlistment – for three years – appeared. Rewards for constables who successfully recruited were raised, and so were penalties for default.

There followed for a time gradual improvement, and by March 1710 the shortage of men had fallen below 5,000. However, by the end of the next year 5,000 were needed for Flanders alone, and in Spain regiments were being broken up. By this time too the first of the three-year men (and their local authorities) were demanding their release.

The 'voluntary' system may be said to have worked in that operations never in fact became impossible for lack of men. Nevertheless the problem of recruitment was never solved, and throughout the war the British relied heavily on foreign mercenaries. Of the original parliamentary vote of 40,000 men for Flanders in 1701, only less than half, 18,000, were to be 'subject' (i.e. British) troops, and the rest mercenaries, mostly from the states of Germany. Of the 'Augmentation' (further help pledged to the Dutch) only 3,000 out of 20,000 men were 'subject' troops. There were in fact four kinds of troops on the British pay-roll: 'subject' troops; foreign troops under their own commanders but on establishments and rates of pay laid down by the English (after 1707 the British) Parliament; foreign troops paid for by a lump subsidy to their ruler; and, lastly, refugees and deserters under British or native officers, and on establishment and pay laid down by the British.

It was a curious fact that the British Parliament in its reluctance to create a large British army, for fear of military power in the hands of the monarch, helped German princes in their struggle against their own parliaments by making it possible and profitable for the princes to maintain large forces on hire to the British.

Although Louvois had introduced permanent barracks in France, there were no such things yet in England. The word derived from the French *barraque*, a shelter in the field, from the Spanish *barraca*, a fisherman's hut. To the English Military Dictionary in 1702 a barrack was:

... A hut, like a little cottage, for Soldiers to lie in the Camp. These are made, either when the soldiers have not tents, or when any army lies long in a Place in bad weather ...[11]

There were barracks – really *gendarmerie* barracks – in Ireland after 1697, but none in England to the end of Anne's reign. The only permanent military accommodation was in the form of billets within forts or garrisons like the Horse-Guards in Whitehall.

I was had into the Guard-room, which I thought to be hell [wrote one observer of the Horse-Guards in 1662], some therein were sleeping, others swearing, others smoking tobacco. In the chimney of the room I believe there was two bushel of broken tobacco-pipes, almost half one load of ashes.[12]

Quartering on houses, though illegal, had been inevitable. Under James II private houses as well as public were used; hence the Declaration of Rights re-stated that no soldier could be billetted on a private householder without his consent. Billetting and the subsistence to be provided were regulated by the Mutiny Act of 1703 and subsequent acts. Constables or Justices of the Peace were to arrange billetting, on

inns, livery stables, ale-houses, victualling houses, and all houses selling brandy, strong-waters, cyder or metheglin to be drunk on the premises, and in no other, and in no private houses whatsoever.[13]

This did not make discipline easier, nor raise the moral tone of soldiering.

Throughout the late Stuart period the colonel was responsible for clothing his regiment out of the off-reckonings. The government merely stipulated the scale of clothing and the frequency of issue. The style of dress was largely a matter of the colonel's choice, although the red coat was now fairly general in the British service. In the French army, too, 'uniform' was slow to come, despite Louvois' efforts. There were red coats on some French regiments and blue on some British. At the battle of the Boyne in 1690 both sides still wore field signs. After 1708, however, the Clothing Committee, a sub-committee of the Board of General Officers, began to regulate dress for the whole army.

Clothing was another source of profit to unscrupulous colonels. Although off-reckonings barely covered the cost of clothing, some colonels made £200 to £600 a year out of it. Depending on the colonel, a regiment might be well-dressed, or like Major Archibald Patton's company in 1704 on the eve of departure to the West Indies:

Noe Christian could doe otherwise than Pitty the Poore men to see them Mount the Guard before the Face of an enemy bare footed and bare leg'd.[14]

At this period regiments were running hopelessly into debt to greedy contractors. Under Anne, however, successful attempts were made to remedy the worst of the clothing abuses. A Royal Proclamation of 1708 embodied reforms proposed by the Board of Senior Officers. A Clothing Board was set up to examine contractors' patterns and compare them with sealed patterns in the Board's office, and to examine delivered consignments. Contracts were to be vetted in the light of regimental finances, in conjunction with the Comptrollers of Army Accounts. Nevertheless the Clothing Board's powers did not extend to dealing directly in the supply of the army's clothing. Marlborough himself arranged for shoes to be provided at Frankfurt for the army on the great march to Blenheim. Such local supply was, strictly speaking, illegal, but characteristic of the way in which success depended not on the system, but on the personality of the commander-in-chief in the field.

The transport of units or drafts to the seats of war abroad under William and Anne showed little, if any, advance over the days of Elizabeth. Scouller describes the troopships as 'floating slaughterhouses'. A private soldier at the time referred to 'continual destruction in the foretop, the pox above board, the plague within decks, hell in the forecastle, and the devil at the helm'.[15]

Responsibility for sea transport and for feeding men at the ports and on board was unclearly divided between several bodies and several high officers of state. The chain of responsibility is obscure. The body immediately responsible for ships was the Commissioners of Transport, who hired vessels on contract. It was not an attractive commercial proposition for ship-owners, because in 1708, for example, they were two years in arrears.

The wastage of men and horses in sea transit was appalling. This must always be remembered in considering the potentiality of seapower in this era. In 1706 a force sailing from Lisbon to Valencia lost half its strength of 8,000 men. Of 5,000 men shipped from the West Indies to Newfoundland in 1702–3 only just over 1,000 survived the voyage. Large-scale British movement by sea was in fact as advantageous to the French as a victory.

The soldier was expected to provide his own food and his horse's fodder out of his pay, even on active service. Private sutlers followed the armies. Each regiment had a grand sutler; each troop a petty sutler. The supply of English armies was made more of a problem by the internationally renowned gluttony of the English, especially for flesh, and by their equally renowned inability to fend for themselves in the field. The government was forced to take over distribution of large items of supply in the field. In Ireland both bread and hay were supplied under contract.

Since the abolition of the old Elizabethan Treasurer at War, there had been no single authority over all the functions of the commissariat. In the field the task of supply fell on the Commissary-General, who lacked the necessary authority and powers, and the staff. He was responsible both to the Commissioners of Victualling at home and to the Commander-in-Chief; an unenviable position. Nobody seemed sure to which officer of state the Commissioners of Victualling themselves were responsible.

In Ireland the army starved while a few miles away food rotted in the supply ships in Belfast Lough. The financial confusion was total, there being no system of accounts or payment. Corruption and graft prospered.

In food supply as in so many things, most really depended on the personal capacity of the Commander-in-Chief in the field. It also depended on the local agriculture. In the barren dust of Spain, the Commander-in-Chief, Peterborough, worked vainly to provide food and fodder, while his troops starved and sickened, and his army could hardly move for want of beasts for transport, artillery and cavalry. Marlborough, on the other hand, campaigned in rich agricultural lands, with plenty of green forage or hay and plenty of animals to ride, to harness or to eat.

Administration was perhaps the most important single ingredient of Marlborough's genius. It was the supply system that he created and watched over, rather than the sketchy and chaotic government machinery, that supported the war. He signed long-term contracts on behalf of the whole army with local contractors of high standing, knowledge and resources. He himself followed through all the detail of performance; made all the special arrangements for particular marches. Marlborough's supreme feat was the 250-mile march from Flanders to the Danube in 1704. His troops were amazed by their general's care:

As we marched, commissaries were appointed to furnish us with all manner of necessaries for men and horse. These were brought to the ground before we arrived, and the soldiers had nothing to do, but to pitch tents, boil their kettles, and lie down to rest. Surely never was such a march carried on with more order and regularity, and with less fatigue both to men and horse.[16]

One article was absolutely essential if even Marlborough was to keep, and move, an army in the field – money. An officer on Marlborough's staff noted:

And to make things yet more easy both to the Armies and the Countries it marched through, his Grace was not unmindfull to provide money and order Regular payments for everything that was brought into the camp; a thing hitherto unknown in Germany ... and to prevent any failure herein he order'd the Treasurer of the Army to be always in cash to answer Bills, and daily to have a Month's Subsistance before hand, and that supplies should be laid from Frankfort to Nurenberg, and that he should lose no time in sending credit to these places.[17]

Regiments might be owed arrears of pay going back fifteen years; Peterborough in Spain might write home despairingly for money; but Marlborough's friend Godolphin, the Lord Treasurer, ensured that money in adequate quantity flowed constantly to Marlborough in Flanders.

On the outbreak of war the medical service also hardly existed. Medical care was normally organized and paid for by each regiment: it took the form of a low-grade chirurgeon appointed by the colonel. This remained the basis of any medicine throughout the war. There were seventeen doctors at Blenheim, one to every 600 men, lacking the support of any kind of nursing or hospital services. On the whole, it was better not to fall sick or be wounded.

In considering the late Stuart military organization and the familiar results of hasty English expansion of a neglected army, it would be easy to condemn too harshly. Corruption, for example, was a universal but accepted evil of the age, permeating all aspects of government. The Speaker of the House of Commons himself was involved in one pay scandal. The seventeenth century faced no other administrative problem of similar scale to the raising and supply of armies. The English lacked the immediate advantages of autocracy as a spur to efficiency. In the French absolute monarchy, however, confusion, corruption and failure were not absent, despite ruthless drives for efficiency. The novelty and scale of the British effort in seventeenth-century terms may be compared with total national mobilization in the two twentieth-century world wars – mobilizations not free from error, confusion or, indeed, corruption.

In the event, the British did better than the vaunted French monarchy. They produced and maintained military forces of comparable efficiency, and of an equivalent size relative to population. More than this, they evolved financial and commercial expedients for nourishing the war without increasing social tensions or misery, and without impairing national prosperity. These achievements, springing freely out of the life and talent of the nation, were quite beyond the French monarchy, where one man at the top was the prime mover of the state machine – a man who thought too much of purely military power and glory.

*

During both William III's and Anne's wars against Louis XIV there was lively controversy in England over the correct grand strategy to follow. The old arguments of Elizabeth's reign were revived between a 'continental' school and a 'maritime' school. The continental school believed that a great land power like France could only be exhausted through defeat of her armies by the European coalition. A British land force on the Continent was therefore seen as essential, both to enhance the military strength of the coalition and to cement it politically together. Sea warfare against French trade and colonies could only be, in the opinion of the continental school, secondary to the main effort.

The maritime school believed that a British land force as a mere component of a coalition army on the Continent was less effective than similar strength transported by sea to the exposed coastlines of the enemy or his allies, or to his colonies. The maritime school also believed that a land war in a place like Flanders was in any event slow and indecisive, exhausting and costly.

Thus the crude strategic dispute of Elizabeth's reign took a more sophisticated form. The argument was to continue throughout the eighteenth century, pulling British strategy first one way and then another. In the reign of Anne it was of importance in political history, because emerging political parties took shape round (among other things) the two strategic beliefs. The Tories were 'maritime', the Whigs 'continental'. However, 'maritime' strategy against Louis XIV was a wasteful failure compared with its success against Napoleon in the Peninsular War.

For whereas after 1808 the British were aiding and stimulating Spanish and Portuguese resistance to France, after 1706 the Spanish people were largely on the French side. Whereas after 1808 there was no European coalition and no main theatre of war, and Britain originally went to Spain for want of anything better, after 1706 troops for Spain meant milking Marlborough's army in the main theatre of war. And lastly, after 1808 there were not the appalling shipboard losses of men and horses between England and the Peninsula that there were after 1706: consequence of a hundred years of gradual progress in shipbuilding, seamanship and organization.

In fact, therefore, Spain became to the British after 1706 what it became to the French after 1808 – a bottomless maw into which men and treasure were poured without commensurate result. In 1708, of 29,395 men voted for the Peninsula only 8,660 reached the battlefield of Almanza. At one time there were more troops allotted to the Peninsula than to Marlborough. Battalions could lose 300 out of 800 men on shipboard.

In 1707 the extraordinary rag-bag of an army so expensively maintained by the British in Spain had met the French and Spaniards at Almanza. The British force included Dutch, Germans, Huguenots and Portuguese. The commands of the two armies illustrate the tangled political and religious loyalties of the time, and indicate that modern national notions of 'loyalty' did not yet exist. The British army was commanded by a French Huguenot, de Ruvigny, ennobled as the Earl of Galway. The French army was commanded by a Roman Catholic Englishman, the Duke of Berwick, James II's bastard son. Since the Portuguese, half Galway's army, took flight, Galway was involved in a disastrous defeat which essentially shattered British hopes in the Peninsula, although the war still dragged on.

Smaller attempts to exploit sea-power in the Mediterranean, such as the project to take Toulon in conjunction with the Austrians (Imperialists) failed. The conquest of Gibraltar in 1704 proved an empty glory, for the British fleet continued to base itself on Lisbon, or, later, Minorca, which proved the one valuable European prize gained by maritime operations during the war.

'Pure' maritime war – that is, against seaborne trade – in fact on balance went against Britain, which was more vulnerable than France because her overseas trade was greater. In another contribution to 'blue water' strategy the perennial expedition to the West Indies was sent, and as usual failed to collect anything but yellow fever.

The contribution of sea-power was negative. The destruction of French sea-power at La Hogue in 1692 ensured that the British Isles would be safe from invasion; and that British and Dutch seaborne trade could continue to nourish the war, despite the harassing attacks of French commerce-raiders.

*

William III's contribution to eventual victory has been cast into the shade by Marlborough's brilliant successes. As Stadtholder of the Netherlands, William had been fighting Louis XIV since 1672. As King of England in 1689 he found that, except at sea, his new country could not at first contribute much to the war. Although a small contingent of English troops was sent to Flanders (where they dismayed the Dutch by their unreadiness for war), the Irish Catholic rebellion, now led by James II and supported by French power, absorbed all British efforts. The Protestant cause in Ireland shrank to a toe-hold: the besieged towns of Derry and Enniskillen. After their eventual and belated relief, however, the Protestant regions of Ulster were recaptured. In the struggle for Ireland that followed, it was William and his Dutch generals who suffered from the standard English performance in the first year of a war: breakdown of supply, the inability of ill-trained officers and troops to fend for themselves or carry out the simplest tasks of a soldier in the field. Ireland in fact proved a successful French exercise in maritime war, for a French force of some 7,000 men kept William himself and over 30,000 English, Dutch and mercenary troops busy for over two years. William's victory of the Boyne in 1690 was the turning point of the campaign. Once more James deserted his followers and fled to France. The war became a prolonged Irish–

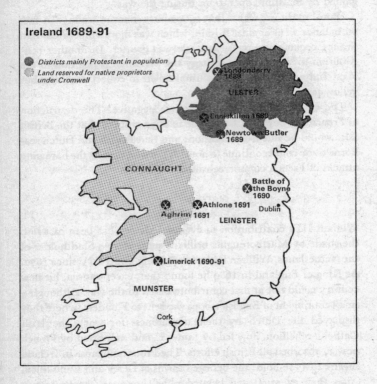

French fighting retreat. Although Dublin was captured, Athlone held out, and the Irish commander Patrick Sarsfield saved besieged Limerick by a daring ambush of the approaching siege train. In 1691, however, Athlone fell and then at Aghrim the Franco-Irish forces were broken decisively in a hard-fought battle that had at one point nearly ended in their victory. After a second siege

Limerick fell, and the war was over. At last William could concentrate on the main war in Flanders.

In the sixteenth century the Spanish Netherlands (roughly
modern Belgium) had served as the base for Spanish offensives
against both the Netherlands and France. Now they provided
merely an arena in which France could fight her enemies.

The maintenance and movement of armies required bulk transport, and bulk transport in the seventeenth century required waterways, for roads were bad and prone to collapse in wet weather.
Although Flanders was well-provided with large and small rivers,
every important crossing or confluence point was dominated by a
town fortified according to the intricate designs of Vauban or his
Dutch rival Coehorn.

Campaigns therefore took the form of the step-by-step siege and
capture of fortresses and the gradual conquest of strategic river
lines. Armies were expensive and difficult to recruit. Battles
were thus events neither lightly entered into, nor frequently repeated.

The campaigns of 1691 to 1693 marked a gradual French capture
of the line of the Meuse. Even in 1693, when the British contingent
had risen to just over 17,000, William III was outnumbered by
119,000 men to 71,000. In cavalry, the decisive arm, he was outnumbered by nearly two to one; and his British troops were particularly short of horse. He attempted to overcome these handicaps
by forcing the French to fight while at a disadvantage, but his skill
in tactics was not equal to his talent as a strategist and organizer.
At Steenkirk (1692) an attempted surprise march on the French
camp failed because of a mistake by a Dutch subordinate, who left
the English advanced guard to fight a desperate and unsuccessful
battle before the main body could support them. At Neerwinden
(or Landen, after two villages on the battlefield) in 1693 William
offered battle on ground unsuitable to the French cavalry. However, there was a marshy stream at his back, and he was heavily
outnumbered. His opponent (as at Steenkirk) was the last of a
great generation of French generals, Marshal de Luxembourg.
Luxembourg's persistent attacks broke William's line, and his army
collapsed in rout.

Nevertheless even apparently unsuccessful warfare, grimly pursued for years, can exhaust an opponent. Because of the glamour of great victories, it is easy to over-estimate their effects in comparison with mere endurance and attrition. The French monarchy was beginning to run out of resources. During the winter of 1693–4 the French failed for the first time to stock forward depots for the next campaign; for the first time they took the field in the spring after the allies. The British contingent with William III had now increased by nearly two-thirds. While the allied army was 89,000 men strong, the French were weaker than in earlier campaigns. Although Luxembourg had hoped to capture Liége, the French campaign was instead purely defensive, redeemed only by a famous march from Huy to the Scheldt by which Luxembourg outwitted William. While William and the main army was thus wearing the heart out of a French army of 84,000 men, the British attempted one of their favourite maritime diversions down the ages – an attack on a French Channel port. Ten British regiments landed near Brest and were repulsed with heavy losses that included the force commander.

During the winter Luxembourg died. France was now desperately short of money and was forced to resort to the poll tax, a highly unpopular tax that fell on the poor majority of the population. Under a new and inferior commander, Villeroi, the French stood on the defensive. In the campaign of 1695 William used the initiative he had so doggedly won to besiege and re-capture the great fortress of Namur. The final two campaigns of the war in 1696–7 were indecisive and uneventful.

William III had fought the French monarchy at the peak of its power and military excellence, when the allies – particularly the British – had yet to develop their potential strength. He had succeeded in permanently dulling the French cutting edge; and Marlborough was to draw the benefit.

Marlborough inherited the same kind of problems and disadvantages that had worn out William III; he overcame them with such skill and success that he stands to this day the most able of all British soldiers.

France, compact, close-knit, enjoyed interior lines; it was relatively easy to switch troops from Flanders to the Moselle or the upper Rhine, or even to Italy and Spain. The allies were spread loosely round the French periphery, from the Netherlands to Germany, Austria, and northern Italy, and round to Portugal and Spain. France herself constituted the main strength of her side, for her allies, like Bavaria or Spain, were either small powers or moribund. France's enemies on the other hand were each too weak either to stand alone or to dominate the alliance. Marlborough

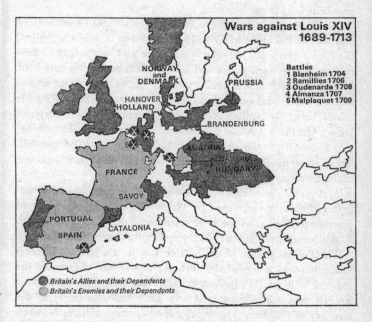

Wars against Louis XIV 1689-1713

Battles
1 Blenheim 1704
2 Ramillies 1706
3 Oudenarde 1708
4 Almanza 1707
5 Malplaquet 1709

● Britain's Allies and their Dependents
● Britain's Enemies and their Dependents

therefore faced all the classic agonies of the management of alliances, both in terms of high policy and of military execution.

By comparison with the French marshals, Marlborough's military experience had been limited: service for two years in Tangier, service under Turenne in 1674, the defeat of Monmouth, and then, after the Revolution, service in Flanders. He had spent much time at court; and urbanity and tact, discretion and diplomacy were as valuable qualities in an allied supreme commander as leadership in a battle. Despite Marlborough's slight experience, William III thought highly enough of him to appoint him both Commander-in-Chief of the British contingent and ambassador to the United Provinces on the eve of the renewal of the war. It was Marlborough who conducted the political negotiations that led to the main treaties of alliance. At the age of fifty-two (six years older than Wellington and Napoleon at their last battle) he embarked on his first great command, carrying a heavier load of responsibility than any British soldier has carried before or since.

Marlborough's talents had no flaw. As a strategist he saw clearly and simply the great issues – the relationship of war and policy, the interdependence between one theatre and another, the inter-relation between sea-power and land war. He constantly outwitted his enemies, one success paving the way for the next. As an organizer, he made a nonsensical military system work. His care for his troops, his understanding of them, led to his nickname of 'Corporal John'. On the battlefield his grasp of confused tactical situations was uncannily clear and accurate; he kept cool and thought fast. To all these qualities he added unflexing will and resolution, and unflagging energy.

And yet his personality remains elusive. There is none of the pungent individuality conveyed by Wellington's correspondence and conversation; none of the brisk anecdotes told about Wellington. Marlborough presented a smooth, perfect, flawless surface of ability.

The French seizure of the barrier forts in the Spanish Netherlands that had preceded the outbreak of war had obliterated the gains of William III's patient struggle. Except for Maastricht, the French now controlled the Meuse. They had also occupied the territory of Cologne, threatening allied communications between the Netherlands and Austria. They once more held the initiative. Marlborough resolved to seize the initiative back, although his polyglot army was smaller than the French. During the campaigns of 1702 and 1703 Marlborough several times manoeuvred the French into positions where he could have forced them to give battle at a disadvantage. Each time Marlborough was prevented from attacking by the Dutch 'Field Deputies' (civilian deputies from the Netherlands government with full powers over the Dutch contingent), whose cautious prohibitions had to be obeyed. Nevertheless Marlborough cleared the line of the Meuse and its fortified towns from Liége downwards, and thus pushed the French away from the exposed south-eastern borders of the United Netherlands.

Meanwhile, however, his allies, the Imperialists (of the Habsburg or Holy Roman Empire) were being worsted in Italy and southern Germany, where Bavaria had now joined the French side, and where, at the end of 1703, the road to Vienna lay open to the French. There was a very real danger that the Holy Roman Empire might be beaten into a separate peace, thus disastrously weakening the alliance.

For the campaign of 1704 Marlborough therefore planned a stroke that would at the same time rescue the Empire, inflict a decisive defeat on the French, and force them on to the defensive everywhere. The plan was simple. He would lead his main army away from Flanders on a 250-mile march across Germany to the Danube, and there unite with the Imperialist forces. The apparent risks would have daunted lesser generals: exposure of the Netherlands to the French army in Flanders; his own destruction far from his base in the course of the long flank march round the French frontiers. The problems of organizing such a march were immense.

Marlborough quietened Dutch politicians by pretending that he was going no farther than the Moselle.

In May 1704 the army set out: the foot tramping to the tap of drum, firelock shouldered; waggons grinding along behind each regiment; horse and dragoons (still mounted infantry); sutlers' carts; guns and powder waggons; bread waggons; gold-laced redcoats; ostrich plumes rippling in the breeze – ninety squadrons of horse and fifty-one battalions of infantry heading down the Rhine valley amid the May blossom.

Neither Marlborough's troops nor the French knew where he was going; all guessed that he meant to invade France by the valley of the Moselle. This belief kept the French army of the Moselle in its place until Marlborough passed it on his southward march. Now Marlborough deceived the French into thinking that his real objective was Alsace, and one French army in southern Germany hastily recrossed the Rhine. Nothing could now prevent

Marlborough's concentration on the Danube. After a march of six weeks that had kept his enemies entirely paralysed, Marlborough's army united with the Imperialist Prince Eugène and the Land-grave of Baden on the Danube, outnumbering the only enemy army in the region (a Franco-Bavarian army under Marsin), and deliver-ing Vienna from danger. To the wonder of Marlborough's allies, his men and horses were in perfect condition even after so long a march.

At last and in frantic haste the French tried to retrieve them-selves. Marshal Tallard drove his men to exhaustion through the Black Forest to join Marsin.

The combined French forces then camped in an extremely strong defensive position on the Danube, in order to watch for Marlborough's next move. It did not occur to them that this move would take the form of an immediate attack on them, this being outside the accepted norms of warfare.

On the morning of 13 August, the allied army broke camp and advanced on the complacent French. In a flurry of plumes and periwigs Marlborough, Eugène and their staffs rode forward to observe the French: 'We saw,' wrote an English officer, 'all their camp in a motion, their Generals and their Aide-de-Camps galloping to and fro to put all things in order.'[18]

Although it was then between 6 and 7 A.M., it was past midday before the allied army was ready to attack. The deployment of Marlborough's army would have appeared clumsy and slow, even something of a shambles, to a commander a hundred years later or to a modern drill sergeant. Wheelings took place at the halt. Sergeants pushed and jostled their men into line, dressing the ranks with their half-pikes or 'spontons'. The armies themselves, although divided on the battlefield into a centre and two wings, suffered in flexibility because the two-battalion brigade was the only formation between a regiment and the unwieldy body of the whole army.

The French position at Blenheim was extremely strong. Its right rested on the Danube, and was anchored by the village of Blenheim itself, well-garrisoned. The left centre was secured by another fortified village, Oberglau, and between lay the Nebel stream; behind the stream there was rising ground. Beyond Oberglau, on the left, lay woods. Tallard deployed the main body of his horse on top of the rising ground, with nine battalions of infantry in support; he thus chose not to make defensive use of the Nebel stream. His colleague, Marsin, and the Elector of Bavaria continued the line north of Oberglau with a wing of horse, and then infantry and horse. The battle was unique in that both sides deployed in two armies, each of whose interior wings made an overall centre of cavalry, whereas normally the centre was of infantry.

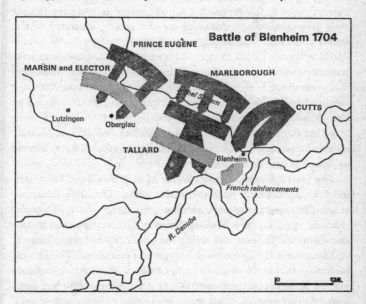

Prince Eugène, commanding the allied right, marched to attack Marsin; a difficult and long approach through woodland. Two-thirds of his infantry were Prussians under Prince Leopold of Anhalt-Dessau, famous in German military history as 'the Old Dessauer'; the remaining third were Danes. Although Eugène's battle with Marsin proved difficult and evenly-balanced, he kept Marsin fixed to his own ground while Marlborough was smashing Tallard.

The village of Blenheim commanded the flank of Marlborough's

assault on Tallard. Marborough therefore masked it with a special
assault force under 'Salamander' Cutts. But Cutts's savage attacks
did more than mask Blenheim – they locked up a disproportionate
French force that was to be badly needed elsewhere at the crisis of
the battle. This crisis turned on the contest of Marlborough's and
Tallard's horse and foot between Blenheim and Oberglau. Marlborough adopted an unorthodox tactical formation, with infantry
posted between the first and second line of cavalry. The French
cavalry charged first, broke the allied forward line of cavalry, but
then were themselves shattered by the steady musketry of the
infantry behind. The struggle amid the drifting powder smoke
ended when the British cavalry charged home in Cromwellian style
with the sword. The French cavalry gave a wavering pistol-fire,
but when the solid weight of the allied horse crashed into them, all,
even the *Maison du Roi* (the French Household Cavalry) fled. The
French infantry were surrounded and cut down. A great French
army became a panic-stricken swarm of fleeing individuals. Marsin,
now threatened in flank by Tallard's collapse, retreated just in time
to escape destruction as well.

The total French loss is not known, but it may have amounted
to over 30,000 killed, wounded and missing. The allies lost some
10,000. The spoils were immense: guns, mortars, colours, standards,
generals' coaches, cases of silver, more than three thousand tents –
and Camille d'Hostun, duc de Tallard, Marshal of France himself.

The impact of Blenheim on Europe was enormous. The French
monarchy had never suffered such a disaster since its rise to greatness in the seventeenth century. No such crushing victory had been
won by any general – not even by Condé or Turenne – since
Gustavus-Adolphus's two battles of Breitenfeld and Lützen seventy
years earlier. The prestige of Louis XIV and his armies had been
shattered. The initiative in Europe had been wrenched from him.
The remainder of the war saw France more and more thrown on
the defensive, gradually yielding ground to the relentless Marlborough and his great comrade Eugène.

The bulk of the fighting took place in Flanders, where France
was most directly threatened. Almost every year's campaign illustrated Marlborough's genius for confusing the enemy by threatening

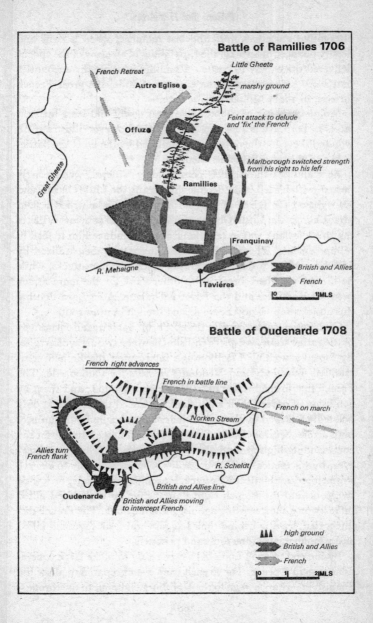

Battle of Ramillies 1706

French Retreat

Little Gheete

Autre Eglise •

marshy ground

Offuz

Feint attack to delude and 'fix' the French

Marlborough switched strength from his right to his left

Ramillies

Great Gheete

Franquinay

R. Mehaigne

Taviéres

| | British and Allies |
| | French |

0   1 MLS

Battle of Oudenarde 1708

French right advances

French in battle line

French on march

Norken Stream

Allies turn French flank

R. Scheldt

Oudenarde

British and Allies line

British and Allies moving to intercept French

▲▲▲	high ground
	British and Allies
	French

0   1   2 MLS

alternative objectives until the last moment, when a swift and deadly pounce (in terms of the capabilities of an army of the epoch) delivered the enemy to battle – Ramillies in 1706, the encounter-battle of Oudenarde and the capture of Lille, the great French fortress, in 1708, Malplaquet in 1709.

Malplaquet was Marlborough's most costly and least brilliant victory. Both Ramillies and Oudenarde however illustrate his wonderful eye for the opportunities offered by the lie of the battle-field and the mistakes of his enemy.

At Ramillies the French commander, Villeroi, was strongly posted, with his left behind a marshy stream, the Little Gheete, and his right on the River Mehaigne. Marlborough launched a feint attack across the Little Gheete strong enough to convince Villeroi that his left flank was in real danger and to induce him to feed in reinforcements. The marshy Little Gheete was then utilized by Marlborough as a defence against French counter-attacks, while he himself switched forces to his other flank for the main attack between Ramillies and the River Mehaigne. After hard fighting this attack swept away the weakened French in utter rout.

Oudenarde was a rarity for the epoch, in that it was an encounter-battle rather than a set-piece collision between two arrayed armies. By forced marching Marlborough intercepted the French commanders Burgundy and Vendôme *en route* for Oudenarde. The French first formed a line of battle on high ground; and then, by confusion of orders, their right flank advanced to the attack, only belatedly followed by the rest of their army. Gradually the units of both armies became involved one by one in a fierce struggle for the commanding high ground above Oudenarde. Marlborough how-ever, by his tactical skill and eye for ground, was able to reserve strong forces for his decisive attack. He sent Dutch cavalry on a wide sweep behind the French right flank, while he himself led allied infantry on a shorter swing against the same flank. The French dis-integrated, leaving behind their baggage train, six thousand killed and wounded, and nine thousand prisoners.

By the end of 1708 Louis XIV was ready to make large conces-sions to gain a peace. The French were even prepared to allow the Spanish inheritance to go to the Habsburg claimant to the throne –

the principal allied war aim. However, the allies now demanded that Louis should actually help to turn his own grandson from the throne of Spain by force, if the grandson should fail to leave Spain within two months. The allies also demanded French fortresses as pledges of good faith. These allied demands leaped beyond even Marlborough's achievements in the field. They changed the French mood from one of concession to defiance and patriotic resistance. They constitute a classic example of how a misjudgement in high policy can throw away the rewards of military success. The war went on. Despite Marlborough's continued victories, which included the swift and easy forcing in 1711 of the supposedly impregnable '*Non Plus Ultra*' lines protecting northern France, there was an increasing weariness on the allied side.

The new British government that followed the Tory victory in the general election of 1710 was bent both on ousting Marlborough and ending the war, even at the expense of Britain's allies. At the beginning of 1712 Marlborough was replaced. The new administration evacuated the Iberian Peninsula, where French successes had done something to counterbalance Marlborough's victories, and opened separate peace negotiations with France in breach of the original treaties of alliance. Britain's allies – especially the exhausted Dutch – had no alternative but to follow suit.

The Treaty of Utrecht reflected the shift in the balance of success in the war between 1708 and 1713, and the folly of the allies in not making a profitable but realistic peace in 1708–9. Louis XIV's grandson was accepted as King Philip V of Spain; in return, Louis undertook that the crowns of France and Spain should never be united. The Spanish Empire itself was divided: Spain and the Indies to Louis' grandson, and the Spanish Netherlands and north Italian lands to the Habsburg emperor. France no longer faced Habsburg encirclement by Habsburg monarchies both to the south in Spain and to the north and east in Flanders and Germany. The Dutch came worse out of the war. Although they had preserved their own independence and also the independence from French control of the old Spanish (now Austrian) Netherlands, and won some barrier fortresses, they were left exhausted and without commensurate commercial rewards or opportunities. Commercial reward fell to the British. An agreement with Spain opened the Spanish Empire legally to one trading ship and 4,000 slaves annually, but in fact to many more. Britain also won Nova Scotia and Newfoundland from France, and Gibraltar and Minorca from Spain. Whereas the Dutch were now in rapid decline as a naval and commercial power, the British emerged from the war as the world's greatest sea-power and most buoyant commercial nation. As a centre of finance she now stood second only to the Netherlands. And her Protestant succession was safe, formally recognised by France.

All this was the result indirectly of the stimulus of a long war and directly of the victories won on land by Marlborough and his allied army, of which the British contingent had been the cement.

Yet Marlborough's achievements are not only to be seen in the terms of the Treaty of Utrecht. A treaty is only a piece of parchment, a formal recognition of a temporary equilibrium in power between nations. A treaty cannot long outlast the real equilibrium it reflects. Utrecht marked the end for eighty years of the ambition of the French, largest nation in Europe, to achieve mastership over the Continent. This was the measure of the crippling damage done to the French state and society by Louis XIV's defeat, whose mortal effects are to be traced in French history down to the final collapse of the French monarchy in 1789, and which deeply weakened the French war effort in the limited dynastic and colonial wars of the eighteenth century.

III

The Army
and the Empire
1714–1902

8

Militia, Army
and
Georgian Politics

THE war against Louis XIV was ended by a government which, when in opposition, had always opposed a continental strategy, and disliked the large army that this required. To the normal haste with which the British dispersed their forces after a war was added the spur of party feeling. Before the Peace of Utrecht had even been signed, the Tory administration of Bolingbroke and Harley had broken up thirteen regiments of dragoons and twenty-two of foot. The estimates of 1713 called for no more than some 8,000 men for Great Britain itself (excluding Ireland), a figure last seen during the brief Peace of Ryswick and before that in the reign of Charles II. In 1714 the British establishment was fixed at 22,000 men – of whom two-thirds were taken up by the troops in the colonies or still needed in Flanders. However, once more, as in 1661, a fresh emergency arrested the process of reduction – the Jacobite rising of 1715. Then the forces dwindled again. In 1722 the figure became fixed at 18,000 men, and there it stayed until 1739. Although Britain was now a major European and colonial power, the standing forces on the British establishment were only double what they had been under Charles II. However, a large force was also carried on the establishment of the Irish kingdom. Yet the British forces were small compared with 133,000 men in the peacetime French army, a figure that in French terms was low, and reflected the penury of the French state after Louis XIV had finished glorifying it.

Thus under the early Hanoverians little was left behind in the way of an army by the great wars of William and Anne. Nor was it even now universally accepted that Britain had an 'army' in peacetime. The parliamentary estimates referred not to 'the army', but to 'guards and garrisons', the traditional formula since the reign of Charles II. The Mutiny Acts, now an annual occurrence, spoke of 'a number of troops, not exceeding' whatever figure had been fixed for that year. The supposedly temporary basis of such forces in peacetime was carefully cherished, and each year the mutiny bill provided an opportunity for diehard Members of Parliament to demand the reduction or destruction of what they horridly referred to as 'a standing army'. It was not until 1755 that 'the army' achieved official recognition when the first of the continuous series of army lists was published.

The army in the first half of the eighteenth century was therefore not a major national institution or a primary career for national talent like the French or Prussian army; it was small in numbers, a collection of scattered regiments, themselves further scattered in troops and companies. Every year that passed consolidated the social and constitutional settlement of the Glorious Revolution. In that settlement, the army – military power – had been allotted its place, minor in extent and firmly under the direct or indirect influence of Parliament. This was at a time when parliamentary checks on the sovereign and control over the army and military expenditure had already been eclipsed in France and Prussia, and were seriously threatened in other German states.

The army remained nevertheless an important factor in the petty British politics of the eighteenth century. In the hands of the Secretary-at-War it formed a useful reservoir of government patronage. Since it was, in the absence of a police force, the only reliable means of maintaining public order, the army sometimes found itself moved into boroughs during sharply and alcoholically disputed elections. It was alleged that governments subtly interpreted 'keeping order' as coercing opposition supporters. A newspaper reported in 1722 that in Coventry the soldiers named two men for Parliament and the sheriff duly returned them. Then there was the old question of quartering. Eighteenth-century ministers discovered, like seventeenth-century monarchs, that nothing was more upsetting to opponents or unfriendly boroughs than having a regiment of dragoons quartered on them.

Thus the small military manoeuvres of parliamentary faction were denounced by those out of office in the traditional language of the great struggles of the past: arbitrary power, danger to liberty, to the constitution, and to the rights of the subject. However the critics of standing forces acknowledged that the realm could not remain entirely without protection on land; and hence they argued the superior constitutional and military qualities of the militia. In the shapeless politics of the first half of the eighteenth century, the question of the militia versus mercenary forces became one of the few genuine political issues that distinguished factions in opposition from factions in power. The arguments derived from a pamphlet war on the matter waged between 1697 and 1699, when the censorship was first relaxed. The pamphlets were written when the Revolution had already really put paid to the problem of absolute kings and royal armies, but while the blood was still hot and the memories still keen. They were full of mixed but hopeful references to history that had never been and to a Utopian future that was equally unlikely. By 1750 the arguments were thus becoming doubly remote from reality.

The writers who attacked a standing army saw the militia as a cheap, militarily effective and constitutionally safe alternative. Various kinds of ideal militias were sketched, from something like the defunct 'select' militia to vast schemes for annual and universal military training in peripatetic camps. Their essential common feature was that the militia should be removed entirely from royal control and placed in the hands of men of property, the *ipso facto* guardians of English liberty. Historical and current foreign examples of the connexion between militias and liberty and between armies and slavery abounded. It was particularly important to preserve England from a standing army because

in this unhappy Age, when an universal Deluge of Tyranny has overspread the face of the whole Earth; so that this is the Ark out of which if the Dove be sent forth, she will find no resting place till her Return.[1]

The case made by court hacks in reply rested on the contention that no militia could be militarily efficient. Wild tribesmen or backwoodsmen with warrior qualities from primitive societies in

Scotland or America or the Balkans could not be compared with
members of British society, occupied with trade, industry and
agriculture, unaccustomed to arms and fighting, and unable to
leave their ordinary occupations for long. Defoe pointed out that
to make a new army from scratch took three years and 30,000
lives; a point that was in essentials to be as true in 1914 and 1939
as it was at the end of the seventeenth century. He also argued with
acuity that the English were 'the worst raw men in the world and
the best when once got over it'.[2] British experience, it was contended,
showed that a standing army did not necessarily lead to royal
despotism. Hence, while a standing army was militarily essential,
it was not constitutionally dangerous so long as Parliament
remained true to its responsibilities.

The court pamphleteers also pointed out that the more efficient
the militia and the more permanent its system, the more it resembled a standing army, so what was gained?

These arguments over the standing army and a reformed
militia echoed with increasing hollowness down to the 1750s:
slogans marking those in parliamentary office from those out of it.
Perhaps the most important and unfortunate result of this continued
controversy was that once again the concept of a militia and the
concept of a professional army were placed in diametric opposition,
militarily and constitutionally. There was less and less chance of
the evolution of a single military system comprising both militia
and army, whereby the militia might serve as a reservoir of partly
trained men for the army, and as an administrative framework for
recruitment. There was less and less chance that the ancient
obligation – or right – to bear arms in defence of the realm would
find modern expression in a national army based on some system
of conscription. This ancient obligation only found expression –
but to a lesser and lesser extent – in the militia. The army hardened
into an institution set apart from the common duties and obligations of the citizen.

It was not only traditional fears of despotism and new apprehen-
sions of government patronage that maintained the antipathy of
the country gentlemen – in and out of Parliament – to the standing
army; nor even dislike of taxes. The whole social evolution of

Britain in the early eighteenth century, consolidating the Revolution settlement, left little scope for importance to an army, which is essentially an instrument of state power. For the English state was withering away. Once the most centralized and strongly governed country in Europe, Britain had now become almost without administration from the centre. Except for taxation, government had devolved to the counties, where the country gentry, in collaboration or rivalry with their great noble neighbours, administered, decided and judged. In the independent local worlds of the counties, busy with improving agriculture and country amusements and building fine houses, there was little place for military affairs. The British gentry were waxing far too fat off good land well-farmed and buoyant overseas trade to look to the King's coat for profit and prestige, like the poor *noblesse* of France or Prussia. The tiny army of peacetime might serve as an episode in the life of a son; but as a career it attracted only a few. The militia on the other hand 'belonged' to the counties, to the gentry. This did not save it from falling gradually into total inanition after 1714, unmustered, untrained; name without substance.

The army was not more popular with the town middle class or the common people. It remained true to the tradition established under the late Stuarts – recruited from wastrels and delinquents, paid little and robbed of much of that by government and officer, and lashed into discipline from which it easily lapsed into drunkenness. Dr Johnson bracketed lifeguardsmen with felons and horrible stinks as equally unwelcome presences in private lodgings. His was a universal valuation. However, the townsfolk had their special reasons for disliking red-coats. In the absence of police, soldiers provided the only instruments by which the government could quell riot. It was an age of violence and sharpening class distinction. Maintenance of public order became one of the principal reasons given by government spokesmen for keeping a standing army in peacetime. The army played a large and unpopular part in combating the widely approved activity of smuggling. The British people's relationship with its army was illustrated by street affrays, fierce local quarrels over the boundaries of Common and Martial Law, protection of deserters by magistrates, ceaseless complaints to the Secretary-at-War about the horrors of quartering.

Thus by the middle of the eighteenth century the army had shrunk from a fundamental constitutional issue, at the heart of political life, to a grudgingly accepted but unpopular minor excrescence, in no way to be compared with national institutions like the Bank of England or the Navy.

But wars would keep breaking in. As a result of two of them – the War of the Austrian Succession and the Seven Years' War – the question of military power flared briefly once more into a major political issue.

Although the development of the domestic issue was closely affected by strategy, for the sake of clarity the strategic history of these wars will be sketched separately later. Sufficient here to say that in neither war did Britain enjoy the advantages of Marlborough's time. Instead of the support of a great European alliance, she had only one or two hard-pressed partners; instead of facing virtually only a single power, France, she herself faced alliances. British resources were therefore thinly spread – at sea, in Europe, in the colonies. The army in particular proved far too small, even when hastily expanded, properly both to fulfil all its commitments abroad and to protect the home island from a French invasion that the over-stretched navy could not be sure of preventing. There was a colossal flutter of alarm in 1744 when the French prepared an armada in the Channel ports. In 1745 French sea-power landed Prince Charles Edward Stuart in Scotland for the second Jacobite attempt to regain the British throne. In the absence of the British army abroad and in the face of the total uselessness of the militia, Charles Edward got as far south as Derby. It was only by bringing the British contingent home from Flanders that the Jacobites were destroyed at Culloden in 1746. In 1756, at the beginning of the Seven Years' War, another vast French armada in the Channel ports pinned British troops in England while the British base of Minorca, under-manned and vainly awaiting reinforcements, fell. Apprehension of invasion became a continual British emotion. In 1759 yet another ostentatious French preparation caused stout British hearts to flutter again.

Under the spur of these re-awakened fears of invasion after 1744, a new movement to revive and reform the militia sprang to life. The old arguments of the 1690s were brought out of the cupboards and dusted down. However, the weight of the arguments this time rested primarily upon functional military grounds rather than on constitutional issues. The performance of the Highland tribesmen in the '45, to say nothing of American and Croatian irregulars, provided topical proofs of the effectiveness of citizen forces. A reformed militia could, it was argued, protect the home island and thus free the regular army to fight abroad, preferably in colonial areas rather than Europe – somewhere where the trade pickings were good. A militia would diminish the need of the navy to watch the Channel, freeing it for more profitable activities. Finally, to base the defence of Great Britain on a reformed militia would cost far less than increasing the regular army.

There were also the high-minded garnishes. Wide military training and service would help to regenerate a nation softened by peaceful pursuits. It would avert in the future disgraces like those of 1744 and 1756, when German mercenaries or the King's Hanoverian troops had to be brought in to save the human sheep of England from French wolves. Some reformers even looked towards the kind of national obligation for service expressed in the French militia and the Prussian canton system (see p. 179).

Another furious exchange of cogently argued pamphlets ensued. Blue-prints for ideal militias abounded.

In the schemes of the 1740s and 1750s there was one great difference from those of half a century back: the continued existence of the regular army was accepted by all. The militia was seen not as an alternative that could entirely replace a regular army, but as a supplement. The army had thus at last become part of the permanent structure of British society. However, while ministerially-inspired militia schemes looked on the militia as essentially subordinate to the army, both in importance and in command, the opposition preferred the militia to be separate and of equal importance. They carried forward even further the traditional dichotomy between militia and army. The governments of the years 1744–56 were tepid towards militia reform. They doubted whether even a reformed militia could serve as a substitute for an increase in the regular army, or save money. Their opponents, on the other hand, saw enhanced opportunities for ministerial patronage and pressure in a bigger army.

Militia reform thus became the first genuine political issue to divide politics since the reign of Anne. It drew the disparate opposition groups together. It was an aspect of a growing 'radicalism' later to find its detonator in Wilkes. At the same time a new county militia, as against an expensive professional army under the control of the administration, appealed to the back-bench squires, the repositories of old Tory and Jacobite sentiment and of true if muddle-headed patriotism. The militia was one of the issues on which Pitt based his relentless attacks on Newcastle's government, attacks which led in 1756 to Pitt's becoming chief minister.

It was not until 1757 that Pitt's government was able to carry its Militia Bill through Parliament, after endless argument and tortuous political manoeuvres and deals.

The Militia Act of 1757 abolished the system set up by the Restoration Militia Acts whereby property-owners supplied men, equipment and horses according to a graduated scale. Instead, each county was to pay for the militia out of the rates, to raise a fixed quota of men, and select the men by compulsory ballot. Although command of the county force was vested in the Lord-Lieutenant, this royal or ministerial appointment was balanced by twenty or more deputy lieutenants or colonels for each county force, appointed from land-owners worth £444 a year, or heirs apparent of men worth double; the rest of the officers down to ensigns were to be drawn from land-owners of lesser value. The new militia was thus very firmly placed in the hands of the county squirearchy. The rank-and-file were to be provided by men aged between fifteen and fifty, but substitutes were once again allowed. The comfortably-placed could still pay the poor to serve for them. Thus even in the new militia the principle of universal *personal* obligation was compromised.

The passing of the Act, after so much agitation, proved only a beginning. The enthusiasm of the county for militia service was not equal to that of its propagandists. After two years only about half

Officer, Norfolk Militia, 1759. The militia embodied the ancient English principle of the citizen's duty to defend the realm. Its supporters looked on it as 'the Constitutional Force', as against the standing army, which 'belonged' to the King's government and hence was a threat to liberty and the constitution.

the 32,000 men originally hoped for were under arms. The county gentry were slow to become officers; this was one bottleneck. Another was the equal distaste among the classes who were to furnish the rank and file; a distaste expressed by a wave of militia riots in 1757. The riots were caused by a misunderstanding that the new Act did in fact mean true conscription for foreign service. The making of a list of those liable for service by the parish constable was the signal for local protest. The protests took the form of trying to seize the lists from the Chief Constable and destroy them, or burning down the Chief Constable's house, or descending on the Lord-Lieutenant in an armed mob to coerce him into not applying the Act. It was ironical comment on the whole militia issue that some militia riots had to be quelled by regular troops and others by volunteer corps of gentry. However, the riots also showed that a national army, based on universal obligation to serve, would have been socially and politically impossible. The British mercenary army, with all its shortcomings, was the result of a national choice.

In 1759 a new French threat of invasion at last filled out the militia's ranks. For the moment a red coat and Prussian drill became fashionable. The militia was embodied for the duration and concentrated in camps, where it lived and trained just like a second army and under martial law – an army just as costly as the regulars and led by amateurs. To an extent impossible to calculate, the militia both tapped sources of recruits not available to the army, and at the same time competed with it for men. The militia never of course fired a shot in anger throughout the war, except in the Channel Islands.

Despite later vigorous attempts to abolish the militia, it survived into peacetime after 1763; but like the old militia of the first half of the century, it survived hardly more than in name. Only a hostile army encamped across the Channel was ever able to focus the British attention on military affairs. The now set British attitude to military institutions may be contrasted with that of contemporary France, where the peasants both paid for the army in taxes and formed its rank and file, while the *noblesse* paid nothing in taxes and enjoyed the glory and reward of command; or with

Prussia, where a whole society had come to accept that it was the obedient instrument of the King's personal military ambition.

*

For most of the eighteenth century, British military organization remained largely fixed in the form set by Queen Anne's wars. At the top, parliamentary control was firm, and even the Articles of War promulgated under the royal prerogative for the interior discipline of the forces were sent down to the Commons for discussion and approval. Military and strategic policy continued to be the responsibilities of the two principal Secretaries of State. In this transitional period between royal and ministerial rule, the King himself remained an important source of policy and decision, partly because in Hanover he enjoyed an alternative army and state machine, partly because of his personal interest in armies and experience of war, particularly in the case of George II.

The royal prerogative of military administration continued to be exercised through the Secretary-at-War. Since there was no Commander-in-Chief between Ormonde, Marlborough's successor, in 1715 and Lord Stair, appointed in 1744, the Secretary-at-War enjoyed unchallenged the place of executive head of the army. In the King's name he corresponded direct with all ranks and persons without regard to the niceties of seniority or hierarchy; issued orders, even down to military minutiae; gave leave; plunged happily into the muddy waters of promotion. In 1733, during a political crisis over Walpole's proposed Excise Bill, the Secretary-at-War was the instrument through which the King, at Walpole's persuasion, dismissed hostile politicians from their colonelcies. Yet despite the real executive power enjoyed by the Secretary-at-War, he remained a junior minister, unable to decide policy, unable to sign warrants, and dependent on the Secretaries of State for both of these functions.

In 1748, after the War of the Austrian Succession and the usual initial British displays of dire muddle and stoical gallantry, the Duke of Cumberland, himself a soldier of the German school, took the internal organization of the army in hand. Although a man unpopular personally and politically, his reforms were useful; for example, he established a recognized hierarchy of command and communication, and put an end to the indiscriminate by-passing of seniors by the Secretary-at-War. In 1751 William Kent's new Horse-Guards building in Whitehall was first occupied by the higher organs of military bureaucracy; and henceforth for more than a century 'the Horse-Guards' was to be a convenient though not always justified abbreviation for every kind of limitless incompetence.

Divided responsibility for military administration continued: pay and finance remained under the Treasury; supply under the Ordnance Department. The Ordnance failed to better their performance as the century advanced. In 1741 transports for the West Indies had to put into Cork because the water was foul and the food uneatable. The Earl of Stair was sent to the Netherlands in 1742 without artillery or engineers.

In peacetime during the eighteenth century the army as a combined and organized fighting force hardly existed. Barracks of the new continental kind, large buildings concentrating the troops in their own military world, were opposed in Britain as smacking of European modes and standing armies. So the British army lay scattered through the villages and towns, living in the strict disciplinary atmosphere of public houses. There were no regimental depots; no kind of base system at all. Far from an army ever being seen assembled and exercised in peacetime, it was a wonder to see a regiment. It was difficult for officers, impossible for men, to see beyond the immediate world of the regiment to any larger loyalty. In other armies too the regiment was the largest permanent body, and cherished distinct traditions; but British conditions were giving a special importance and independence to the British regiment. However, cross-posting of officers and men was still customary; it was only in the nineteenth century that the British regiment became a completely insulated world, in which a soldier spent his entire career. In wartime in the eighteenth century regiments at home served as reservoirs for drafts to other units abroad. Regiments abroad that nevertheless needed recruits had to send their own recruiting parties home. At Lord Stair's suggestion, an experimental regimental depot system was briefly tried, by which every regiment kept two extra companies (or one troop) always in Britain.

Regimental organization, economy and tactics equally showed only gradual evolution from those of Marlborough's time. George I tried to introduce German methods into his British army, with mixed success. Although he failed to abolish purchase, stoppages from pay were regulated by warrant after 1717. Even so, special expense arising out of local conditions of war fell on the soldiers, such as extra blankets to keep out the winter cold of Cape Breton Island. George I also introduced uniform arms-drill throughout the army. Uniform drill in the movement of formed bodies of troops had to wait until the 1790s. In the meantime tactical drill depended on the choice made by the regimental colonel out of the available text-books. Although precision and sophistication of movement gradually improved during the century, the lack of uniform drill led, according to Wolfe, to '... the variety of steps in our infantry and the feebleness and disorderly floating of our lines'.[3] It would be wrong to see even in feats of discipline like Fontenoy or Minden the faultless mechanics of the modern Royal Tournament.

In the infantry, now all armed with flintlocks and bayonet, there were two developments between 1714 and 1760. In 1743 the grenadier companies were massed together in battalions – no longer true grenadiers, but simply shock troops of selected tall men. In the same decade light troops were introduced in most European armies. As the tactics of the infantry of the line became more rigid and mechanical, based on mass volley-fire, there was a need for skirmishing and scouting troops able to use ground, to delay, and to shoot accurately at individual targets. The Austrians employed Hungarians and Croatians, often irregulars. The various armies of the German states relied on companies of *Jäger*, or gamekeepers from the boar and deer hunts of the great forests, first-class woodsmen and crack shots with rifled fire-arms. The French army too, under Saxe, raised some 5,000 light troops. The *Chasseurs de Grassin* at Fontenoy combined both light infantry and light horse. Although there were some light troops in the British army in the 1740s – Highlanders, for example, at Fontenoy – it was really Wolfe and Amherst in America who began the history of light infantry in the British army. In the wilderness of the American frontier the sharp-shooting tradition of the *Jäger* had found a new expression. Swiss and German gunsmiths in Pennsylvania adapted the rifles of their homelands into the long 'American' rifle. British, European and American developments in light troops were all fused in 1756 when German and Swiss immigrants in Pennsylvania were formed into the Royal American Regiment, later the 60th Foot and later still to become the King's Royal Rifle Corps.

In the cavalry as well, light troops were the great eighteenth-century innovation. Once again it was the Austrians who were the innovators, fielding from their outer provinces troops with strange and barbarous names – hussars, pandours, Croats – and no less barbarous costume and manners. The French army had had its hussars since the late seventeenth century, and under Saxe possessed Polish scouts. In the British service there were at first only light *troops* of horse, although later they were formed into regiments. The continuous history of light horse (as opposed to true dragoons, or mounted infantry, now becoming merged with ordinary horse) in Britain began in 1756 with the raising of the 15th Light Dragoons.

By the end of the Seven Years' War there were nearly 8,000 light troops in the allied army in Germany under Prince Ferdinand of Brunswick, ten per cent of the force. The popular stereotype (in the older history or school-book) of eighteenth-century war as being a matter only of stately parade-ground drill does not represent the facts.

The foundation of a permanent corps of artillery in the British service took place in 1716. It was named the Royal Regiment of Artillery in 1727. In 1741 the Royal Military Academy, Woolwich, was opened to teach gunnery and engineering. In Prussia, Frederick the Great introduced horse artillery for service in combination with cavalry. Brunswick's own light artillery was also effectively handled.

The role of cavalry tended to diminish as the rate and destructiveness of infantry fire grew; and by the 1740s battles no longer turned like those of Marlborough primarily or generally on the collision of horsemen.

It was the Prussian infantry that set a new standard for Europe; it was Prussia that was now the rising military power of the

Continent.. Prussia was a state without natural frontiers. Like so many German states, it had been helplessly marched over during the Thirty Years' War. Survival, let alone expansion, could not derive from geography, as with Britain. It derived from a sequence of strong rulers; yet they were less rulers than field commanders of an army. In Prussia constitutional liberties had succumbed to absolute rule. By the eighteenth century, the Prussian state existed round and for the army;* the army protected it, and steadily pushed out its frontiers. Frederick William I ('the sergeant King') during his reign (1713–40) increased the army from 30,000 men to nearly 80,000, an astounding figure for a state of only two and a quarter million people and a revenue of not much more than one million sterling a year. Four-fifths of the Prussian public revenue went on the army. France, despite a population ten times as great and a revenue eight times as great, had an army only about twice as large.

In 1733 compulsory military service was introduced in Prussia, after twenty years of gradual evolution from older obligations to serve in the local militia. Each regiment was assigned a canton whence to draw its Prussian-born recruits. Cantonal headmen and the captains of companies jointly chose recruits from a general roll of all males. The principle of universal obligation to serve was re-stated in all subsequent decrees. Thus, whereas in Britain the ancient universal obligation to serve had come to mean service (if at all) only in the militia, and never in the army, in Prussia the ancient obligation had found full modern expression in the professional defence force of the state. However, conscription was not applied universally: the Prussian state, like Britain in the two world wars of the twentieth century, recognized that thriving industry and good administration as well as armed forces were the foundations of successful war. There was a wide range of reserved occupations. In practice, it was the poorer peasant who went to war: hardy, obedient, patient. Even with conscription there were never enough Prussian peasants, and from two-thirds to one-half of the army were mercenaries, recruited – to put it elegantly – in other German states. The native Prussians themselves, although

* Indeed, the state bureaucracy was based on the army administration.

enlisted for life like the mercenaries, in fact only served for two or three months in the year; once trained they were sent back to their farms, a formidable and ready reserve.

The Prussian officer corps was without professional rival. It was the creation most of all of Frederick William I, who virtually conscripted the sons of the Prussian *noblesse*, the *Junker*. He ordered lists to be made of all nobles between twelve and eighteen, and personally chose from them cadets for the Berlin cadet corps, which combined secondary education with military training. Unwilling candidates were rounded up by police or troops. There was not only compulsion. The King offered a career that was rewarding in terms of pay and prestige to members of a mostly very poor class. An officer stood first in the Prussian state; the King himself wore an officer's blue coat, and met his officers on terms of comradeship. By 1724 most Prussian aristocratic families had a son in the army. By 1740 the Prussian nobility and the army were deeply fused. Because of the austerity of their background and the rigour of their education, the Prussian officer corps displayed a frugality and a professionalism unmatched in the French or the British service, and approached only by some other German state armies. Promotion was by seniority combined with merit, not by favour and family. Not much less important to Prussian efficiency was the corps of under-officers (sergeants and corporals), also well-trained men of high quality.

The infantry tactics and organization of the Prussian army in the first half of the eighteenth century were largely created by Prince Leopold of Anhalt-Dessau ('the Old Dessauer'), who had fought with Marlborough at Blenheim. He demanded 'good shooting, quick loading, intrepidity, and vigorous attack'.[4] It was to be a tradition for two centuries. The Old Dessauer replaced breakable wooden ramrods with iron – perhaps the major technical development of the century in infantry equipment. He trimmed off loose, full-skirted clothing so that files could stand closer. Ranks were reduced from four to three. These changes, together with meticulous individual fire-arms drill, raised the Prussian rate of fire to three or four shots a minute. A Prussian regiment was a machine of mass-fire, instantly obedient to its officers, swiftly and impeccably changing front, direction or formation according to standard drill.

Like the Swedes of Gustavus-Adolphus, the Prussians combined all arms – cavalry were stiffened by infantry and artillery, while hard-pressed infantry were supported by horse. The Prussian army was designed for swift and decisive attack in the field. The full potential of Prussian precision and flexibility was realized by Frederick the Great (1740–86). His attack in 'oblique order' was a brilliant invention for use against slow and clumsy adversaries; and in his own hands never degenerated into a fixed and diagrammatic model to be applied regardless of circumstances. Frederick explained:

You refuse one wing to the enemy and strengthen the one that is to attack. With the latter you do your utmost against one wing of the enemy which you take in flank. An Army of 100,000 men taken in flank may be beaten by 30,000 in a very short time. ... The advantages of this arrangement are 1) a small force can engage one much stronger than itself; 2) it attacks the enemy at the decisive point; 3) if you are beaten, it is only part of your army, and you have the three-fourths which are still fresh to cover your retreat.[5]

Two great battles illustrate the Frederician system: Rossbach and Leuthen in 1757.

At Rossbach, the French under Soubise (after whom the onion sauce is named) outnumbered Frederick by nearly two to one. The earlier part of the campaign had gone heavily against Frederick, and overwhelmingly superior forces were closing on Prussia. Soubise and his commanders believed the tide was flowing for them, and that they had only to outflank Frederick to force him to withdraw. The French army marched in dense columns, without an advanced guard, round the left or southern flank of Frederick's army encamped on a north–south axis by the village of Rossbach. Far from outflanking Frederick, the French exposed their own dense columns to a flank attack from the Prussian army, nimble and well-trained enough to change front swiftly. Covered from the French by east–west hills, the Prussian army led by Seydlitz's cavalry countermarched eastwards and deployed facing south. Suddenly, the undeployed columns of the French and their allies were struck with devastating surprise by the Prussian cavalry advancing 'compact like a wall', said an eyewitness, 'and at an incredible speed',[6] by relentless fire from guns posted on a hill, and by infantry coming up at the double and then pouring in the machine-like Prussian volleys. Seydlitz charged again, and the

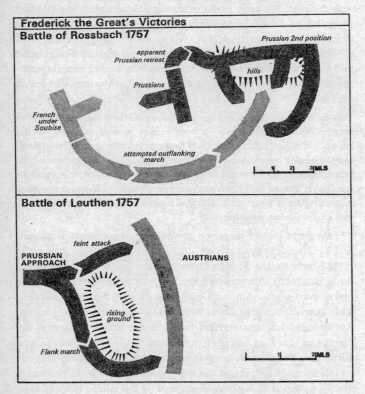

Frederick the Great's Victories

Battle of Rossbach 1757

Prussian 2nd position

apparent
Prussian retreat

hills

Prussians

French
under
Soubise

attempted outflanking
march

1 2 3 MLS

Battle of Leuthen 1757

feint attack

PRUSSIAN
APPROACH

AUSTRIANS

rising
ground

Flank march

1 2 MLS

French army broke up into a rabble that spread itself over forty miles of country. The booty was enormous, but the Prussians lost only 165 killed. Rossbach shattered into splinters the rotten façade of French military greatness.

A month later Frederick with 36,000 men attacked the Austrians at Leuthen. This time the enemy, 60–80,000 men, were strongly posted defensively. Frederick feinted towards the enemy's right flank with a strong attack that carried a key village; and Austrian reinforcements drained away from the opposite wing to reinforce the apparently threatened point. The main Prussian force swung away to attack the Austrian left flank. An eyewitness wrote:

It is impossible to witness a more beautiful sight; all the heads of the columns were parallel to each other, and in exact distances to form line, and the divisions marched with such precision, that they seemed to be at a review, ready to wheel into line in a moment.[7]

The watching Austrian command interpreted the Prussian change of direction as a retreat, especially as the Prussians disappeared from view (in fact into dead ground). Too late the Austrians saw them again only when they were about to attack their weakened left flank in overwhelming force. In violent fighting the Austrian line was rolled up under infantry and cavalry attack covered by furious artillery fire. The Austrians lost some 10,000 killed and 21,000 prisoners, against Prussian losses of some 6,000 killed. Frederick had preserved his kingdom by these battles and established it as the first military power in Europe.

To turn from the Prussians to the French army of the Regency and of Louis XV is to leave the barracks of a guard-grenadier regiment and enter a salon decorated with the works of Watteau and Fragonard.

The decadence of the army created by Louvois and led by men like Turenne had begun during Marlborough's wars. After the death of Louis XV himself, the army decayed with the rest of the great state machine. Partly because of the skill of Marshal de Saxe in giving the French army the sort of battles that suited it, there was a long afterglow of military success: Fontenoy in 1745, Raucoux in 1746 and Lauffeld in 1747. But Saxe himself wrote:

Our infantry, though the bravest in Europe, is not fit to stand a charge in a position where infantry less brave, but better drilled and in a better formation, can close with it; and the successes we have had in battles can be attributed only to chance, or to the skill our generals have shown in reducing engagements to sudden dashes or affairs of posts ...[8]

The French army, unlike the Prussian, was still officered by the purchase system. In 1744 the chief of Saxe's staff wrote:

The officers do not know how to command or to secure obedience, and those who do know are often afraid to do it, lest they should bring on themselves the hatred of their comrades, who believe punishment makes the men desert, or should incur blame from their colonels, who are not aware of the importance of discipline, and usually have no idea of it.[9]

By the time of the Seven Years' War decadence had gone far indeed. In retreat before the Prussians a French army left behind it: 'Pommades, perfumes, powdering and dressing-gowns, bag-wigs, umbrellas, parrots... whining lacquays, cooks, friseurs, players and prostitutes....'[10]

There was also an extraordinary superfluity of officers owing to promotion by favouritism. The French in Germany in 1757 enjoyed the services of forty-four lieutenant-generals, sixty-one camp-marshals and eighty-six brigadiers for an army of only thirty-six brigades. Command was therefore rotated, at the cost of its effectiveness. The administrative system that had been Louvois' pride had disintegrated: no money, no supplies. The army lived by pillage. One French army commander was known as '*Père La Maraude*'. Lieutenant-General St Germain wrote from Germany:

I command a band of robbers, of assassins to be broken on the wheel, who take to their heel at the first gunshot and who are always ready to mutiny. The king has the worst infantry under heaven and the most ill-disciplined.[11]

It is in contrast to Prussian austerity on the one hand and French laxity on the other that the British field armies of the mid-eighteenth century have to be considered.

No observer, friend or enemy, could fault their courage and steadiness on the battlefield, nor their musketry. The French commander at Dettingen (1743) wrote that the British and allied infantry were like a wall of brass 'from which there issued so brisk and well sustained a fire that the oldest officers owned that they had never seen anything like it, incomparably superior to our own'.[12] Contades, the French commander at Minden (1759), wrote of the advance of the British and Hanoverian infantry: 'I have seen what I never thought to be possible, a single line of infantry break through three lines of cavalry ranked in order of battle and tumble them to ruin'.[13]

However, there was more to the professional performance of an army than bravery and discipline on the infrequent battlefields. There were all the continuous duties and responsibilities, tedious and unglamorous, of long campaigns: reconnaissance; making and striking of camps; catering and supply; health and hygiene; staff work, especially march planning and march discipline; outposts and skirmishing. These were the real test of professional knowledge and zeal. Too few British officers passed it. The biographer of Ferdinand of Brunswick, the allied Commander-in-Chief in Germany during the Seven Years' War, believed that it followed from the purchase system that British officers

do not trouble their heads about the service; and understand of it, very few excepted, absolutely nothing whatever, and this goes from the ensign up to the general. Their home customs incline them to the indulgences of life; and, nearly without exception, they all expect to have ample and comfortable means of sleep. This leads them often into military negligences, which would sound incredible were they narrated to a soldier.[14]

An Austrian officer and a historian of the Seven Years' War perhaps made the fairest contemporary judgement of national military virtues:

The English are neither so lively as the French nor so phlegmatic as the Germans; they resemble more, however, the former, and are therefore somewhat lively and impatient. If the nature of the English constitution permitted some degree of discipline, a more equal distribution of favours, and an abolition of buying and selling commissions, I think they would surpass, at least equal, any troops in the world.[15]

However, the effects of purchase on military dilettanteism were mitigated in war by one of the abuses it created: absenteeism. A long hard campaign or an unpleasant station in the tropics found officers flocking home. By a process of natural selection this left behind at the seat of war the able and professionally keen.

Cumberland tried hard to improve the calibre of the officer corps, bringing forward not only his own favourite German-style commanders like Braddock and Hawley, rough *sergeants de bataille*, but an unorthodox and eccentric man like Wolfe, and first-class all-round intelligent soldiers like Amherst and Howe. Perhaps more than most the British officer corps was a mixture of extremes.

*

At mid-century, therefore, the British army was still small even in wartime compared with continental armies with land frontiers to defend; in peace it still barely existed, although it was at last accepted by the nation as a permanent institution, if outside the mainstream of national life. The professional zeal and skill, the cream of national talent, that Prussians put into the army the British put into politics, trade, or the law, or all the rich and diverse life of an English county; or perhaps the navy. For all its faults the British army was better than the nation's lack of concern merited; it was to prove more equal to its role than the French army of the mid-eighteenth century. The growing riches and the comfort of Georgian England depended indeed on distant war-torn red-coats that the Georgian squires rarely saw.

9
The
Seven Years'
War

THE leading theme of seventeenth-century British military history had been constitutional: the place of military power within society. The leading theme of the eighteenth century was strategic. The century opened with a war to thwart the continental ambitions of Louis XIV, and it ended with a similar war against Napoleon Bonaparte. In between there took place a ruthless world struggle between Britain and France for trade and colonies. The weapons of this fierce rivalry were wealth (from trade), fleets, armies and allies. At three to six months' sail away from the homelands in America, in India, the struggle was obscure, local, tenacious and continuous. Three times the struggle exploded into open war between the contestants, involving the full resources of the homelands: in the War of the Austrian Succession (1740–48), the Seven Years' War (1756–63) and the American War of Independence (1775–83).

Throughout these wars the strategic argument between the 'continental' and the 'maritime' schools burned high; indeed it has burned ever since. It is a mistake to subscribe to either school in its full doctrinal rigidity. All depends on particular cases.

The wars against Louis XIV and Napoleon were essentially fought to prevent French hegemony over Europe, and to curb the power of the French state. Since France was a self-sufficient land power, these objectives could not be achieved by picking up colonies, however rich, or by sinking French merchant ships, however many. The existence of Britain, on the other hand, was very vulnerable to such a strategy. The maritime wars against both Louis XIV and Napoleon were in fact barren of decisive result and not very successful in detailed execution. Instead France was beaten each time in continental Europe itself by great armies that wore out her manhood over years of struggle.

The three wars of the mid-eighteenth century, on the other hand, were fought not over the hegemony of Europe, but over world predominance in commerce and colonies. They were truly maritime wars; and therefore rich colonies and seaborne trade were primary objectives.

Yet even in these wars, land campaigns in Europe could not be ignored by the British. Since the days of Bacon it has been claimed that, safe in their island, the British can take as much or as little of a war as they like; that they have a free choice whether or not to intervene on the Continent. In fact this has never been so, from the time when Elizabeth I was forced to aid the Dutch to the time in 1914 when even a Liberal government was forced to fight for Belgium. The eighteenth century in particular is seen by 'blue water' historians as the heyday of maritime extra-European strategy. However, the British Kings were also Electors of Hanover. It thence followed that for the first time since the Middle Ages the British monarchy was tied by inescapable continental responsibilities in fact, if not in constitutional law. British policy had to make provision for the defence of Hanover against the French and thus for continental war – by subsidies to allies or by mercenaries, perhaps by a British expeditionary force. The balance of world strategy could be affected equally in America or in Europe.

France, as a continental state, was even more inescapably committed to the purely European struggle. Disaster in Europe could expose her to invasion. Despite her much larger population France was fatally weakened by this strategic ambivalence. Her combined military and naval strength would have given her victory in a purely colonial struggle with Britain. However, she was forced at the same time to wage major campaigns in Europe with great armies *and* fight a world-wide sea war against the British; she had to find soldiers for the Rhine as well as for the St Lawrence and the Hooghly. Therefore, the 'continental' school of British politicians thought it essential to keep European warfare going against France by means of limited British military intervention. Some French statesmen equally believed that pressure on Hanover could counterbalance British successes far across the oceans.

By seeking allies and opportunities in Europe, therefore, France and Britain connected their world struggle to continental rivalries. For France this European connexion had to be of primary importance; for Britain it was only secondary. This, in a sentence, was the reason for the eventual British triumph.

*

The imperial struggle between France and Britain began indirectly in 1739 with war between Britain and Spain. The Spaniards claimed the right to search British ships in supervision of their imperial trade; Britain denied the right. The ear of one Captain Jenkins, cut off by the Spaniards, provided the needful atrocity story, and British bellicosity, born of a long peace and ancestral hatreds of Spain, propelled Walpole reluctantly into war. A daring stroke by Admiral Vernon and a small force captured Porto Bello on the isthmus of Panama, and encouraged the government into yet another, and full-blown, Caribbean operation against Cartagena. However, this venture was a failure. The climate supplemented the effects of Spanish fire, and the British hospital ships provided a picture of maritime war not usually emphasized by 'blue water' historians. Smollett, himself a surgeon, wrote:

The men were pent up between decks in small vessels where they had not room to sit upright; they wallowed in filth; myriads of maggots were hatched in the putrefaction of their sores, which had no other dressing than of being washed by themselves in their own allowance of brandy; and nothing was heard but groans and lamentations and the language of despair invoking death to deliver them from their miseries.[1]

Meanwhile a separate conflict had begun in Europe. The Austrian Emperor died. His daughter Maria Theresa's claim to inherit all his dominions had been previously guaranteed by all the great powers. Since she was young and inexperienced and the Austrian state was weak in money and soldiers, the great powers ignored their guarantees and set about carving up her inheritance.

Frederick II of Prussia was first to move. The Prussian army beat the Austrians at Mollwitz (1740), and all Silesia was lost to Maria Theresa. France, despite her state of governmental and social decay, revived the ambitions of Louis XIV and aspired to the Austrian Netherlands and Luxembourg, while her old ally Bavaria looked to increase of territory and to the Imperial crown. Britain entered the war on the side of Austria, partly because of fear of French designs on the Low Countries or even Hanover, partly because Britain was already fighting a sister Bourbon monarchy, Spain.

Hostilities between France and Britain opened before war was formally declared in 1744. In 1741 the British began again to raise a large field army virtually from scratch. In 1742 the estimates called for 62,000 men on the British establishment. John, Earl of Stair, an able though elderly veteran of the wars of William and Marlborough, was appointed to command in the Low Countries. In 1743 he marched into Germany and joined Hanoverian and Austrian forces. At Dettingen on the Main the combined armies under the command of George II himself were manoeuvred by the French into a bottleneck between the river and the hills blocked by the French army posted in a strong position. However, a French commander disobeyed his orders and advanced to the attack, when his ill-disciplined troops were broken by those steady volleys of the British infantry that so impressed Noailles, the French Commander-in-Chief (see p. 184). The French rout was completed by the charges of the British cavalry. Dettingen was without strategic result, but illustrated that the qualities of the British army were unchanged after thirty years of peace; it was also the last time that a reigning monarch led British troops into battle.

In 1744 war between France and Britain was formally declared. The major maritime event of the year was a vast French preparation for the invasion of Britain, which, since the British army was now largely overseas, gave rise to the militia reform movement. A British fleet was denied the chance of fighting the French invasion fleet because a gale forced the French to return home. The remainder of the War of the Austrian Succession, so far as it concerned Britain and France, consisted of French successes in

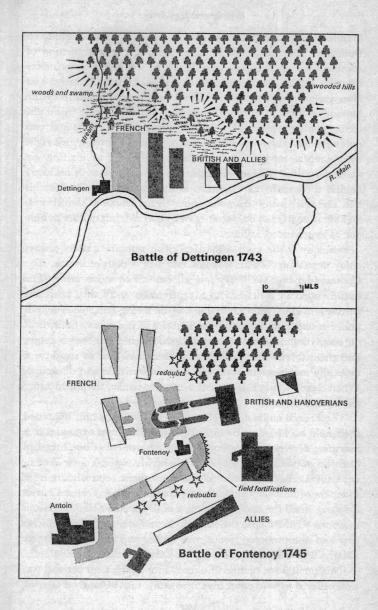

woods and swamp

wooded hills

stream

FRENCH

BRITISH AND ALLIES

Dettingen

R. Main

Battle of Dettingen 1743

0   1 MLS

FRENCH

redoubts

BRITISH AND HANOVERIANS

Fontenoy

field fortifications

Antoin

redoubts

ALLIES

Battle of Fontenoy 1745

Flanders, British successes in North America, and stalemate in
India. All illustrated the inter-dependence and inter-action of
continental and maritime war. In 1745 a French army under
Maurice de Saxe was fighting a British, Dutch, Austrian and
Hanoverian army in Flanders. At Fontenoy, Saxe, aware of the
human weaknesses of the French army, offered battle in an extremely strong position. His left was covered by a forest and two
redoubts, his centre by the fortified village of Fontenoy, his right
by redoubts and high ground, and, at the end of his line, by
another fortified village. He massed the main weight of his army
behind the narrow gap between Fontenoy and the woods to his
left. The allied army was commanded by the Duke of Cumberland,
an able enough man only twenty-five years old, but neither as able
nor as experienced as Saxe.

Fontenoy is the kind of battle British military writers always
enjoy describing. There was not much of a plan of attack. The
Commander-in-Chief early lost all control over his army. The
battle ended in a defeat. As a centrepiece to all this, however,
British and Hanoverian battalions made a long and steady march
under converging fire up to the muzzles of the enemy guns, beat
off enemy infantry and cavalry attacks, reached the enemy camp,
and then, totally unsupported, marched back just as steadily; a
tactically meaningless display of extreme fortitude and discipline.
When Saxe at length launched a counter-stroke, the allied army
fell back in retreat.

The French enhanced their success at Fontenoy and tightened
their hold on Flanders by one of the most brilliant examples of a
maritime diversion in history. For the investment of one brig and
one ship of the line, they gained as a dividend the Young Pretender's invasion of England and the consequent return home from
Flanders of most of Cumberland's British troops. Prince Charles
Edward raised the savage tribesmen of the Scottish Highlands and
marched south. Cope, the British commander in Scotland, with
raw and outnumbered troops, was routed at Prestonpans. Prince
Charles Edward, with 6,000 men, decided to march on into England.

This small force plunged England into panic. Cumberland was
now ordered to send home his entire army, thus instantly rendering

the strategic situation in Flanders perilous. The Dutch were called on to furnish troops under their 1678 treaty of alliance; and Dutch troops and Hessian mercenaries arrived to save England before Cumberland's own men. Seven out of ten battalions committed to Marshal Wade for the defence of the kingdom were foreign. The militia was called out in every county, those county forces along Charles Edward's line of march providing hapless spectators of his

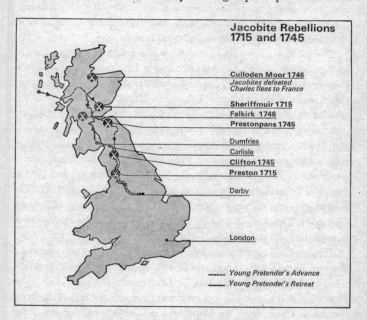

**Jacobite Rebellions
1715 and 1745**

Culloden Moor 1746
*Jacobites defeated
Charles flees to France*

Sheriffmuir 1715
Falkirk 1746
Prestonpans 1745

Dumfries
Carlisle
Clifton 1745
Preston 1715

Derby

London

------ *Young Pretender's Advance*
—— *Young Pretender's Retreat*

passing. The nobility raised their own volunteer corps of horse. The Bank of England paid in sixpences to gain time in order to avoid collapse. There was the spectre of a French invasion directly across the Channel. It was a great time for British phlegm.

Although Prince Charles Edward got as far south as Derby, British forces gradually closed round him. He retreated unscathed back into Scotland. In 1746, Cumberland nominated General Hawley, one of his favourite *sergeants de bataille*, as Commander-in-Chief in Scotland. But in a fight at Falkirk in a rainstorm that damped English musketry the Highlanders once again panicked some of the less experienced British troops. Hawley reported, 'Such scandalous cowardice I never saw before.... The whole second line of foot ran away without firing a shot.'[2] Cumberland took command in person, re-organized and re-trained his army and began a relentless and systematic hunt for Charles Edward. He found him on Culloden Moor. This time the steady volleys of Dettingen and Fontenoy swept away the turbulent onrush of the Highlanders; the English horse rode through the human wreckage, and Charles Edward's army dispersed to its tribal lands.

The success of the French use of Charles Edward was emphasized in September and October 1746 when a British force of six battalions was landed on the coast of Brittany and re-embarked after three weeks without accomplishing anything at all.

Meanwhile Saxe in Flanders had been taking the offensive against an allied army now much weakened by the loss of most of its British contingent. In 1746 he crowned a successful campaign with a victory at Raucoux. In 1747 the British under Cumberland were once more present in force, but Saxe outgeneralled him in manoeuvre and then beat him at the battle of Lauffeld. The campaign – and the war – ended with the French capture of Bergen-op-Zoom. The French had added much of Dutch Brabant to their occupation of the Austrian Netherlands.

However, when it came to peace-making, this French success in Europe had to be set against British success in North America, where a blockade by the Royal Navy combined with a siege by New England provincial troops brought about the fall of the great fortress of Louisbourg, on Cape Breton Island, which commanded the eastern sea approaches to the St Lawrence river and the French colony of Canada. There were no British regular troops present at the siege. Regular troops had been promised for a joint British and colonial invasion of Canada, but instead had been kept back for the luckless tip-and-run raid on Brittany. A French fleet sent in 1746 to recapture Louisbourg was ruined by Atlantic storms, while a second fleet in 1747 was defeated by the Royal Navy outside La Rochelle. Louisbourg and Acadia (Nova Scotia) remained in British hands until the peace.

The Peace of Aix-la-Chapelle itself (1748) illustrated that the war, as between Britain and France, had been primarily over colonies and trade. France was willing to give up all her conquests in the Low Countries in return for Louisbourg, while the British on their side were willing to let Louisbourg go so long as they regained Madras, one of their principal trading bases in India, which had been captured by the French.

The war had marked only the beginnings of a great struggle; the peace marked merely a temporary halt in formal hostilities between the homelands themselves. In India the French and British, acting as 'auxiliaries' of Indian princes, continued to intrigue and fight. In North America frontiersmen of the British and French colonies clashed along the rivers, lakes and valleys that gave access to the interior of the continent. After 1750 the colonial and commercial strife gradually sharpened again towards open war.

The British colonies in North America formed a chain of more or less continuous settlement along the Atlantic coast, between the ocean and the Alleghenies and the mountains that divided New England from New France (Canada). Their population was now some two millions against a mere 60,000 in French Canada. It was a settled population engaged in trade and farming, with numerous townships – in contrast to the scattered trappers and hunters and peasants of French Canada. However, each colony was separated by long distances and bad communications; each jealously guarded its separate independence. Combined action was near to impossible, while the French enjoyed the unity that came from a single authority, the royal Governor-General. It was French strategy to block the westward expansion of British settlement over the Alleghenies by a series of strategic posts and territorial claims extending from Canada to Louisiana, the southern French colony in America. Economically, however, North America was much less important either to Britain or France than their rich sugar islands in the West Indies. French Canada meant furs; British America meant above all supplies for the Royal Navy – such things as spars and rigging – otherwise obtainable only at some hazard from the Baltic.

In India there were no French or British colonies, but only trading posts; no government representatives, but those of the two national East India Companies, both of which raised their own very small forces of European troops and sepoys.

British regular troops had become only gradually entangled with the growing empire. Some troops had been sent to Virginia in the 1670s to quell a rebellion among colonists; others had been turned over to the East India Company in the 1680s for service in India. However, even by the mid-eighteenth century regiments of the British army were not permanently stationed in the colonies in peacetime. The colonies were looked on as extensions of the British garrison-and-fort system, whereby each garrison town or fort had its own permanently attached company of men; part soldiers, part caretakers of the fabric. Colonial garrisons, usually of independent companies until the mid-eighteenth century, were often made up by drafts from regiments; and since this meant exile for life, such drafts were unpopular. During Anne's wars a whole regiment was sent to the Leeward Isles, and in fact was passed over to the colony at the peace. It thus became a garrison, and therefore permanent. The 38th Foot spent sixty years in the Leeward Isles.

The defence of the colonies against major attack rested with the Royal Navy and with military expeditions specially sent. In the case of North America its defence was normally the responsibility of the colonial militias, modelled on the British militia, but owing to American conditions rather more effective in the field.

It was an expedition of the Virginia militia under Colonel Washington, together with the British garrison companies from New York and Carolina, that in fact opened the main struggle for North America, a struggle that expanded into the Seven Years' War. The French defeated Washington's attempt to build a fort on the Ohio, and built one themselves, calling it Fort Duquesne, after the current and able governor of Canada. As a result of this setback the British government decided to send an expeditionary force of regular troops under General Braddock to take Fort Duquesne. Instead of brushes between colonials, it was now to be direct intervention by one of the home powers: war eventually and inevitably. The government decided also to raise two regular regiments in America. Once again the process was begun of re-building an army from a peace establishment of only 8,000 to 10,000 men.

Braddock arrived in Virginia in April, 1755. In May the French, having learned of his dispatch, also sent a force of regulars to America: 3,000 men to Braddock's 800. A squadron of the Royal Navy was ordered to intercept the French, and although the British attempt failed, it remained a blatant act of war. It opened a year of undeclared hostilities between Britain and France by land and sea.

Meanwhile Braddock had set off to Fort Duquesne through the forests and untouched wilderness of inland America. Braddock did not attempt rigidly to apply parade tactics to this new theatre of war. His column was preceded by local guides and scouts, and covered by scouting groups thrown out into the forest on both flanks. Nevertheless the French and their Indian allies succeeded in ambushing him just beyond a ford on the Monongahela. To the terrifying sounds of Indian war-whoops a deadly fire cut from the undergrowth into the column trapped in the narrow trail. For a time the British volleys roared steadily back into the unheeding trees, and then the ranks melted in the face of an unnerving and unorthodox attack. The survivors struggled out of the trap, carrying the dying Braddock with them. It was not the best of beginnings to a great war for world empire.

The war came home to Britain herself at the end of 1755. British naval strength, already reduced by peace, had been worn down by commerce raiding, while the French fleet remained strong. From St Malo to Dunkirk flat-bottomed boats were assembling for the invasion of England. British ministers belatedly began to recreate British strength: 5,000 marines were to be raised for direct service under the Admiralty; treaties were signed with Hesse and Russia for 8,000 and 40,000 men to defend Hanover against the French; and the British army was to be expanded to over 34,000 on the home establishment and 13,000 for the colonies. The militia reform movement took wings again.

The same strategic factors as in the War of the Austrian Succession became apparent. When both army and navy had been left weak by the negligence of peacetime governments, a direct French threat to the home island could paralyse British action in all parts of the world. Strategy was a world-wide web; a tug anywhere could distort the entire fabric.

The French preparation for invasion was in fact only a cover plan to pin the British fleet in the Channel and the British army at home. While the plan was succeeding in this purpose, the Toulon fleet escorted a French army to the island of Minorca, the main British base in the Mediterranean, and captured it from a weak garrison.

Formal declaration of war could hardly be delayed much longer. It would be a war for the defeat of the French in North America. Such a war turned on command of the Atlantic crossings as well as on land campaigns in America. France was rich enough in population and resources to match and perhaps overmatch any British effort by land and sea if the war was limited to the two nations alone. The British government again faced a fundamental British dilemma. It could not avoid some commitment to Europe because of Hanover. On the other hand, if this commitment could be made part of a coalition against France, it would prevent the French from concentrating on the maritime and colonial struggle. Even the Admiralty itself saw the need for a continental alliance if undiluted French strength were not to prove too great for Britain at sea. In May 1756 Britain therefore concluded an alliance with Prussia.

The French government now played into British hands by an act of utmost but gratuitous folly. It concluded an alliance with Austria, France's traditional enemy. While this tied France to Maria Theresa's ambitions and her thirst for revenge against Frederick the Great, it could serve no French interest. It went clear against France's need to prevent a great continental war in order to concentrate against England. And since France could hardly invade the territories of her new ally, all traditional British fears for the Low Countries – now the Austrian Netherlands – were removed.

Thus the colonial struggle between France and Britain, which had already broken into open conflict, was now joined to war in Europe, primarily between Prussia on the one hand and Austria and Russia on the other.

In the face of heavy odds and concentric dangers, Frederick the Great struck first, as in 1740, and in September 1756 invaded Saxony. The Seven Years' War was in full career.

The British chief minister between 1754 and 1756, the Duke of Newcastle, has been heavily blamed for all the initial British setbacks, and for want of leadership and strategic acumen. He was the target of William Pitt's patriotic oratory, attacked in particular for committing Britain to war on the Continent. The criticisms were unjust. When Pitt himself came into office he realized that the continental commitment was an essential part of global strategy,

preventing the French from building a larger navy and from pouring troops into Canada and the West Indies. Pitt, indeed, in office regarded Frederick the Great as 'the Protestant hero'. The foundations of Pitt's victories were in fact laid by Newcastle. He arranged the Prussian alliance and the defence of Hanover. In 1756 he raised ten new regiments, and light troops later to be formed into eleven regiments of light dragoons. The Royal Americans were raised during his ministry. In September 1756, a fresh expansion of the army was set on foot: 15,000 men were to be raised to form second battalions to existing line regiments, battalions which two years later became regiments themselves. To all this Pitt, becoming chief minister in December 1756, was heir. Pitt's own contribution during the following year was no more than three new regiments and the reformed militia (existing so far only as an Act of Parliament).

Pitt was chief minister throughout 1757, except for three months between April and July. It was he who was responsible for the strategy decided upon and the orders given early in that year. It seems illogical to blame Newcastle therefore – or not to blame Pitt – for the disastrous course of the war during 1757.

In March the French invaded Hanover and defeated the Duke of Cumberland at Hastenbeck. Cumberland's consequent retreat ended with the Convention of Kloster Zeven. It provided for the disbandment of the mercenaries, the retirement of the Hanoverian army to a northern corner of the state, and the occupation by the French of large areas of Hanover. Although it was a shattering humiliation, it was later repudiated by both sides.

In America there was failure and defeat. Pitt's intention was to attack the French fortress of Louisbourg, commanding the sea approaches to the St Lawrence. Pitt ordered seven battalions from Britain to America in January, but they arrived in July, some two or three months later than need be. Meanwhile Loudoun, the Commander-in-Chief in America, had withdrawn his troops from the Canadian frontier region to New York to await these reinforcements and the accompanying fleet that would transport all to Nova Scotia for the siege of Louisbourg. When Loudoun at last got to Louisbourg, it was seen that the French fleet in the harbour numbered sixteen sail to the fifteen British. The British armada therefore returned to New York. Pitt had neglected to ensure British command of the sea.

Meanwhile in the key strategic valleys that led from New York to Montreal by way of Lakes George and Champlain, the French, under a new and able Commander-in-Chief, Montcalm, took advantage of Loudoun's absence to capture Fort William Henry, at the head of Lake George.

Pitt's special contribution to strategy in this and later years took the form of landings on the French coast – not as in earlier British exercises of this kind, in strengths of up to 5,000 troops, but more like 10,000. The intention was to divert French resources from America or Hanover or both. Sixteen sail of the line and ten battalions of good troops were committed to an attack on Rochefort. The expedition took a small island fort, found that Rochefort was too well garrisoned, and so sailed vainly home again. These forces – or part of them – would have enabled Loudoun to take Louisbourg or hold Fort William Henry.

The one British success in a gloomy year owed nothing to either Newcastle or Pitt. This was the battle of Plassey, fought in the course of the East India Company's private struggle with the French and with Indian native potentates. It marked, however, the beginning of the long association of the British regular army with India, for Clive's little army of 3,000 Europeans and sepoys included the 39th Foot. It was not much of a battle. The enemy army was a medieval horde of 50,000 men – horse, foot, guns and elephants. Eleven years earlier a Swiss officer in the French service, Paradis, with only 230 Europeans had destroyed a similar Indian army of 10,000 men, demonstrating that numbers were meaningless in Indian warfare. Clive's victory at Plassey over Siraj-ud-Daulah, Nawab of Bengal, at the cost of eighteen dead, opened the whole of northern India to eventual British conquest. It was perhaps the single event that changed the British destiny in India from commercial exploitation to the creation of an empire, with all that this implied for the future of the British army.

In Pitt's first and dismal year of power, it was Frederick the Great who saved the cause and made possible the later tide of success. His twin victories of Rossbach and Leuthen preserved both Hanover and his own kingdom, and ensured that the French involvement in a long and exhausting European war would both continue and grow deeper.

In the aftermath of Rossbach and Leuthen, the Hanoverian army, under a new commander, Prince Ferdinand of Brunswick, a former officer in the Prussian service, took the offensive against the occupying French. Brunswick gained strategic surprise by marching and fighting throughout the depths of winter in an era when armies normally retired to snug winter quarters. By the beginning of January 1758, Hanover was clear of the French. In late February Ferdinand of Brunswick took the offensive again, crossing the Rhine and inflicting enormous damage on the ill-disciplined French army. Brunswick's operations protected Frederick the Great's western flank. His 40,000 men occupied two French armies that together outnumbered him nearly two to one. Germany was a colossal drain on French resources, and it went on continuously for the rest of the war.

Although Brunswick's command was known as 'His Britannic Majesty's Army in Germany', since it was composed partly of the King's Hanoverian subjects and partly of mercenaries on British pay, the first British contingent – five regiments of foot, fourteen squadrons of horse – arrived only in September 1758.

Pitt's strategy for the American campaign of 1758 was an improvement over that for 1757. The navy was now stronger, so that the fleet component of the renewed attack on Louisbourg numbered twenty-two battleships. Other squadrons watched Toulon and Rochefort, so that the French navy was unable to intervene in American operations. Loudoun was replaced by Abercromby as Commander-in-Chief in North America, with the brilliantly promising Lord Augustus Howe as second-in-command. Their task was to advance up the valleys of Lakes George and Champlain on Montreal, taking Fort William Henry and Ticonderoga on the way. While this advance threatened the heart of French Canada from the south, the expedition against Louisbourg was to open up the eastern approaches via the St Lawrence. It was hoped that the capture of Quebec would quickly follow the capture of Louisbourg. The command of the Louisbourg force was given to Jeffery Amherst, an able and zealous officer who had been at Fontenoy, and more recently with the Hessians in Ferdinand of Brunswick's army. Amherst was allotted some 11,000 regular British troops. Abercromby, on the other hand, was given 10,000 regulars and 20,000 American militia for the long thrust at Montreal. A third, and subsidiary, operation was aimed at Fort Duquesne, with troops comprising 1,900 British regulars and 5,000 American militia. The strategy was thus of a three-fold advance against the extremities and the centre of French settlement. The ulterior aim of the 1758 campaign was the total extinction of French power in Canada.

The expedition to Louisbourg went well. On 8 June the troops went ashore from ships' boats covered by gunfire. Boscawen, the admiral, found only five French ships of the line at Louisbourg, as against fifteen the year before, and sank them all. The isolated

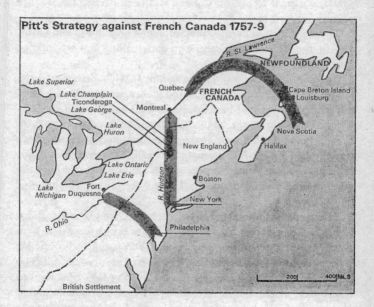

French garrison fought well, but surrendered on 27 July. It was the first British success in three years of hostilities; the first effective British contribution (except for subsidies) to the war. It was also at last a wholly successful use of sea-power and a model of interservice co-operation. But there it stopped. Boscawen refused to go up the St Lawrence to Quebec, believing such an operation to be impracticable. Abercromby's own advance overland to Montreal therefore now took place in isolation. At Ticonderoga at the head of Lake Champlain in a wilderness of forest and mountain, he came up with Montcalm. Having only 4,000 men, Montcalm had felled the forest to make a field of fire, and formed barriers from logs and sharpened stakes. Howe was killed in a skirmish, a critical loss, and Abercromby ordered a direct assault. The British and Americans struggled bravely forward under destructive French musketry. The attack was pressed three times; then morale snapped, and the battle ended in a British rout. When Abercromby retreated, the overland danger to French Canada had been parried for another year.

The expedition to Fort Duquesne found it abandoned and burnt, and so the British built their own fort, calling it Fort Pitt, or Pittsburgh.

As some compensation for the failure at Ticonderoga and the failure to go on from Louisbourg to Quebec, another British force unexpectedly captured Fort Frontenac on Lake Ontario.

Since the aim of the 1758 campaign had been to extinguish French power in America, it must be accounted a failure. Pitt's strategy had split British strength between three divergent thrust lines. Louisbourg, though a great prize, led nowhere. Perhaps the able Amherst and his troops would have been better employed at Ticonderoga.

In Europe Pitt attempted three more of his sea-borne diversions along the French coast. 13,000 men, a larger British force than with either Amherst or Abercromby or with Ferdinand of Brunswick, were escorted to the French coast by a fleet of twenty-four sail. The expedition first burned some small vessels in St Malo, then went to Cherbourg, where, the weather being poor, and provisions giving out, it was decided to go home again. In August a similar force landed near Cherbourg, captured the unfortified town and destroyed the docks. It re-embarked and sailed to St Malo, but found it fortified. It therefore marched on to St Cast, where it re-embarked under fierce French attack. The rearguard of some 1,400 men was killed or captured.

The achievements of these raids do not seem proportionate to the employment of forces larger than Pitt was committing to the main operations of the war. Contemporaries described them as 'breaking windows with guineas'. Because this strategy of diversions has proved so seductive to British leaders from the age of Elizabeth to the Second World War, it is important to note its inherent miscalculations. The aim always was to divert enemy troops from a main theatre; and, because the British army was always smaller than the enemy's, to divert more enemy troops than the British force employed. If 10,000 troops could be put ashore by surprise to take and *hold* some vital objective, which could then be supplied by sea, many more than 10,000 men would be needed to turn them out again. However, it was essential that the British sea-borne expedition should remain *in situ* long enough for the enemy command to feel it a serious danger, long enough for the enemy to order the recall of troops from a main theatre, and long enough for those troops to march home: say, three months at least. A stay of three days, about the usual average, made little impact. It was only when sea-power was employed to open up a true second battle-front, a permanent running sore to the enemy – as in the Iberian Peninsula after 1808 – that maritime operations created an effective strategic diversion. Under Pitt, the Channel combined operations represented an enormous waste of resources: in 1758 the 12,000 men allotted to them saw active service on French territory for a total of about one month out of twelve.

Although the year 1758 had not vindicated Pitt's ability as a grand strategist, the total strength of the Royal Navy was growing, while Ferdinand of Brunswick and his 'British' army of Germans was holding in play nearly 90,000 Frenchmen, thus preventing France from matching the British effort overseas. In these combined underlying factors lay the foundation of ultimate British victory. In 1759 they led to a series of British successes.

The French sought escape from their dilemma through a real, not feigned, invasion of Britain. They were too late: the Royal Navy was now strong enough simultaneously to deploy strong squadrons in the Atlantic, in the Mediterranean and in the Channel. The French were closely blockaded in their own ports. However, the invasion scare led to the heyday of Pitt's militia. While the militia thrilled to the novel squeal of the bugle, the year's reinforcements for America sailed away in February, accompanied by a squadron of twenty-one sail of the line.

With commendable persistence Pitt proposed to carry out in 1759 the uncompleted portions of his plans for 1757 and 1758. Once again there would be a threefold attack on Canada: in the west, via the Mohawk river and Lake Ontario to Niagara; in the centre, the familiar advance on Montreal by Ticonderoga; in the east, combined operations against Quebec.

The western thrust was subsidiary. Amherst, the Commander-in-Chief in America, retained some 11,000 men, of whom 5,000 were American, under his own command for the central advance to Ticonderoga and beyond. Amherst was an able tactician who had formed his own bodies of light infantry, and a thorough and experienced organizer, both of an army and of its supplies and communications, without which expeditions in the American wilderness wilted from starvation. His talent and achievement have been obscured by the striking, not to say eccentric, personality of his subordinate James Wolfe, entrusted with the expedition against Quebec. Wolfe had had no experience of independent command; he was only thirty-two years of age. He was a passionately keen professional, and bitterly contemptuous of the frivolity and negligence bred by purchase. He himself was an original tactical thinker and trainer of troops. Since he was killed at the beginning of his first battle as a commander, it is impossible to assess how good he might have proved in a great command. The romantic glory of his death may have inflated his reputation beyond his deserts.

At the beginning of June 1759 the expedition stood out of Louisbourg: 170 sail, including twenty-two ships of the line. Wolfe was lucky in his naval colleague, Admiral Saunders. Saunders was as dauntless and cheerful as he was modest. Until the army was safely on shore and fighting its battle, the expedition was in his sole charge; his was the responsibility of conducting a great fleet along the narrow and uncharted waters of the St Lawrence; his the daring that took English ships where no Frenchman believed that enemy men-of-war could pass.

Montcalm, the French commander, could muster only five regiments of French regulars and a rabble of a militia for the defence of Quebec. The French administration of Canada itself reflected all the rottenness of the French monarchy at home. Yet Montcalm offered a tenacious and skilful defence. He thwarted one attempt after another to approach Quebec, on its promontory into the St Lawrence, from different directions. He repulsed one major attack in a near rout of the British. Montcalm placed his hopes in keeping the British off until the Canadian winter forced them to retire. For two months, until the end of August, he seemed to be succeeding. Wolfe, baffled and disappointed, fell ill and took to his bed.

It was Amherst, advancing step by step from the south, organizing his communications as he went, who helped to unlock the door. After the French had blown up Ticonderoga, he pressed north towards Crown Point. The outnumbered French abandoned this too. The approaching danger to Montreal and the area from which the French in Canada drew all their supplies induced Montcalm to detach his most able subordinate to Montreal.

It was not Wolfe himself, but his three brigadiers who together invented the daring plan that finally won Quebec. All Wolfe's thwarted moves had been made downstream of the city. His brigadiers proposed to pass upstream of the city and land above it, taking its defences in reverse and cutting its communications with Montreal. Wolfe accepted the outline plan, and himself chose the place of landing and gave the detailed orders.

The night landing and the scaling of the cliffs that led to the battlefield on the Heights of Abraham have passed into British legend. Montcalm, with some 1,400 French regulars against Wolfe's nearly 5,000, attacked in column and was swept away by close-range British volleys. The heroes' deaths of both Montcalm and Wolfe, mortally wounded in the fight, ensured that the taking of Quebec would become a romantic set-piece of popular or school-book history.

However, the fall of Quebec did not mean the conquest of French Canada. Wolfe's troops advanced no farther. Meanwhile Amherst's own advance had come to a halt at Crown Point. In Quebec during the icebound winter British morale sank as sickness mounted. In the spring of 1760 the French launched a dangerous counter-offensive. The British failed to drive them away, and lost a third of their strength. Now it was the turn of the British to be besieged in Quebec. They held out until a British fleet appeared in the St Lawrence in May.

In Canada, 1759 had brought further progress towards final conquest. Elsewhere too the year marked the ebb of fortune away from France. At the beginning of the year, Goree, in West Africa was taken. Another expedition invaded Guadeloupe, the richest of French West Indian sugar islands. It took five months of bitter fighting in a fever-ridden environment to complete the conquest. This was a deadly blow at French commercial wealth, but, not as some Britons had hoped, at French capacity for war. In India, Madras held out against the French until a British fleet relieved it and threatened in turn the French base of Pondicherry. Farther north a British force that included two regular regiments took Masulipatam from the French, and French predominance in the state of Hyderabad was replaced by British.

And in Germany Ferdinand of Brunswick's British contingent had taken the field in its first campaign. Ferdinand, with nearly 80,000 men (including nearly 5,000 British foot and fourteen British squadrons of horse), faced two French armies: under Contades, 66,000, and under Soubise, 31,000. The scale of operations in Europe was thus very much larger than in Canada.

Ferdinand was beaten at Bergen in April in an attempt to take Frankfurt-on-Main, one of the main French bases. In July the manoeuvrings of the armies brought them to Minden, on the Weser.

The French commander, Contades, was strongly posted defensively, his right on the Weser and the fortified town of Minden, his left covered by marshes. However, his government was pressing him hard to attack. He also feared he was being deeply turned by a detached force, and so he decided to advance.

The plans of both Ferdinand and Contades for the battle foundered when a single corps of Ferdinand's army advanced to the attack unsupported, having apparently misunderstood its orders. It formed the extreme right of Ferdinand's line, and it was composed of six British infantry regiments and a battalion of Hanoverian guards. In its rapid march it passed French guns on its outer flank, which, as at Fontenoy, blasted the ranks in enfilade. The advance inclined away from the guns, crowding out the corps to the left, and heading straight for the massed French cavalry in the French centre. Two further Hanoverian battalions found space to join the advance, which went on before the astonished eyes of both armies unbroken, indeed unflurried, by the terrible fire of field-guns and musketry directed at its flank and front.

In succession the massed squadrons of the French heavy cavalry charged the red-coated British and Hanoverian infantry; each time they came tumbling in heaps of men and horses before the reeking muzzles of levelled muskets. Only the last charge, ebbing round

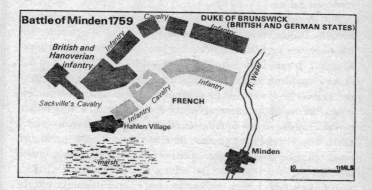

Battle of Minden 1759

DUKE OF BRUNSWICK (BRITISH AND GERMAN STATES)

Cavalry
Infantry
British and Hanoverian infantry
Infantry
R. Weser
Infantry
Sackville's Cavalry
Infantry Cavalry
FRENCH
Hahlen Village
Minden
marsh
0   1 MLS

the flanks of the infantry, threatened to succeed. But the British held steady, fired again, and then Hanoverians and Hessians came up to shatter the French horse with another murderous volley. It was an amazing performance for unsupported infantry to defeat cavalry in this way.

The French centre had been broken; elsewhere too, heavy fighting began to go against them. Now was the time for the British cavalry, under Lord George Sackville, to charge home and complete the victory of the infantry. The cavalry never moved; Sackville disobeyed repeated and anguished orders from Ferdinand. The disobedience cost him his command, but unfortunately not his career.

The French army scrambled away in retreat, leaving behind some 10,000 men killed, wounded and missing.

Minden took its place in British military legend alongside Fontenoy as a display of discipline and steady musketry. The anatomy of British military legend was becoming clear: the British came to admire imperturbable discipline, unshakeable courage and endurance – even if, perhaps sometimes even because, it was all in pursuit of a tactical blunder.

Such displays of battlefield steadiness can give a false impression of eighteenth-century warfare. In the marches and manoeuvres that made up most of a campaign, it was the detached forces of light troops – fast-moving, able to scout, screen, raid or fight – that saw most action.

The decisive victories of 1759 took place at sea. In August the French Toulon fleet got to sea in the hope of reaching the Channel, uniting with the Brest fleet and covering the invasion of England. It was intercepted off Portugal by the British Mediterranean squadron and destroyed. In November it was the turn of the French Brest fleet, while attempting single-handed to rendez-vous with the troop transports of the invasion force. It was caught by Admiral Hawke, who followed it into Quiberon Bay in a rising north-westerly gale. The relentless chase ended amid shoals and rocks with the final destruction of French maritime power in this war. All the French colonies lay isolated now, helpless while British sea-power enabled Britain to concentrate superior military force against them.

The year 1760 saw the completion of British success. In Canada the patient Amherst advanced on Montreal from the west, while another British force marched from Quebec. On 8 September, Montreal surrendered, and French Canada passed into British hands. In India, British command of the sea enabled the British to extinguish French power. At Wandiwash on 22 January a British force under Eyre Coote broke the French in a hard battle. There remained the gradual elimination of pockets of French resistance in India, and the eventual capture after a long siege of Pondicherry, on 5 April 1761. In Germany in 1760, Ferdinand of Brunswick continued to grip powerful French armies through mixed fortunes in the field; at the battle of Warburg the British cavalry magnificently redeemed its inaction under Sackville by routing the

French horse and foot. The British commander, the Marquis of Granby, lost his hat and his wig in the charge and thus gave birth to the expression 'going for them bald-headed'.

Although for Britain the Seven Years' War had already proved a completely successful war of aggressive imperial expansion, the heart went out of it after 1760. The great objectives had been achieved, while the cost of the worldwide effort was ever mounting, and increasingly resented. Pitt was one of those leaders who thrived on the drama of great conflict. The economic and financial underpinning, the patient organization of parliamentary support, were beneath his notice. His ambitions soared to the total extinction of French power everywhere. When Spain appeared increasingly unfriendly, Pitt decided to destroy the Spanish Empire too. At home, however, his ministry disintegrated amid growing weariness with the length and cost of war. Pitt resigned in October 1761. Nevertheless war began with Spain in December. In 1762, expeditions were sent to Portugal, to Havana, to Buenos Aires and to Manila in the Philippines. Martinique and other French West Indian sugar islands were added to the swelling bag.

In Europe the death of Elizabeth of Russia, one of Frederick the Great's relentless enemies, saved Prussia at a moment of desperation. The tide towards peace grew stronger.

The Treaty of Paris in 1763 between France and Britain reflected the extent of the British victory. Lost to France altogether were Canada, Louisiana east of the Mississippi, and valuable islands in the West Indies. French military and political power in India was ended, although France was allowed to retain some trading stations. From Spain Britain regained Minorca and gained Florida.

Force, by land and sea, had delivered two great continents, North America and India, into British hands. The victory rested equally on two strategical pillars: the land war in Germany and the maritime and colonial war across the globe. Only the raids on the French coast had been irrelevant.

Although Pitt's supreme political objective in the war had been the elimination of French power in Canada, there were those who even at the time thought this shortsighted. For as the Duke of Bedford wrote to Newcastle (two of the politicians Pitt despised):

... I don't know whether the neighbourhood of the French to our North American colonies was not the greatest security for their dependence on the mother country, which I feel will be slighted by them when their apprehension of the French is removed.[3]

10

The
Loss of
America

AT their peak during the Seven Years' War, in 1760, the land forces on British pay (including German mercenaries) rose to some 203,000. The number of regiments in the British regular army had passed a hundred. The weight of such forces on the national finance and on the country gentlemen who paid taxes and sat in the House of Commons was very heavy. Peace was therefore welcome. The receding tide of this war, like others, left behind, however, a permanent accretion of the army. In 1764 the peace establishment was fixed at seventy regiments of foot: over 17,000 men for Great Britain, 10,000 for the vastly increased colonial empire, over 4,000 for Gibraltar and Minorca, 1,800 men in the artillery and 12,000 on the Irish establishment – 45,000 men in all.

The Seven Years' War had not marked radical reform of the British military organization. No attempt was made to unite the divided responsibilities of Secretaries of State, Secretary-at-War, Master-General of the Ordnance, Treasury and Commander-in-Chief. It happened that an able veteran soldier – Lord Ligonier – personally united the posts of Commander-in-Chief in England and Master-General. Because of his own capacity Ligonier became responsible for general military advice to Pitt and for drafting instructions to theatre commanders. In many ways he was like a modern Chief of the General Staff. Ligonier exercised his control of home military affairs through military districts.

Billetting and movement of troops at home remained the responsibility of the civilian Secretary-at-War. The army lacked its own transport throughout the eighteenth century, and depended on impressment of beasts and waggons from local authorities.

'Impressment' meant unwilling and inefficient collaboration. Making the army thus dependent on civil authorities for movement was a potent curb on military power.

There were only tentative and temporary reforms in the system of supply in the field. As in the time of Marlborough, successful supply depended not on the system, but on the personal talent of the Commander-in-Chief in the theatre. Although Germany was near at hand, a rich, well-populated country – very different from colonial America at one to two months' sail away – the breakdown of the commissariat prevented Ferdinand of Brunswick taking the field in 1760 as soon as he wished. Ferdinand put his finger on the ancient shortcomings:

I have a monster of a commissariat independent in some respects of me, and composed of several heads, independent of each other, each with its own chief or protector in England, but together as ignorant and as incapable, as they are avid to line their own pockets.[1]

There was still no permanent supply organization, with trained and experienced personnel. Commissaries were appointed only once war was in progress. Although they were supposed to supply the needs of the local Commander-in-Chief, he had no formal powers over them since they were civilians responsible to the Treasury. Ligonier, at Pitt's instigation, did something to sort out the troubles in Germany by militarizing the commissariat on the German pattern under a single officer, an Intendant-General on Ferdinand's staff. The choice of incumbent was unlucky, and there was little improvement. The Commander-in-Chief of the British component in Ferdinand's army, Granby, was himself a gallant man for a charge, but not a great housekeeper. As he himself put it, ' ... sudden marches, Alarms etc. drive the Commissariat business sometimes right out of our heads ... '.[2]

The commissaries too had their difficulties. One wrote pathetically to Granby: 'The British troops under your command are so divided that I cannot find them; therefore inform me that I may take the appropriate measures.'[3]

These shortcomings in Germany illustrate how prodigious was Amherst's achievement in America, campaigning in vast spaces, thinly, if at all, populated. The local American authorities were unco-operative; waggons and draft animals were not made available in European abundance. The advance on Montreal by Lakes George and Champlain involved laboriously stocking a chain of magazines through the forest. The supplies came by trail or by boats that had to be carried overland past rapids.

Divided responsibility for supply – in England and in the field – was the British defence against concentration of power in military hands. In any event, efficient organization was hardly a mark of any aspect of mid-eighteenth-century government in Britain.

*

In view of their physical separation, environmental differences, and their divergent social development, it was perhaps inevitable that the American colonies would drift away from Britain. However, the specific issues that led to the American Revolution lay in strategy and military finance.

Victory over the French in North America had been paid for almost entirely by Great Britain. Hers was now the huge financial burden; hers remained the major cost of dealing with Indian incursions. From George Grenville's Stamp Act of 1765 forward to 1775, when the first shooting took place, the slide towards a breach between Britain and the colonies was impelled by British attempts to get the Americans to pay for their salvation in the Seven Years' War and for their current security. Now, however, the Americans were no longer frightened or grateful for British protection. No matter how ingeniously framed the British imposts were, they were uniformly unwelcome. The old arguments of the reign of Charles I came up again: no taxation without representation. Words like liberty and tyranny were bandied about.

The immediate cause of the American War as well as its general cause was military. In 1775 General Gage, commanding British troops in Boston, sent a detachment to collect arms stored by the American militia at Concord. At Lexington the British detachment ran into the militia, and was forced to retire painfully into Boston while being shot at from trees and hedgerows. The 'battle' of Lexington caused American hearts to pound with patriotic frenzy.

The Americans attempted to wall the British into Boston itself, and into Charleston, which stood on a peninsula in Boston Harbour. The British attacked the Americans on this peninsula. Two assaults on the American defences on Breed's Hill were gallantly and steadily repulsed by the American militia, while the third succeeded because the Americans ran out of ammunition. The British lost two-fifths of their force. Breed's Hill passed into American history as the battle of Bunker's Hill (the hill adjacent to Breed's). As the first major collision of the war, it was not promising for the British. General Burgoyne sombrely noted:

The defence was well conceived and obstinately maintained; the retreat was no flight; it was even covered with bravery and military skill, and proceeded no further than to the next hill, where a new post was taken.[4]

The American performance made a deep impression on General Howe, in command of the attack, and who was later to play a major part in the war.

The Americans convened a Continental Congress in the hope – not entirely fulfilled – of co-ordinating the efforts of thirteen jealously independent colonies. They appointed George Washington, the companion of Braddock on the Monongahela, as Commander-in-Chief. The issue between America and Britain was now committed to the decision of war.

Both sides had their own special difficulties. The American difficulty was that of producing a united and sustained effort. The British problem was that of space and numbers. The four million colonists were scattered between the mountains and the sea along the whole eastern coastline of the continent south of New Brunswick. Communications, where they existed, were poor, and political, industrial or social nerve-centres were few. Wherever it marched, an army could be swallowed up like a fist in a bog. However, British sea-power provided easy movement up and down the coast.

The British counted heavily – as it proved, far too heavily – on the influence and numbers of American loyalists. In fact the loyalists were suppressed everywhere except under the immediate shield of a British army. Although most Americans lost their fervour when the fight for liberty became long, personally inconvenient and unprofitable for trade, it was the active rebels, not the loyalists who dominated American society. The rebels controlled the militia and local administration – and as in Britain itself under the late Stuarts, the militia ably performed the function of rooting out political dissent. The British therefore faced the task of coercing four million people, the majority of whom were hostile, in a vast country. The resemblance between the British predicament and that of those who choose to invade Russia was strong.

The two essential strategic tasks were to destroy the American field armies and to occupy territory in order to restore effective British and loyalist control of American life. As always in such situations the two tasks conflicted in their demands on scarce means. The problems were sharpened by the 3,000 miles of slow sea communications between Britain and the seat of the war, and by limited shipping capacity. Only a fraction of the British land forces was ever in America, and only a fraction of that fraction was ever with the main field armies.

Even before Lexington had taken place, Gage, the British Commander-in-Chief, wrote home: 'If you think ten thousand men enough, send twenty; if a million is thought enough, give two; you will save both blood and Treasure in the end.'[5] Military diagnoses of this kind are rarely well received by politicians. Optimistic statesmen saw easy salvation in the loyalists and in recruiting large numbers of troops in America itself. Instead of the massive military effort right at the start suggested by Gage, there was to be a gradual build-up that barely kept pace with the worsening situation.

The British compounded their difficulties by their method of organizing and controlling the war. Grand strategy was placed in the hands of the Secretary of State for the Colonies, Lord Germain, a month's or two months' sail away from America, and further still from the armies up country. Under the name of Sackville, Germain was the cavalry commander who had failed to charge at Minden; he had been dismissed in disgrace and later convicted by a court martial. He was an arrogant, awkward man.

He shared direction of operations with the Commander-in-Chief in America (first Gage, then Sir William Howe). However, the

Commander-in-Chief in America did not enjoy complete command over other generals and armies in America, who tended to look to Germain for instructions. In fact it was Germain, 3,000 miles away and bone-lazy, who 'co-ordinated' the operations of the separated British armies. Strategy was evolved, so far as it was at all, by three- and four-cornered correspondence between the generals and each other and Germain, the letters sometimes crossing and on occasion crossing disastrously. By the time a dispatch vessel had crossed the Atlantic twice, the military situation might have entirely changed, leaving generals to carry out instructions that were out of date.

Britain once more made gold take the place of men. German mercenaries, Hessians, Waldeckers and Brunswickers again brought their fighting qualities and professional expertise to a British quarrel. Recruitment of loyalists in America proved somewhat disappointing, but, as the war went on, the British were able to recruit from Washington's deserters – just as he recruited from British prisoners or deserters. Ulster and Scottish immigrants played a considerable part on both sides, especially in the rougher kinds of irregular fighting.

The war hardly opened well for Britain in 1775. The only soldier of genius in the conflict – and that of a demonic, erratic kind – emerged on the rebel side in Benedict Arnold. With speed and daring he captured the strong places that guarded the route between New York and Montreal – Ticonderoga and Crown Point. While a colleague advanced directly on Montreal in Amherst's footsteps of 1758–9, Arnold thrust on Quebec through the mountainous wilderness to the east. Canada, the British stronghold in America, was itself in danger. Montreal fell, and Carleton, the British commander, retired on Quebec, where Arnold was only repulsed after a bitter fight in a snowstorm. The rebel stroke against Canada only just failed.

Sir William Howe, now Commander-in-Chief in America, was penned into Boston by Washington. At the beginning of 1776 he evacuated by sea and shifted his force first to Halifax and later to a strategically central point at New York, which he took from Washington without a battle. These movements were an early example of the mobility conferred by English command of the sea.

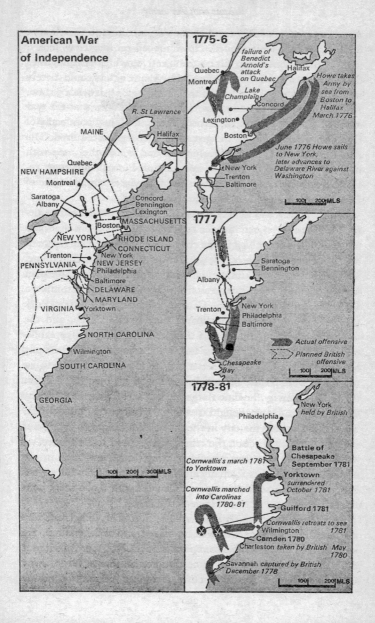

American War of Independence

1775-6

failure of Benedict Arnold's attack on Quebec

Quebec
Montreal
Halifax
Lake Champlain
Concord
Lexington
Boston
New York
Trenton
Baltimore

Howe takes Army by sea from Boston to Halifax March 1776

June 1776 Howe sails to New York, later advances to Delaware River against Washington

100 200 MLS

1777

Saratoga
Bennington
Albany
Trenton
New York
Philadelphia
Baltimore
Chesapeake Bay

Actual offensive
Planned British offensive

100 200 MLS

1778-81

Philadelphia
New York held by British

Battle of Chesapeake September 1781

Cornwallis's march 1781 to Yorktown

Yorktown surrendered October 1781

Cornwallis marched into Carolinas 1780-81

Guilford 1781

Cornwallis retreats to sea 1781
Wilmington
Camden 1780
Charleston taken by British May 1780

Savannah captured by British December 1778

100 200 MLS

R. St Lawrence

MAINE
Halifax
Quebec
NEW HAMPSHIRE
Montreal
Saratoga
Albany
Concord
Bennington
Lexington
Boston
MASSACHUSETTS
NEW YORK
RHODE ISLAND
CONNECTICUT
Trenton
New York
PENNSYLVANIA
NEW JERSEY
Philadelphia
Baltimore
DELAWARE
MARYLAND
VIRGINIA
Yorktown
NORTH CAROLINA
Wilmington
SOUTH CAROLINA
GEORGIA

100 200 300 MLS

Another example was General Clinton's expedition to Charleston, South Carolina, which failed. Howe moved on into New Jersey, with Philadelphia as an ultimate objective, while Washington's dwindling army fell back before him. Washington could barely muster 10,000 men, and half of those sick, against Howe's 30,000. American patriotism had subsided when it was seen that the war entailed privations and sacrifices. The squabbling politicians of Congress failed to rise to the greatness later legend required. The American cause shrank to Washington and a few other men with both capacity and resolution. Washington himself, however, revived the dying cause by a successful mid-winter stroke at one of Howe's outlying posts at Trenton, New Jersey.

British power was slowly gathering itself together. Howe demanded another 20,000 men for 1777 and got 2,500. A master plan of campaign was evolved in the course of complicated correspondence at great delay between Howe, Germain and General Burgoyne, who visited England during the winter from Canada. The plan was a good one. While an army from Canada advanced south via Lake Champlain and Lake George, an army from New York (Howe's) would advance north via the Hudson valley, and the two would meet at Albany. New England, the heart of the revolution, would be cut off from the rest of the colonies. Unfortunately Germain forgot to have the letter confirming the plan dispatched to Howe, while Howe himself had changed his own mind about the outline plan by the time Burgoyne had set off from England for Canada again. Howe thought it essential to move on Philadelphia. This he did, taking the city in the face of Washington's army, but without decisive effect on the rebels, who retired to Baltimore.

While Howe was thus marching away from New York in the opposite direction from Albany and farther distant from Burgoyne, Burgoyne set off southwards from Canada with 8,000 men, confidently expecting to meet Howe at Albany.

Burgoyne was an efficient and intelligent soldier, fully trusted by his men. His advance was well-organized and well-handled. He manoeuvred the American commander out of Ticonderoga without difficulty and followed him some distance south-eastwards, away from Lake George. At this juncture, Burgoyne elected to continue his advance by this overland route through a wilderness instead of taking the easier route to Albany by water and waggon trail. Despite his utmost efforts he could not reach his next objective, Fort Edward, before the Americans had had time to re-organize and concentrate. It had been a terrible march, from which Burgoyne's army emerged exhausted and with its transport worn out. Henceforth the problem of supply tightened its grip on Burgoyne. A raiding party of his Hessians was routed at Bennington, an action inflated into a great victory by American newspapers. Burgoyne pushed on farther and farther from sanctuary in Canada. By now he knew that Howe was away in Pennsylvania. He wrote to Germain: ' ... I little foresaw that I was to be left to pursue my way through such a tract of country, and hosts of foes, without any co-operation from New York...'.[6]

An attempt at rescue by General Clinton with such forces as remained in New York failed to reach him. After two fierce fights at Freeman's Farm, Burgoyne had no alternative but to surrender at Saratoga on 16 October, for he was hopelessly outnumbered and surrounded, without supplies, and without means of moving his army.

Saratoga was a catastrophe. It convinced France that the American cause was a solid investment. In February 1778 France and the United States signed an alliance. The private quarrel between Britain and America expanded into a general war. It was a war whose strategic factors were very different from those of the Seven Years' War. This time the British had no stout European ally to keep the French busy. France herself was no longer the rotten power of Louis XV. Even before the end of the Seven Years' War, a great minister, Choiseul, had begun to re-organize her army and navy and the rest of her state administration. The British on the other hand had neglected their navy as well as their army in the interests of economy; a less understandable dereliction, and therefore less forgivable. The command of the sea no longer rested in British hands; it passed locally first to one side and then the other. In 1779 Spain and then Holland joined in against Britain. The outnumbered Royal Navy had to fight for its life, in the Channel, in the Atlantic, in the West Indies, in the Bay of Bengal. Arms and men flowed from France to aid Washington. It was a terrifying illustration that in a war against a great continental power, even for colonial purposes, Britain could not do without land war in Europe. As the Admiralty itself noted: ' ... England till this time was never engaged in a sea war with the House of Bourbon thoroughly united, their naval force unbroken, and having no other war or object to draw off their attention and resources ... '. [7]

The entry of France altered the war's entire shape. America

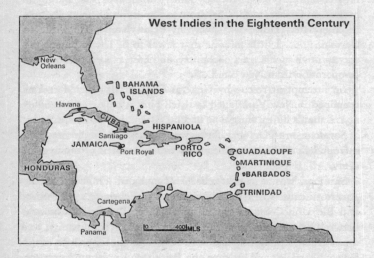

West Indies in the Eighteenth Century

itself became secondary. It was the wealth of the West Indies that was now at stake; for sugar islands were to the eighteenth century what oilfields were to be to the twentieth. The very basis of British prosperity was threatened by the fleets under d'Estaing, Guichen and de Grasse and the white-coated troops they carried. And in the East another great French sailor, Suffren, threatened British trade and dominion in India. Not again until 1940–41 would British neglect of their armed forces deliver Britain into such a desperate plight.

The French alliance came just in time to rescue the American cause from internal collapse owing to disunity and crumbling faith. In two years the Americans had repeated English military history by moving from faith in a militia to reluctant recourse to a regular army. 'To lean on the militia,' wrote Washington, 'is to lean on a broken reed. Being familiar with the use of the musket they will fight under cover, but they will not attack or stand in the open field.'[8] One-year enlistment was hardly better; it meant that the continental army had to be re-raised and re-trained every year. As Washington put it, 'There is not time to drill the men before they are gone, and discipline is impossible because if it was enforced they would go.'[9]

During the winter of 1777–8 Washington was reduced to a few thousand starving men at Valley Forge. He hung on, and with the aid of a Prussian veteran, Baron von Steuben, began to create a regular, well-disciplined army on the European model. At this juncture came the French alliance. More than any other commander on either side Washington saw that victory would turn on sea mobility. This, thanks to the French navy, he might now enjoy equally with the British.

However, the very mobility conferred by sea-power proved a temptation to shift thrust points instead of keeping up a sustained major effort. The fleets of both sides commuted between the Atlantic coast of America and the Caribbean, and played hide-and-seek amid the sugar islands of the West Indies. Sir Henry Clinton, now Commander-in-Chief in America in succession to Howe, had employed sea mobility to abandon Philadelphia and New Jersey and sail back to New York. Germain in London similarly gave way to the temptation. His plan for late 1778 and 1779 was to shift the weight of operations to the southern American states, nearer to the Caribbean theatre. Germain believed the southern states to be highly loyalist. He was convinced that with the aid of these loyalists, the British army could re-conquer America from south to north.

The new strategy opened brilliantly with the capture of Savannah and the conquest of Georgia. At the beginning of 1779 Clinton from New York landed in South Carolina with his main body, and besieged and took Charleston. Clinton believed that South Carolina had been firmly conquered, and went back to New York, leaving Cornwallis in command. However, Cornwallis became involved in a confused succession of marches and fights in the damp heat of up-country Carolina. He beat the Americans at Camden and Guilford, but his force was so diminished that he then retreated to the coast at Wilmington. Once again, the Americans seeped back behind a departed British army. The British detachments in South Carolina were mopped up one by one. Germain for his part assumed that South Carolina was now firmly in British hands, and that Cornwallis should now move north to Virginia. Germain, Cornwallis and Clinton sharply disagreed with each other about the relative importance of Virginia and New York and the strategy now to be followed. The kind of misunderstandings that had led to Burgoyne's surrender now led to Cornwallis's. Relying on reinforcements from Clinton and on British control of the sea, Cornwallis marched into Virginia and formed a base at Yorktown, on the tidal York river. There he was boxed in by Americans and French under Lafayette and Nathaniel Greene. Unfortunately the sea, instead of being a means of rescue, became the other wall of Cornwallis's prison. A British fleet under Admiral Graves not only failed to destroy a French fleet under de Grasse in the battle of the Chesapeake but then sailed back to New York.

Washington feinted at New York to pin Clinton, and then raced south to join Lafayette round Yorktown. Cornwallis, hoping in vain for Clinton's arrival with a British fleet, conducted an obstinate siege. On 17 October 1781, his defences breached, he surrendered. It was the anniversary of Burgoyne's surrender at Saratoga, and it was the end of the real war for America. There was a slow and dreary anti-climax, while the war raged more fiercely elsewhere.

Britain, alone, faced the envious hostility of Europe. Gibraltar and Minorca, far from being bases for British offensive power in the Mediterranean, were now besieged and isolated posts, but although Minorca fell, Gibraltar held out.

With British ships outnumbered in the Channel as well as in distant oceans, the threat of invasion became immediate and real. The militia came to life again. However, it was not the British themselves who prevented invasion, but muddling and indecision on the part of the French and Spaniards. They missed their one opportunity in history of invading Britain while they held command of the Channel.

In India British regular troops were among the Europeans and sepoys that Sir Eyre Coote led to victory in hard campaigns against the Mahrattas. In the West Indies, however, one British island after another fell to the French.

Further disaster, perhaps a great national defeat, was averted by acknowledging American independence in order to free British resources. Britain was then able to offer her enemies the choice of a compromise peace or continued war on worsened terms. Britain's enemies chose peace, and the treaties were signed in Paris in 1783.

The British defeat in America was not primarily owing to the qualities of the British army and its German and American loyalist auxiliaries, nor to British generals. It is probable that to restore British authority in America was a problem beyond the power of military means to solve, however perfectly applied. Clinton, Burgoyne, Howe and Cornwallis conducted their own individual operations if not brilliantly, at least ably and intelligently enough, often outmanoeuvring or beating their enemies in the field. The two critical disasters – the surrenders of Saratoga and Yorktown – were the results of poor liaison and faulty strategy, not of lost battles. The troops performed well in the unusual conditions of America. There was no attempt to adhere to the solid, rigid formations of great European battles; loose, open formations were quickly adopted. The infantry of the line fought in two ranks instead of three, and in open order. The British were in no way behind their opponents in forming special fast-moving units of mounted infantry. Colonel Banastre Tarleton's 1,000-strong Legion and Simcoe's Rangers became famous for the daring of their marches. Tarleton once rode 105 miles in fifty-four hours with his men to overtake and beat an enemy force. The British infantry of the line and gunners had victories in pitched battle they could be proud of: Brandywine Creek, Camden, Guilford. It was not the army that lost America.

*

Although the American colonies had been lost, the peace establishment after 1783 was no smaller than before the war. It was a sign that as one great British dominion disappeared, a new one was already taking its place – India. Over 6,000 regular troops now formed part of the British forces in the provinces controlled by the East India Company. The remainder of the British empire – Gibraltar and the 'plantations' – also required over 15,000 men. The British home establishment was just above 17,000, and the Irish 12,000. The British standing army had thus steadily increased during the eighteenth century. Nevertheless in peace as well as in war the larger part of the army served outside the United Kingdom. The army's destiny was already becoming entangled with colonial security and imperial expansion; a destiny that was to stamp it with a special character and tradition, and at the same time keep it out of the mainstream of national life at home.

The nine years of peace between the American war and the wars of the French Revolution and Empire were a time of rigid economy, financial re-organization and reform under the younger Pitt. The result was a decline in the efficiency of the army more rapid and complete than under Walpole. No Commander-in-Chief was appointed and the Secretaries-at-War were political hacks. For want of recruits the regiments became skeletons. The worst of eighteenth-century military abuses flourished: promotion by favouritism, promotion of rich playboys by purchase, drunkenness, absenteeism, all kinds of military ignorance and negligence. A satirist in 1792 only slightly exaggerated the truth about far too many British officers:

Dry books of tactics are beneath the notice of a man of genius [he wrote. If] the major or the adjutant advises you to learn the manual, the salute or other parts of the exercise ... you may answer, that you do not want to be a Drill-sergeant or corporal – or that you purchased your commission and did not come into the army to be made a machine of.

The satirist's advice to majors was:

Whenever you are to exercise the regiment, get the adjutant or sergeant-major to write out on a small card the words of command in proper order; and if you cannot retain the manoeuvres in your head, you may at least keep them in your hat.[10]

Nevertheless there was some reform and progress. In 1788

Colonel (later General Sir David) Dundas published his *Principles of Military Movement*. It was Dundas's belief that the loose formations and tactics of the American war would prove dangerous against well-disciplined troops in Europe. He believed that the army required the even pace and exact evolutions of the Prussian army, whereas at that time there was not even a standard British tactical drill. In 1792 an abridgement of Dundas's book was made the first official drill manual of the British army, the *Rules and Regulations for the Movement of His Majesty's Army*. Dundas's drill was ridiculed as being too mechanical and pedantic. It certainly neglected light infantry. Yet Wolfe, himself no pedant, had noted thirty years earlier how British lines 'floated' in the absence of uniform drill movements. The steady infantry of the line that formed the essential ingredient of Wellington's victories was a product of Dundas's adaptation of Prussian drill.

In France the last years of the *ancien régime* saw a military renaissance. The deep-seated faults of the French army – purchase, domination by the *noblesse*, suppression of bourgeois talent – were rooted in the society of the *ancien régime* itself, and could only be cured by revolution. However, in organization, equipment and tactics the France of Louis XVI prepared for the victories of Napoleon. The renaissance began even under Louis XV. In 1758 the effects of purchase were mitigated when it was decreed that no officer was to take command of a regiment under seven years' service, of which five had to be in the rank of captain. In 1762 Choiseul ended the system by which regiments were scrapped wholesale at the end of a war, with consequent unemployment among the *noblesse*. Instead all regiments were to be retained in being in peacetime as cadres for future expansion. At the same time the colonels and captains were turned fully into state servants. All responsibility for clothing, supply, payment and recruitment was taken over by the state. In 1763 Choiseul established thirty-one recruit depots which in 1768 were consolidated into four. All private proprietary powers of colonels over cavalry regiments were abolished, thus enabling commanders to order a charge without colonels objecting to possible damage to their property. In 1771 the militia was replaced by 'provincial' regiments assimilated to line regiments. A uniform tariff for purchase was established, and henceforth promotion, even by purchase, was only to be on the basis of recommendation by a commission of senior officers.

The technical reforms in the artillery under Louis XVI were the basis of Napoleon's later success as a gunner. They were the work of Gribeauval, who had served with the Austrian artillery in the Seven Years' War, and became French Inspector-General of Artillery in 1776. His objects were accuracy and rapid mobility. Better accuracy came from improved methods of manufacture and improved quality-control of barrel, ball and powder, as well as from cloth cartridges and from a new mechanical system for aiming the gun. Gribeauval achieved lightness by reducing the barrel-length of his standardized weights of guns (twelve-, eight- and four-pounders) to seventeen calibres, and by making gun carriages stronger and lighter. He introduced the limber box.

St Germain, minister of war under Louis XVI, carried out further reforms. Each regiment was allotted a second, or drafting, battalion. St Germain divided the army into twenty-two divisions, each an independent unit of all arms under a lieutenant-general. In 1788 the French divisions were made permanent and allotted their own territorial districts. It was a major development in the organization of armies – both in supply and movement, and in battle. As a French officer noted in 1794:

No more first line, no more second line, no more cavalry on the wings; the army was broken up into divisions of ten or twelve battalions; the cavalry was distributed among these divisions, four to six squadrons to each, except one-fourth of it which was kept together, and formed the reserve of the army.[11]

In tactics, too, the last years of the *ancien régime* in France were a time of innovation. Ever since Malplaquet there had been controversy in the French army over the relative merits of the line and the column. Saxe in his *Rêveries* argued that vigorous onslaught with the bayonet in close column suited the French better than the rigidity and passivity of fire tactics in line. The controversy was re-lighted in 1770 by an officer only twenty-seven years old, Guibert, in his *Essai Général de Tactique*. Guibert reckoned that troops should attack with the bayonet without firing at all, because firing tended to reduce the momentum. Although Guibert conceded that columns might be used in certain circumstances for attack as well as for manoeuvre, his chosen fighting formation was the three-deep line. The French regulations of 1776 reflected this priority.

Another French theorist, Menil-Durand, followed Saxe in wanting dense, heavy columns instead of a line for attack. Menil-Durand believed that his dense formations should only deploy and open fire if some obstacle stopped their inital rush. In 1778 a competitive trial was carried out at Bayeux by troops using Menil-Durand's system and by others operating according to the 1776 regulations. The verdict went against Menil-Durand. Guibert himself reckoned that Menil-Durand's opponents in the trial had shown that

the modern system of tactics is capable of everything, adapts itself to everything, employs columns when needed – and columns simpler than those of de Menil-Durand – combines them, and intermixes them with deployed battalions, supports a line with them etc.[12]

The French regulations of 1776, based on Guibert and the primacy of the line, were reproduced almost in entirety in 1791, and in all the regulations of the Republic and Empire. In his later book, *Défense du système de Guerre Moderne*, Guibert himself was careful not to make line and column exclusive and opposed conceptions; all depended on the particular situation and terrain. He thought that columns were able to deliver a rapid succession of attacks on a given objective, while giving confidence to the attacking troops and intimidating the enemy by their weight and size. At the same time, in a passage prophetical of French battles against Wellington, Guibert warned of the dangers of the column in attack:

It is subject to undulation, tumult and disorder. If its flanks are struck by fierce fire, if it does not surmount the obstacles it encounters at the first attempt, the men close up and press on one another, the ranks become confused, the officers are not heard, the mass sways, scatters, and cannot be rallied except a long way off, and even then not as a column.[13]

Despite its technical renaissance, the army of Louis XVI reflected the deep social tensions of the old regime. The spirit of reason and scientific inquiry in France that was undermining the anomalies of privilege and absolutism had penetrated the minds of the best French officers. While they were serving with Washington's armies in America, the French officers themselves had seen liberty and equality – revolution itself – in action. There was a strong current inside the officer corps in favour of opening the corps to the talent of the nation. This current, like other currents of reform, was dammed up by an arch-reactionary group round Louis XVI's brother, the Count of Artois. Indeed in 1781 the dam of privilege in the French army was raised higher. A royal ordinance required that henceforth new entrants to the officer corps must prove four generations of noble blood. This dam, like all the others, collapsed under the flood of revolution in 1789.

*

After 1789 it was the general European opinion that the Revolution had ruined the French army; in truth, however, the Revolution had transformed the nature of war.

The scope and intensity of war is determined by its social and political frame. The wars of the eighteenth century had been fought by small ruling groups – the king, the court, even in parliamentary England by the gentry. War had been a matter of limited liability and limited purpose. The new doctrine of liberty and equality burst this narrow frame. With the Revolution, the masses with all their passions, frustrations, ignorance and idealism stepped into politics. The French armies were no longer the instrument of a limited materialistic policy, but of an ideological crusade. They were now the vehicle of all the physical and emotional resources of the French nation. Ruthless leadership was to enlist these resources by means impossible to the *ancien régime*: conscription, requisition, central direction. The objectives of war became no less far-reaching: instead of a town or a colony or a province, the very survival of opposed ideologies and social systems. The French Revolution imparted to war a new and appalling power.

The new French war machine took shape between 1789 and 1800. A National Guard, middle-class citizen soldiers loyal to the new regime, was formed to replace the old militia. In 1791, when the monarchies closed on revolutionary France, the National Assembly called for 101,000 volunteers to man the frontiers. The volunteers formed their own battalions, separate from the regular regiments bequeathed by the old royal army, and they chose their own officers. Some chose badly, but others chose such men as Davout, Jourdan, Lecourbe, Marceau, Masséna, Oudinot, Pichegru and Victor. The volunteer battalions gave openings to men of hitherto small military experience – like Lannes, Moreau, St Cyr and Suchet. The Revolution was already tapping the unused talent of the French nation.

In July 1792 generals were authorized to requisition recruits, euphemistically known as *Volontaires Forcés,* although substitutes were still allowed. The volunteers enlisted for one campaign – not a sound system. In February 1793, under heavy threat of invasion, the Committee of Public Safety decreed a levy of 300,000 men. By August the army of the Republic numbered 500,000 men, fit material for the organizing genius of Carnot, the Minister of War.

In the winter of 1793–4 the old royal army and the volunteers were amalgamated. The infantry were divided into demi-brigades, each of one regular and two volunteer battalions. The regulars gave up the Bourbon white coat and donned the blue of the National Guard. The old regimental names disappeared in favour of numbers.

The volunteers were often intelligent and educated citizens, very different from the human material common in monarchical armies. Loose skirmishing tactics suited the volunteers best, for to fight in line required drilled discipline beyond their power. Despite Guibert and the official regulations, the column therefore came strongly into fashion. Even raw troops can rush forward impetuously in a mass. By 1795 a novel kind of army had emerged in France. It was characterized by high individual intelligence, morale and enthusiasm – by flexibility and mobility. Even its uniforms were looser than those appropriate to the mechanical puppets of the Prussian army. The French army now marched at a rapid pace both off and on the battlefield. It fought in battalion columns behind a cloud of skirmishers, or sometimes in a line backed by columns. Its new fighting style was of incessant activity and alacrity.

In supply there was often a return from eighteenth-century methods of magazines and supply lines to foraging along the line of march. Where adopted, foraging gave greater speed and flexibility to strategic marches, but it also meant that a French army so subsisting must move on or starve. Some historians have exaggerated the degree of this change in supply. In the eighteenth century armies had also lived by pillage, while on the other hand the armies of the Republic and later of Napoleon often had highly organized systems of magazines and waggon-borne supplies.

The new French army was a formidable instrument. Technically it incorporated the later reforms of the old regime, particularly Gribeauval's artillery. It had a solid spine of old soldiers, an inherited military system. It had behind it the dynamism of great ideals and of a nation unbound.

After 1789 the mechanical armies of the monarchies, perfectly drilled in narrow rules and procedures of war, prepared to defend the societies they so well represented against the reforming violence of the Revolution. As the French bands exultantly crashed out the *Marseillaise* and the *Ça Ira*, the slow parade steps of the old regime were heard again: the 'Hohenfriedberger March', '*Fridericus Rex*', and later 'The British Grenadiers'.

11

The Army against Napoleon

In 1791 the French revolutionary government embarked on a combined policy of national expansion and ideological crusade by declaring war on Austria. In 1792 the French army invaded the Austrian Netherlands (now Belgium). The French army was then in transition between the old military system and the new, and it was beaten back into France so easily that the monarchies formed a fatal opinion that the Revolution had destroyed French military power. Gradually the armies of Austria and Prussia, together with troops from smaller German states, converged on France. At Valmy, in September 1792, the Prussian army under the Duke of Brunswick encountered the French under Dumouriez: 34,000 to 52,000. Brunswick was accounted the first soldier in Europe. However, his troops were riddled with dysentery, and the weather was dire. His advance was slow. Brunswick, expecting the French to be in full retreat, was surprised to find them deployed for battle. There was a cannonade between the Prussian guns and the French artillery under Kellermann. Brunswick examined the steady French line and decided that an attack would not be propitious. Instead he retreated. Although combined casualties of both sides at Valmy were fewer than 500, it was a decisive encounter; it opened the way to a long war and to the eventual rise of Napoleon. It gave the new French army confidence in itself. However, the infantry and cavalry that had daunted Brunswick were mostly units of the old royal army: Picardie, Navarre and twenty-two other infantry regiments; *La Reine, Royal-Cravates* (one of the units defeated by the British infantry at Minden in 1759) and four other royal cavalry regiments.

In 1793 France declared war on Britain and launched a new and successful invasion of the Low Countries.

The younger Pitt, the British Prime Minister, had yet to take the measure either of the war or of revolutionary France. In 1793 Pitt and most British politicians believed that the war would be short, and that Britain's role in Europe would be secondary. Pitt thought in terms of his father's strategy against the France of Louis XV. While British guineas helped to cement a coalition that would grip France in Europe, British sea-power would enable Britain to scoop up the French colonial Empire. Pitt saw the conflict as another episode in the Franco-British trade and colonial struggle.

As a consequence of Pitt's mistaken diagnosis, the weight of the scanty strength of the British army was loaded not on the vital theatre of Flanders, but on the West Indies. Between 1793 and 1796 the taking of French sugar islands cost the British army no fewer than 80,000 men, of whom 40,000 died and the rest were rendered unfit for service. This was a higher mortality than in all Wellington's campaigns in the Peninsula. It was the most costly of all the many British adventures in the deadly Caribbean climate, where malaria, yellow fever and dysentery were but three of the available diseases. The direct impact of such losses on a small army like the British, hard to swell by voluntary recruitment, was enormous. In addition, there were the secondary effects, once the mortal nature of a posting to the West Indies dawned on the British lower classes. The West Indies became a major deterrent to recruitment. At the same time British military weakness in Europe (in 1793 the British expeditionary force at first numbered three battalions) meant that British policy could carry little weight. Under Pitt in the 1790s the British army in Europe was a minor contingent in the allied army, not the binding cement that it had been under William III and Marlborough when Britain had led the great coalition against Louis XIV. Finally, there was the failure of Pitt's strategy in itself. Although Britain conquered the French colonies, France grew ever more formidable in Europe instead of being reduced, as Pitt hoped, to making peace.

The campaign of 1793 offered another chance of beating the French armies while they were still disorganized by revolutionary change. The Austrians and Prussians under the Duke of Coburg, an ancient veteran, turned the French out of the Low Countries. France seemed once more open to invasion. However, old Coburg proceeded to besiege fortresses in the approved eighteenth-century style instead of lunging at Paris, the heart of the Revolution. His campaign petered out. The Duke of York's army (mostly Hanoverians and the old reliables, Hessian mercenaries), was sent by the government to besiege Dunkirk. Unfortunately, the Ordnance Department was unable to supply York with siege guns, so the Duke sat helplessly before the fortress while his opportunity slipped away.

On the French side, it was a time of heroic re-organization under Carnot. A French counter-offensive in the north – clouds of skirmishers, furious onslaughts pushed regardless of losses – rolled the allied armies back. In the south, British sea-power had enabled the capture of the fleet-base of Toulon. But the allied garrison was unable to withstand a counter-offensive, in which an artillery officer named Bonaparte distinguished himself, and Toulon was evacuated. In the west a royalist revolt in the Vendée was crushed while the British government dithered over sending troops.

In 1794 the full power of the re-created French army now made itself felt. An allied force including a British contingent of some 5,500 under York was badly beaten at Tourcoing. Although York's own initial attack made more ground than those of his allies, his clumsy and flustered units were outfought by French skirmishers – 'as sharp-sighted as ferrets, and as active as squirrels', as a British officer put it.[1] Coburg was narrowly defeated by Jourdan at Fleurus, and the allied armies began to retreat away from each other: the British and Dutch to cover Holland, the Austrians eastwards.

The Dutch people now proved receptive to French ideals of liberty and equality and to the French army that bore them forward. Great Dutch fortresses fell with lamentable ease. The British army was in a state of moral collapse, partly alcoholic. There was heavy rain and bitter frost. A third of the British army was sick. York, who had done his not inconsiderable best, was recalled to take the public blame. Early in 1795 the campaign in Holland came to an end with incessant French attacks, the continued fall of Dutch fortresses, and the final dissolution of the

British and German forces. Walmoden, the Hanoverian commander, wrote encouragingly to York: 'Your army is destroyed;
the officers, their carriages, and a large train are safe, but the men
are destroyed.'[2] At last the government took the decision to evacuate. Fifteen thousand demoralized individuals eventually went on
board the transports at Bremen. The British, as islanders, could
make good their escape like this; the Hanoverians and the Austrians
could not. The Hanoverians did not regard the British evacuation
as comradely. The Prussians, for their part, prudently made peace
with France.

In 1796, Napoleon Bonaparte, now commanding the French
Army of Italy, swept the Austrians out of northern Italy in a series
of brilliant tactical and strategic improvisations. In 1797 Austria
signed the Peace of Campo Formio, by which she yielded Belgium,
Lombardy and the Rhine frontier to the French Republic. The
first coalition had collapsed. The Spaniards and the Dutch now
declared war on Britain, stretching British sea-power to the utmost
again. Britain was forced to evacuate the Mediterranean. Only
Britain and Portugal stayed in the war against revolutionary
France. Britain's overtures for peace, based on the customary
eighteenth-century kind of swaps, were brushed aside. Pitt's short
and limited war had turned into a single-handed life-and-death
struggle. On the one hand there was the anomalous and ramshackle
old structure of the British state, and the patchwork of individual-
istic privilege that made up British society; on the other the ruthless centralized leadership of France, sustained by the national will.

*

Never since the Commonwealth had Britain sent a battle-worthy
expeditionary force to Europe at the beginning of a conflict. The
failure was a necessary result of British suspicion of military
institutions in peacetime. All British wars opened in unreadiness
and improvisation. Nevertheless, the army that campaigned in
Flanders and Holland in 1793–5 had been peculiarly awful. The
Duke of York's Adjutant-General wrote to a colleague at home:

That we have plundered the whole country is unquestionable; that we
are the most undisciplined, the most ignorant, the worst provided army

that ever took the field is equally certain: but we are not to blame for it ... there is not a young man in the Army that cares one farthing whether his commanding officer, the brigadier or the commander-in-chief approves his conduct or not. His promotion depends not on their smiles or frowns. His friends [i.e. family] can give him a thousand pounds with which to go to the auction rooms in Charles Street and in a fortnight he becomes a captain. Out of fifteen regiments of cavalry and twenty-six of infantry which we have here, twenty-one are commanded literally by boys or idiots ... we do not know how to post a picquet or instruct a sentinel in his duty; and as to moving, God forbid that we should attempt it within three miles of an enemy.[3]

Subsequent opinion has generally agreed with this view of the evil effects of the purchase system. Purchase disconnected what should have been an essential relationship between merit and rank. Another pernicious contemporary system of promotion – that of rewarding successful recruitment by rank – also created officers lacking knowledge or capacity. From Marlborough's day through to the Waterloo campaign the general professional standard of British officers, senior and junior, received a bad press from British and foreign critics. Keen professionals like Wolfe and Amherst always formed an embattled minority. However, the purchase system had gradually altered in its effects during the eighteenth century. The regiments had become less and less their colonels' own 'private enterprises', although the colonel still clothed his own regiment under government supervision. Purchase therefore ceased to mean the purchase of a profitable business; rather, because of government economy, officers often found it necessary to contribute to the support of their units out of their own pay. Private means gradually became more and more essential to an officer. Rather than an investment, purchase became the *entrée* to (and means to pursuit of) a fashionable and exciting career for young men of the aristocracy and gentry. The very conception of a 'gentleman' had itself altered. The country gentry were ceasing to speak with the accent of their shire, or educate their children at the local grammar school. A gentleman now was not simply a person of a certain rank and property, but a distinct type. It was the change from Squire Western to Mr Darcy. A new ideal of manners and polish, of a caste apart, had percolated down from the grandees. By the 1790s the purchase system was providing the British officer corps not merely with gentry, but with gentlemen.

However, the separate 'army' run by the Board of Ordnance (the Royal Artillery and the Royal Engineers) continued to promote without purchase, and continued to have a strong careerist and technical flavour. Similar types of officer, without family or fortune, were indeed still to be found in the infantry and cavalry as well, especially during the swift expansion of the Napoleonic wars. However, Wellington himself had a strong prejudice in favour of gentlemen. As Commander-in-Chief at home after the wars, he was to lend his weight to the final domination of the officer corps by gentlemen, by the rich, with their code of manners and their professional – or rather non-professional – outlook.

The performance of British officers during the Napoleonic wars presents a paradox. Critics of purchase and the gentlemanly amateur cannot ignore that the British army outfought the French, by repute the most formidable of all contemporary armies. Nor can critics ignore the further fact that some of the most notably able British soldiers of the time were aristocrats. It is dangerous therefore to generalize about the effects of purchase. Bearing in mind the kind of criticism Wellington himself made of his officers and his reluctance to delegate much to their independent judgement, the guess might be hazarded that while the general standard of the British officer corps was well below that of the French, a minority of officers was so good as to be able to carry the rest – at least, under a general of Wellington's calibre.

Throughout the conflict the British higher machinery of war remained much what it had been under Anne.* In 1794 Pitt made the one major innovation by creating a full Secretaryship of State responsible for military affairs. However, the first Secretary of State for War, Henry Dundas, was also Home Secretary, Treasurer of the Navy and President of the Indian Board of Control. He could thus hardly perform the work of a Louvois. The Secretary-*at*-War remained the executive head of military administration;

* See A. H. Burne, *The Noble Duke of York* and Richard Glover, *Peninsular Preparation* for British military administration in the Napoleonic era.

his department, the War Office, controlled movements, establishments, rates of pay, while he also had to answer to Parliament for the cost of the army and settle disputes arising from the clash of civil and military interests (as over quartering). The Secretary-at-War did not, of course, administer the Ordnance Department or the ordnance forces (Royal Artillery and Royal Engineers), which still fell under the separate empire of the Master-General of the Ordnance. The Master-General himself was a soldier, but sat in Parliament as a civilian minister, where he answered for the Ordnance Department. His empire was itself divided into a civilian side – a source of supply and munitions to both army and navy – and the military side, the other 'army' of artillery and engineers, which he commanded as a soldier.

The Master-General until 1795, Charles Lennox, Duke of Richmond, was an able and energetic administrator. He reorganized the financial system and drew a logical division between civilian and military personnel; created a Royal Corps of Artificers (a building construction corps) and a Royal Corps of Artillery Drivers to replace civilian gun teams. He founded the British Horse Artillery and the Ordnance Survey. Under his administration the problems of shortage of ammunition and powder were solved. Powder manufactured in the government mills at Faversham and Waltham Abbey eventually supplied three-fifths of the nation's requirements, at a lower cost than through private contracts. Richmond also instigated research that led to a more efficient gunpowder.

Control over the army itself (cavalry and infantry) was still partitioned between Secretary-at-War, the Treasury, and the Commander-in-Chief. In 1795 the King's son, the Duke of York, unlucky commander in the Flanders campaign, became Commander-in-Chief in the place of Amherst, the now senile conqueror of Canada. The Commander-in-Chief was now for the first time provided with a proper headquarters staff (at the Horse-Guards). This in itself tended to limit the responsibility of the Secretary-at-War to financial matters. Although young, York was a devoted professional soldier. Since radical structural reform was politically and practically impossible, York instead intelligently improved what existed. His prestige as a royal duke lent weight to his instructions and example.

York tried to ensure that despite purchase and recruiting for rank, all officers were professionally competent. New candidates for commissions were required to produce recommendations by a field officer. No man could purchase the rank of captain until after two years' service as a subaltern, nor purchase the rank of major until after six years' service as an officer. By setting the lowest age for an ensign's commission at sixteen, York ended the abuse of infant officers. He began the system of periodic confidential reports on officers. He promoted indigent but talented officers by keeping a list from which he could make selections for commands to which purchase did not apply. The founding of the Royal Military College in 1802 to train young men as subalterns in a Junior Department (later the Royal Military College, Sandhurst), and older officers in staff duties in a Senior Department (later the Staff College, Camberley) also owed itself to York's support.

However, the system of confidential reports and of recommendations for a commission by field officers eventually tended to have an unlooked-for effect. Officers brought forward men on personal and social grounds as well as professional. Gentlemen tended to choose gentlemen. The web of family connexion became perpetuated. After the war, under Wellington, the choice of gentlemen was to become more conscious and deliberate.

York completed Cumberland's work in establishing standard procedures and fixed channels of command and communication. The functions of the Adjutant-General swelled in importance. Recruitment, the clothing and arming of troops, field exercises and discipline, and the interior administration of regiments, were brought under centralized regulation. The Military Secretary, a post created in 1793, became the channel of all business relating to promotion and appointments. This was another aspect in which the importance of the Secretary-at-War declined during the war.

Scope for reform in discipline and what is now known as 'man-management' was limited by the nature of the human material in the British ranks. In the new French army conscription had raised the general level of intelligence and self-reliance. This allowed a much lighter rein, and an intimate and informal relationship between officers and men. By contrast, the British army did not reflect the balance of British society. Since the restrictions on recruitment of Catholic Irish had been removed in the 1780s, there had been a flood of Irish peasants – to the extent that the Commander-in-Chief hesitated to send troops to Ireland in 1797 to put down the feared rebellion because whole regiments were full of Irish. Although the Irish were hardy and brave, they were also ignorant, mad for drink, violent, and without self-discipline. The jails of England continued to yield the army their drunks, felons, debtors and psychopaths. There was a leavening of 'respectable' and intelligent men in the ranks who had enlisted because of some single social lapse, like getting a girl with child, and of men who chose a soldier's life either for the bounty or delusions of military glory, or for other reasons not readily apparent.

Only later in the war did the 'respectable' working class join the army in large numbers via the militia. For there was little reason for men of solid background or character to wish to join the army in normal times. In the 1790s a soldier's gross pay was raised from the 8*d.* a day first established under the Commonwealth to 1*s.* Although his country now provided him with bread, he was expected to buy the rest of his food, as well as the pipe-clay to whiten his equipment, and other articles. Deductions from gross pay left him just over 18*s.* net per annum. This may be compared with the bricklayer's 3*s.* 9*d.* a day. This was in an age of soaring inflation. Soldiers cried in their bunks from hunger they could not afford to appease; they deserted in the desperation of starvation. The general quality of British soldiers and officers alike was the price the nation paid for an army that was cheap and offered no danger of subverting the constitution.

This army was kept in its ranks by the lash – and not always then. Sentences of 1,000 lashes and more were not uncommon. Later opinion has been shocked by the fearsome severity of these flayings. However, in the context of an age of brutality, where in civilian life children were hanged or transported for petty theft, military flogging was not so specially cruel as it may appear in retrospect. That it was absolutely essential to prevent the army dissolving into a criminal mob was believed not only by generals like Wellington, but by those members of the rank-and-file who were themselves of good character and background. James Anton, quarter-master-sergeant of the 42nd Highlanders, wrote:

Philanthropists, who decry the lash ought to consider in what manner the good men – the deserving, exemplary soldiers – are to be protected; if no coercive measures are to be resorted to in purpose to prevent ruthless ruffians from insulting with immunity the temperate, the well-inclined, and the orderly-disposed, the good must be left to the mercy of the worthless ... [4]

John Stevenson, author of *A Soldier in Time of War*, had had some experience of soldiering, for he described his career on his title page as 'Forty years a Wesleyan Class Leader, twenty-one years in the British Foot Guards, Sixteen a Non-Commissioned Officer'. 'They talk of the lash,' he wrote ,'I never was any more afraid of the lash than I was of the gibbet, no man ever comes to that but through his own conduct ... '.[5]

The obverse of the stoical courage on a bloody field like Albuera, or of the silence and stillness of a British line waiting to fire, was the animal violence of the sacks of captured fortress towns. Those carnivals of drink, rape, robbery and blind destruction were illustrations of what the British soldier was capable of once he slipped the iron chains of brutal discipline. It was the considered retrospective opinion of one private on Wellington's harsh regime that: '...the army...could not be kept in the order so essential to its well-being if some examples had not been made ... such punishments are necessary to deter others'.[6] The more humane methods of Sir John Moore are always held up for admiration, but on the retreat to Corunna in 1808–9 it was floggers like Crauford who held their own units together, when Moore's appeals to the soldiers' better nature had failed. Only in the light infantry (which Moore had trained) was less severe discipline successfully applied.

If there was little York felt able to do with discipline, it was otherwise with training. He put the weight of his authority behind compliance with Dundas's infantry-training manual, and he laid down through his Adjutant-General an army training programme.

In 1795, Dundas's later manual for the cavalry was distributed to all cavalry regiments.

The cavalry presented a particular problem. In a country whose land was divided up among jealous freeholders there was no space to train *en masse* in large-scale evolutions. Nor had there ever been any training in the use of the sword, and in Flanders British cavalry had tended to cut up their own horses' heads instead of the enemy. Colonel Le Marchant (who was responsible for the original scheme for the Royal Military College) filled the gap with his *The Rules and Regulations for the Attainment and Practice of the Sword Exercise*. It was printed by York's order in 1797 and all cavalry officers were required to have a copy. York sent Le Marchant himself on tours of instruction. The cavalry inherited the feudal and cavalier tradition; it was the arm of fashion and wealth. Its officers, although brave to the point of foolhardiness, too often affected a careless and arrogant nonchalance towards the duller aspects of their work. In 1826 Wellington was to reflect that his cavalry had been useful 'first ... upon advanced guards, flanks etc. as the quickest movers and enable me to know and see as much as possible in the shortest space of time; secondly, to use them in small bodies to attack small bodies of the enemy's cavalry'. But 'they would gallop ... could not preserve their order'. Wellington thought them

so inferior ... to the French [that] although I consider one squadron a match for two French squadrons ... I should not have liked to see four British squadrons opposed to four French squadrons; and as numbers increased, and order of course became more necessary, I was more unwilling to risk our cavalry without having a greater superiority of numbers.[7]

York and others thought that Dundas had unduly neglected light infantry. He had felt their lack in Flanders in the face of the swarming French skirmishers. In 1797 he began to reform the light troops of the British army. As a first step he issued instructions that commanding officers were to take out the light companies of their regiments on separate training exercises and shooting practice. In March 1798 his able Assistant-Adjutant-General, Sir Harry Calvert, submitted a memorandum on the formation of special 'corps of Light Troops'. In the summer a trial exercise was held in Essex of a combined experimental unit of light infantry, light cavalry and horse artillery. It was the germ of the Light Division that performed so well and so usefully in the Peninsula. In 1803 the threat of French invasion forced the concentration of the army in large units in southern England, which helped training. York took the opportunity to appoint Sir John Moore to train the troops in Shorncliffe Camp. Moore, like Wolfe, was to ensure his own legend by dying at the climax of his first campaign as an army commander. It is probable that Moore's reputation likewise exceeds his talents or achievements. The credit for creating the light troops of the Peninsular War belongs to several, including York. Moore's ideas on light-infantry training and tactics derived largely from a book by a German officer. The book, by Major-General Baron de Rottenburg, was published in English translation in 1798 under the title *Regulations for the Exercise of Riflemen and Light Infantry*. Moore himself acknowledged that he used de Rottenburg as 'the ground-work, noting in the margin whatever changes we make from him'.[8] What Moore supplied were the personal powers of leadership of a great trainer of troops.

It was York, too, who in 1800 called 'for the formation of a Corps of Riflemen by detachments to be returned to their Corps when properly trained'.[9] While these men were gathered for training in Windsor Forest, they were called on in a body to join an expedition to Ferrol. They went as an *ad hoc* regiment, and stayed together afterwards as the 95th Foot, which later gained two more battalions. In 1816 its three rifle battalions were, as the *Gazette* put it, 'taken out of the numbered regiments of the line and styled THE RIFLE BRIGADE'.[10]

The *Jäger* of Germany and Austria had used rifles in the Seven Years' War, as had their emigrant cousins in the Royal Americans. They were all irregular troops, really foresters using hunting rifles made by craftsmen. The muzzle-loading rifle fired more accurately than the smooth-bore musket and at longer ranges, although its rate of fire was slower owing to the difficulty of ramming the ball down the rifling.

The formation of the British 95th Foot followed competitive

tests at Woolwich Arsenal of European, American and British rifles. The Ordnance Board selected the British Baker rifle as giving the best balance of qualities for service in the field. It shot accurately up to ranges of 200 yards and beyond. The ball was wrapped in a patch of oiled leather to engage with the rifling. At first a wooden mallet was provided to tap the ball and patch home, but was soon found to be unnecessary. The riflemen of the 95th were dressed in *Jäger* green, a precursor of khaki as a camouflage in the field. In the Peninsula, British skirmishers with rifles dominated the French *tirailleurs* and *voltigeurs* that had so confused European troops.

There was not much weapon-training in the infantry of the line. The annual training allowance of ammunition was thirty ball and sixty blanks – hardly enough to produce phenomenal musketry. Since the flintlock musket was inaccurate and misfired twice out of five shots, it followed that volleys had to be delivered at point-blank range to kill. It has been calculated that during Wellington's crushing victory at Vittoria only one musket-ball out of every 459 issued took effect.[11]

The bayonet is an essential part of military legend, not only in Britain but elsewhere, especially in France. In fact a bayonet charge was more intimidating than lethal. It was the opinion of a surgeon who served in the Peninsula that

Opposing regiments when formed in line and charging with fixed bayonets, *never* meet and struggle hand to hand and foot to foot; and this for the best possible reason, that one side turns and runs away as soon as the other comes close enough to do mischief.[12]

In any case, there was little training in the use of the bayonet in Britain.

The Duke of York resigned as Commander-in-Chief in 1809 after a campaign to ruin him by his ex-mistress Mary Anne Clarke and others. Mary Anne had tricked men into giving her large sums of money on the assumption that she could and would influence her lover to award them commissions or promotion. The Duke's traducers accused him of conniving at and profiting from this traffic. A prolonged public inquiry completely cleared him of these charges. In fact no promotions or commissions followed Mary

Anne's promises. Although York's resignation was a very great loss, his work of reform was largely complete. Wellington himself summed up York's achievement in evidence to the public inquiry:

I know that since his Royal Highness has had the command of the army, the regulations framed by him for managing the promotion of the army have been strictly adhered to, and that the mode in which promotion is conducted has given general satisfaction ... the officers are improved in knowledge; that the staff of the army is better than it was ... and everything that relates to the military discipline of the army has been greatly improved since His Royal Highness was appointed Commander-in-Chief.[13]

However, the internal reforms carried out by York inside the army and Richmond inside the Ordnance Department could not put right the fundamental weakness of British military organization: the division of high responsibility between Secretary-*for*-War, Secretary-*at*-War, Treasury, Commander-in-Chief and Master-General of the Ordnance.

Such a 'system' had worked against Louis XIV because William III and later Marlborough in their own persons had supplied the unifying and directing force. Marlborough united in himself, as Captain-General and later Master-General of the Ordnance, authority over both the army and the Ordnance Department. Through his friend and devoted colleague Godolphin at the Treasury, he could largely command the Treasury's part in the military effort. He was virtually war-lord over diplomacy and grand strategy. No equivalent of Marlborough existed during the Napoleonic wars. Neither a person, nor an organization united the disparate sections of the British war machine, nor gave a single direction to strategy. The war against Napoleon was therefore less well organized and directed than the war against Louis XIV.

*

After 1797, Britain was left struggling on her own but for Portugal, and without a toehold in Europe except at Lisbon. France now occupied Holland, which had become the puppet Batavian Republic, and Belgium, which was incorporated into France; the Rhineland, and northern Italy. The Mediterranean was a French lake. The French Republic had achieved in five years of war what the old French monarchy had failed to achieve in two hundred years of wars. The British Isles themselves were directly threatened. As in 1689–90, Ireland was a point of weakness. French promises of armed assistance found ready ears among Irish who dreamed of an independent Ireland. In 1797 a small French force landed in south Wales and was rounded up by the Pembroke militia. British ministers pondered with alarm the consequences of such a landing in Ireland. French invasion preparations in Channel and North Sea ports might be aimed at either Ireland or Britain itself.

In 1798 the Irish broke into full, but as it happened, premature rebellion. The rebels enjoyed early successes against the militia, but were beaten and dispersed by General Lake and regular troops at Vinegar Hill before French help could arrive. When the small French force of 900 men under General Humbert landed, it found itself without an Irish rebellion to support. After beating off General Lake at Castlebar, it was surrounded and forced to surrender.

Defensive isolation was the price Britain was now paying for inability to send a large and well-found army to Europe in 1793. Without a continental army it was impossible to have a continental policy. Reduced now to sea-power alone Britain was like a shark fighting a lion. As long as the lion did not venture on the water, it was hard to see how to get at him. But what if the lion, with all the shipyards of Europe at his disposal, should eventually build a greater fleet? Nevertheless Pitt and the solid squires behind him were tenacious enough. They hung on. In 1798 Napoleon Bonaparte, now a member of the French Directorate and France's leading military commander, took to the sea with extraordinary visions of conquering an empire in the East from a base in Egypt. It was Britain's opportunity. The Royal Navy re-entered the Mediterranean; a squadron under Nelson found Napoleon's fleet in Aboukir Bay and destroyed it. Napoleon's army was marooned in Egypt. Sea-power enabled Britain to extend her influence in the Mediterranean once again, for Minorca was taken, and the kingdom of Sicily brought into the war. The news of the battle of the Nile created the Second Coalition against France.

The year 1799 brought high promise. The Austrians swept the French out of northern Italy. An Austrian–Russian army under old Suvorov invaded French-held Switzerland. The British contributed 12,000 men (a small fraction of the coalition) to a joint British and Russian expedition to the Helder Peninsula in Holland. Once again, however, Pitt and his colleagues fatally dispersed the available British land forces. There were plans (for which 80,000 troops were held back) for middling-sized expeditions to Walcheren, Belleisle, Cadiz, and Tenerife; later again to Brest and the mouth of the Seine. Ministers constantly changed their minds. In the end two expeditions took place, to Ferrol and Cadiz, neither of which damaged the enemy.

Meanwhile in Holland the Duke of York and the Russians conducted an unhappy campaign in country so cut up by water as to be ideal for the defence, which was energetically led by Brune, the French commander in Holland. This campaign too ended in failure and re-embarkation.

Meanwhile Napoleon had returned from Egypt without his army. France swung furiously to the counter-offensive. Suvorov was thrown out of Switzerland by Soult. At Marengo in June 1800 Napoleon smashed the Austrian army of Italy in a near-run battle whose balance might very probably – even certainly – have been swung by only a few thousand of the British troops standing about in England waiting to go on a day trip to the French coast. Moreau broke the Austrian army in Germany at Hohenlinden. The Second Coalition fell apart. Spain invaded Portugal and deprived Britain of that toe-hold. As a consolation prize, the British took Malta from the French.

In February 1801 Austria made another humiliating peace at Lunéville. Britain was once more left on her own.

The Second Coalition failed because of British government strategy, not because of want of readiness in the forces. Historical tradition led Pitt and his colleagues to think that the mobility of sea-power meant tip-and-run raids, instead of the capacity to land a major force at some single place where the enemy least wants it or expects it. At the very end of the episode of the Second Coalition, the British stumbled on the correct use of sea-power. The fleet conveyed an army under Sir Ralph Abercromby to Egypt where it fought and beat the marooned French at the battle of Aboukir. It was the first victory of the army that the Duke of York had re-built. However, the Near East had already become a strategic backwater.

There was consolation too from India, where Marquis Wellesley, a governor-general of Roman ambition, set about the expansion

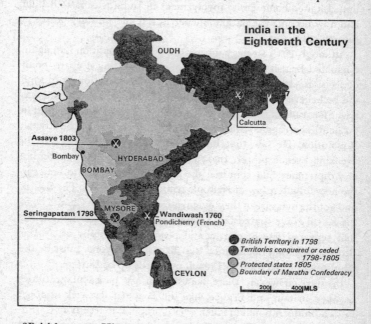

India in the Eighteenth Century

OUDH

Calcutta

Assaye 1803

Bombay

HYDERABAD

BOMBAY

MADRAS

Seringapatam 1798

MYSORE

Wandiwash 1760
Pondicherry (French)

● *British Territory in 1798*
◉ *Territories conquered or ceded 1798-1805*
○ *Protected states 1805*
○ *Boundary of Maratha Confederacy*

CEYLON

200   400 MLS

of British power. His younger brother, Arthur Wellesley, saw to the military aspects of imperial assertion. Once again the indirect enemy in India was France, the new revolutionary France. She had sent agents, money and later small numbers of troops to Indian potentates, including Tippoo Sahib, Sultan of Mysore. In 1799 a British army under Colonel Arthur Wellesley (aged twenty-nine) made a brilliantly organized march to Tippoo's capital, Seringapatam, and destroyed his army during a successful siege in which Tippoo himself was killed. With Mysore eliminated,

Hyderabad too became a British puppet-state. Later, in 1803, the Governor-General was to turn his attention to the Mahratta Confederacy, one of the most formidable of Indian military powers. Once more Arthur Wellesley (now a major-general) took the field. In a major battle at Assaye in 1803, Wellesley with 7,000 men smashed a well-drilled and equipped native army of 40,000. Two years later the Grand Moghul himself accepted British protection. Limited commercial involvement in India was past: Britain had now become the paramount territorial and military power in the sub-continent.

Although Pitt's strategy during the Second Coalition had again dissipated British strength instead of concentrating it at the point of decision – Italy – Pitt was gradually learning. No longer in 1798 did he believe that the British role was secondary; nor that this was a war for trade of the old kind. He saw that Britain was engaged in a relentless struggle with the ideals and the power of the French Revolution. He saw that Britain must play the leading role in breaking French power. In 1798 it was Pitt who by his subsidies and diplomacy had conjured the Second Coalition into being in the hopeful afterglow of Nelson's triumph at the Nile. The British had got the measure of their enemy now. The English Channel and the Royal Navy spared them the massive onset of French armies, that repeated fate of continental powers. Geography as well as British resolution determined that Britain, if anyone, must be the mainstay of opposition to French overlordship of Europe.

In 1802, however, there was a delusory pause in hostilities between Britain and France, like the Peace of Ryswick in 1697. Pitt's administration had fallen over a proposal to free Irish Catholics from Stuart penal laws and his successor, Addington, concluded peace by the Treaty of Amiens.

*

In Napoleon Bonaparte as First Consul and later (in 1804) as Emperor, all the dynamic energies released by the Revolution found a director able to channel them into the service of his own boundless personal ambitions. Bonaparte's talents – his intellectual calibre, his ruthless will, his administrative and military genius –

impressed and intimidated foreigners and French alike. The flaws in his character – the insatiable ambition and the egotism – would reveal themselves later. In 1800–1804 the unleashed powers of the Revolution and the talents of the new dictator seemed terribly well-matched.

The evolution of the French revolutionary army was now completed. Conscription provided 80,000 recruits a year. When Napoleon became Emperor, his army numbered 500,000 men. Casualties thus ceased to be of great importance. Massive onslaughts to produce quick results, no matter the cost – this was the foundation of the new method of waging war. Such great masses could no longer march as a single column, but were divided into independent army corps, which followed separate routes on the march, only to unite before the chosen battlefield was reached, or on the battlefield itself. The heavy cavalry was grouped in a separate corps. Massed guns under the direction of the army commander became a decisive instrument of victory instead of an adjunct to the other arms. Guns supplied the destructive effect on enemy infantry in place of the old close-range musket volleys, for the French infantry (despite Guibert and the official regulations) tended more and more to neglect their own fire-power. They attacked with the bayonet in column, relying on momentum and impact to smash through enemy lines already torn in holes by the guns. The handy battalion columns of the Republican era were replaced by ever more massive formations, and the initiative of subordinate commanders suffered accordingly. In 1799 Napoleon as First Consul founded the Guard, of 2,000 men. By 1813 the Guard was to grow to an *élite* army-within-the-army of eight infantry divisions – 72,000 men.

In 1803 the Peace of Amiens foundered in British suspicions of Napoleon's good intentions and general trustworthiness. The colossal engine of French power was turned directly against Great Britain. British resistance alone now stood between Napoleon and unchallenged enjoyment of empire over Europe. Britain – and British gold – was a standing encouragement to countries like Austria who were restless under French domination. So Napoleon decided to crush Britain like other powers by direct invasion. There was the preliminary problem of getting the *Grande Armée* across the Channel. For two years Napoleon devoted his great executive powers to organizing a fleet of transports. He applied his strategic skill to the problem of getting the British fleet out of the Channel while the combined French and Spanish fleets convoyed the French army over. In Britain it was a time of heroic exertions and occasional invasion scares. The measures adopted by the Elizabethan government in 1588 were examined for useful tips. The citizens of a nation that detested armies flowered into the fanciful uniforms of volunteers, fencibles and militia. Their capacity to help the regular army to defeat the victors of Marengo was never put to the test, thanks, as in 1588, to the Royal Navy. At the denouement of Napoleon's maritime combinations and diversions the French fleet found the Channel not empty but covered by the concentrated naval forces of the British.

Meanwhile Pitt (again Prime Minister) had been patiently trying to create another coalition. He was able to reach an understanding, later an alliance, with Russia. Austria hung back – until Napoleon imposed a fresh humiliation she found herself unable to bear. He had himself crowned King of Italy as well as Emperor of the French, thus expunging Austrian influence from Italy as well as from Germany.

Austrian belligerence put an end to Napoleon's plan of invasion. By 1 September 1805 the invasion camps were empty: 200,000 men were making forced marches eastwards across Europe to destroy the resurgent Austrians and their Russian allies. Although Nelson's victory at Trafalgar on 21 October may have finally relieved the British from anxiety about French invasion, it was without relevance to Napoleon's already implemented decision to abandon the present invasion attempt; it was also without the least effect on the subsequent land campaigns of the Third Coalition. These were fought without aid from Britain except in guineas. Despite plans for an Anglo-Russian landing in Hanover, the British army remained locked in the home island until too late. By his speed Napoleon was able to force the surrender of one main body of the Austrians at Ulm before the Russians could join them. He occupied Vienna itself and marched on to meet the Russians and the remnants of the Austrians in Bohemia. At Austerlitz 73,000 Frenchmen utterly routed 85,700 Russians and Austrians after a grim battle.

In December 1805 Austria made another, even more humiliating, peace with France at Pressburg, which robbed her of three million subjects. The Third Coalition was broken. In 1806 Prussia foolishly declared war on France when it was too late to join an allied combination. The military machine of Frederick the Great, which had degenerated into a mechanical toy of parade drill under aged commanders, was shattered at Jena and Auerstädt. In 1807, after two bloody battles at Eylau and Friedland, Napoleon imposed a humiliating peace on Russia too. The French triumph seemed final and complete. Only a completely successful combined operation by the British redeemed the gloom. The navy landed the army near Copenhagen, and the army marched to capture most of the Danish fleet frozen in at its moorings.

Pitt died in January 1806. After a short ministry Charles James Fox too died. The war against Napoleon fell henceforth into the hands of governments headed by run-of-the-mill politicians and political aristocrats, who in fact waged it rather better than Pitt. But in 1807 it was not easy to see how to prosecute the war. The lion and the shark faced once more the baffling problem of how to get to grips. Mutual blockade, the one closing Europe off from the markets and raw materials of the world and the other closing off Europe to British manufacturers, seemed the only and self-destructive answer. In 1806–7 British naval and military power was employed in such oblique attempts to harm Napoleon as attacking the South American empire of his Spanish ally. Although Montevideo was taken, an assault on Buenos Aires was beaten off in rout, serving only to decorate the cathedral of Buenos Aires with British colours.

However, Napoleon could not keep still or rest content. In 1808 he deposed the Spanish king and placed his brother Joseph on the throne of Spain by trickery. The Spaniards rose spontaneously in revolt. For the first time the forces awakened by the French Revolution – the passions of the mass of a nation – reacted against them. For the first time the French were fighting not merely a monarchy and its paid army, but a people. At last the British were offered the opportunity of intervening effectively on the Continent – and in a region where sea-power gave them better communications than the French could enjoy by land.

The command of the British expeditionary force of 13,000 men was given to Sir Arthur Wellesley, the returned victor of Assaye. Its purpose, in the words of the instruction written by Lord Castlereagh, the Secretary of State for War, was 'the final and absolute evacuation of the Peninsula by the troops of France'. It was an order that took six years to fulfil. The little army landed in French-occupied Portugal. Sir Arthur began promisingly by beating off French attacks at Vimiero with heavy loss. By the Convention of Cintra the French went home to France – in English ships. This feeble Convention was the product of the supercession of Wellesley by generals of ever increasing age and seniority as the British army in Portugal grew in size. When it reached some 40,000, another able commander was appointed – Sir John Moore, the one-time trainer of light infantry at Shorncliffe. Moore was instructed to take 30,000 of these troops and, in co-operation with the Spanish army, throw the French out of Spain.

The Spanish army seemed at that time a promising collaborator, for at Bailén it had surrounded and forced the surrender of a French army under Dupont, the first French surrender in the field for a decade. This defeat, together with British intervention, brought Napoleon himself across the Pyrenees with 250,000 men. For the first time the British army was in a position similar to that of the Austrian army on repeated occasions – exposed to the undiluted force of the Emperor's aggression.

Although Moore's command in Spain had been increased to 35,000 men, it was a small army by European standards. However, in the words of Canning, the Foreign Secretary, it was 'not merely a considerable part of the dispensable force of this country. It is, in fact, the British army.'[14]

That such should be the case after fifteen years of war was an illustration both of the government's dispersal of forces on random projects overseas and of the problems the government had faced in tapping British manpower. The population of Great Britain was

Supplementary-Militia, turning out for "Twenty Days Amusement";—"The French Invade us Hay?—damme, who's afraid?"

The Supplementary Militia (part-time local defence forces) failed to inspire confidence in their ability to repel the French army. A cartoon by Gillray, 1796.

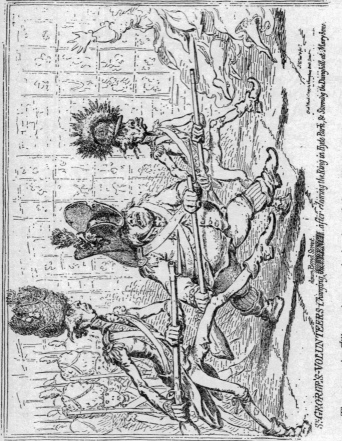

ST GEORGE'S-VOLUNTEERS! Charging down Bond Street, after Clearing the Ring in Hyde Park, & Storming the Dunghill at Marybone.

The cartoonist Gillray takes a sardonic view of the military worth of the volunteer movement, 1797. Here a gallant charge clears female shoppers from Bond Street.

now over eleven millions, twice what it had been in Marlborough's day, yet the available field army was smaller. There was plenty of military zeal and spirit in Britain, not least during the invasion threats of 1797–8 and 1803–5; but it did not extend to joining the regular army, or to the creation of a straightforward system of a field army and a reserve army (for home defence and as a reservoir of trained men), both based on universal conscription. The very fact that conscription was the French system made it less, not more, attractive; universal military service, an ancient English tradition and obligation, now appeared as an aspect of Jacobin democracy or Napoleonic tyranny. The gentry and the middle classes poured their military enthusiasm into the rivals of the regular army – the militia and the volunteers, which were both under local control. The lower orders – increasingly restless under revolutionary ideas and the sharpening industrial and agricultural revolutions – rioted in 1796, as in 1757, at mere apprehension of the conscription of militiamen for foreign service. The intensely localized nature of British administration and the amateur, part-time manning of its machinery made it hard enough to raise and organize the militia, let alone operate full conscription.

Since 1793 therefore, successive Secretaries of State for War and their governments had struggled ingeniously with a variety of fancy systems for getting men directly into the regular army, or out of the militia and into the army. There was bitter and traditional resistance to any reform that seemed to aim at making the militia a reserve force to the army, rather than the present independent and equal military institution. A variety of separate 'armies' grew up in Britain. The volunteers were privately raised and paid by patriotic associations. Their heyday was during the invasion threats; they faded away after 1805. They drained off manpower from the militia. The militia was itself eventually divided into the 'Old Militia', embodied for the duration, and therefore virtually a home army, and the 'New Militia', an extra force only to be called on for emergencies. The militia drained off manpower that might have gone into the regular army. Then there were the 'fencibles' – new regular regiments, but raised for the duration only and for home service only – which also competed for manpower. It was

hardly surprising that with all these alternatives to dying of fever in
the West Indies or on a battlefield, the regular army lacked recruits.

It was Castlereagh, the first really able War Secretary, who
during and after 1806 abandoned the haphazard structure of fancy
recruiting measures piled up by his predecessors. He tried as far
as was politically and socially possible to turn the militia into a
straightforward army of reserve and a reservoir of trained men for

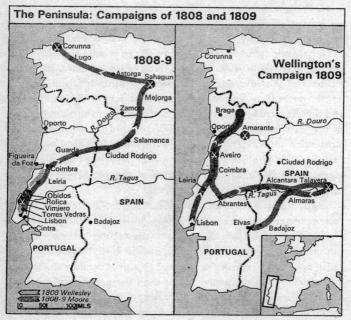

The Peninsula: Campaigns of 1808 and 1809

the regulars. He called on the militia to furnish 28,000 volunteers
for the line in 1806 and got most of them; in 1809 he was able to
get another 28,000; in 1811 his successor Lord Palmerston got
over 11,000. Since the adult male population was compelled to
serve in the militia if balloted (normally only in the part-time
'Local Militia') Castlereagh's system was a further step towards
true conscription. During the remainder of the war some forty per
cent of army recruits came from the militia. The regular forces
rose eventually to 237,000 men at home and abroad.

Napoleon's intention in 1808 was to sweep across the Iberian Peninsula to Lisbon and deal with the Spaniards and the impudent English in one of his single, swift strokes. Napoleon never liked long, patient campaigns. However, after he reached Madrid he learned that Sir John Moore's small army was across his single main line of communication with France and threatening an isolated French corps under Soult. Instead of continuing westwards to Lisbon, Napoleon marched furiously northwards to destroy Moore. Moore got away just in time and began a long retreat to the port of Corunna. It was a retreat in appalling conditions of winter weather and hunger, and it broke the discipline and cohesion of all but a few units of Moore's army. Napoleon left the tedious pursuit to Soult. Nevertheless the army was able to stand at bay at Corunna, and by defeating Soult's attack, get safely aboard its transports for home. The British success on the battlefield itself did not render an evacuation a victory. In Britain there was harsh criticism of Moore despite his hero's death in battle. However, by drawing Napoleon away from his main objective and causing a fatal delay and dislocation in French plans, Moore saved the Spanish cause from immediate extinction.

Meanwhile Sir Arthur Wellesley* had been returned to the command of the troops in the Peninsula. It was probably fortunate that he rather than Moore fought the Peninsular War. Moore was a prim, priggish, prickly Scot, whose relations with such worldly people as politicians were bad. Wellington was an aristocrat, a broadminded man of the world, who had been a Member of Parliament and had served as Chief Secretary in Ireland. His relations with the government at home were generally excellent, despite his battles with it over particular questions. He and Castlereagh enjoyed special accord. As a soldier, too, Wellington was very different from Moore; an iron disciplinarian where Moore had been something of the scoutmaster; a stronger character with a cooler nerve. He was also a patient, longheaded practical strategist. Above all, Wellington was a master of the problems of supply and movement over long distances in barren country; this he had

* Wellesley became Lord Wellington in 1810 and Duke of Wellington in 1814. In this narrative he will henceforward be referred to as 'Wellington'.

learned in India. The secret of his victories was not only to be found
in brisk orders on the battlefield but in dreary correspondence
about bullock-carts and mules.

The division of responsibility for the British land forces at home
(see pp. 238–9), extended to armies in the field.* Although the
Officer Commanding Royal Artillery was Wellington's artillery
adviser, he *commanded* the guns on behalf of the Master-General of the
Ordnance, not Wellington. Neither the artillery nor the ordnance
stores and transport 'belonged' to Wellington; nor did the Royal
Engineers, for the Commanding Royal Engineer was also responsible to the Master-General of the Ordnance. The Commissary-
General, who was supposed to meet the requirements of Wellington's
operations for food, forage and supply-transport, was responsible
and accountable to the Treasury. Even Wellington's own
principal staff officers, the Adjutant-General and the Quartermaster-General, were by the custom of the time appointed as
delegates from their departments at home to the army commanded
by Wellington rather than to Wellington in person. They were free
to correspond about their own departmental matters directly with
superiors in London.

Such divided responsibilities, meeting in ill-defined or overlapping borderlands, were pregnant with disastrous muddle. As
with Marlborough on the higher plane of running a whole war, so
it was with Wellington in the more limited field of a theatre commander. It was his dominating character and talent alone that
made the 'system' work; that made him effectively the single un-
questioned head of the British military machine in the Peninsula.
It was his powerful mind and will that impelled every department,
and most vital of all, that of supply.

At first, the Treasury commissaries were little help, as Wellington bitterly complained: ' ... the existence of the army depends
upon it [the commissariat], and yet the people who manage it are
incapable of managing anything outside of a counting-house'.[15]
After 1810, however, he enjoyed the collaboration of a most

---

* S.G.P. Ward, *Wellington's Headquarters: A Study of the Administrative Problems
in the Peninsula 1809–1814* (Oxford University Press, 1957) is the best modern
work on the subject.

energetic and enterprising Commissary-General in Robert Kennedy.

Wellington was badly served by his engineering branch in all his sieges. Although the Ordnance Department supplied him with trained engineer officers, he enjoyed none of the lavish establishment of trained sappers and miners and all kinds of equipment that every French corps enjoyed. Wellington also had to improvise field intelligence and a network of spies, and have his own maps of the country made after survey.

In the course of five years of hard campaigning, the Peninsular army became a lean, hard, highly efficient force, with perfected organization and staff. This was not the result of radical innovation, but of Wellington's talent for inducing order and system, for gradual but always immediately practical improvement. By 1813–14 Sir George Murray, his Quartermaster-General, had become virtually a Chief of Staff in the modern sense, although strictly as a channel for plans and decisions emanating from Wellington alone. The organization of the army into divisions, a novelty in the British service in 1809, had progressed by 1814 almost to that of a century later, with all kinds of attached specialist troops, including signals, and only lacking cavalry. However, the unfussy efficiency of the British army which so impressed European soldiers in France after 1815 was only the product of a long war and of Wellington's personal powers of command; it did not stem from a reformed and sound military system.

In Spain, supply and transport formed the basis of Wellington's victories. Although the French had by no means abandoned supply by waggon trains and magazines, they depended very greatly on what they could strip from the country. Spain was not a good country for stripping. With that plain sagacity of his, Wellington put his finger on the French dilemma even before he landed in the Peninsula:

Buonaparte cannot carry on his operations in Spain, excepting by means of large armies; and I doubt much whether the country will afford subsistence for a large army, or if he will be able to supply his magazines from France, the roads being so bad and the communications so difficult.[16]

The French were also forced to disperse to hold down the Spanish people and to fight the implacable *guerrilleros*. By the end of 1809 Wellington was clear how he could in the end beat the French despite their numbers:

My opinion is, that as long as we shall remain in a state of activity in Portugal, the contest must continue in Spain; that the French are most desirous that we should withdraw from the country, but we know that they must employ a very large force indeed in the operations which will render it necessary for us to go away; and I doubt whether they can bring that force to bear upon Portugal without abandoning other objects, and exposing their whole fabric in Spain to great risk.[17]

Wellington himself at first faced major problems. The government at home only gradually came to see that the Peninsula was the one theatre where the British could apply continuous and effective pressure on the French. The government still hankered after the old strategy of descents on European coasts, and Moore's returned troops (except the Light Division) were not sent to reinforce Wellington, but on a fruitless and fever-stricken expedition to the island of Walcheren. Wellington, like Moore, discovered the unpredictable joys of collaborating with the Spaniards. After the campaign of 1809, when he narrowly escaped destruction by a successful fight against heavy odds at Talavera, Wellington refused to have anything further to do with Spanish plans or Spanish armies. He made his base in Portugal (which he had cleared for the second time in a brilliant stroke against Soult in Oporto). His colleague, William Carr Beresford, re-organized and trained the Portuguese army, which, when partly brigaded with the British, fought well.

In 1810 the Peninsular army was organized into five infantry divisions and the Light Division (which was a development of Sir John Moore's brigade at Shorncliffe), independent infantry brigades and army cavalry. A tenth of British strength was made up of Hanoverians from the King's Hanoverian army, dissolved by the French when Hanover was occupied in 1803. By 1812 the number of infantry divisions had risen to seven.

The history of the Peninsular War is of the gradual working out of the French strategic dilemma that Wellington had so acutely divined; of battles on well-chosen positions where Wellington's outnumbered army in line repulsed French attacks in column; and of the growth of confidence in Wellington and his campaign both among his own army (his officers were prone to croak) and at home.

Even before he landed in the Peninsula Wellington believed that the French system of assault in column would fail before the volleys

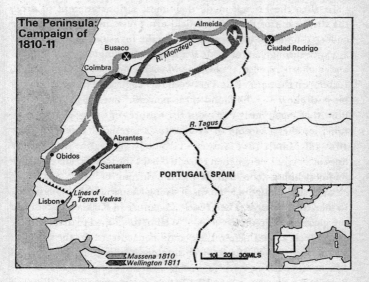

The Peninsula: Campaign of 1810-11

of steady infantry in line. And indeed in battle after battle Guibert's pre-war diagnosis of the weaknesses of the column (see p. 229) was exactly borne out. A French general described the typical collision of the French and British tactical systems:

... cries of '*Vive l'Empereur! En avant à la Baionette!*' broke from our mass. Some men hoisted their shakos on their musket, the quick-step became a run: the ranks began to be mixed up: the men's agitation became tumultuous, many soldiers began to fire as they ran. And all the while the red English line, still silent and motionless, even when we were only 300 yards away, seemed to take no notice of the storm which was about to break upon it. ... At this moment of painful expectation the English line would make a quarter-turn – the muskets were going up to the 'ready'. An indefinable sensation nailed to the spot many of our men, who halted and began to open a wavering fire. The enemy's return, a volley of simultaneous precision and deadly effect, crashed upon us like a thunderbolt. Decimated by it we reeled together ... Then three formidable *Hurrahs* terminated the long silence of our adversaries. With the third they were down upon us, pressing us into a disorderly retreat ...[18]

In 1810 the French made their most serious attempt to drive the British out of Portugal. A field army of some 70,000 men was collected together under Masséna for the invasion. After a painful advance through countryside stripped by Wellington of all supplies and a sharp repulse at Busaco, Masséna neared his destination, Lisbon, on the neck of land between the Tagus and the sea. Barring his path, however, he found three powerful lines of field fortifications that ingeniously exploited the features of a very difficult terrain; another example of Wellington's foresight. From October 1810 till March 1811 Masséna resolutely starved in front of the lines of Torres Vedras, then retreated back into Spain. His offensive had cost him 25,000 men. It was the turning point.

In 1812 Wellington felt himself strong enough (with 45,000 men) to take the offensive. The French adventure in Russia had reduced the garrison in Spain to 230,000. Wellington hoped to defeat one of the French armies before they could concentrate. In the dry dust and relentless heat of a Spanish summer Wellington and Marshal Marmont manoeuvred for each other's communications. At Salamanca Marmont gave Wellington an opportunity. Wellington watched the French marching fast across his front to turn his flank. As they marched, they became extended, one corps separated from another. Wellington struck the French a succession of blows, breaking them up and destroying them in forty minutes. Salamanca was a brilliant manoeuvre battle like Oudenarde or Rossbach. It raised Wellington into the ranks of the greatest commanders. Although his subsequent siege of Burgos failed (partly because of a lack of adequate siege artillery), and he had once more to retreat to Portugal, the balance was swinging further against the French. In 1813 it swung against them heavily and finally. In another brilliant

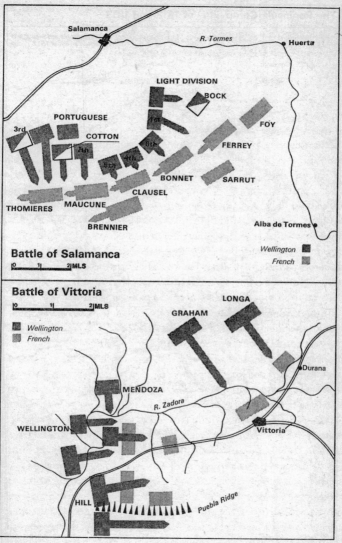

Salamanca

Salamanca •

R. Tormes

• Huerta

LIGHT DIVISION

BOCK

PORTUGUESE

FOY

3rd

COTTON

FERREY

7th

1st

6th

4th

5th

BONNET

SARRUT

CLAUSEL

THOMIERES

MAUCUNE

BRENNIER

Alba de Tormes •

Battle of Salamanca

0   1   2 MLS

Wellington

French

Battle of Vittoria

0   1   2 MLS

Wellington

French

LONGA

GRAHAM

• Durana

MENDOZA

R. Zadora

WELLINGTON

Vittoria

HILL

Puebla Ridge

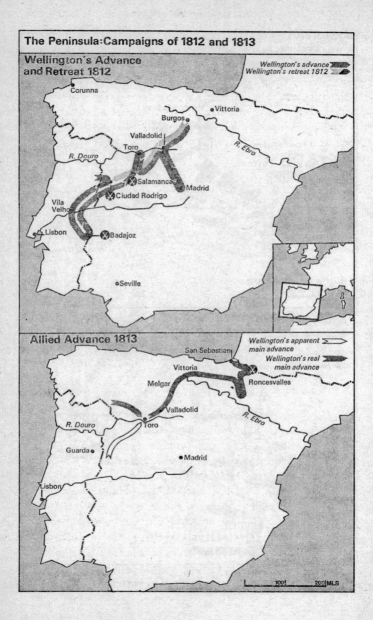

The Peninsula: Campaigns of 1812 and 1813

Wellington's Advance and Retreat 1812

Wellington's advance
Wellington's retreat 1812

Corunna

Vittoria

Burgos

Valladolid
Toro

Salamanca
Madrid

Ciudad Rodrigo

R. Douro

R. Ebro

Vila Velho

Lisbon

Badajoz

Seville

Allied Advance 1813

Wellington's apparent main advance
Wellington's real main advance

San Sebastian

Vittoria
Melgar

Roncesvalles

Valladolid

R. Douro

Toro

R. Ebro

Guarda

Madrid

Lisbon

100   200 MLS

strategic march Wellington constantly outmanoeuvred the French by the right flank across northern Spain, and utterly shattered them at the battle of Vittoria in another manoeuvre battle, this time of converging assaults. It was the end of French dominion in Spain; the campaign of 1814 was fought in southern France and ended with the capture of Toulouse.

Wellington's achievement was very great. It is no slight, however, to place it in the context of the whole war. Vittoria in 1813

was the first of Wellington's battles to make a decisive impact on the European situation and on European policy. In 1809 (the year of Corunna and Talavera), the Austrians had again taken the field, after being re-organized by their most able soldier, the Archduke Charles. At Aspern the Archduke inflicted a partial defeat on Napoleon; a few days later, at Wagram, Napoleon turned the tables and once more smashed the Austrian army and forced Austria to a crippling peace. However, the numbers – and the casualties – involved in these two battles were immense by Peninsular standards. The Austrian army numbered 80,000 (Wellington's at this time numbered some 20,000), and it inflicted 20,000 casualties on Napoleon at Aspern. The victory of Wagram cost

France another 18,000 dead. Repeatedly defeated though they were, it was the Austrians who throughout the war faced the main strength of France under the Emperor himself, and successively weakened it in great and bloody battles.

On the other hand, it was Wellington who kept the anti-French cause continually alive from 1809 until 1812, and steadily drained French power. Finally, in 1812, the Russian army and the Russian winter inflicted the greatest loss on the armies of France and her puppet-states of any single campaign of the war: of some 500,000 men who marched on Moscow, only 20,000 came back. This colossal catastrophe, coming on top of other cumulative losses, eviscerated French power. In 1813 Prussia once more came into the war, along-side Russia. The Prussian state and army had been reformed and revitalized under the sting of Jena and Auerstädt. Prussia was now the standard-bearer of a Germany re-awakened to national con-sciousness. Yet, despite the swelling strength of his enemies and the weakening of France, Napoleon managed to create another army and narrowly beat the Prussians and Russians at Lützen and Bautzen.

Austria hesitated to expose herself yet again to the risk of defeat at Napoleon's hands. Then came the news of Wellington's victory at Vittoria, the flight of Napoleon's brother King Joseph and the collapse of the French fabric in Spain. The Austrian ministers there and then decided to declare war on France. At Leipzig a gigantic battle was fought between Napoleon and his three enemies, where upwards of half a million men were involved; not so much a single battlefield as history had so far known it, but a series of connected battles, a prototype of future warfare. Napoleon was crushingly defeated. The way was open for the campaign of 1814, fought in France itself, where Napoleon by brilliant manoeuvres, with a miniature army of ragged men, tried in vain to parry the remorse-less advance of his enemies on Paris. In vain, too, Soult fought on against Wellington, yielding Toulouse only after a stubborn fight. The adventure of the Empire seemed to end with Napoleon's abdication and exile in Elba.

His escape and return to Paris in 1815 in an attempt to repair his fortunes led to three more battles – battles fought where the wars

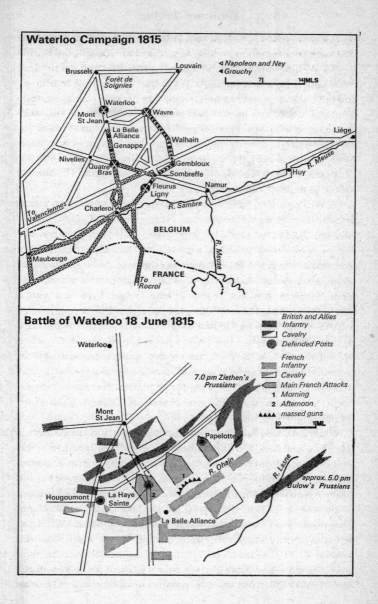

Waterloo Campaign 1815

◄ Napoleon and Ney
◄ Grouchy

7 | 14 MLS

Louvain

Brussels

Forêt de Soignies

Waterloo

Mont St Jean

Wavre

La Belle Alliance

Genappe

Walhain

Liége

Nivelles

Quatre Bras

Gembloux

Sombreffe

R. Meuse

To Valenciennes

Fleurus
Ligny

Namur

Huy

Charleroi

R. Sambre

BELGIUM

R. Meuse

Maubeuge

FRANCE

To Rocroi

R. Meuse

Battle of Waterloo 18 June 1815

British and Allies
Infantry
Cavalry
Defended Posts

French
Infantry
Cavalry
Main French Attacks
1 Morning
2 Afternoon
▲▲▲▲ massed guns

0 | 1 ML

Waterloo

7.0 pm Ziethen's Prussians

Mont St Jean

Papelotte

R. Ohain

R. Lasne

approx. 5.0 pm Bulow's Prussians

Hougoumont

La Haye Sainte

La Belle Alliance

against the French Republic and Empire had begun, in Flanders. By a swift concentration and advance, Napoleon caught the British (under Wellington) and the Prussians (under Blücher) before they could concentrate and unite. At Wavre the Prussians were beaten, and fell back in retreat. At Quatre Bras the British, coming up unit by unit, fought a confused encounter battle, and then too fell back, to the forest of Soignies, covering Brussels. Napoleon believed he had succeeded in driving the British and Prussians away from each other. He detached 33,000 men under Grouchy to follow the Prussians, as he believed, on their retreat eastwards. He himself meant to destroy Wellington.

Of Wellington's 67,000 men at Waterloo, only some 24,000 were British. The rest were Hanoverians, King's German Legion, Brunswickers, Nassauers and Dutch-Belgians. The British were not Peninsular veterans (who had gone to fight the Americans in a war over maritime rights) but inexperienced troops. Some of the allied contingents were of very doubtful quality. Against this nondescript force Napoleon brought 74,000 veteran troops, keyed up with a sense of desperation. For Wellington there could be no question of a battle of manoeuvre. He had to return to the tactics of the early days in the Peninsula – the two-deep line kept back out of gunfire behind the crest of a ridge, musket-fire against the onslaught of columns. A French general warned Napoleon before the battle that it could be like one of the Peninsular battles. Napoleon took no heed; he meant to shiver the mixed fabric of Wellington's line into fragments by direct impact.

While the dense French masses climbed again and again towards the allied position, Wellington held the allied line together by his icy nerve, his clear tactical sense and his force of leadership. British troops in square fought off successive charges by massed French heavy cavalry. The line began to thin dangerously; the crumbling point was near. But already Napoleon had had to make large diversions to his right flank, where Blücher's Prussians, far from retreating away eastwards, were coming up to keep Blücher's promise to Wellington to join him at Waterloo. As the afternoon wore on, more and more French troops drained away to stop the continued Prussian advance. Napoleon waited in vain for Grouchy and his 33,000 men. Finally he launched the Old Guard in a last attempt to smash through Wellington's crumbling line. It was the final charge of the Empire; a repetition of every encounter of a French column with a British line. When the cheering Frenchmen in their huge bearskins drew near, Wellington told the commander of the Brigade of Guards: 'Now, Maitland, now's your chance!'

The volleys crashed, the Imperial Guard reeled back. The 52nd Foot swung out of the British line and poured a volley into the French flank. The red lines swept the blue masses down the slope. Wellington waved his cocked hat towards the enemy, and the whole allied line charged. The wars of the French Revolution and Empire were over.

*

British prestige and influence in Europe had become paramount. Castlereagh, now the Foreign Secretary, was able to dominate the peace conference of the Congress of Vienna. Britain had been raised to this pinnacle by the feats of Wellington and a British army that it had taken twenty-two years of war to create and mature; an army which was now promptly broken up.

Diplomatically, Britain was to use Wellington's victories for half a century. Their lingering prestige formed the leverage behind the foreign policies of Castlereagh, Canning and Palmerston. Only when the Crimean War revealed to Europe the current truth about the British army was the spell of Wellington and Waterloo broken – on the eve of Prussia's rise as the great modern European military power.

To the British at home Waterloo marked the culminating moment of the long struggle with France since 1689; the end to a century and a half of wars and national danger. Until the close of the nineteenth century there was to be no other great power in sight to disturb Britain's enjoyment of the world empire she had won, or prevent her from enlarging it further. Waterloo cast its protective mantle over the pacifistic optimism of the Victorian age. It receded in the national memory, until it had become the distant, the legendary event that ended the last of the great wars and ushered in perpetual peace, ever-growing prosperity and continual progress.

12
Decay
and Reform
1815–70

TRAFALGAR and Waterloo had consummated final success in the long struggle with France for colonial and trade supremacy. The aims of William III, Marlborough and the Pitts had been achieved. The mercantilist empire begun by Cromwell had been completed: a self-sufficient system whereby colonies and home country exchanged tropical and temperate products for industrial goods. Yet at this very epoch of completion, new economic theories and the industrial revolution destroyed the basis of the imperial structure. British supremacy in manufacturing technique and free trade together destroyed mercantilism and the *raison d'être* of the empire. In the early nineteenth century Britain wanted free access to all markets for its vigorous exporters, not a closed system of colonial trade.

By the 1840s the empire had become an unprofitable and unwelcome responsibility. The largest markets for British goods now lay mostly outside the empire, in Europe, America, China and South America. Here too were the richest fields for British investment. Of British possessions only India could compare with these in economic importance. Trade no longer followed the flag, it went ahead, or it went where the flag would never go.

The British relationship to Europe also completely altered in the first half of the nineteenth century. The days of continental alliances and great wars seemed over for good.

After 1815 therefore the British army's role was very different from in the century after 1715. It was no longer needed, however intermittently, in struggles against great powers, or in deliberate imperial expansion. Nevertheless the existing empire, irrelevant though it now seemed, had to be garrisoned and its frontiers protected against native unrest. The peacetime strength of the British standing army rose to the unprecedented figure of over 100,000 men. However, up to three-quarters of the infantry were overseas, in the empire. The army now became for the first time a largely colonial army, whose units might be exiled for a decade or more at a time.

Although the empire seemed an encumbrance, it nevertheless kept on expanding by a piecemeal but irresistible process. This process is illustrated by the case of India, the greatest single 'colony'. Corrupt or warlike Indian potentates on the fringes of British territory would threaten trade or order; the British would therefore take military action against the potentates. This would lead to a further extension of British rule, and by thus bringing the British up against yet another set of native potentates, the forward process would begin all over again. Long before the renewal of deliberate imperial expansion in the 1880s and 1890s, the British Empire therefore expanded in Africa, India, Burma, Malaya and China, despite hapless attempts to arrest the process. The army even more than the navy was now the instrument of expansion. In the nineteenth century the history of the British army is the history of British colonial policy and British involvement overseas.

Thanks to their mercenary army, the British people as a whole never felt the burdens of world power during the Victorian age. The middle class in the prosperous suburbs were not called upon to furnish officers to die in China, the Gold Coast or Egypt; the respectable lower middle class in neat red-brick streets were not called upon to furnish non-commissioned officers or privates to expire of enteric fever or cholera or heatstroke in the Sudan or India or southern Africa. The British could rage at military incompetence when the army they neglected (and never joined) suffered some disaster – they could presume to take pride in victories won despite their indifference. War became a noise far away. The national sense of danger, the sense of struggle between nations, was atrophied. The mercenary army made possible Victorian pacifistic optimism; it permitted the creation of the mental climate where the British were ready to project their own sense of law and civic docility into the jungle of international rivalry, and believe that a treaty between powers was as safe a guarantee as a British legal contract.

Yet in Europe it was only the prestige conferred by Waterloo that provided British foreign policy from Castlereagh to Palmerston with weight. In the absence of a European super-power from 1815 until the rise of Prussia, British prestige was enough to tip the balance in crises involving powers roughly equal. The success of Palmerston's foreign policy hardly outlived the British army's débâcle in the Crimea. In 1864 Palmerston tried in vain to work the old bluff against Prussia on behalf of Denmark. Bismarck was reported to have said that, if the British army landed on the Prussian coast, he would send a policeman and have it arrested.

Nevertheless the British were able to continue to ignore Europe militarily (except for periodic scares which will be noted) throughout the nineteenth century. The key to British foreign policy and grand strategy after 1815 was not Flanders but India. Indeed British world power revolved round India until its disintegration after 1945. In the eighteenth century the axis of the British Empire lay westward from Britain to North America and the West Indies. The main imperial line of communication had passed across the broad Atlantic, commanded (except in 1779–82) by the Royal Navy. In the new nineteenth-century empire the main lines of communication were both much longer and more exposed to interruption by hostile land powers. Although the Cape route to India was secured by British sovereignty over Cape Colony (a fruit of the Napoleonic Wars), the direct route via the Mediterranean and the Red Sea was not so secure. Napoleon had shown the vulnerability of the route to India when he went to Egypt in 1798. In the nineteenth century it was exposed to French attempts to re-build their lost influence in the Near East, and to hostile local regimes in Egypt or other provinces of the decrepit Turkish Empire. It was also exposed to Russian expansion via the Bosporus and Dardanelles into the Mediterranean, or to Russian control or conquest of Turkey. The opening of the Suez Canal in 1869 did not mark the beginning of British preoccupation with the Near East, but merely a sharpening.

It was the fear of Russian designs on British communications with India through the Near East, and later on India itself (via Afghanistan) that made the personnel of the Victorian Foreign Office pale behind their whiskers. It was concern for India and the route to India that involved Britain in the Eastern Question, that tangled saga involving (at different times) Russian, French, Austrian, Bulgarian, Egyptian, Rumanian and Greek designs on Turkish territory. It was India that led Britain (via the Eastern Question) into the Crimean War, her one nineteenth-century war against a European power.

India involved Britain even farther afield. Although India was ultimately ruled from London, the Governor-General (later the Viceroy) and his government enjoyed some independence of policy. Therefore, the government of India, although British, came to treat foreign relations partly from an Indian point of view. It looked west to Arabia and the Persian Gulf, north-west to Afghanistan and Russia beyond, north to Tibet and China, east to Burma, Siam, Malaya and the French in Indo-China. From time to time the security of India required punitive expeditions outside India or even conquest and occupation; and these expeditions involved British troops as well as Indian.

In 1815, there were two armies under British control in India; troops of the Crown and the army of the East India Company ('John Company's army'). The forces of the East India Company were raised and administered by each of the three 'Presidencies' into which British India was divided, Bengal, Madras and Bombay. The three Presidency armies consisted of Indian troops under British command and a minority of European troops enlisted either in Britain (in fact mainly in Ireland) or from white mercenaries or adventurers in India itself. The armies were organized and trained in imitation of the British army of the epoch, with numbered regiments of the line, in which Indians of various races and religions were indiscriminately mixed. Except for certain Asiatic touches, the uniforms were also European in style. John Company's army was entirely separate from the British or army of the Crown in India. Its officers were recruited separately, and were educated not at

Sandhurst or Woolwich, but at the Company's own military academy at Addiscombe in Surrey. There was no cross-posting between the two forces. Although the two armies had to work closely together, there was hard feeling if officers of one were given command over forces of the other.

For these two British armies in India, the European victory year of 1815 was irrelevant to their continual conquests. The red-coats marched ever deeper into the power vacuum caused by the disinte-

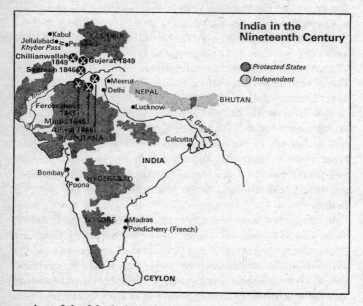

India in the
Nineteenth Century

● Protected States
○ Independent

gration of the Moghul empire. In 1815–16 the Gurkhas of Nepal were defeated after a hard war, and surrendered the provinces of Kumaon and Garwhal. In 1817–19 a war against the Pindaris and Mahrattas brought British power to the line of the River Sutlej. Only Sind and the Punjab remained independent of British para-mountcy. In 1814–15 Ceylon had been finally annexed to the British crown, although most of the island had been taken earlier from the Dutch. To the east, when the kings of Burma threatened British dominion in Assam in 1824, a British and Indian expedition

captured Rangoon and forced the Burmese to yield coastal territories from the Irrawaddy to Chittagong. In 1839 a wish to supplant
Russian predominance with British in Afghanistan led to the occupation of Kabul. In 1842 there followed the retreat from Kabul,
one of those disasters beloved of British legend-spinners. The
Afghans rose in rebellion and the British, encumbered by their
families or camp-followers, began to fall back through the mountains in savage weather. Gradually the army melted away, amid
the scenes customary on such retreats. Only one man, Dr Brydon,
reached safety at Jellalabad. The disgrace was redeemed by a
punitive army that marched on Kabul, released British prisoners,
and marched back.

In 1843 the British were advancing again, this time against
Sind. With 3,000 men against 20,000, they won the province in a
muddled battle at Miani. In 1845 the Sikhs of the Punjab crossed
the Sutlej into British territory. The Sikhs were warriors by
temperament and religion, the most formidable troops the British
had met in their Indian conquests. Nevertheless they were beaten
at Mudki and Ferozshah in 1845 and at Aliwal and Sobraon in
1846, and forced to conclude a peace, which, however, they broke
in 1848. The Second Sikh War was another hard struggle. The
bloody battle of Chillianwallah in 1849 saw, for once, British
bravery and discipline outweighed by their lack of tactical cunning.
It took another, better-conducted battle, at Gujerat, to break the
Sikhs and give the Punjab to Britain.

Three years later the British were at war again in Burma,
taking Rangoon once more, and this time annexing it and the
surrounding province. These conquests, coupled with other, peaceful annexations, completed the British control of the Indian sub-
continent from the borders of Afghanistan and Persia, along the
Himalayas, and down the Burmese coast to the delta of the
Irrawaddy.

None of those who fought the British and their sepoys – not even
the Sikhs – could match a European army in discipline, tactical
cohesion or leadership. Therefore the British were not called upon
for the tactical and technical skill required against a European
enemy. It was the superior courage, discipline and fire that

triumphed in these Indian battles, in frontal attacks or charges pushed relentlessly home. At Gujerat for instance:

... the right brigade of cavalry was ordered to charge, which they did in splendid style, cutting the enemy down in all directions, and driving them back in disorder. By this time, the fight had become general along the whole line: roll after roll of musketry rent the air, and clouds of smoke rose high and thick, while death was dealt out without mercy; and now was heard the well-known cry of 'Victory'. With levelled bayonets we charged; but they could not stand the shock of cold steel. They gave way in all directions; although some of their officers showed most daring courage.[1]

Such fighting bred an emphasis on 'regimental' qualities – discipline, personal bravery and boldness in combat – as the principal ingredients of military success, while on the other hand it led to a relative neglect of the intellectual requirements of the conduct of war.

Life in India in garrison also threw emphasis on the closed family world of the regiment, for only 40–60,000 British troops were scattered across a sub-continent. By 1850 India had become the greatest formative influence on the life, language and legend of the British army, for most British soldiers could expect to serve there, and for a long time. India, with its heat, stinks and noise, its enveloping dust, its glamour and poverty, became the British army's second home – perhaps its first. In the earlier nineteenth century Indian mistresses – 'native dictionaries' – brought officers and men even closer to Indian life. Later, stern memsahibs, stiffly corsetted with Victorian morality and etiquette and resentful of the voluptuous competition of sari-ed brown bodies, stopped all this, with lasting damage to British relations with Indians, which now became more distant and aloof.

At home after 1815, the army once more shrank under the familiar impulses of national economy and fear of militarism. By 1820 its strength at home had fallen to 64,426 men and only twenty-two field-guns. If it had not been for the sharp fears of the governing classes about the revolutionary danger from radical agitation, the army would have shrunk even further. As it was, its old peacetime role as a substitute for a police force was more important than ever before. The only other reliable armed force in the country was the mounted volunteer corps of the Yeomanry, recruited from the gentry and their tenants and servants, such as the corps that broke up the radical mass meeting in Manchester in 1819 in the 'massacre of Peterloo'. It was only with the establishment of borough police forces in 1839 and county police in 1855 that the army ceased to be the main prop of public order.

Despite the shrinking of the army after 1815, ancestral British fears that the victorious army of Waterloo and its officers might become a dangerous social and political force remained lively. The innocent enough foundation in 1816 of the United Service Club in Pall Mall caused the Prime Minister, Lord Liverpool, to write to a colleague:

A general military club with the Commander-in-Chief at its head is a most ill-advised measure, and so far from its being serviceable to the army it will inevitably create a prejudice against that branch of our military establishment, and we shall feel the effects of it in Parliament.[2]

When the political roles of the French and German officer-corps in the nineteenth century are borne in mind, the constant English vigilance against the emergence of an influential military caste appears less alarmist and absurd.

The peacetime home army was not only shrunken; it had disintegrated again into its constituent regiments. The requirements of public order scattered them throughout the country. No nucleus of higher organizations remained: no brigades, no divisions, no corps, no field army. There was no systematic training in formations larger than a battalion, no annual manoeuvres. By 1830 the army in the United Kingdom was down to 50,856 men. This was all the power behind British European policy. In 1840 and twice in 1846 there were scares of impending war with France. In the latter year Major-General Burgoyne reported to the Master-General of the Ordnance that after garrisons had been found for forts and ports, only 5–10,000 men could be found for a field army. As a consequence, Palmerston, the Foreign Secretary, reported to the Cabinet that 'this Empire was existing only by sufferance and by the forbearance of other powers'.[3] A reply from the Commander-in-Chief, the Duke of Wellington, leaked out and was published by *The Times* in 1848; he described the defenceless state of the country with his usual bluntness. However, the tide of commercial growth and pacifistic optimism was running too deep and fast for the British public to worry long about outmoded topics like defence and war. No re-armament was politically possible. Instead, attempts were made to bring home some of the high proportion of the army dispersed in odd battalions throughout the colonies. Some colonies were called upon to contribute towards the cost of their British garrisons. However, in 1854 there were still more troops abroad than at home.

The short-service enlistment of the Napoleonic war was abandoned. Until 1847 men enlisted for life; then for ten years, with the option of serving twenty-one years to qualify for a pension. Such long service had two results – soldiers in the ranks who were worn out by age and drink, and an army without a reserve of discharged soldiers in civilian life to fill out the regiments in the event of a major conflict. Once more the human material of the army reverted to the most primitive elements in British society. Although the troops were now mostly housed in barracks, these reflected the value placed on soldiers, for they were less luxurious than jails. A convict enjoyed 1,000 cubic feet of air; a soldier 400 cubic feet, in some cases only 300. In 1858 the Commons were told that the mortality rates in the Foot Guards were 20·4 per thousand, in the line regiments eighteen per thousand and in the cavalry eleven per thousand, whereas the average for the civilian population of military age was only about nine per thousand. The death rate among troops from tuberculosis was five times that of civilians.

The British people provided their soldiers with one pound of bread and three-quarters of a pound of meat a day, and supplied two coppers for each mess to boil the meat in – the only cooking equipment. Just before the Crimean War in 1854, a third daily meal was provided – at the soldier's own expense. Out of the gross pay of 7s. a week, half was deducted to pay for food extra to the bread and meat, and 1s. 10½d. for general maintenance and laundry. The soldier was left with 2¾d. a day to spend or save.

The early Victorian army – fixed in the mould of Waterloo. A review of the Grenadier Guards in Hyde Park by the Duke of Wellington, 1843.

Welfare facilities and recreation consisted of wet canteens and drinking. High standards of personal character, intelligence and conduct could hardly be expected. Army recruitment came to depend heavily on desperate Irishmen escaping from famine.

Between 1815 and 1854 the officer corps (a convenient misnomer, because in Britain there was no officer corps, but instead the tight little exclusive circle of each regimental mess) became ever more stiff-necked and haughty, rigid in social etiquette and distinctions, and dominated by a hierarchy of birth, wealth, kinship, connexion and fashion. In colonial battles such officers displayed physical courage and iron self-control; 'character' rather than intelligence and professional education.

At the Horse Guards, old men, active and able in their time, stultified progress. The Duke of York's second term as Commander-in-Chief lasted from 1811 until his death in 1827. Wellington was briefly Commander-in-Chief in 1827. In 1828 Lord Hill, his Peninsula colleague, became Commander-in-Chief for fourteen years. Finally, in his old age, Wellington returned to the Horse Guards until his death in 1852. Under their ancient and hallowed hands, the army remained preserved like a garment in a bottom drawer, sentimentally loved, but rotted and rendered quaint by the passage of time. Even its uniforms in 1854 were still essentially those of Waterloo.

The only stir in this stagnation was provided by the re-organization of the militia in 1852–3. It was occasioned, like earlier militia reforms, by renewed apprehension of a danger from France, Louis Napoleon having proclaimed himself Napoleon III, Emperor of the French. The Militia Act of 1852 fixed the strength of the militia at 80,000 men, to be raised by voluntary recruitment with liberal bounties and rewards to successful recruiters. Nevertheless, the ballot from a list of all males between eighteen and thirty was retained in case military ardour and patriotic zeal were lacking. The Act of 1852 succeeded in reviving the militia both in numbers and performance, and in the Crimean War militia battalions were to carry out useful service as garrisons of bases in the Mediterranean and Ionian Islands.

So long as the army had only Indians or other natives to fight, it remained professionally adequate. However, in 1854 the unthinkable occurred again – a war against a great European power.

It was one thing to improvise an expedition against the Afghans or the Sikhs; another to improvise an expedition to the Black Sea to take on a first-class military state like Russia. Yet British resources for the latter task were the inferior in some ways. In India, there were permanent field forces; there was a background of continual war; British commanders enjoying untrammelled control over the resources of the country. In Britain, on the outbreak of the Crimean War, all preparations – material, organizational and psychological – started once again from nothing.

*

The war with Russia arose out of bullying Russian diplomacy towards Turkey over the question of the protection of the Sultan's Christian subjects and of the Holy Places in Jerusalem. For Napoleon III of France, the Russian claim to be protector of the Holy Places was a challenge to himself as self-appointed champion of Roman Catholic interests. There was also the opportunity to enhance the traditional French interest in the Levant in Napoleonic fashion. For Britain Russian diplomacy aroused fears of a Russian partition of the Turkish Empire – Russian command of the Bosporus and the Dardanelles, and danger to the Near East and to the imperial route to India.

In fact the real grounds for war were slender. Confused diplomacy and tardy communications led the combatants haplessly into combat. By the time the French and British expeditionary forces were ready to expel the Russians from Turkey's Balkan provinces (the ostensible reason for hostilities) the Turkish army had unexpectedly evicted the Russians without help. France and Britain cast about for something their armies could do, and finally settled on the capture of the Russian Black Sea naval base, Sevastopol, on the Crimean Peninsula.

The Crimean War is one of the compulsive subjects of British historical writing. Few have heard of Granby's charge at Warburg, or the charge of the Union Brigade at Waterloo; few have not heard of the charge of the Light Brigade at Balaclava, or of

Essential equipment to enable an officer to withstand the rigours of the Crimea, 1854.

1 English musket exercises, 1600. Effective use of fire-arms required complicated and well-practised drill – which contributed to the rise of regular armies in Europe and diminished the usefulness of militia.

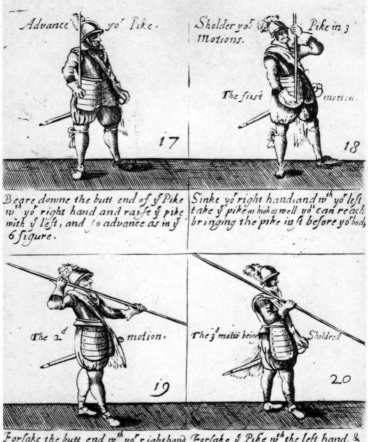

Advance   yo.ʳ Pike.

Sholder yo.ʳ   Pike in 3
          Motions.

The first   motion

17   18

Beare downe the butt end of y.ᵉ Pike
w.ᵗʰ yo.ʳ right hand and raiſe y.ᵉ pike
with y.ᵉ left, and ſo advance as in y.ᵉ
6 figure.

Sinke yo.ʳ right hand, and w.ᵗʰ yo.ʳ left
take y.ᵉ pike as high as well yo.ᵘ can reach
bringing the pike in ſt before yo.ʳ bod.

The 2.ᵈ   motion.

The 3.ᵈ motiō being   Sholdred

19   20

Forſake the butt end w.ᵗʰ yo.ʳ right hand
bring forward yo.ʳ Pike in the left
hand, and take the pike backward
in y.ᵉ right hand as farr as well
you may reach.

Forſake y.ᵉ Pike w.ᵗʰ the left hand, &
with the right only ſet vpon your
ſhoulder or: as in y.ᵉ 12 figure.

2 English pike exercises, 1600. It was the pikemen who formed the backbone of a seventeenth-century army, protecting the musketeers from
hostile cavalry until the invention of the bayonet.

3 William Blathwayt (1649–1717). As Secretary-at-War from 1683 to 1704, he was to the army what Samuel Pepys was to the navy – a great creative administrator.

4 John Churchill, Duke of Marlborough, Captain-General and Master-General of the Ordnance, victor of Blenheim (1650–1722). He completed the task begun by William III of preventing French hegemony in Europe. Marlborough was a flawless blend of strategist, diplomat, administrator and battlefield commander.

5 The Battle of Oudenarde, 1708. Marlborough intercepted the French on the march, and defeated them in an encounter battle.

6 (*Right*) The principal conqueror of French Canada 1758–9, Major-General Jeffrey (later Field-Marshal Lord) Amherst, Commander-in-Chief of the British forces in North America. A cartoon by C. Bretherton, 1782.

7 (*Below*) His Royal Highness the Duke of York. As Commander-in-Chief, 1795–1809, he reformed and reorganized the British military system and laid the foundations of Wellington's victories in the field.

8 (*Above*) Not a true cross-section of society – recruits *c.* 1780–90, caricatured by Bunbury.

9 (*Top right*) An uncharitable view of the Duke of York and his staff in the Flanders campaign of 1793, by Gillray. Though not the fault of York himself, the British army's performance was amateurish to the last degree.

10 (*Below right*) A British army on the march at the time of the Napoleonic wars, in a caricature by Rowlandson. A proportion of the regimental wives marched with their husbands to battle to provide what nursing services there were. The custom died out during the nineteenth century, as proper medical services were gradually created.

FATIGUES OF THE CAMPAIGN IN FLANDERS

11 Major-General Arthur Wellesley (later Field-Marshal the Duke of Wellington, victor over the French in Spain and at Waterloo) (1769–1852), painted by Robert Home after his early victories in India against the Mahrattas.

12 (*Top*) Military life in India in the early nineteenth century – in the army of the Honourable East India Company, not the army of the Crown. An engraving from *Tom Raw, the Griffin*.

13 Flogging on the triangle, 1822. The military aspect of a brutal age. However, decent men in the ranks as well as the army's leaders believed that flogging was essential to enforce discipline among the sweepings of society found in the army. It was abolished in time of peace in 1868, and in war in 1880.

14 (*Top*) Early Victorian conquest in the East – the occupation of Afghanistan in 1839. However, in 1842, an Afghan rising forced the British troops into a retreat in mid-winter from which only one man reached sanctuary.

15 The early Victorian army on manoeuvres, 1853. Unfortunately such exercises were rare.

16 A mid-Victorian military hospital. The Royal Family visit sick and wounded from the Crimea in the Brompton Hospital, Chatham.

17 (*Above*) Coldstream Guardsmen in the Crimea. Their weapons were muzzle-loaders fired by a percussion cap instead of the earlier flintlock.

18 (*Top right*) Huts, tents and houses round the harbour of Balaclava, 1854–5. The field army on the plateau south of Sevastopol enjoyed no such good lodgings and, owing to appalling communications, often went hungry while ships full of food lay in the harbour.

19 (*Below right*) Life in the Crimea – in fine weather. Although the muddles of the Crimean War were nothing unusual in the history of the army, British public opinion for the first time cared about the soldiers' suffering.

20 His Royal Highness the Duke of Cambridge (1819–1904) photographed at the time of the Crimean War. As Commander-in-Chief of the army from 1856 till 1895, he became progressively more obstructive to change and reform as he grew older.

21 Edward Cardwell, Liberal Secretary of State for War, 1868–74. The importance of his reforms of the army and the War Office, though considerable, has been exaggerated.

22 Army life in the United Kingdom in the late Victorian era – a barrack room in 1875. Austere though it was, it was a better lodging than many recruits had ever known in their lives.

23 (*Top*) Garrisoning the ever-expanding Empire – troops ready to go on a route march. Port Elizabeth, Natal, 1871.

24 The army's life in India, its second home, in the Victorian age. Officers of the 93rd Highlanders with some trophies of the hunt, 1864.

25 Hiram Maxim with the gun he invented in 1884 – the true machine-gun utilizing its own gases to re-load and fire the gun automatically. It transformed infantry tactics by its range and rate of fire.

26 A Maxim machine-gun detachment of the King's Royal Rifle Corps on the North-West Frontier, *c.* 1898. Field operations in the hills of the Frontier rarely looked as neat as this posed photograph.

27 (*Top*) General (later Field-Marshal) Sir William Robertson, Chief of the Imperial General Staff, 1915–18. Working class by origin, he was shrewd and blunt of speech and deeply suspicious of politicians.

28 Scapegoat and victor: Field-Marshal Sir Douglas (later Earl) Haig, Commander-in-Chief of the British armies in France, 1915–18. He was the principal architect of the defeat of the German army in 1918, but was blamed subsequently for British losses and failure to win in 1916–17.

29 What wartime propaganda did not reveal was British dependence on foreign, especially American, technology for her war effort.

30 Patriotic fervour, 1915. Apart from its general unfairness, the voluntary system of recruitment led to factories being denuded of skilled men.

31 (*Top*) The Battle of the Somme, July 1916. Until 1917 the British lacked enough heavy artillery like this eight-inch howitzer to cut the German wire and smash their defences.

32 The Somme, November 1916. Digging a position for a sixteen-inch howitzer. Many shells produced in 1915 and 1916 failed to explode or exploded in the breech. By 1917, however, the British had created huge battering-engines of artillery to clear the ground ahead of the infantry – the slow, ponderous but only available answer to barbed wire, machine-guns and field fortifications.

33 Field-Marshal Lord Kitchener, the Secretary of State for War, inspecting men of the 'New Army' on 1 June 1915. The 'New Army' (or Kitchener's armies) was the product of the enthusiastic volunteering of 1914. It was brave, but ill-trained, ill-officered and ill-equipped. Efficient modern armies cannot be quickly improvised.

34 (*Above*) The first official photograph of a tank on active service (the Somme, September 1916). Note the crew-member's leather helmet, and the huge wheels (soon discarded) that were supposed to help steer the tank. The unreliable early tank's speed was half a mile an hour.

35 (*Top right*) British and German wounded walking back together, the Somme, July 1916. The refusal of the peoples and governments at home to make a compromise peace drove the armies into battle again and again in search of victory.

36 (*Below right*) A stew-up in a steel helmet: Royal Field Artillery and Royal Engineer officers near Miramont-le-Grand, March 1917. Note the elegant dining-chairs – not War Department issue.

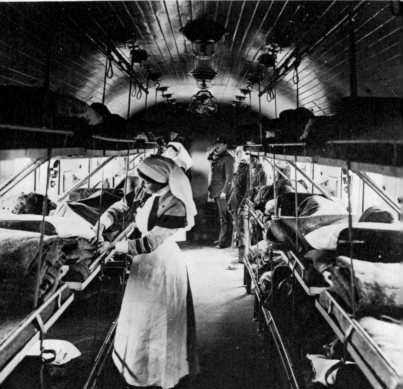

37 (*Above left*) 'Jocks' of the 15th Division meet the members of a concert party near Blangy, October 1917. Behind the Western Front were the best welfare arrangements the British soldier had ever enjoyed – cinemas, sport, regimental institutes (shops and canteens) and canteens organized by private charity.

38 (*Below left*) 'Blighties' – wounded on a hospital train for evacuation to England, near Doullens, April 1918. For the first time in any war medical and surgical services in the British army were efficient and on a large scale.

39 (*Above*) 'Let him kip on' – trench warfare on the Somme, September 1916. Note that the rifle's mechanism is wrapped to keep out the ubiquitous mud. The combination of machine-guns, barbed wire and millions of men created the trench stalemate of 1914–18.

40 Western Front attack. In 1916 and 1917 there was apparently little to show for the British offensives. But from August to November 1918, offensives under the same generals and Commander-in-Chief drove the German armies back seventy-five miles and took nearly 200,000 prisoners.

41 The cost of victory. British casualties in the Great War were in fact proportionately lower than those of France, Russia or Germany.

42 (*Top left*) Army recruiting, 1936. During the long slump in Britain between the world wars the regular army reverted to its traditional role as a rescue service for the jobless, the destitute or the unfortunate.

43 (*Below left*) Territorial Army camp – kit inspection for the Inns of Court Regiment, 1936.

44 (*Above*) Field-Marshal Earl Wavell. As Commander-in-Chief Middle East in 1940–41, he was responsible for the conquest of Italian East Africa and for the first British victory in the Western Desert.

45 (*Left*) Field-Marshal the Viscount Montgomery of Alamein photographed on 25 July 1945 on an Arab stallion formerly belonging to his opponent Field-Marshal Erwin Rommel. Montgomery won the second Battle of Alamein (October–November 1942). His greatest achievement, however, was the victory in Normandy (June–August 1944).

46 Field-Marshal Earl Alexander of Tunis. In August 1942 he succeeded Sir Claude Auchinleck, who had won the first Battle of Alamein in July 1942, as Commander-in-Chief Middle East. Alexander was responsible for the allied victories in Tunisia in 1943 and in Italy in 1943–5.

47 (*Above*) Waiting for the German invasion – General Sir Alan Brooke (later Field-Marshal Lord Alanbrooke), Commander-in-Chief Home Forces, on a tour of inspection, May 1941. From 1941 to 1945, as Chief of the Imperial General Staff, Brooke was Churchill's principal strategic adviser.

48 (*Top right*) E.N.S.A. concert, Western Desert, September 1942. In the Second World War travelling concert parties, film shows and lavishly equipped clubs and leave camps were included in the welfare services for the troops.

49 (*Below right*) The Western Desert, a waste of gravel and scrub. British tanks near Tobruk, September 1941. Not until the American Sherman tanks arrived in August 1942 was British tank equipment equal in quality to German.

50 The cook-house queue, Egypt, 1941. The feeding of millions of men in desert and jungle, in transit or in the middle of great battles, was an administrative triumph of the two world wars.

51 (*Top*) D-Day, 6 June 1944. The largest and most successful example of maritime strategy in history. Five out of twelve of the seaborne assault divisions and one out of the three airborne divisions were British.

52 Lieutenant-General Sir William (later Field-Marshal the Viscount) Slim, 14th Army commander. He commanded Burma Force in the retreat from Burma in 1942, beat the Japanese at Imphal-Kohima in 1944 and reconquered Burma in 1944–5.

53 (*Top*) The battle for India, 1944, round Imphal and Kohima. A British tank on the Imphal–Ukhrul road. In such country, air supply became the key to victory.

54 The Burma front: the men who believed themselves the 'forgotten army' – their appalling hardships and difficult achievements were eclipsed in the eyes of the home public by the war in Europe.

55 Air mobility in the Malayan jungle, 1957. Close co-operation between the R.A.F. and deep-penetration groups of the army was a major factor in the defeat of the Communist revolutionary forces in Malaya.

56 Post-1945 retreat from Empire. While British governments dithered, the army had to preserve order until the eventual evacuations. Here the 5th (Royal Northumberland) Fusiliers remove a grenade-throwing terrorist in Aden in 1967. It was the kind of scene already played out in Palestine, Egypt, Cyprus, East and West Africa and elsewhere.

Florence Nightingale. In fact the suffering and incompetence were not in the least bit novel, but standard form. Every harrowing detail of the Crimea had been seen before, many times, since Elizabeth's expeditions to the Netherlands and France. The Crimean War has received attention much out of proportion to its interest or importance on any score.

What was novel about the Crimea was not the experiences of the troops or the workings of the military system, but that for the first time the home public was really aware of these things, and that for the first time such things had become unacceptable by the general standards of the epoch.

In the Napoleonic wars the circulation of *The Times* had been about 5,000 a day; during the Crimean War, it was over 40,000. And now it was only one among several newspapers, morning and evening, with large circulations that were stimulated by the end of newspaper stamp duty in 1855. The railway carried these papers overnight to the breakfast tables of an influential middle class that had hardly begun to exist as a coherent force in 1815. Although there had been newspaper correspondents with the armies in the Napoleonic wars, it was William Russell, the correspondent of *The Times* in the Crimea, who invented the techniques of the interview and of the vivid pen-portraiture of the life of the army. The fast steamship brought the Crimea closer in time to Britain than the Peninsula had been in 1808–14. For the first time in history the nation knew what its soldiers were going through, and cared.

General progress had made the traditional horrors of war no longer acceptable. Filth and disease in civilian life had retreated before the advance of science and social reform. Chaotic and ramshackle administration was being largely swept away in favour of efficiency and new ideals of professional competence. The military system was one of the few corners of the old structure that had escaped early Victorian re-building, since few reformers and no voters in peacetime were interested in it. Now, under the shock of war and in the glare of aroused public opinion, the pre-industrial-revolution military system was exposed to the nation's horror.

There was one further, and a personal, factor about the Crimea. In the Crimea there was no Marlborough, no Wellington to make the chaotic system work despite itself. Instead there was Lord Raglan, a man of sixty-six, once Wellington's military secretary in the Peninsula, a man who had never commanded in the field, and appointed for no much better reason than the feeling that he was the repository of the Wellingtonian spirit. Raglan manifested to a remarkable degree the characteristics of the ideal Victorian gentleman. He was dignified, brave, courteous, gentle and honourable to the point of saintliness. Unfortunately these virtues do not make for success or survival in a tough world. They did not make for success in the Crimea. It would have been better had Raglan been a bloody-minded careerist bastard, as were Napoleon III's generals. No driving will-power united the disparate parts of the British military machine.

In any event, the Crimea had fewer resources of food, beasts and waggons than even Spain. A supply system whose basic premise was local hiring instantly collapsed. Raglan himself committed the error unthinkable in Wellington of spending the winter in the open country before Sevastopol instead of in snug billets round the port and base of Balaclava. The one road between Balaclava and the front became a bog. There were copious ship-borne supplies in Balaclava while the beasts and men of the army were starving.

As the nation became generally conscious of the sufferings of its soldiers and the breakdown of the inadequate military system it had tolerated in its fear of military power, there was a colossal scandal. The hunt was up for scapegoats. A Select Committee of the House of Commons inquired into the state of the army before Sevastopol. Later in 1855 came the *Report of the Commission of Enquiry into the Supplies of the British Army in the Crimea*. The Report stated that from 1 October 1854 until 30 April 1855 mortality was thirty-five per cent of the active strength of the army.

... this excessive mortality is not to be attributed to anything peculiarly unfavourable in the climate, but to over-work, exposure to wet and cold, improper food, insufficient clothing during part of the winter, and insufficient shelter from inclement weather.[4]

Some of the curiosities of the British military system were exposed

Balaclava helmets, original version, 1854. This engraving was optimistic; the army suffered terribly from exposure, hunger and disease in the bleak Crimean winter.

to the gaze of the commissioners. The Commissary-General (a Treasury officer) gave evidence that it was not the custom in the British service to keep the commander-in-chief informed of the available stock of provisions in depot, but only of provisions already in possession of the troops or in the hands of divisional commissaries. Nor was it the practice to issue fuel in the field, but only in home garrisons; which satisfactorily explained why men froze or lived soaking wet, and why the Commissary-General had strongly resisted Raglan's plea to issue fuel. Nor was cooking equipment issued, for the troops were supposed to cook over fires. On the other hand there must be some sympathy for Filder, the Commissary-General. As in all previous wars, the Commissary-General had only been appointed – without instructions – when it had been first decided to send out an expeditionary force. It was his task to improvise in the field a complete supply organization. Owing to civilian demand for economy after 1815, not even a nucleus of Wellington's waggon train had been retained.

The recruiting system – the long-service army – similarly failed once more. After the first 25,000 men had been sent to the Crimea, all that remained were young recruits. In November 1854 the heights of Inkerman were defended by only 8,000 British infantry. A first reinforcement of seven battalions consisted of 6,000 men; but a second reinforcement of eleven battalions of only 6,500 men. By midsummer 1855 the French army in the Crimea numbered 90,000 men; the British only about a quarter of this figure.

Even before the customary beginning-of-a-war breakdown of the military system became a national scandal, it had forced the start of the radical reconstruction that had been pending since the reign of Anne. The old separation of functions under different authorities was ended. In June 1854 the Secretaryship of State for War was separated from that of the Colonies, and for the first time Britain possessed a full-time Secretary of State for military affairs. All purely military departments were placed under his supreme authority. At last the old constitutional attitude that the army 'belonged' to the sovereign and must therefore be weakened by external checks and by divided administration was abandoned. Parliamentary and civilian control was now fully achieved. In December 1854, supply and transport were transferred from the dead hand of the Treasury to the War Secretary. In February 1855 the post of Secretary-*at*-War – an increasing anomaly – was amalgamated with that of Secretary *of* War. In March 1855 control over the militia and yeomanry was transferred to the War Department from the Home Office. In May 1855 came the turn of the Master-General of the Ordnance's private empire. The supply of munitions and field equipment and of supervision of fortifications at home were turned over to the Secretary of War. The Master-General lost his military command over the engineers and gunners to the Commander-in-Chief. The War Department also took over the Army Medical Department and – from the colonels – direct responsibility for clothing the infantry and cavalry.

Thus only the Commander-in-Chief, with purely military responsibilities for the internal discipline, promotion and training of the army, remained outside the new consolidated War Department, and even he was in fact supposed to be responsible to the War Secretary.

The reforms came too late to help the army in the Crimea. It was only after Sevastopol had been captured, during the winter of 1855-6 while the armies were waiting for a peace treaty to be signed, that the troops were at last well-hutted, well-clothed and well-fed.

From the point of view of strategy, tactics and military technique the Crimea War offers little of interest. The industrial revolution had made small impact on either armies or navies. The allied battle-fleets were still composed of 3–4,000-ton wooden sailing ships. Steamships were only used for supply and communications with home, while steam-tugs hauled the battleships into bombarding station. Although the allied troops were all armed with muzzle-loading Minié rifles, the artillery were still smooth-bores. The new rifles could be loaded and fired as fast as a musket. Like the latest muskets they replaced, they were fired by a hammer hitting a percussion cap instead of by the old unreliable flint and priming-pan of powder. The bullet did not have to be rammed down the rifling, because the force of the discharge against a hollow at the base of the elongated bullet expanded it into the rifling at the moment of firing. In loading, the new bullet could therefore be dropped home under its own weight. In fact it was not Minié, but another Frenchman, Delvigne, who invented the principle of the expanding bullet. Minié developed it further. It was the various national armouries who finally developed the 'Minié' rifle used in the field, and in Britain the new Royal Small Arms Factory at Enfield began producing the first 'Enfield' rifles on American machinery.

There was thus now no real difference between rifle regiments and other infantry, except that the rifle regiments were trained to act as skirmishers. In the cavalry, lances had come back into fashion during the Napoleonic wars for the first time since the sixteenth century. Except in costume, all distinction between dragoons and hussars had disappeared, for all cavalry but lancers charged with the sword. There was no mounted infantry of the type seen in the American War of Independence.

As a war-time expedient, a 'Land Transport Corps' was raised to replace the haphazard local hiring of civilian waggons. It was kept standing in peacetime after 1856 as the 'Military Train'.

The British army of the Crimea was simply the Peninsular army brought out of its cupboard and dusted down: four infantry divisions, the Light Division and the cavalry. The tactics were unchanged. Dundas's infantry training manual of the 1790s had been virtually re-printed in 1824, except for a two-deep line instead of three-deep. The French regulations of 1831 had similarly carried forward Guibert's regulations of 1791. The British attacked and defended in line with close-quarters musketry; the Russians used the massive columns appropriate to an army of peasants; and the French used battalion columns as well as line.

In none of the combatant armies was there a commander of real strategic and tactical talent. The best were rough and tough Frenchmen like Bosquet and Pélissier, trained in the wars against the Arabs in Algeria. In the main battles (the Alma, Balaclava and Inkerman) allied success turned on the sheer fighting quality of the troops in disconnected close-range encounters. It is curious that one incident in one battle of the war – the charge of the Light Brigade at Balaclava – should loom so large in British legend. Only

673 men were involved, and they lost 157 men out of 20,000 war dead. Why have the British chosen to make a sentimental legend out of a pointless effort arising from muddled orders? The entirely successful and equally gallant charge of the Heavy Brigade earlier on the same day is generally forgotten, as is the charge of the *Chasseurs d'Afrique* on flanking Russian batteries that helped the Light Brigade's eventual retirement.

Sevastopol eventually fell in September 1855 after repeated bloody repulses. In 1856 the Treaty of Paris made a compromise settlement of the kind that was already in the air when the nations stumbled into war.

In Britain the impulse to reform the military system was by no means exhausted. In 1856 a Commission, after visiting the major military powers of Europe, recommended changes in military education. In the same year His Royal Highness the Duke of Cambridge became Commander-in-Chief, a post he was to hold until 1895. Cambridge was at this time young and keen. In 1857 he laid down new educational qualifications for staff officers and doubled the number of students at the Senior Department of the Royal Military College, Sandhurst, which now burgeoned forth into a separate existence as the Staff College. Soon a splendid building in the Italian style began to arise at Camberley. The study of military history and past strategy was inaugurated, and became the most interesting and best-liked part of a course perhaps too much devoted to theoretical mathematics and surveyors' work.

The Staff College was intended to repair the ignorance of staff duties and the personal incompetence displayed in the Crimea, for Indian warfare and regimental soldiering had not proved an adequate preparation for the problems of handling a large army in the field. Whereas Wellington's army in the Peninsula in 1808 had been able to profit from fifteen previous years of bitter war experience, the Crimean army had plunged straight out of peace into war. In 1856 it was seen to be clearly necessary to follow continental armies in giving staff and technical officers systematic training in peacetime.

It was the beginning of twenty years of fitful reform. Commissions or committees of investigation were loosed on the British military system and combed Europe for lessons. The scope of inquiry varied from major questions like recruitment and reserves to such matters as the re-shuffling of departmental responsibilities inside the War Department. Nor did world events in the 1850s and 1860s allow the British to sink back totally into complacent relaxation. Hard on the Crimean War came a sudden and fearsome shock to the fabric of British rule in India, when sepoy troops of John Company's Bengal army erupted in widespread mutiny. There were fewer than 40,000 European troops (Crown and 'Company's') scattered across the whole sub-continent to represent the power of the British conqueror. British rule had rested too confidently on the loyalty of more than 200,000 native sepoys; on a moral ascendancy that was now brutally challenged. While the Bengal native army numbered 137,000 men, the British forces in India had been reduced by a campaign against the Persians and by garrisons in Burma and Aden. When the Mutiny was extinguished after great anxiety and immense exertions, it had administered a shock to British confidence from which it never really recovered.

The Mutiny caused reconstructions both of British administration and of the British military system in India. The territories directly administered by the East India Company were transferred to the Crown under a Viceroy. The East India Company's army was likewise transferred. The sepoy troops were re-organized and by 1864 reduced in strength to 120,000 men. An Indian Staff Corps was set up to provide the Indian army with British officers. The East India Company's European troops were incorporated into the British army. In 1864 the European garrison in India had risen to 65,000, while the proportion of European troops to Indians had increased from one to eight before the Mutiny to one to three.

Thus more troops had to be found for India at a time when governments were trying to reduce British commitments in the empire. Ten thousand men were brought back from New Zealand after a war with the Maoris. In North America the American Civil War and later the menace of a private army of Fenian expatriate Irishmen in the U.S. demanded a garrison of 17,000 British troops in Canada. Only in 1867 was it possible to withdraw all but 3,500

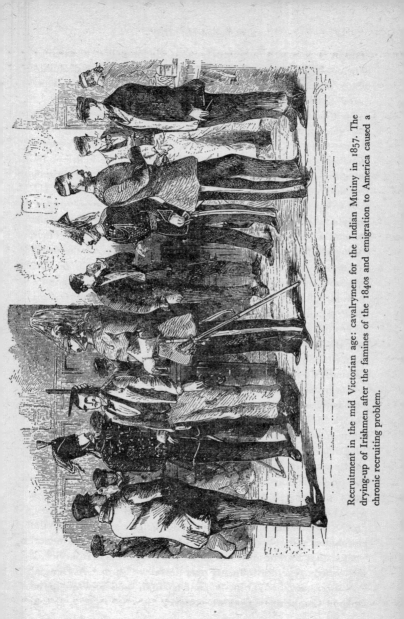

Recruitment in the mid Victorian age: cavalrymen for the Indian Mutiny in 1857. The drying-up of Irishmen after the famines of the 1840s and emigration to America caused a chronic recruiting problem.

of these. It was partly motives of economy that impelled this attempt to bring the army home from the empire; it was partly to stimulate white colonial self-reliance; and it was partly strategic apprehension about Europe.

For the Crimean emergency had exposed British weakness. The later years of the 1850s and the decade of the 1860s did not diminish the sense of anxiety felt by statesmen, if not always by the people. In 1859 Napoleon III had followed in his uncle's footsteps by defeating the Austrians in northern Italy, and there was a scare in England that, with the aid of steam-navigation, Napoleon III might now succeed where his uncle had failed, and swiftly throw an army ashore in England one dark night. Peaceable Victorians put on the dashing uniforms of a new volunteer movement. Their week-end gatherings performed the same disservice to the army as did the militia in former times by convincing public opinion that 160,000 Sunday soldiers rendered Britain safe. In 1864 Bismarck ignored Palmerston's hints of war in protection of Denmark, and the Prussians and Austrians swiftly exposed British military helplessness by beating the unsupported Danes. Danish naval success over the Prussian fleet could be read in two ways: while it proved to an island people like the British that sea-power was still potent, alternatively it proved that sea-power alone could not affect land events in Europe. The same ambivalence applied to the war of 1866 between Prussia and Italy, and Austria. The Austrians' naval victory of Lissa over the Italians did not preserve them from shattering defeat in Bohemia at the hands of the Prussian army. This defeat, at Sadowa, was one of the decisive battles of history, yielding predominance in Germany to Prussia, and opening the way for German unification under the Prussian monarchy. Britain was a spectator. Had she wished it, she could not have been otherwise. Lissa demonstrated that sea-power could still, if necessary, protect Britain from invasion, but Sadowa again pushed home the eternal lesson that sea-power alone could not influence continental events; that Britain must have an army for continental service, if she wished to exercise influence over the fate of Europe. As General Peel (Secretary for War in 1859 and again in 1866–7) wrote to the Duke of Cambridge apropos Denmark:

If when the Prussians and Austrians entered Holstein as they SAID only
with the intention of preserving peace, we COULD HAVE SAID; 'Well,
we highly approve of this and we will send 60,000 men and our fleet to
the Baltic,' the gross robbery that was afterwards committed would never
have been perpetrated.[5]

By 1868 the various investigations into military affairs had
accumulated a great deal of useful information and recommendations. Concrete progress in reform had been made in two directions: reserve forces, and organization of the War Department.
The traditional long-service recruitment meant that there were no
reserves of trained soldiers in civilian life to swell the army in an
emergency. In 1867 the total reserve forces in Great Britain were
put by one observer at less than 5,000 men. Yet the Prussians had
been able to put 400,000 men into the field (the majority of them
reservists) in 1866. A War Office committee investigated all the
continental systems of recruitment and terms of service. The Prussian system seemed to have most to offer. It was based on service
of only three years with the colours (as against twenty-one in
Britain) and four years in the reserve. The Prussian standing army
had become simply a training *cadre* for intakes of conscripts. The
Prussian army's organization for peace and war was virtually the
same. Prussia was divided into army-corps districts for the purposes
both of administration and of recruitment. On the outbreak of war
the command organization of the district became that of a corps
in the field. 'Localization' of the army and of its recruitment gave
the districts pride and interest in their 'own' corps.

However, the Prussian system was based on universal obligation
to serve. Long historical process had now made conscription unthinkable in Britain, despite the chronic shortage of troops both to
fulfil imperial commitments and to back British foreign policy. In
1866–7 a Royal Commission reported on the problems of recruitment. The eighteenth-century combination of a bounty on enlistment and the lying blandishments of recruiting sergeants in pubs
was found to be not enough in an age of buoyant trade and emigration. The Irish reservoir was drying up now that famine and
emigration to America had emptied the country. Nor could traditional recruitment begin to draw in the kind of intelligent and

educated men conscripted in Prussia. An Under-Secretary for War acknowledged: 'Our system of recruitment has, I believe, swept to a great extent the refuse of large towns.'[6] He defended the system on the grounds that otherwise 'better members of the community' might be wasted in the army. The result of all the argument was an Army of Reserve Act of 1867 – a characteristic British attempt to have the benefits of a continental system without any of its distasteful comprehensiveness or obligation. Two reserves were to be set up: the First Reserve of (it was hoped) 50,000 men and the Second Reserve of 30,000 men. Each was subdivided into two. The First Reserve was to consist of 20,000 regulars who would pass the last five years of their first term of service in reserve, and of 30,000 militia reserve recruited by a bounty of £12 spread over the five years of reserve service. This First Reserve was to be liable for recall to the colours and for service overseas. The Second Reserve was for home duties only, and was to consist of regulars completing their second term of service, and of present and future pensioners. The Act was not much of a success, for three years later the First Reserve consisted of under 2,000 regulars instead of 20,000.

During the 1860s, departmental responsibilities within the War Department and the Horse Guards were re-shuffled. In 1868 the commissariat, purveyors, barrack, military store, clothing and contract departments, and munitions of war and their manufacture were all grouped under a single Controller-in-Chief, a second Military Under-Secretary of State.

The effect of all the departmental re-organizations since 1854 was to consolidate two 'empires' within military administration in place of the previous five. The Secretary of State for War controlled all aspects of supply and finance, while the Commander-in-Chief was responsible for the internal administration of the army and its preparation for its military tasks. Although the Commander-in-Chief's constitutional responsibility to the Secretary for War had been restated in 1860, he was in practice independent, and the Horse Guards and War Department corresponded with each other as separate departments. In the division of responsibilities between Secretary for War and Commander-in-Chief there therefore remained a serious and unfortunate anomaly.

In 1868 the second great reforming administration of the nine-teenth century came into office under Gladstone.

The new Liberal Secretary of State for War, Edward Cardwell, was an exemplar of Victorian intellectual ability; a product of Winchester and Balliol, with a double first in classics and mathematics. He possessed the capacity to relate detailed reforms to clear fundamental principles of organization and function. He aimed not at further patchwork improvement, but at the creation of a complete, coherent and effective military system. It is important not to lose perspective in considering Cardwell's work at the War Office. Cardwell's name sometimes appears as a kind of signpost designating army reform in the nineteenth century, and marking a single point at which the Wellingtonian army gave way to the modern. In fact the changes of 1854–5 were more fundamental than any of Cardwell's. The further improvements of 1856–68 and in particular the close study of military problems by committee and commission provided Cardwell with a basis for action. And the results of Cardwell's reforms proved less (and later) in practice than on paper.

When Cardwell took office his primary object was to save money by improved efficiency, rather than to give Britain a more powerful military instrument. Two years were spent in detailed investigation of the problems. From 1869–70 he tackled what he considered to be the root of the military problem – the size of the forces overseas in the empire, and the long-service system. Cardwell was more thorough than his predecessors in bringing home troops from the colonies. In 1869 he brought back over 15,000 men; and in 1870 another 10,000 men – colonial garrisons now stood under 24,000 (excluding India), as against nearly 50,000 in 1858. In 1870 Cardwell brought forward a bill to bring in short-service on the continental model, although based on volunteering instead of conscription. On the passage of this Bill and on all Cardwell's subsequent measures impinged the events of the Franco-Prussian War.

The Prussian victory was a further fine advertisement for their system of short-service and 'localization'; it was a shock to those who had continued to look on France as the first military power in Europe. It did not at first cause apprehension in Britain, for German unification seemed a worthy fulfilment of liberal ideals, and the Prussian army, after all, had fought alongside Wellington against the French at Waterloo. The war was seen as a victory of austere Protestant patriots over the dissolute, Roman Catholic and expansionist French empire. But even while the war was still impending, it raised acutely the question of British military weakness. The British government felt the traditional British concern for the security of Belgium. Thought had to be given therefore to defending Belgian neutrality or at least Antwerp. It was found that only by keeping back drafts from India could 20,000 men be scraped together – 20,000 men in under-strength battalions, not a cohesive army, to meet a situation where the main belligerents were to field over a million and a half. Luckily French and Prussian assurances of respect for Belgian neutrality allowed Britain to relapse into her customary role of spectator.

Behind the immediate implications in the Franco-Prussian war for Britain and for Cardwell's plans there was a wider lesson. The conflict demonstrated with vivid force the enormous changes in the character of war that had now been brought about by the industrial revolution, by social progress, and by scientific invention.

13

Cardwell
and the Late
Victorian Army

WAR had always been a pacemaker of technology. The demand for ever more powerful and accurate artillery had stimulated advances in metallurgy and manufacturing technique. The making of cylinders for steam-engines grew out of the making of cannon-barrels. The demand for accurate and reliable small-arms had similar effects on technology. In the nineteenth century accelerating technological development in turn made possible new weapons of enormous power. In 1853 a Russian fleet destroyed a squadron of wooden Turkish frigates with explosive shell. In 1862, during the American Civil War, there was an epoch-making though indecisive fight between two experimental armoured ships, the Confederate *Merrimac* and the Federal *Monitor*. In 1859 and 1860, the two great naval powers, France and Britain, launched armoured steamships, *La Gloire* and the *Warrior*. Each alone could have sunk the fleets at Trafalgar unscathed. More powerful explosives demanded stronger metal to resist their impact or pressure; a chain reaction drove forward technical change faster and faster. The Bessemer process, for example, was the direct result of a reward offered by Napoleon III for a cheap process for making steel capable of withstanding the new shells.

The general adoption of rifling and breech-loading revolutionized small-arms and artillery alike. Although there had been experiments with both rifling and breech-loading since the sixteenth century, it only now became technically possible to achieve a gas-tight breech and a simple, reliable method of loading and firing. The breech was sealed at the moment of detonation by the expansion of a soft metal base to the cartridge: the invention of a

Frenchman named Pauly. It was a German, Johann von Dreyse,
who invented the bolt action for inserting the round in the breech,
locking the breech during firing, and extracting the spent cartridge.
There had been various experiments to unite the percussion cap
with the cartridge as a means of detonation: centre-fire cartridges,
rim-fire cartridges. Dreyse placed his detonating charge at the
head of the cartridge (behind the bullet), rather than the base. A
long needle released from the front of the bolt pierced the length
of the cartridge and exploded the cap, giving Dreyse's rifle its
name of 'needle-gun'. Adopted by the Prussian army as early as
1843, it was the first service breech-loading rifle. Infantry armed
with the needle-gun enjoyed two great advantages over opponents
with muzzle-loaders – a rate of fire six times faster, and ease of
loading while lying down. Effective musketry no longer depended
on close-order drill. In the war against Austria in 1866 the Prussian
infantry swept away the Austrians as they stood up in their dense
old-fashioned formations.

By 1870 the French army introduced a far better weapon than
the needle-gun in the Chassepot rifle, which had almost three times
the range and was more reliable. However, the Prussians had now
revolutionized their field artillery by replacing muzzle-loading
smooth-bores with rifled breech-loaders. In accuracy, range and
speed of fire they dominated the French smooth-bore artillery and
largely nullified the superiority of the Chassepot over the needle-
guns. The French themselves nullified the effects of their own new
weapon, the first effective service machine-gun, the *mitrailleuse* –
which worked by hand rotation of multiple barrels – by treating it
as an artillery piece instead of an infantry weapon. Kept back from
the front line, and outranged by Prussian artillery, it was destroyed
in battery.

New weapons were only one aspect of the mid-nineteenth-
century revolution in war. After 1830 the railways put an end to the
era of the horse and the carriage which had lasted for thousands of
years. An army's supplies could now move at an average speed of
twenty miles an hour instead of ten miles a day, and in vastly greater
quantity. The railway enabled the battlefront easily to tap the
entire resources of the nations behind it – and those resources had

been multiplied many times by the speeding growth of industry and trade.

Prussia, a country without natural geographical frontiers in the heart of Europe, saw the railway as a means to German unity and national power. Railways would enable her to make use of her central position to throw an army swiftly to any threatened frontier. An economist, Friedrich List, prophesied how railways might bind a united Germany. In 1846 the Prussian army conducted its first experiment in large-scale troop movement by rail. The German railway system was from the start developed on strategic lines approved by the general staff.

By the development of long-distance telegraphy (first used in war in the Crimea) orders and information could be transmitted swiftly over great distances, and no longer at the speed and range of couriers on horses.

By 1870 war lacked only one other major element of the new industrial era – the participation of mass society. The war of the French Revolution and Napoleon I, though pre-industrial, had been an ideological peoples' war, fought for the unlimited aim of total victory, and fed, through conscription, with the entire human resources of the nations. It was the belief of military writers after 1815 that there could be no going back to the 'cabinet' wars of the eighteenth century, fought with limited forces to achieve limited political ends. The German Carl von Clausewitz, in his great book, *On War*, derived from the Napoleonic wars a complete philosophy of war, believing that it must always tend towards extremes, to a struggle to the death between whole peoples. In fact nineteenth-century European wars were all 'cabinet' wars – even the Prussian victories of 1866 and 1870 – waged in the service of a circumspect foreign policy.

It was in America that industrial power and peoples' war were first combined. In the American Civil War (1861–5) the North and South fought for completely irreconcilable principles – preservation of the Union versus the right to secede, and later the abolition of negro slavery versus its preservation. The Civil War was a struggle for survival between two opposed kinds of society and ways of life, a fight to the finish. The war revealed the gigantic force modern invention and modern social organization gave to war. The industries of America and Europe were tapped for munitions. The adult manpower of America was conscripted into the armies. The railway united nation and army, hinterland and battlefield. The railway network permitted rapid strategic combination over long distances, and rail junctions became the objects of attack or manoeuvre like the river fortresses of old. The war was ended only by the extinction of the military power of the South and its occupation. To achieve this 'total' objective took four years, although the South was outnumbered five to one in population and heavily outweighed in industrial resources. The casualties numbered half a million. The final campaign of 1864–5 took the form of continual battles of attrition; of trench warfare. This was the scale of industrial peoples' war and the cost of total victory.

In Europe the lessons of the American Civil War were ignored or misread. The swift victories of the Prussians over the Austrians in 1866 and the French in 1870 were thought to show that modern techniques meant short wars, economical in blood and financially profitable.

The Prussian government tapped the national manpower more effectively than the Americans. The Prussian army had been completely re-organized since 1859. Before 1859, although the obligation of all Prussian citizens to serve had never lapsed, the Prussian army had been a force of mostly long-service professionals, to be supplemented in war by the *Landwehr*, equivalent to the British militia. Under Scharnhorst's reforms at the beginning of the century, conscripts had passed to the *Landwehr* after service with the line, thus forming a trained reserve. Latterly men had joined the *Landwehr* directly as they did the British militia; and like the militia the *Landwehr* was not militarily efficient. The *Landwehr* was also, again like the British militia of the eighteenth century, a separate 'civilian' army, independent of the army high command. The Prussian military reformers proposed a new military system, whereby the professional army would become a permanent cadre for training intakes of conscripts, who after three years' service with the line and four with the regular reserve, would pass into the *Landwehr*. In time of war Prussia would be able to call on large reserves of trained men. At the same time the *Landwehr* was to lose its independence (this caused a bitter political and constitutional struggle) and be merged into a single military system under regular officers. In 1870, the new Prussian system quickly mobilized over one million men, an unheard-of figure.

Until 1868, the French, like the British, still held largely to a long-service professional army, partly because conscription would have been politically unpopular. Even in the face of Prussian success against Austria, the French felt able to only create a half-baked kind of reserve system without full national service, so that in 1870 France, with more than Prussia's total population, was only able to put into the field less than half the number of troops. It had been the argument of those in favour of a long-service army (in France and earlier in Prussia) that conscript troops could not stand against professionals. The event proved that with modern weapons three years' service was as good as twenty.

The Prussians also ushered in the modern era in terms of staff methods and organization. The movement and supply of even the best of the old armies had been something of a shambles. However, with millions of men to mobilize and move by rail, a collective brain, using scientific methods of study and evaluation and new techniques of statistical analysis, was required. Under the guidance of Helmuth von Moltke the Prussian Great General Staff evolved into this kind of brain. It learned from its mistakes by systematic study. It mastered the problems of mass organization and movement so brilliantly that in 1870 1,183,000 men passed through the barracks into the army in eighteen days, and 462,000 were transported to the French frontier in the same time. No contemporary operation of civilian industry or public administration could compare in scale with this. The Prussian General Staff paved the way for later techniques of industrial management; the staff college preceded the business school, while the 'war game' was to become an accepted device in commerce and industry.

By contrast, the French mobilization was typical of the pre-industrial era. After three weeks only half the reservists had reached their units, which themselves often lacked supplies and equipment. During the campaign too, the efficiency of the German supply system contrasted with the old-style improvisation and marauding in the French army. The French failure was partly owing to their tradition of colonial warfare, with its romantic legends. Small campaigns against Arabs in North Africa led the French, like the British, to emphasize the ability of commanders to improvise. Military skill in the French army, as in the British, came to be seen as a swift eye for ground and bold personal leadership of small units, rather than as 'big-business' management.

It was against the background of these fundamental changes in the nature of war that Cardwell carried through his reforms.

*

Cardwell faced two major and inter-related problems: one was recruitment, and the other was Britain's dual strategic roles as both a European and a world-imperial power. Possible intervention in Europe required a nucleus organization of a field army backed by ample and quickly mobilizeable reserves: the Prussian system, although on a much smaller scale because Britain was an island. However, the Prussian system was founded on the sure base of an annual intake of conscripts, while any reformed British system would have to depend on voluntary recruitment. Cardwell abolished bounties as an incentive to enlist in 1869 as now ineffective, but Gladstone and the British tax-payer were unlikely to sanction such costly improvements in pay and conditions as to make the army a competitive occupation. In any case, a short-service army, even with steam-navigation, could not garrison India and the empire, for which long-service troops were needed. It was the kind of problem that had troubled the French before 1870, and the resulting unhappy compromise between European and colonial demands had contributed to the French army's defeat by the Prussians.

Cardwell tried to find an answer with his Army Enlistment Act of 1870. Enlistment was henceforth to be for twelve years: six with the colours and six in the reserve. However, while men in India would serve the full six years with the colours, men in Britain could pass into the reserve after three years. Cardwell hoped that eventually this Act would produce a reserve of 80,000 men. Under another

Below decks in a 'trooper', 1873. Unlike European soldiers, the British soldier spent much of his service abroad in the Empire. This overseas service deeply influenced the history and character of the British army.

Act of Cardwell's, men of bad character could be discharged from the army. It was hoped that the two Acts together would improve the quality of the rank-and-file without actually spending more money on them.

Cardwell's reforms are often, though wrongly, said to revolve round the 'linked-battalion' system, by which one battalion served abroad, while its pair was at home in the depot as a training and reinforcement unit. In fact two-fifths of the pre-Cardwell regiments already possessed two battalions, and since 1825 all battalions had been so divided as to provide a number of companies for duty abroad (the service companies) and one or more for duty at home (the depot companies). The key to Cardwell's reforms of the regimental system was in fact recruitment; and the best hope for recruitment at a time of dearth of Irish lay in the militia, composed of volunteers already partially accustomed to a military life. Thus 'localization' of the military system in territorial areas, where line regiments could be linked to militia regiments, was the essential frame of the Cardwell reforms. Although the model was Prussia, in Britain the place of army-corps districts was taken by districts of an administrative (not a field) brigade. There were sixty-six of these districts, fitted so far as possible into the British county map. The district and its brigade, under a lieutenant-colonel and a depot staff, welded together regular army, militia and volunteers into one system. The district comprised two regular battalions (one, and quite often both, away from the depot), two militia battalions and the volunteers. For the first time, regiments of the line were to be given fixed, permanent homes. Once new barracks had been built, it was hoped that through local pride the gulf between the army and the nation might be bridged, and recruitment stimulated by the close local association of militia and regulars. Thus Cardwell's 'localization' of the army was only made possible by the revival of the militia itself by the re-organization of 1852–3. For the district depots to be of adequate size and for ease of reinforcement, it was necessary to have two-battalion regiments. As Field-Marshal Lord Hardinge wrote at the end of the Crimean War:

The experience of the last two years affords a practical proof of the inefficiency and danger of relying on small regimental depots as a reserve for the field battalions, when the country may be suddenly involved in war.[1]

Since the British regiment was self-contained and 'independent', single-battalion regiments well under strength could not be combined to make full-strength battalions. By contrast, the Royal Artillery, whose regiments had never been self-contained, could post men freely where needed. However, because of the strength of sentiment about the infantry regiments, with their individual customs and history, it was out of the question to form a Corps of Infantry on the lines of the Royal Artillery. Cardwell hoped instead to find some kind of answer by linking single-battalion regiments in pairs, one to be at home as a drafting and training unit, the other abroad, in alternation. However, his linkings demanded that very different kinds of regiment should work in double harness. Cardwell, by reforming too little, demanded too much. In 1881 another Secretary for War, Hugh Childers, took the final step of fusing the linked units permanently into new two-battalion regiments, with territorial designations of the style Cardwell had already applied to much of the remainder of the army. The cherished post-1881 county names often replaced sometimes very different county titles given to the numbered regiments of the line during the American War of Independence. In Cardwell's own time territorialization existed mainly on paper. For troubles in Ireland meant that the 'home' as well as the 'overseas' battalion of a linked-pair would sometimes be away from the depot. Depot buildings had to be constructed throughout the country before the regulars and the militia could really share a common local home and loyalty. And, in the event, an unexpected bonus to recruitment was provided by the agricultural depression of the 1870s.

Before Cardwell's master-plan for 'localization' could be carried through, two obstacles had to be removed. The first was the control of the militia (extending to the issue of commissions) by the Lords-Lieutenant. The second was the institution of purchase. Both were dealt with in the Regulation of the Forces Bill of 1871.

Because of the bitter and prolonged fight over the abolition of purchase, it has excited more notice than its importance in Cardwell's reforms merits. It was not so much for its own inherent evils that Cardwell wanted to abolish purchase, but because it stood squarely in the way of all his other reforms. Purchase blocked regimental re-organization and led to rigidity in the army's structure, because it made each regiment not simply a unit in an army but a colonel's private property. Two colonels' private properties could not be amalgamated or linked because of the possibility of financial loss. As Cardwell himself told the Commons:

Do you wish to increase the number of double battalions with a view to the Indian branch of the army, and to short terms of service – a point of the greatest possible importance? If you do so wish, you will be met immediately by difficulties arising from the purchase question.... Do you wish to unite closely the militia and the regular forces? If you do, one of the first things you will have to do will be to give subaltern officers of the militia, commissions in the line without purchase, and how can this be done if there remain any conditions in reference to the purchase system?[2]

The effects of purchase on the professional quality of officers was a lesser question than that of organization. Nevertheless there was wide agreement (except among the diehards) with the view expressed by the 1856 Royal Commission that purchase was

... vicious in principle, repugnant to the public sentiment of the present day, equally inconsistent with the honour of the military profession and the policy of the British Empire, and irreconcilable with justice.[3]

Although Cardwell persuaded a thrifty government to pay over-regulation (black market) prices instead of the official tariff in buying out owners of commissions (which involved, for example, paying up £14,000 to buy out the owner of a cavalry regiment instead of £6,175), he failed to win over the opposition. A violent parliamentary struggle ended with the House of Lords throwing out the Regulation of the Forces Bill. To the diehards' fury, Cardwell turned their flank by inducing the Queen to end purchase by royal warrant, on the grounds that purchase had officially existed only by virtue of regulations established under earlier royal warrants. The Lords now passed the Bill, which, as well as abolishing purchase, transferred control over the militia and volunteers from the Lords-Lieutenant back to the Crown (and hence to the Secretary for War and the Commander-in-Chief). At last regular army and militia had been brought into one military system and the Lords-Lieutenant were deprived of their Tudor *raison d'être*. The Regulation of the Forces Act also gave the government powers of control over the national railway system in time of threatened invasion.

Cardwell's three great reforms (the Army Enlistment Act of 1870, the Regulation of the Forces Act of 1871, and the localization and linked-battalion scheme of 1872) provided the blue-print of the late Victorian army: short service, a reserve, a comprehensive military system based on the local depot. Cardwell was also responsible for other reforms, such as the abolition of flogging except in time of war, an increase in privates' pay to 1s. a day on top of free meat and bread, and some improvement in living conditions. In 1871 the first large-scale manoeuvres ever to be held in Britain were organized and repeated annually for several years before petering out again.

The War Office and Horse Guards also received the benefits of Cardwell's intellect and energy. By the War Office Act of 1870 and subsequent Orders-in-Council, Cardwell tried to complete the piecemeal reforms since 1854, and re-organize army administration on clear principles. The subordination of the Commander-in-Chief to the Secretary for War was placed beyond doubt by the new Act, which on behalf of Parliament and the Crown vested direct responsibility for every branch of the army in the Secretary of State. The army was no longer even residually under the royal prerogative, and the constitutional ghosts of the seventeenth and eighteenth centuries had at last been laid. The Horse Guards and the War Office were now to constitute a single department, although they remained physically separated. The work of the combined department was divided between three executive officers: the 'Officer Commanding-in-Chief' (the strictly military aspects of all regular and irregular forces); the Surveyor-General of the Ordnance (all aspects of supply and equipment); and thirdly a financial secretary, responsible to the Secretary for War for pay, for all estimates and accounting, and for checking expenditure.

Cardwell's new consolidated War Office was marred by the hesitancy and compromise of all his schemes. There was only a partial approach to a general staff on the Prussian model (without the name). In practice, the Commander-in-Chief still ran the army independently of the Secretary for War. The forming of a general staff and the abolition of the personal power of the Commander-in-Chief were measures that went together, but there was an immovable obstacle in their way in the person of His Royal Highness the Duke of Cambridge, the Commander-in-Chief. Although Cambridge had given tepid support to Cardwell's other reforms, his taste for improvement did not extend to the abolition of his own unchallenged control over the army, or the loss of his job. Behind Cambridge stood his cousin, the Queen, and the court. Cardwell did not even attempt the impossible, and so instead of a general staff Britain continued to have Cambridge for another quarter of a century.

When Cardwell left office in 1874 his work remained unfinished in some respects, and half-baked in others. Even a double first at Balliol had found British institutions intractable material for the application of clear fundamental principles. His work does not therefore stand alone as a great turning-point of reform; it marks only one important stage in a continual, if spasmodic, process.

*

In the late Victorian age, the strategic role of the British army and its place in the sentiments of the nation both altered. The industrial revolution had crowded the British into drab towns and suburbs. The Reform Act of 1867 extended the vote to the lower middle classes and the 'upper' working classes in towns. The Education Act of 1870 began compulsory education. The rise of the lower middle and working classes created a new climate of national opinion. A new kind of journalism sprang up to exploit it. Patriotism, imperialism and war provided exciting reading, a compensation for the drabness of life, a vicarious outlet for suppressed aggression.

At the same time there was a national feeling that other nations, envious of Britain, were striving to catch her up. These factors led to the mood known as Jingoism, and the policies known as Imperialism. In the late Victorian age the music-hall had become a mirror of mass sentiment. In 1877, when there was again a possibility of war against Russia on the side of Turkey, the music-hall launched Jingoism with a song that began:

> The Dogs of War are loose and the rugged Russian Bear,
> Full bent on blood and robbery has crawled out of his lair,

and went on:

> As peacemaker Old England her very utmost tried,
> The Russians said they wanted peace, but then those Russians
>   lied,
> Of Carnage and of trickery they'll have sufficient feast,
> Ere they dare to think of coming near our Road unto the East.

Then came the well-known chorus that became a leitmotif of the age:

> We don't want to fight, but by jingo if we do,
> We've got the ships, we've got the men, and got the money too.
> We've fought the Bear before, and while we're Britons true,
> The Russians shall not have Constantinople.

In a later version criticisms of Jingoism were rebutted by the argument that 'If it's Jingo to love honour, then Jingoes are we'; and the refrain assured Europe:

> So we're waiting for the signal; directly up it runs,
> Clear the decks for action, stand by the guns,
> Our Army and our Navy, true British dogs of war,
> Will make them cry 'Peccavi', the same as they did before.

For the first time since Waterloo British world power was threatened by the rivalry of other great states. British commercial supremacy was being eroded – especially by united Germany. In these new circumstances the British empire ceased to appear a costly encumbrance and began once more to seem a source of power and opportunity. It was a boom period for ideas of imperial federation. Unavoidable involvement in colonial wars gradually altered into more or less open imperial expansion.

By the 1890s, thanks to the Cardwell reforms and to the prevailing public mood of imperialism, the soldier had at last ceased to be a figure of national suspicion or contempt.

Although the Royal Navy remained the symbol of British world supremacy, it was the army that did the fighting. 'The Soldiers of the Queen', as the title of another rousing music-hall song had it, were continually engaged on active service – and for the first time in history, right in the eye of a proud public. In its red coats and spiked helmets of Prussian model (it survives without the spike in the modern policeman's helmet), the late Victorian army found a place in national pride and affection never accorded to its predecessors. The nation cheered victories like Tel-el-Kebir, were stirred by such gallant stands as at Rorke's Drift, groaned at disasters like Isandhwana and Majuba Hill. The army's leaders became folk-heroes – Sir Garnet Wolseley ('All Sir Garnet'), Lord Roberts ('Bobs'), and Kitchener of Khartoum ('K of K'). When Cardwell's localization of the army gradually took shape, there developed, as he had hoped, a strong local pride in the Royal Barsetshires that had rarely been felt for the Umpteenth Foot. The local depot became one of the institutions of town or country life. The gulf of sympathy between army and nation was at last nearly closed.

It was not, however, closed to the extent that men from all sections of British society joined the army. The feeling that it was a disgrace to a family for one of its members to go for a soldier died hard. Although the gradual reform of the conditions of army life and discipline had put an end to a rank-and-file of felons, drunks, and pathological outcasts, the army was still recruited mostly from the very poorest and most ignorant. The army was, in a real sense, the only welfare service provided by the British state for the rescue of such unfortunates. It followed that standards of physical fitness, intelligence and education could not be high; that discipline had still to be stern and rigid. This was a rough and tough army that could endure a campaign or a battle stoically enough under the orders of its officers, but not always display individual initiative and quick response.

The officer corps also failed to reflect the great changes in British society. Despite the abolition of purchase, the life of a regimental mess still reflected the life of the country's upper classes. After the 1880s the Victorian public schools began to infect the officer corps with their own very narrow snobbery and rigid sense of form. Such sons of the rich middle class as reached the army did so by courtesy of their private income and a public-school conditioning. The need for private income was an excellent substitute to purchase as a social filter. A life of racing, polo, hunting, balls and parties required an income much greater than an officer's pay, which was in any case not competitive with those of other professions. The control of the army remained in the hands of men out of touch with, and out of sympathy with, the social and technical changes of the age. Secondly, since both officers and men were recruited from unrepresentative social groups, the nation as a whole had little directly to do with the army. The human cost of imperial responsibility did not fall on the audiences who sang so patriotically in the music-halls, or damned lesser breeds at suburban tennis parties. What cheaper or less troublesome way of running a great empire could there be than a professional army whose officers all had private incomes, and whose rank-and-file were all paupers?

Many traditional institutions of the British way of life trace their present character no further back than the late Victorian period: organized cricket and football, mass tea-drinking, the popularity of the monarchy, the Labour movement – and the army. The army's principal homes today – like Aldershot – were then being built. The intense regimental spirit that has been so jealously defended in the face of amalgamations since 1945 owes more to Cardwell and Childers than to the era before the Crimea. The familiar full-dress uniforms of the Foot Guards and Household Cavalry in their present form are late Victorian. In Rudyard Kipling the army found a poet to express its own private values and record its way of life in India, the country that marked it so deeply.

The characteristics of the late Victorian army, the type of opponents it had to face, and the kind of leader it threw up are illustrated by the careers of three national heroes: Wolseley, Roberts and Kitchener. The span of their careers also covers most of the campaigns that mark the transition from unwilling involvement in colonial wars to overt imperialist expansion.

All three heroes came, like many British officers, from the Anglo-Irish gentry, the nearest thing Britain ever possessed to the

Prussian *Junker* class. Often poorer than their English brethren owing to Irish rural poverty and consequently low rents, the Anglo-Irish lived a horsey life particularly remote from the modern world of industry and towns. As with the *Junker*, son followed father into the army down the generations. Roberts, Wolseley and Kitchener were all sons of soldiers, none of them rich like many English officers, although possessing sufficient private income to live on; all therefore highly ambitious.

Roberts succeeded in entering the East India Company's cadet college at Addiscombe and thence the Company's army in India. During and after the era of 'John Company's' army, the Indian service offered a better career to the less affluent but able than the British. Later, it was those entrants to Sandhurst with the highest marks who were creamed off for the Indian army. Expenses were lower, pay and allowances more generous, opportunities for advancement wider than in the British army. Roberts's career therefore represents that other great strand in Victorian military history – the Indian army.

Both Roberts and Wolseley served in – and learned from – the war in the Crimea. Both served in the campaign to quell the Indian Mutiny, and were at the relief of Lucknow and the taking of Delhi.

After ten years as a staff officer and in minor expeditions against Indian tribesmen, Roberts was with the Indian contingent in the British force that invaded Ethiopia in 1868 to rescue some British and other European prisoners of the mad King Theodore. This too-often-forgotten Abyssinian expedition was entirely successful. The British force under Sir Robert Napier routed the Abyssinians at Arogee almost without a fight, took the Abyssinian fortress of Magdala (whereat King Theodore committed suicide), and released the prisoners. The Abyssinian expedition is interesting in that it was particularly cheap in life and treasure, suffered no setbacks or even awkward moments, and was fought largely by the Indian army. This showed that India might be a source of imperial military power instead of a drain on it.

Roberts was now given the post of First Assistant Quartermaster-General at army headquarters in Simla. Roberts was learning much about organizing forces in the field, but he learned, in characteristic British fashion, on the job, for there was no staff college in India. In 1869 he organized the transport for a column that was off to punish a hill tribe near the Burma border. As Quartermaster-General he was also responsible for the elaborate and faultless arrangements for the great Imperial Assembly of New Year's Day, 1877, at which the absent Queen was proclaimed 'Empress of India'.

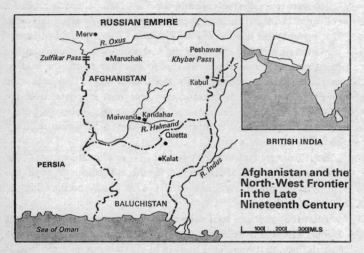

Afghanistan and the North-West Frontier in the Late Nineteenth Century

In 1878 Roberts commanded a field force in the Second Afghan War. The war illustrated the change in British imperial policy from unwilling local involvement into rivalry with other great powers. Russian expansion eastwards in Asia had carried Russian power to the northern borders of Afghanistan. An apparent Russian threat to India was now added to the traditional British involvement (because of India) with the internal politics of Afghanistan and even Persia. The Afghans having failed to show themselves sufficiently pro-British, the British invaded their country in three columns. Roberts's command consisted of six battalions, which, characteristically, he had himself to organize into a field force, and for which he had to find transport. The invasion was successful.

However, the Afghans later murdered the British mission in Kabul and beleaguered the British garrisons. Roberts was put in charge of the 'Kabul Field Force', a punitive expedition to restore British authority. He led its advance with relentless activity and boldness. However, his chief of staff noted:

The march was a lamentable instance of the carelessness and happy-go-lucky style in which we do things. There was a small advanced guard, a few men with guns, others scattered about, and the rest in the rear; no attempt was made to keep the baggage and troops within a reasonable space, and the consequence was, the whole line of march was sprawling along three times as long as it need.[4]

Nevertheless the Afghans did not take advantage, and Roberts finally beat them outside the city of Kabul (1879). In 1880 came news of a disaster to a British force in southern Afghanistan at Maiwand, followed by retreat into Kandahar, where it was besieged.

The relief of Kandahar made Roberts a national hero. His force consisted of under 10,000 men and eighteen guns. His march was a supreme example of the kind of campaign the British and Indian armies habitually fought. In the words of a correspondent with Roberts:

... we are marching day after day through a half-desolate land, with no supports to fall back upon in case of disaster, and uncertain of what lay before us; with nothing but thin tents to shield us from a sun which laughed to scorn 100° in the shade, and with a water-supply so uncertain that we never knew in the morning where our camping ground in the evening might be.[5]

Despite exhaustion and dysentery among the troops, Roberts drove his force the 300 miles to Kandahar, routed the Afghan army and relieved the town. Roberts received the thanks of the Houses of Parliament, a baronetcy, a G.C.B. and an autographed letter from the Queen. In late Victorian England the relief of Kandahar counted as a great military achievement. In 1885 Roberts became Commander-in-Chief in India, the culmination of the career of an officer of the Indian army. He himself was more aware than the nation that his successes had been won against ill-equipped irregulars, and that the enemy might not always be such. As Commander-in-Chief he set to work to re-organize the recruitment, training and transport of the Indian army.

Wolseley's career, in the British service, followed a similar alternation of staff appointments and leadership of small expeditions. In 1869–70 Wolseley in Canada led a force 1,200 miles through a wilderness of forest, rivers, rapids and lakes to crush a minor rebellion on the Red River. Wolseley displayed great powers of improvisation and personal leadership. In 1871, as an assistant adjutant-general in London, Wolseley was Cardwell's military mentor. Wolseley by temperament and professional conviction violently attacked all that was inefficient and old-fashioned. By earning him bitter enemies (including the Duke of Cambridge), his well-publicized attacks served to slow rather than hasten the reform of the army for which he strove throughout his career.

In 1873–4 Wolseley commanded an expeditionary force against the Ashanti tribe of West Africa. The Ashanti under their king, the Kofi, based on their up-country capital Kumasi, terrorized the tribes on the fringes of British rule. The Ashanti military system was based on universal conscription and lavish human sacrifice to the gods. The successful capture of the Ashanti capital required the improvisation of a field force and of its logistics, the construction of a road through the thick fever-ridden jungle and forest and of no fewer than 237 bridges, and an advance through unfamiliar country against an elusive and capable enemy. Wolseley picked his own staff from young officers of his own zealous type. Later, as he rose in the army, he tended to choose members of the same group of officers for key positions. They became known as the 'Ashanti ring' or the 'Wolseley ring'. Moltke in Germany too had stamped a common method and mind on the Prussian army partly by means of staff officers who would be vehicles of his ideas. However, Moltke was trying to create a professional system, while Wolseley's 'ring' was purely personal.

Wolseley returned home from the defeat of the Ashanti to a hero's reception by Queen and nation. Although it was understandable, the late Victorians were getting things slightly out of proportion. Wolseley's enemies, though ferocious, had only been equipped with matchlocks.

Wolseley's next military assignment was in South Africa. Adjacent to the British colony of Natal and the Boer state of the Transvaal was the Zulu nation of King Cetewayo, in whose warriors the martial spirit was kept high by sexual repression, leading to marked irritability vented on the enemy by means of the assegai. The Zulus were well-disciplined and incredibly fleet of foot. In 1879 they lured Lord Chelmsford, the local Commander-in-Chief, away from his camp at Isandhlwana, and then destroyed it and all who were in it. Isandhlwana struck the British public as if it were a catastrophe like the surrender of Yorktown; another indication that the late Victorians were getting a little out of perspective. The successful defence of Rorke's Drift, a small group of houses by a ford, by just over 100 men later that day was treated like a battle of Talavera. So 'Britain's only general', Sir Garnet Wolseley, set forth. However, he arrived only to find that Chelmsford had redeemed himself by beating the Zulus at Ulundi. It was left to Wolseley to break up Zululand between petty chiefs.

In 1881 the Boers went to war to regain their independence after the British annexation of their territories in 1877. Wolseley had gone home, but one of his 'ring', Sir George Colley, took the field against the Boers with 1,500 men. It was the first time the British army had fought white men since the Crimea. Colley was beaten at Laing's Nek, advanced again and tried to turn the Boer position by installing 359 men on the top of Majuba Hill. Instead, the Boers, pitting excellent fieldcraft and musketry against the wooden discipline of the British, drove them off the hill with heavy loss, including Colley himself. Majuba Hill, involving fewer than 400 troops, equally struck the British at home as a major disaster. In its aftermath the independence of the Boer Republics was recognized.

In 1882 Wolseley was involved in what was perhaps the first purely imperialist British military expedition, undertaken by Gladstone of all people, although reluctantly enough. The Khedive of Egypt had been lent vast sums of money by European financiers

The price of Empire that the nation as a whole never paid – sick and wounded from Wolseley's campaign in Egypt in 1882.

at rewarding interest rates, with Egypt as the pledge. Later, in order that the interest should be paid, the European financiers and their governments suggested, among other things, economies in the Egyptian army. A Colonel Arabi Pasha led a nationalist revolt against foreign domination and made a tool of the Khedive. Europeans were killed in riots. There was a danger to the Suez Canal as well as to the pockets of the holders of Egyptian bonds.

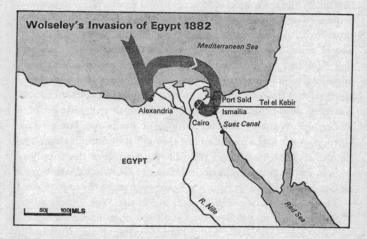

The British government therefore sent an expedition under Sir Garnet Wolseley, then Adjutant-General at the War Office.

This expedition was the largest and most elaborate of all Wolseley's small wars. It involved over 40,000 soldiers, and sixty-one steamships carried the army and over 41,000 tons of supplies from Britain to Egypt. It was a credit to Wolseley that the movement was quickly mounted and smoothly performed. He feinted at Alexandria, then landed at Ismailia, half-way down the Suez Canal, and lunged towards Cairo across the desert. However, transport and supply arrangements in the field once more proved inadequate. There was a limit to improvisation, and Wolseley found it in Egypt. Only after a pause longer than an eager nation liked, did he move on to smash Arabi at Tel-el-Kebir. Egypt became a British protectorate.

Now, however, the British became further involved in the Sudan, an Egyptian territory, where a dervish chief, the Mahdi ('Messiah'), had raised the people in revolt against Egyptian rule and all foreigners. Gladstone sent General Gordon (who had made his reputation during another British involvement on the mainland of China in the 1860s) to evacuate the garrisons and civilians of the Sudan. Instead, Gordon resolved to hold Khartoum, the Sudanese capital. While the nation read anxiously the news of his heroic and prolonged defence, opinion waxed hot in favour of sending a relief expedition. After months of havering, on the score of cost and liberal principles, Gladstone gave way. 'Our only general' was sent back to Egypt. Once again there was an expedition through appallingly difficult country for Wolseley to organize and lead – another long line of communication to build, this time a railway. However, despite his improvisation and furiously energetic personal leadership, Wolseley arrived forty-eight hours too late to save Gordon. A fortnight had been lost through staff muddles over coal for the river steamers and the railway, and over the supply of camels. Public fury at Khartoum's fall and Gordon's death turned on Gladstone; Wolseley returned home even more the hero.

Then followed five weary years inside the War Office, where Wolseley, as Adjutant-General, fought an open battle for reform with the Commander-in-Chief, a battle fought both departmentally and, on the part of Wolseley, by fierce public propaganda. After largely failing, he spent five years as Commander-in-Chief in the military backwater of Ireland. In 1895, already a field-marshal, Wolseley at last took Cambridge's place at the head of the army, but he was now well past the prime of his intellect and energy.

Herbert Kitchener, the youngest of the three heroes, began his army career as an engineer. Kitchener, like Wolseley, had driving ambition and professional zeal. Kitchener's careerism was more ruthless and single-minded, more cold and egotistical than that of Wolseley. Able survey work in Palestine and Cyprus (then Turkish territory) between 1874 and 1880, and admirable intelligence reports in 1884 on the state of upper Egypt founded his reputation. More intelligence work and the leadership of Arab irregulars in the Sudan, well put about by Kitchener's father, further helped his rise. After seeing action against the dervishes, he was appointed Adjutant-General to the Egyptian army in Cairo in 1889 – astoundingly rapid promotion that did not help his popularity. Nor did his cold and arrogant manner. He commanded the cavalry in a brisk action against the dervishes at Toski. In 1892 Kitchener, still only a colonel in the British service, was appointed Sirdar, or Commander-in-Chief of the Egyptian army.

When at last in 1896 the British government, in the full tide of imperialism, decided to re-conquer the Sudan, Kitchener commanded the army. The conquest took two years, in which Kitchener advanced up the Nile by stages, deliberately organizing his rail and river communications behind him. His command included river steamers and gun-boats and some 15,000 men, British and Egyptian. It was the largest of all the long-range penetrations organized and carried out by British soldiers since Wolseley's Red River expedition of 1870. It went forward through shaking white heat, and, less expectedly, through fierce rain-storms and floods. The advance to Khartoum was a supreme exercise in personal leadership, the more so because Kitchener was an intense and secretive egotist who refused to delegate. Kitchener carried to its ultimate that late Victorian British military tradition of personal improvisation, which stood in such contrast to the collective, 'big-business' staff systems of Europe. Kitchener's office methods were absolutely chaotic; everything was in his head, and his head alone. Nevertheless the dervishes were beaten first at the battle of the Atbara, and finally destroyed under the walls of Khartoum at Omdurman (2 September 1898).

The battle of Omdurman was the climax and the final curtain of Victorian colonial war and the kind of leadership and tactics it produced. The British and Egyptian troops were drawn up in formal battle array and fired by volleys, just as if 1898 were 1815 or 1704. They could afford so to do, for their enemies had no modern artillery and only short-range fire-arms. The fire of British field artillery began to destroy the dervish charges at a range of nearly two miles. British rifle and Maxim machine-gun fire (at ranges of up to a mile) completed the destruction. No dervish got nearer the British line than 800 yards. A well-conceived dervish counter-stroke against the flank of the British advance was similarly broken up. Eleven thousand dervish dead lay on the field, while British and Egyptian casualties numbered only forty-eight. The completion of the re-conquest of the Sudan won Kitchener a peerage.

A little later, it was the presence of his army – and, for once, his own tact – that forced the French to yield the claims to the Upper Nile represented by Colonel Marchand, who had marched across Africa to Fashoda with a tiny party: a notable moment in imperialist rivalries.

The campaigns of the three Victorian heroes, Roberts, Wolseley and Kitchener, represented essentially all the British people knew of modern war. It was in fact a highly specialized form, which contrasted sharply with war as fought between great industrial powers. There was emphasis on the man rather than the system, on smallness instead of greatness of scale, on great variety of task and terrain instead of a single eventuality, on overwhelming superiority of instead of equality of armaments, and on minute casualties and easy victories instead of heavy losses and prolonged fighting. War against savages could not really test an army. These colonial triumphs created a dangerous impression at home that wars were distant and exotic adventure stories, cheaply won by the parade-ground discipline of the British line; that to win a modern war, you called for a hero.

14
Stagnation
in an
Age of Change

SINCE Waterloo – since the Crimea even – British military experience had thus diverged further and further from European. After 1870 especially, European soldiers became concerned not with a multiplicity of minor expeditions, but with a single gigantic task: preparing for the moment when national policy or survival called for the mobilization of the entire trained manpower of the nation and its launching into battle. Each European general staff ceaselessly worked to evolve and perfect a single plan of campaign that would solve the problems posed by its nation's diplomatic and geographical position. Victory might depend as much on speed of mobilization as on the course of battle itself. Such mobilization and deployment required deep technical knowledge and high managerial skills. The general staffs had to study the implications for tactics and organization in the field of the swift development of weapons; they had to evolve standard tactical doctrines so that the whole vast mass of a conscript army would be animated by the common principles and procedures.

The last thirty years of the nineteenth century saw continued rapid technical change in warfare. In 1884 Germany modified her single-shot Mauser rifles into tubular-magazine rifles. In 1885 the French introduced the tubular-magazine Lebel rifle. In 1886 the Austrians adopted the first magazine rifle of the kind that was to last until after the Second World War. This was the Mannlicher, with a box magazine held by a spring clip under the barrel forward of the trigger guard. Two years later the British followed suit with the ·303-inch Lee-Metford. A spring inside the magazine forced up the rounds in turn into the entrance of the breech. These rapid-fire rifles were accurate and lethal beyond a mile. The replacement of black by smokeless powder in the 1880s was equally important. Since the Middle Ages an exchange of musketry of cannon-fire had caused thick clouds of stinking smoke. The close-range volleying of the eighteenth century (the summit of muzzle-loading smooth-bore musketry) had shrouded the whole battlefield in fog. In the

The Gatling machine-gun, terror of lesser breeds during imperial expansion in the last quarter of the nineteenth century. Its cluster of barrels was rotated by a hand-crank.

Prussian wars against Austria and France in 1866 and 1870, the cloud of powder-smoke had given away the position of infantry firing prone from otherwise concealed positions. Now, with smoke-less powder, the well-trained infantrymen melted into the terrain, and dispensed death invisibly at long range.

A new invention, the machine-gun, dealt the final blow to close-order tactics. The Gatling gun (first introduced towards the end of the American Civil War) and the French *mitrailleuse* of 1870 were the first successful service machine-guns, despite centuries of

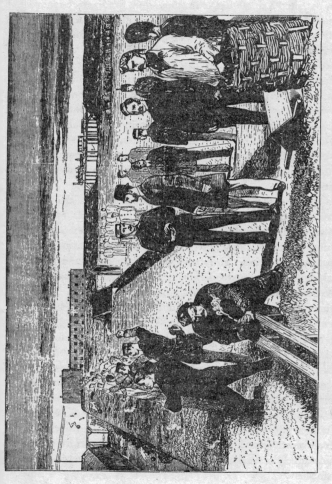

A hazardous occupation – hand-grenade training at Chatham in 1877, watched by the Prince Imperial, son of Napoleon III, the former Emperor of the French. Grenades did not become a major infantry weapon again until the trench warfare of the First World War.

experiment. However, they were hand-cranked and clumsy, and their rate of fire was less than 200 rounds a minute. In 1884 Hiram Maxim patented a single-barrel machine-gun, fired and re-loaded continuously by its own recoil. Maxim's machine-gun was fed by cartridges on a moving belt and cooled by water. It fired at the astounding rate of 600 rounds a minute.

In 1889 field artillery caught up with the new infantry weapons. The French and German armies introduced field guns whose barrels alone recoiled (against a progressive buffer action) instead of the whole carriages. This made possible a far faster rate of fire, and, by using shrapnel shell (which burst in the air above the enemy), enabled artillery to inflict heavy casualties beyond the range of infantry weapons. At the same time, smokeless powder permitted guns as well to remain concealed behind ground or vegetation.

As a result of these developments in powder, small-arms and artillery, the traditional battlefield now disappeared. Modern fire-power made close-order formations suicidal. A given frontage could now be held by a fraction of the old numbers. The armies of the past, manoeuvring tightly under the close command of the general, gave place to extended fronts – detached groups of men close to the ground engaged in unnumerable small fights. For the first time, barrack-square drill and battlefield tactics became different things. Even in the Franco-Prussian war of 1870 the formal columns had tended to melt into the skirmishers to form an irregular line of groups, a kind of skirmishing swarm. Modern weapons meant that decisive leadership on the field was devolving from commanders of corps or divisions, or even brigades, down to the commanders of battalions or even of companies and sections. The lesson was rammed home in the war between the Russians and the Turks in the Balkans in 1877–8. Skobeleff, the Russian commander, drew the conclusion: 'The only formation in which troops can successively assault entrenched positions is in successive lines of skirmishers. . .' .[1]

The disintegration of the traditional battlefield also spelt the end of the pageant of war, and the support given by it to the morale of the individual. Gone too was the moral support afforded by being in a mass, by the close presence of comrades and officers. Thus, the moral virtues required of the soldier were also changed. He no longer had to stand unflinching and obedient in the ranks, but to endure a shapeless torment of fire from invisible enemies.

By the 1880s the Germans, although not the French, had finally abolished volley-firing and the mass advance in formal order. Instead their regulations of 1888 called for a fire-fight in extended order and an advance by short rushes under covering fire. No fixed tactical drill was imposed; instead the initiative and alertness of individual officer and man were to be developed.

The French, on the other hand, came to believe that the moral effect of a resolute charge would 'disarm' defenders. This French school of thought was founded in 1880 by the publication of a book called *Etudes sur le Combat*. The book was based on the writings of a Colonel Ardant du Picq, who died of wounds during the Franco-Prussian war. He believed that

In battle, two moral forces, even more so than two material forces, are in conflict. The stronger conquers .... With equal or even inferior power of destruction, he will win who is determined to advance .... Moral effect inspires fear ... the Moral impulse lies in the perception by the enemy of the resolution which animates you ... [2]

When the memories of slaughter by Chassepot or needle-gun faded away, nonsense like this was elaborated by various French military writers. One exponent of this extraordinary myth before 1914, later to become famous, was Ferdinand Foch, who became a professor at the French Ecole de Guerre in 1894 and afterwards its commandant. He saw numerical or material superiority as nullified by moral superiority. Moral superiority was established and demonstrated by the attack, headlong and frontal. Foch describes the culmination of such an attack in a future war over a mile of ground in the face of machine-guns and rifles thus:

Here begins ... the action of infantry in masses. They march straight on to the goal ... speeding up their pace in proportion as they come nearer. ... The consideration of what fire one may oneself receive now becomes a secondary matter; the troops are on the move and must arrive; moreover, there is but one means to extenuate the effects of enemy fire:

it is to develop a more violent fire oneself [*author's note*: in the open, while in rapid movement!] ... another means consists in rapid advance. To march, and march quickly, preceded by a hail of bullets; in proportion as the enemy is hard pressed, to bring forward more and more numerous troops, and, moreover, troops well in hand, such is the fundamental formula for the formations to be taken and tactics to be adopted.[3]

The general progress of invention also had profound effects on the organization and control of armies – faster methods of printing, the introduction of the typewriter, the canning of food, the telephone. The telephone enabled commanders to speak directly with subordinates or superiors miles away. The telephone and telegraph together, by linking armies to the government at home, put an end to much of the independence once enjoyed by commanders-in-chief in the field.

The late nineteenth century was also an era of increasing international tensions, both because of imperialist and commercial rivalry and because of the sentimental animosities of the new mass public opinions. The general staffs of Europe stood ready to begin mobilization at any moment. In this constant, watchful readiness, too, there was a striking contrast with the British military situation.

The European nations paid a heavy political and social price for the great armies which their land frontiers made essential. In Britain the army – military power – had long faded away as a political or social issue. In Germany and even to some extent in France, the army was a focus of constitutional strife during the nineteenth century. The old problem of military power was posed again in the new society produced by the industrial revolution. The problem was complicated everywhere by the impact of that new society, with its urban middle-class values, on that most rural and conservative of social groups, the officer corps.

In France, it was under the Third Republic after 1871 that the class nature of the officer corps and the place of the army in French society gradually became a political issue. Ever since the Revolution of 1789 the *noblesse* had continued to send its sons into the army, because it was the traditional occupation consonant with their conception of honour and with their way of life. Nevertheless poor pay and prospects had led to a steady decline in the proportion of noble officers between 1815 and 1860. From about 1860 the trend was reversed. Under the Second Empire, with its reflected Napoleonic glory, the army once more became a cherished institution and a worthwhile career. Paradoxically the coming of the Third Republic in 1870 hastened this return of the *noblesse* to the officer corps. The republicans barred all those suspected of monarchical sympathies from civil branches of the state service, and thus left the army as the only public-service career open to the *noblesse*. Thus the *noblesse* came to dominate the officer corps (especially its higher ranks) of a middle-class republic. In 1898 twenty-three per cent of the 110 divisional generals and 220 brigadier generals had names *à particule* (with the prefix 'de'), signifying a noble family. What was more, the *noblesse* – and the officer corps – were strong in loyalty to the Roman Catholic Church, an institution with which the lay republic carried on a bitter struggle about such questions as control over education. The French army gradually became a conservative, Catholic, noble enclave within a lay, radical and bourgeois republic.

In the Dreyfus case the army became the cause and the centre of a conflict between the lay republic and the Catholic conservatives that almost brought down the republic. Dreyfus was a Jewish bourgeois officer. He was accused of selling secrets to Germany, and condemned on somewhat feeble evidence. Under attack by republican politicians, the officer corps closed its ranks and tried to maintain that the army's internal discipline and justice was no affair of civilians. The army was accused of being a Catholic and monarchist institution seeking the downfall of the Republic. The Dreyfus case involved a fundamental issue: the place of an army in a modern democracy. Before Dreyfus was finally cleared, the true culprit (a noble and Catholic officer) found, and the issue finally settled by a republican 'purge' of the officer corps, the French state and army had been shaken to their foundations.

In Prussia in the 1860s the army was the centre of a constitutional struggle that in some ways resembled the English struggle against the Stuarts two centuries earlier.

In the late eighteenth century the Prussian officer corps had been almost entirely noble; the officers had owed allegiance personally and feudally to the monarch, not to the nation or state. During Scharnhorst's reforms in the Napoleonic wars it had seemed possible that universal conscription and the throwing open of the officer corps to the middle-class talent might merge army and nation. Instead, as an aspect of European reaction after 1815, the Prussian officer corps closed its ranks and preserved its *Junker* origins and code of honour, and its personal obedience to the king. In 1848, the year of revolutions in Europe, the Prussian monarchy was forced to grant a constitution that gave the new Prussian parliament the right to grant and supervise state expenditure. In the 1860s the King and his army became ranged against the Prussian parliament in a fierce struggle over the reform and expansion of the army. The proposed reforms involved raising army expenditure by a third and abolishing the *Landwehr* as an independent force under constitutional, not royal, control and officered by the middle class. The Prussian parliament eventually refused to vote supplies for the maintenance of the army, leading to a constitutional deadlock.

The army crisis had raised the question of whether king or parliament was to be the supreme authority in Prussia. The generals saw the conflict indeed as a repetition of the parliamentary rebellion in England against Charles I and of the French Revolution against Louis XVI. There was talk of force. However, instead of force, there was Bismarck as Minister President. In four years, 1862–6, he brilliantly outmanoeuvred the Prussian parliament, finding alternative funds for the army in place of their grants, offering the liberals what they had always wanted, a united Germany – but through war. When patriotic feeling during the war with Austria swamped the last of liberal doubts, Bismarck was able to wrap up a neat constitutional package that under cover of concession left control of the army and military expenditure, indeed all executive government, firmly in the hands of the monarch and his chief minister. It was a fateful result, because after 1871 the new German Empire was governed by a constitution no more parliamentary and representative than that of England under the late Stuarts. The army and its officer corps formed a state-within-a-state of enormous and growing influence. The technical modernization and re-organization of the Prussian military system between 1860 and 1870 had been without effect on the social and political outlook of the officer corps. The German officer corps in the late nineteenth century thus presented an astonishing paradox: while technically it was the most modern in the world, it was otherwise still living in the Potsdam of Frederick the Great. It was a dangerous combination of qualities to find in the most influential social group within a Germany growing fast in might and ambition. For by 1900 the military values of the aristocratic officer corps had permeated the entire German nation. Scholars were more proud of being promoted to captain in the reserve than of being made a professor. Germany by 1900 was a living example of what the British had fought so hard and continuously (and sometimes it even seemed, absurdly) to prevent – the militarization of a whole nation and the concentration of executive government in the hands of the army's commander, the monarch.

On the other hand, in Britain during the last thirty years of the nineteenth century there was a failure to carry out long-overdue reforms of the armed forces. Yet Britain was now the centre of a world empire of coloured subject races and white colonists, and it was upon her that fell responsibility for imperial defence by land and sea. The potential military danger to the empire from ambitious rival powers was first perceived by writers on military and naval affairs rather than by governments. They called for the re-organization of the United Kingdom forces and the small and separate colonial forces into an imperial defence system, to which all should contribute men and women or ships for service anywhere in the empire. The Australian volunteers who served in the Sudan in 1885 seemed to offer a pattern. There was a great deal of discussion between the British and colonial governments. In 1885 the British government even set up a Colonial Defence Committee. Unfortunately this Committee failed to tackle broad questions of imperial strategy and devoted itself to petty matters, such as the defence stores of minor colonies. By 1900 little progress had been made towards imperial forces. Growing nationalism in the white colonies made them in fact reluctant to merge their own forces in a general pool, or to lose control over them to some imperial

authority. Wide differences in pay and conditions and legal obligation between one colony and another also made common forces
difficult to achieve. There was much aspiration, a lot of talk, but
little result.

In Britain itself, despite the delusory successes in little wars, an
educated minority was aware how ramshackle the British military
system remained even after Cardwell's reforms. It certainly was not
for want of examination of the problems that the British army
remained unfit for war against a great power: between the late
1860s and 1880 no fewer than eighty-nine official bodies of one
kind or another pried into military affairs. The spate of investigation continued through the 1880s. The Cardwell system itself began
to reveal its weaknesses. There was an imbalance between battalions
at home and abroad, and a new recruiting crisis, while the depot
battalions had become inadequate training cadres instead of a strategic reserve. From 1885 to 1890 Wolseley, as Adjutant-General,
was struggling with the Duke of Cambridge for reforms in weapons
and equipment. He tried to arouse a complacent public opinion
by announcements or articles of uncompromising rigour. On one
occasion he assured the House of Lords that the army would be
unable in the event of war even to guarantee the safety of London.

However, all attempts to awake national alarm and drag the
armed forces into the modern world failed to penetrate public
complacency or the sloth of governments. Within the army there
was a special obstacle to change in the Field-Marshal Commanding-
in-Chief, the Duke of Cambridge. Although Cambridge in his own
old-fashioned way loved the army devotedly, it was to his entrenched position for forty years at the head of the army, together
with court backing, that the British failure to keep pace militarily
was greatly due. His conception of an army was pre-industrial.
The Queen's private secretary from 1870 to 1895 wrote of him: 'At
a time when Army reform was under discussion he was not just
conservative but hopelessly reactionary, and not only opposed
change, but quarrelled with those who proposed it.'[4]

In 1890, a Royal Commission under Lord Hartington charged
with considering the functions of both the War Office and the
Admiralty made its report. It was a document of the greatest

significance. It recommended for the overseeing of imperial defence as a whole 'the formation of a Naval and Military Council, which should probably be presided over by the Prime Minister, and consist of the Parliamentary Heads of the two services and their principal advisers'.[5] This suggestion showed how the empire was again being considered as it had been in the eighteenth century, as a

" WHY, that buckle you are wearing, Miss Thyra, is a regular Army one. Is it a souvenir of some great battle ?"
"No; but I got it in a short engagement."

The officer-corps on the eve of the Boer War, 1899, was an expression of late Victorian upper-class society, rich, snobbish and corsetted by etiquette.

strategic entity. The recommendation foreshadowed the later creation of the Committee of Imperial Defence. In its second report, on the War Office, the Hartington Commission strongly criticized the office of Commander-in-Chief as centralizing all authority in one person and stultifying the responsibility of the various military departments. It called for the abolition of the post of Commander-in-Chief and the establishment of a general staff which would be freed from all executive functions and charged with the responsible duty of preparing plans of military operations, collecting and co-ordinating information of all kinds, and generally tendering advice upon all matters of organization and the preparation of the Army for war.[6]

The Hartington Commission also recommended that control of the army should be vested in a War Office Council, composed of the War Minister, two junior ministers, the Permanent Under-Secretary, and five departmental officers responsible to the War Minister. These officers would be the Chief of the General Staff, Adjutant-General, Quartermaster-General, Director of Artillery, and Inspector-General of Fortifications.

The recommendations of the Hartington Commission formed the basis of reforms to be carried out at long last after 1904. In 1890 they met the stubborn opposition of Cambridge and court. By a coincidence, the Commission's call for a general staff was echoed by the publication of a study of Moltke, *The Brain of an Army*, by Spencer Wilkinson, a prominent advocate of reform. The coincidence looked to Cambridge like a conspiracy. Both Cambridge and the Queen seemed to think that there ought to remain a direct link between sovereign and the command of the army. There was an unholy alliance against the Hartington Report between Cambridge and Wolseley, of all people. Wolseley had his own eye on the post of Commander-in-Chief, and did not wish to see the Commander-in-Chief's authority shared out between a general staff and a partly civilian War Office Council. Wolseley's outlook, although reformist, had been shaped by colonial war, and he did not really comprehend the European general staff system or appreciate its necessity. After complicated in-fighting, the report of the Hartington Commission was added to the other reports stacked on dusty shelves.

Only in 1895 was the aged Cambridge prised loose from his official chair, but even then as part of a compromise. No general staff was set up, nor was the post of Commander-in-Chief abolished. Instead the office of the Commander-in-Chief was reduced to the same importance as departmental heads like the Adjutant-General or Quartermaster-General. Nevertheless, in a vague way the Commander-in-Chief was still supposed to supervise and co-ordinate their work, although they were directly responsible to the War Minister. Soldiers and ministers together constituted a new War Office Council, one fruit of the Hartington Commission. Wolseley as the new Commander-in-Chief described himself as the fifth wheel on the coach; he was by now an elderly and creaking wheel. The results of this failure to give Britain a modern military machine were demonstrated in 1899–1900, when Britain became involved in her first major war against well-equipped white troops since 1856, apart from the brief skirmishes against the Boers in 1881. Although the (Second) Boer War was still small-scale compared with the American Civil War or recent European conflicts, it found the British imperial military system terribly wanting.

*

The origins of the Boer War were imperialist. In 1884, after the First Boer War, the London Convention had made an ambiguous settlement of the relations between the Boer republic of the Transvaal and the British government, by which the independence of the Transvaal was recognized, subject to British control over its foreign relations. British *suzerainty* over the Transvaal, mentioned in an earlier Convention, was no longer specified. In 1886 gold was discovered in the Transvaal. Into a republic of 20,000 scattered, simple, Calvinist farmers poured foreigners of all kinds eager to exploit the new find. A great and turbulent city grew up at Johannesburg. The annual revenue of the Transvaal rose from £200,000 in 1886 to over £4 millions in 1899. While the Transvaal government, under President Kruger, were happy enough with the rake-off from the huge foreign (mostly British) community, they had no wish to see the foreigners ('Uitlanders') swamp their pastoral way of life, or gain control of the government. They therefore denied Uitlanders the rights of full citizens. The Uitlanders appealed to the government of Cape Colony and to the British government at home for support over their alleged wrongs.

Attempts to negotiate a settlement acceptable to British, Uitlanders and Boers drifted towards failure and war. The Boers bought Mauser rifles and Krupp artillery from Germany in ever larger quantities. On 9 October 1899 Kruger in an ultimatum called for the withdrawal of British troops from the Boer borders and of recent reinforcements from South Africa itself. On 11 October the ultimatum expired and the war began. War having been increasingly in sight since the end of 1895, no one could say that Britain was taken by surprise. The British pre-war commander in South Africa, General Butler, who had warned that 200,000 men would be needed to beat the Boers, was recalled for his pessimism and alleged pro-Boer sentiments; he was a Roman Catholic Irishman with Irish nationalist sympathies. Wolseley himself, though he greatly underestimated the force eventually required, warned the government that war would be the most serious business they had ever had on hand. He tried to persuade the government to create and equip an expeditionary force in time. The politicians, however, neglected all warnings for characteristic reasons: first, preparation would cost money, and, second, preparation might annoy the Boers and prevent a peaceful settlement.

When the Orange Free State joined the Transvaal, the combined Boer forces numbered some 50,000 well-armed mounted infantry – mobile, resourceful, crack-shots, excellent at fieldcraft in country they knew intimately. At the outbreak of war there were only 14,750 British regulars in South Africa, because the British government had only agreed a fortnight earlier to the dispatch of the main field force of 47,000 men.

The Boers did not await the arrival of the main British field force, but invaded the British colony of Natal, with the objective of the port of Durban and direct access to the sea. The British Natal Field Force was beaten and forced back into Ladysmith, where it was closely besieged. Other British forces were besieged in Kimberley and Mafeking. In fact, the Boers locked up too much of their strength in these sieges, when a better strategy would have been to sweep straight south into Cape Colony, raising the Dutch inhabitants as they went. As it was, only small Boer forces invaded Cape Colony.

The British main field army, when it arrived, was commanded by Sir Redvers Buller, an old member of Wolseley's 'Ashanti ring' and one of Britain's most respected soldiers. Buller chose to divide his army. He dispatched Lord Methuen with a strengthened division to relieve Kimberley, while General Gatacre with a brigade was to clear the Boer invaders from the north of Cape Colony. Buller himself, with the largest portion of the army, transferred by sea to Natal, with Durban as his base. The British did not expect the Boer farmers to last long.

Methuen won some minor but costly successes; then, in December 1899, a week of disaster – 'Black Week' – stunned British opinion. Methuen was heavily repulsed at Magersfontein; Gatacre

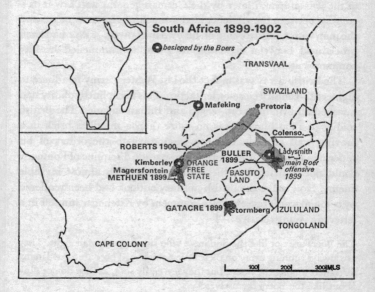

South Africa 1899-1902

was beaten at Stormberg; and Buller himself was defeated at Colenso on the Tugela River, losing his nerve to the extent of ordering the Ladysmith garrison to surrender (an order which was ignored). The British at home followed their usual procedure when disaster overtakes their lack of system and preparation. They sent for a hero – Field-Marshal Lord Roberts of Kandahar. Indeed they sent for two heroes, because Lord Kitchener of Khartoum was appointed his Chief-of-Staff. Meanwhile, Buller tried again, but his attacks at Spion Kop (January 1900) and Vaal Krantz (February) were bloodily smashed. Only General French of the British commanders, by holding off superior numbers round Colesberg, had distinguished himself.

At home, the defeats seemed disasters as great as Sedan or Sadowa. In fact, even at Spion Kop the British had lost only some 1,700 men, in comparison with Austrian losses of 20,000 at Sadowa in 1866. Nevertheless in the scale of colonial war they were still major setbacks. What had happened in these battles? The history of the war prepared later by the German general staff saw it as a contest 'between the soldier drilled to machine-like movements and the man with a rifle working on his own initiative.... War had been proclaimed between rigid formulas and untrammelled healthy common sense'.[7]

The British army was in fact the last Western army to adhere to eighteenth-century close-order tactics. This disciplined solidity had smashed all Britain's arab, negro and Indian enemies. The British soldier of 1899 himself was no more than a mindless brick in a moving wall of flesh, instantly responsive to the orders of his superiors. However, the courage and parade discipline of Fontenoy could not avail against the accurate fire of an almost invisible enemy. How naïve the British military outlook had been rendered by colonial war is revealed by a comment by Kitchener himself in a letter to a young relative:

The Boers are not like the Sudanese who stood up to a fair fight. They are always running away on their little ponies. ... There are a good many foreigners among the Boers, but they are easily shot, as they do not slink about like the Boers themselves.[8]

The average quality of British officer and man as well as tactics and training was shown to be inferior, although performances varied widely between one unit and another. There was a grim similarity between the shortcomings in South Africa and those in the Crimea, in Flanders in 1793–5, in Ireland in 1689, in Germany in 1623, in the Low Countries after 1585 – lack of organization, ignorant and casual officers, inferior human material in the ranks.

The *Report of His Majesty's Commissioners on the War in South Africa,* published in 1903, stated that 'the whole military system as it stood at that date [1899] was tested by the war in South Africa'.[9] It went on to indict almost every aspect of the army and its organization, from Wolseley, the then Commander-in-Chief, down to the private soldier. Only the Director of Military Intelligence and his fund-starved department received commendation, for as early as 1896 the D.M.I. had warned that the Boer war plan would probably be to invade Natal. In 1897 the D.M.I. had warned that in the event of war, two months would elapse before British reinforcements could reach South Africa; that in the meantime a Boer offensive would fall on the troops already there; and that therefore the British ought now to be raising their strength in South Africa. In 1898 the D.M.I. repeated his warnings and recommendations. However, the Intelligence Department was not a general staff. Wolseley, as Commander-in-Chief, was supposed to be a one-man general staff. The Royal Commission observed of Wolseley's performance:

... the general impression to be derived from the whole circumstances must be that the special function of the Commander-in-Chief, under the Order in Council of 1896, viz: 'The preparation of schemes of offensive and defensive operations', was not exercised on this occasion in any systematic fashion.[10]

And the Report also stated that it was 'not altogether remarkable under the circumstances described above that no plan of campaign ever existed for operations in South Africa'.[11]

According to the Report, organized land transport (other than the railway), suitable maps, stores and equipment of all kinds were all lacking.

The Report noted that in 1899, out of a paper strength of 249,466 regulars and a reserve of 90,000, only two corps and a cavalry division (70,000 men) were available for overseas service – yet these also formed an integral part of home defence. India swallowed nearly 70,000 men, Egypt and the rest of the Empire nearly 60,000. It was an indication of how limited in scope and result Cardwell's reserve scheme and his attempted reduction of colonial garrisons had proved.

Witnesses before the Commission sharply criticized the standard of staff efficiency despite the fitful reforms in the Staff College and its syllabus since 1856. In Lord Roberts's opinion

... the absence of a definite system of staff duties, leading sometimes to an overlapping of responsibilities, sometimes to waste of time, and sometimes to a neglect of indispensable precautions, was undoubtedly prejudicial to the smooth running of the military machine ... staff officers cannot be improvised.[12]

The British field artillery, in Roberts's opinion, was inferior to European in range and rapidity of fire. There were muddles over small-arms and ammunition. Sixty million rounds manufactured at Dum-dum in India had to be withdrawn because they stripped in the rifle barrel. Over 200,000 Lee-Enfield rifles were found to have faulty sighting, firing eighteen inches to the right at 500 yards. Peacetime provision and planning for remounts and transport animals proved inadequate. The Royal Commission recorded that while the medical department did its best to care for an army three or four times larger than allowed for in the medical establishment, nevertheless pettifogging red-tape and untrained orderlies caused needless suffering. The hospital equipment was, according to the Commission, 'old-fashioned', and, although campaigning in country where water supply was a crucial question, the British army had nothing equivalent to the German system for testing the purity of new water supplies. Sanitation in the British army was also inferior to the German. The Commission saw, however, some bright spots – in the excellent performance in its first war of the new Army Service Corps, despite the size of its task and shortage of personnel. This corps originated in the 'Military Train', kept in being after the Crimean War. In 1888 the old civilian commissariat system for the supply of food and other necessaries had at last been abolished, and both supply and transport vested in the Army Service Corps.

Of the unfortunate rank-and-file of the infantry, the evidence of witnesses and the final Report of the Commission had gloomy things to say. Reservists were fitter physically than regulars already with the colours. Too many British soldiers were industrial townsmen. Most witnesses thought the British rank-and-file was inferior in intelligence (partly owing to lack of education) both to the Boers and to British colonials who joined the war later. One witness believed that

... his [the British soldier's] mental qualifications are not up to the general run of European soldiers, and the reason of it is, that we get them mostly from a class where education is not looked to as much as it is in Germany and in France.[13]

The Royal Commission in its final Report drew the conclusion:

If the terms offered are attractive only to men whose intelligence is underdeveloped, it is impossible to make them soldiers of the class required in modern warfare, with the same amount of training that will be sufficient for men whose mental calibre is higher at the time when they enter the army.[14]

Roberts and Kitchener both agreed that the British soldier lacked resourcefulness and the ability to look after himself in the field; Kitchener said that 'he was usually too dependent on his officers and lacked individuality'.[15]

However, the officers and non-commissioned officers themselves were heavily criticized by witnesses and by the Commission. There was a shunning of responsibility from the corporal all the way up the hierarchy. Of the officer, Kitchener observed: 'There appears to be too often a want of serious study of their profession by officers who are, I think, rather inclined to deal lightly with military questions of moment.'[16] This opinion was completely endorsed by the *Report of the Committee appointed to consider the Education and Training of the Officers of the Army* (the Akers-Douglas Committee) in 1902. The Committee were impressed 'by the widespread dissatisfaction – a feeling expressed by practically all the witnesses – with the present state of education, both military and general, among the officers of the Army as a class'.[17]

Both the Royal Military Academy, Woolwich (gunners and engineers) and the Royal Military College, Sandhurst (cavalry and infantry) came in for detailed criticism. Of Sandhurst the

Committee observed that 'the cadets cannot be expected to derive much benefit from their instruction ... when it is clearly established that they have absolutely no incentive to work'. The passing-out standard was low enough, and yet 'there is too much reason to fear that even those cadets who fail to attain this standard have been commissioned none the less'.[18]

The training of young officers with their units was called by the Committee 'most unsatisfactory'.

By no part of the evidence laid before them have the Committee been more impressed than by that which shows in the clearest manner the prevalence among the junior commissioned ranks of a lack of professional knowledge and skill, and of any wish to study the science and master the art of their profession.[19]

The Committee was informed that 'keenness is out of fashion ... it is not the correct form'.[20]

Even the minority of keen officers that did exist found it difficult to train themselves or their men in Britain, because

Under the existing system the officer rarely sees the men for whose military efficiency he is responsible. They are largely employed in non-military duties, such as waiting in the canteens and regimental institutes, the charge of cricket and tennis grounds ... in addition to the large number constantly required for ... fatigues ... [21]

Promotion examinations too were a farce.

All these aspects of lack of professionalism derived, as for two centuries, from recruiting the officers from a leisured class to whom professionalism too often appeared as vulgar careerism. The need for a private income to support the lavishness of military life was just as efficient a means as purchase in barring the poor but meritorious. As one witness told the Akers-Douglas Committee: 'I am sorry to say that the officer wanted in the Army is only one who can command from £150 to £1500 a year.'[22]

It was noteworthy that in the cavalry, where living expenses were highest, professional standards were said by the Report to be lowest.

In 1903 yet another Committee specially investigated this

SOCIAL LIFE IN THE ARMY.

ILLUSTRATIONS BY G.M. PAYNE.

100 UP.

UNDER CANVAS. A CANTEEN CONCERT.

AT THE SERGEANTS' BALL.

AT THE REGIMENTAL SPORTS.

CHURCH PARADE.

SOLDIER'S WEDDING IN INDIA.

ON THE STRENGTH.

At the end of the Victorian age, army life at home, even for N.C.O.s, was dominated by the social round. For officers, devoted study and practice of the military profession was not 'good form'.

question of expenses and private incomes*: its final conclusion
was that:

The whole of the evidence before the Committee proves incontestably
in their opinion, that the expenses of the Army form a very serious deterrent to parents in selecting a profession for their sons, and that many
otherwise entirely suitable candidates are precluded from entering the
Service by no other consideration than the insufficiency of their private
incomes.[23]

These expenses were almost entirely unprofessional – a
dandy's wardrobe of uniforms, entertaining, sporting and social
life.

Thus almost all aspects of the British military system had been
found wanting in a war against 50,000 farmers. The deficiencies
had historical roots going back probably as far as the Tudor
militia. However, they were less forgivable in 1900 than they had
been in 1800 or 1700. The army was no longer conceivably a threat
to the constitution, and no longer 'belonged' even residually to the
monarch. The army's poor quality could not therefore be attributed
any longer to the earlier national desire to keep it feeble. On the
contrary, late Victorians had wanted it to be efficient and economical. Nor could the state of the army in 1900 be blamed entirely
or even largely on the army's own leaders, for the British army was
not a self-regulating state-within-a-state like the German army. Its
size, organization and efficiency were the responsibility of a civilian
minister, and beyond him of a government responsible to the
House of Commons, and beyond the House of Commons of an
electorate ever more representative of the people as a whole. The
army's obsolescence and the survival of its traditional weaknesses
were ultimately the responsibility of civilian governments and of
public opinion in general. In fact, neither government nor nation
was very much interested in the army, except to cheer a victory.
The British people did not wish to be conscious of the cost and

* 'The Committee Appointed by the Secretary of State for War to Enquire
into the Nature of the Expenses Incurred by Officers of the Army and to Suggest Measures for bringing Commissions within reach of Men of moderate
means', or Lord Stanley's Committee, 1903.

pains of being an imperial power. Britain, as always, had got the army it deserved.

*

Once more Britain had to forge the instrument of victory after the war had begun. To defeat the Boers some 450,000 troops in all were employed, of which about 250,000 were British regulars. Almost all battalions of the militia were embodied, and they formed the principal part of the home forces during the war, as well as garrisoning the Mediterranean bases. Militia battalions also performed well in South Africa. However, press attention focused on the volunteers. Under the sting of the news of 'Black Week', thousands of British at home made good their Jingoism by volunteering. The colonies also displayed their loyalty to the mother country. Australia sent 16,000 volunteers; New Zealand 6,500; Canada too sent a contingent. It was a sudden demonstration that the British empire really did exist as a collective military power – a by no means overdue demonstration, because there was bitter hatred for Britain and deep sympathy for the Boers among the great European powers. This hatred made the British government abruptly aware of Britain's isolation and vulnerability, at a time when the United Kingdom was stripped of regular troops.

Victory was eventually gained by the overwhelming material and numerical forces that Britain put in the field. Hardly less important was the firm command and simple, excellent strategy of the new Commander-in-Chief, Lord Roberts, and Kitchener, his Chief of Staff. Roberts reached Cape Town on 10 January 1900. A month of heroic exertion was spent in re-organizing the army. Great efforts were made to make good the glaring British inferiority in mounted infantry. The Boer mounted infantry used ponies for swift mobility, but fought on foot. Roberts and Kitchener created British mounted infantry partly out of the cavalry, who turned in their swords and lances, partly by putting infantry on to horses. The best of the imperial mounted infantry proved to be the colonial volunteers, accustomed to horses and wide open spaces; enterprising and intelligent.

The second phase of the war opened on 11 February 1900 with

Roberts's offensive against the territories of the Boer Republics. He concentrated his forces in one thrust, instead of the three under Buller. He manoeuvred a Boer army under Cronje out of powerful field fortifications at Magersfontein, cut off his retreat to Bloemfontein (by an epic march of the British cavalry under French after the relief of Kimberley) and trapped him round a ford in the Modder River near Paardeberg. The Boers, complete with waggons and women and children, dug themselves in. British frontal attacks, launched by Kitchener while Roberts was absent sick, were as bloodily repulsed as Buller's and Methuen's the previous year. Roberts decided instead to starve Cronje out. On 27 February Cronje surrendered. It was Majuba Day. At the beginning of March Buller's luck too turned, and he broke through to relieve Ladysmith. The Orange Free State lay open, and Roberts swept on to capture Bloemfontein, the capital. Now ensued a pause of seven weeks because of shortage of supplies and animals, but even more because of an epidemic of enteric fever born of infected water and poor sanitation. Sixteen thousand men were to die of this fever during the war as against the low battle casualties of some 6,000.

When the army was re-organized and brought up to a strength of 75,000, Roberts advanced on Pretoria, capital of the Transvaal, and captured it on 5 June. Both the Transvaal and the Orange Free State were annexed to the British Crown. It was an astoundingly swift turning of the tables. Roberts returned home to become Commander-in-Chief in the United Kingdom, leaving Kitchener in command. However, it was only the beginning of the third phase of the war, which was to last for two years. The Boers split up into small columns or 'commandos' of about 1,000 men, which pounced on detached British units or on railways. A year and three-quarters after the fall of Pretoria, for example, a force of 1,300 men under Lord Methuen was destroyed by a Boer commando amid scenes of panic, and Methuen himself had to surrender with 600 men and six guns. Kitchener set to work ruthlessly to round up this elusive enemy. The country was divided up by 3,700 miles of barbed wire and 8,000 block-houses. Each section of country so isolated was 'driven' by troops, although often with indecisive results. Finally, to prevent the Boer commandos simply melting back into the farming communities, the farms were burned and women and children herded into concentration camps. Some 20,000 inmates died of disease in the concentration camps. Gradually the scale and relentlessness of Kitchener's hunt wore the Boers down, and on 31 May 1902 peace was at last signed at Vereeniging.

The war had been essentially fought to prevent the Boers establishing a Dutch republic over all southern Africa, including Cape Colony, and instead to extend British sovereignty over the existing Dutch Republics. The result of the generous political settlement made by Britain in 1907 was that fifty-four years later, the whole region became a Boer republic.

IV

The Army
and National Survival
1902–45

15

Radical
Reform
1902 – 14

THE Boer War had shattered the Victorian complacency of the British ruling classes, if not of British public opinion. It had demonstrated the feebleness of the land forces of the British Empire before a gloating world: it had revealed how alone Britain stood in that gloating world. For the first time since 1815 there was an awareness that Britain needed strong friends. And there was now, ever more evidently, a new challenger to British world power – Germany. Since Bismarck had unified Germany in 1871, German industrial growth had swiftly eaten up the lead Britain had enjoyed since the beginning of the Industrial Revolution. The new Germany, restless, ambitious, conscious that she was too late to grab the richest of colonies, looked on Britain with envy and with resolution to overtake her. In 1900 Germany began to build a battle-fleet. Before the alarm caused by the Boer War could fade in Britain, Germany had emerged not merely as a rival, but as a possible enemy. Edwardian Englishmen found themselves in the novel situation of facing the kind of problems their Georgian and Tudor ancestors had known so well. But it was hard to adjust quickly after half a lifetime under the Victorian peace. As recently as 1891, for example, the then Secretary of State for War, Edward Stanhope, in an important memorandum, had stated the tasks of the British army as (in order):

(a) The effective support of the civil power in all parts of the United Kingdom.
(b) To find the number of men for India, which has been fixed by agreement with the Government of India.

(c) To find garrisons for all our fortresses and coaling stations, at home or abroad ...

(d) After providing for these requirements, to be able to organise rapidly for home defence two Army Corps of Regular troops and one partly composed of Regulars and partly of Militia ...

(e) Subject to the foregoing ... to aim at being able, in case of necessity, to send abroad two complete Army Corps ...

However, the Stanhope memorandum had confidently added:

But it will be distinctly understood that the probability of the employment of an Army Corps in the field in any European war is sufficiently improbable to make it the primary duty of the military authorities to organise our forces for the defences of this country.[1]

In hardly more than ten years the basking warmth of Victorian security displayed by this memorandum had been blown away.

It was not only a question of Germany. Other nations too had become great powers during the nineteenth century and, whether unfriendly, friendly or neutral, they were factors British policy had to take account of. America had burst out of her long isolation in 1898 in a war against Spain which won her a colonial empire in Cuba, Puerto Rico and the Philippines; she was now a considerable naval power. Italy was now united into a nation state, and since she was allied to Germany and Austria, her fleet was a potential menace to British control of the Mediterranean. Russia still seemed to pose a threat to the north-west frontier of India. And in the Far East, where forty years before nothing had stood in the way of European domination, a great Asiatic power based on western technology had emerged in Japan. In two decades the Japanese had pulled their society out of the Middle Ages into the modern world, with industries and an army based on German exemplars and a navy based on the British model. In 1894 Japan had smashingly defeated China; in 1904–5 she was to stagger world opinion by inflicting an equally smashing defeat on Russia, a first-class European power. Thus after 1900 Britain's relative power was sharply diminished right across the globe. However, it was the direct threat in Europe from Germany – a threat to British command of the waters round the British Isles – that appeared most serious. Although in the wars of the eighteenth century the French navy might have inflicted serious damage on British seaborne trade, it could not have starved the British at home, because they were fed by their own agriculture. Now, thanks to the industrial revolution and free trade, Britain could neither work nor eat if seaborne suppiles were cut off.

British foreign and defence policy after 1900 therefore attempted to put an end to British diplomatic isolation, to reduce the number of potential threats, and to re-build and modernize the army and navy. In 1902 Britain concluded an alliance with Japan, which left her free to concentrate on European affairs. In 1904 she concluded the *Entente Cordiale* with France, an ancient enemy with whom war had seemed possible as recently as 1898. The *Entente* was not, however, a formal alliance, laying down reciprocal obligations, but a settlement of various contested questions between the countries. In 1905–6 Germany tried to split the new *Entente* by truculent diplomacy in a manufactured crisis over French influence in Morocco. The attempt failed, but war between the great European powers had for a time seemed to grow near.

This thickening European atmosphere was the background and the stimulus of a fresh period of military reform in Britain.

In autumn 1900 St John Brodrick became Secretary for War in the Conservative government. Brodrick, like all incumbents of his office, had to face the fundamental strategic problem posed by the British overseas empire. While the United Kingdom itself required troops for its own garrison and as an expeditionary force in the event of European war, the empire (especially India) also needed garrisons and (as the Boer War had shown) substantial ready field forces as well. The Boer War had been won only by leaving Britain herself absolutely defenceless on land. In 1901 Brodrick produced his answer to the problem:

... my proposition is that besides Home Defence we ought to be ready at any moment to send abroad three Army Corps with the proper Cavalry Division, in fact a force of 120,000 men.

Brodrick's own suggestion for creating such an expeditionary force was ambitious, logical, and copied from the German system.

The proposals I have to make to the House are as follows: I propose to re-organise the Army on a new system of which the bedrock will be that the whole country will be divided into six Army Corps by districts, that each district in times of peace will have the same relative proportions to the various arms that are necessary to make up the corps, and that they will be under the commanders who will lead them in war.[2]

The First Corps at Aldershot was to be entirely composed of regulars, the Second, Third and Fourth partly of regulars, partly of militia and volunteers; the Fifth and Sixth entirely of non-regulars. To economize in regular troops, Brodrick proposed that some minor overseas stations should be garrisoned by old soldiers, while the fleet's coaling stations should be defended by marines.

There was merit in Brodrick's attempt to unite regulars and auxiliary forces in one military organization based on readiness to take the field. However, in a country of voluntary and flagging recruitment (and bearing in mind India, which swallowed on average about half the regular army), Brodrick was hopelessly over-ambitious in planning for six army corps. Critics saw that these could only be achieved by a large increase in the army; a proposal that no British government could present to the voters. In 1903 the six army corps still remained merely imposing titles without reality. Even the First Corps at Aldershot, the only one to take any kind of shape, had no brigadiers.

Although Brodrick's plans remained only a blue-print, his term at the War Office saw one great reform and many detailed reforms and developments. Britain had always lacked effective central machinery for planning imperial defence, although for many years there had been a Colonial Defence Committee concerned with local matters of detail. There was also a Defence Committee of the Cabinet, but this lacked a permanent organization and continuous life. As a later Committee on War Office reform was to report in 1904:

The scientific study of Imperial resources, the co-ordination of the ever-varying facts upon which Imperial rule rests, the calculation of forces required, and the broad plans necessary to sustain the burden of Empire, have, until quite recently, found no place in our system of government.[3]

In 1902, therefore, after the Boer War, Brodrick in conjunction with Lord Selborne, the First Lord of the Admiralty, recommended to the Cabinet that this lack should be repaired. As a result, a Committee of Imperial Defence was set up. Balfour, the Prime Minister, thus described the new Committee to the House of Commons in March 1903: 'The idea the Government had in establishing it is ... to make it its duty to survey as a whole the strategical military needs of the Empire.'4 The Committee was to consist of the Prime Minister, the Lord President, the First Lord, the War Minister, the Commander-in-Chief, the First Sea Lord and the heads of naval and military intelligence. It was the beginning of a development that, despite times of doldrums and frustrations, was to give Britain in the Second World War the most effective defence-planning machinery in the world. Part of the credit for the new Committee belongs to Brodrick; so equally does the credit for important innovations within the army itself.

For Salisbury Plain now became Britain's second military station, and a new barrack complex began to rise at Tidworth. In 1902 the British army abandoned the red coat (except for ceremony) in peacetime, and went into khaki service dress. Quick-firing field guns were bought from Germany as a stop-gap until nine British prototypes had been tested. In 1903 Britain placed large orders for the Mark 1 eighteen-pounder, marrying the best points of the Armstrong and the Vickers designs, while a thirteen-pounder was ordered for the horse artillery. The infantry's long Lee-Enfield rifle having proved too unwieldy for cavalry in the Boer War, a shortened version was now made standard for both infantry and cavalry. Under Brodrick, therefore, the weapons were first ordered with which the British army was to enter the Great War.

In October 1903 Brodrick was replaced by Arnold-Forster, another man with a cut-and-dried scheme of army re-organization not closely enough related to the real situation. Nor had Arnold-Forster himself, a cold personality, the temperament of the successful reformer. Instead of biding his time, disarming opposition with dinners and reason, and above all listening in order to learn, Arnold-Forster plunged in with fixed ideas. He felt that the international situation made haste necessary, and in 1904 he expounded his own scheme for a new army to the House of Commons; or rather, for *two* new armies, a General Service Army and a Home Service Army:

The General Service Army will serve both abroad and at home in time of peace and in time of war.

The Home Service Army will serve at home in peace, and abroad, if necessary, in time of important wars.[5]

Here was another simple, logical answer to the conflicting demands of imperial and European security, of garrisons and field forces.

The General Service Army would be long-service – nine years with the colours, three with the reserve. Instead of Cardwell's linked-battalion depot system, Arnold-Forster proposed that the General Service Army should have large depots, like those of the Guards and the Royal Artillery. The few General Service battalions to be kept in England would be allotted to a striking force at Aldershot. This striking force was a new incarnation of the first of Brodrick's six corps.

The Home Service Army on the other hand was to be short-service – two years with the colours and six with the reserve, approximating to European conscript service armies, though without the conscription itself. The Home Service Army was to be recruited and organized on an entirely territorial basis. Arnold-Forster had little constructive to say about the militia (declining in numbers and efficiency) and the volunteers. He thus ducked the problem of how to combine the various regular and auxiliary land forces into one system. His 'striking force' was to be composed of mature and trained regulars. It was an attempt to cure the present weakness of the First Class Reserve, which instead of supplementing the number of men with the colours on recall, merely replaced regulars too young to be sent abroad on active service. Instead of Brodrick's army corps districts, there would be administrative districts, as recommended by the Esher Committee (see p. 360).

Arnold-Forster's schemes were violently criticized as impracticable, and as once again turning the army upside down. However, their capital point – two kinds of service for two kinds of army –

had to be abandoned not to the critics but to circumstance. The need for long service men for the empire (and above all, India) was so pressing that the existing three-year term of engagement had to be suspended in favour of nine years. Before any other of Arnold-Forster's plans came to fruition, Balfour's administration fell.

However, Arnold-Forster's tenure of the War Office was remarkable for major reforms of the War Office itself and the higher army command structure. These reforms did not emanate from Arnold-Forster himself, but it was he as War Minister and his colleagues in the government who backed them. The reforms stemmed from the three parts of the Report of the War Office (Reconstitution) Committee (the Esher Committee), which were published successively in February and March 1904. The Chairman of the Committee, Lord Esher, was a kind of middle-man in politics – a middle-man in ideas and also in people. He always refused the commitment and drudgery of office, preferring rather to use his connexions, influence and political flair independently. He was a confidant of King Edward VII. The Committee took no public evidence, and its report was crisp, brief and decisive. Its main recommendations were implemented by the government even as the parts of the Report were in turn appearing.

The importance of the Esher Report and its consequences can hardly be exaggerated. It coolly analysed the confusions and ineffectiveness of a military administration that had never been designed, but which had grown piecemeal, with piecemeal demolitions and re-building, ever since 1660. It laid the foundations of the War Office organization and general staff system that has endured in essentials to the present time. Without the Esher Report, and its acceptance by the government of the day, it is inconceivable that the mammoth British military efforts in the two world wars could have been possible, let alone so generally successful. It was the reconstruction of the 'brain' of the army on clear functional lines that followed the Report that made possible the successful reorganization of the body of the army. Unquestionably both Brodrick and Arnold-Forster were ill-judged in trying to reshape the body while the War Office itself remained unreformed.

The three essential recommendations of the Report were: an Army Council on the model of the Board of Admiralty; a general staff; and the division of departmental responsibilities inside the War Office on defined and logical principles.

The Army Council was to provide a single collective body to consider and decide questions of policy in place of the present ill-defined responsibilities of War Secretary, Commander-in-Chief, Adjutant-General and Quartermaster-General. The Secretary of State for War was to be placed in all respects on the same footing as the First Lord of the Admiralty. All submissions to the Crown on military topics were to be made through him: the final consummation of civilian and parliamentary control of the army. The Army Council was to consist of seven members: the War Secretary; the First Military Member (operations and military policy); the Second Military Member (recruitment and discipline); the Third Military Member (supply and transport); the Fourth Military Member (armaments and fortifications); a Civil Member (the Parliamentary Under-Secretary: civil business other than finance); and another Civil Member (the Financial Secretary). The Council was to meet frequently, and its decisions were to be collective. Dissenters might either accept the majority opinion or resign.

It was essential to the creation of both the Army Council and a general staff that the post of Commander-in-Chief be abolished. In 1904 therefore, Lord Roberts, the last incumbent, was evicted. Responsibility for preparation of the army for war was vested in the new post of Chief of the General Staff (C.G.S.).

The Esher Committee divided administration inside the War Office between the Chief of the General Staff, the Adjutant-General, the Quartermaster-General and the Master-General of the Ordnance. The duties of the General Staff itself were divided between a Director of Military Operations (D.M.O.), Director of Staff Duties (D.S.D.), and a Director of Military Training (D.M.T.). The Adjutant-General was made broadly responsible for all that related to the maintenance and welfare of the troops. Under him were the Director of Recruiting and Organization, the Director of Personal Services, the Director-General of Medical Services and (to take care of the militia and volunteers) a Director of Auxiliary Services. The old post of Judge-Advocate-General was replaced by a Judge-Advocate, with more limited responsibilities. All aspects of material supply other than actual manufacture were grouped under the Quartermaster-General. His departmental heads were a Director of Transport and Remounts, a Director of Movements and Quartering, a Director of Supplies and Clothing, and a Director of Equipment and Ordnance Stores. The Master-General of the Ordnance's subordinates included a Director of Artillery, a Naval Adviser and a Director of Fortification and Works.

The clear logical division of responsibility was to be carried right down through the strata of the army. In the Esher Committee's own words:

The line of cleavage between the duties of the several staff officers should be ... rigorously preserved. It is essential to prevent the confusion of staff arrangements which has hitherto prevailed.[6]

Equally:

The principle of the division of training from administration, which we have sought to apply throughout our scheme, appears to us to be fundamental.[7]

Thus the Esher Report re-made the core of the British military system on first principles.

It also re-organized the whole body of the army in the United Kingdom. Administration and policy had become concentrated in the War Office, to the detriment of efficiency and initiative. The Esher Committee was convinced that

... if the Army is to be trained to exercise the initiative and the independence of judgement which are essential in the field, its peace administration must be effectively decentralized. The object should be to encourage the assumption of responsibility as far as possible.[8]

Instead of the existing paper army-corps districts, the Esher Committee recommended administrative districts to which many War Office functions should be delegated. The districts would look after organization and administration and thus leave commanders of field units free for their proper function of training for war. These recommendations too were in principle accepted by the government and formed the basis of army organization at home for the next sixty years.

When the Liberal government took office therefore in 1906, radical reconstruction of the military system had already begun on the lines of the Report of the Esher Committee, while the Committee of Imperial Defence had existed since 1903. The new Liberal War Secretary was also able to profit from the trials and errors of Brodrick and Arnold-Forster, whose proposals had at least pointed the way to the essential requirements of an ever-ready expeditionary force, and of an effective reserve system to back it.

The new minister, however, brought to office all-round personal talents far exceeding those of his predecessors. Richard Burdon Haldane was a Lowland Scot, whose first-class intellect had been trained in philosophy at the University of Edinburgh and, for a brief stay, at Göttingen. From philosophy (in which he retained a deep interest) he passed to law. As a barrister he displayed remarkable capacity for intensive and continuous work, and for 'gutting' the essentials swiftly and accurately out of complicated briefs. He was keenly aware of modern developments abroad in technology, management and education. It was more owing to Haldane than any other single person that new teaching universities other than Oxford and Cambridge were at last being created in England and Wales. His table, cellar and cigar box were renowned, and his social world included many of the interlocking circles that made up the British ruling class. He was deft at handling men and human situations.

Haldane brought no prior military knowledge and no set scheme of reform into office. He was ready to spend months asking questions and listening. As he told his generals,

I was as a young and blushing virgin just united to a bronzed warrior, and that it was not expected by the public that any result of the union should appear until at least nine months had passed.[9]

It was Haldane's great task to implement the Esher Report. The year 1906 was spent in intensive study and planning. The

reforms followed between 1906 and 1909. Haldane gathered about
him a younger generation of professionally-minded soldiers. Ellison
(the Secretary of the Esher Committee) and Douglas Haig were
outstanding among them. Haldane said of his military collabor-
ators:

The men one comes across, the new school of young officers – entitled
to the appellation of men of science just as much as engineers or chemists
– were to me a revelation. ... A new school of officers has arisen since the
South African War, a thinking school of officers who desire to see the
full efficiency which comes from new organisation and no surplus energy
running to waste.[10]

For the first time in its history the British army was provided
with official manuals laying down in detail staff responsibilities
and procedures: *Field Service Regulations Part I – Operations – 1909*;
Part II – Organization and Administration – 1909. When in 1907 the
Imperial Conference agreed to common military forms and
methods throughout the empire, the General Staff became 'the
Imperial General Staff', and the new manuals later became the
basis of standard staff procedures for all imperial forces. Without
these manuals (for which Haig as, successively, Director of Military
Training and Director of Staff Duties, was mainly responsible) the
colossal expansion of the British and dominion armies during the
Great War must have resulted in military chaos.

It was during the same three years 1906–9 that the new War
Office and General Staff were transformed from a blue-print into
an efficient machine.

However, the most difficult of Haldane's tasks (it had defeated
his predecessors) lay in re-organization of the home field army and
reserve system. Here he met the fiercest opposition from entrenched
interests (such as those who feared a reduction in the number of
generals); here in the end he carried out what are generally remembered as 'the Haldane Reforms'.

European events gave an immediate impulse to the creation of
an expeditionary force that his predecessors had not enjoyed. There
was a crisis over Morocco, and during the General Election of 1906
Grey, the Foreign Secretary, asked Haldane what help Britain

could offer the French, if, as persistent rumours suggested, Germany attacked her in the spring. As a result, unofficial and then official contacts were made with the French general staff, with special reference to both powers' treaty obligations to protect the neutrality of Belgium. When the Moroccan crisis died down, the staff talks continued.

Haldane saw the implications of the talks – British military commitment on the continent of Europe. He wrote:

We had therefore to provide for an Expeditionary Force which we reckoned at six great [i.e. with three instead of two brigades] divisions, fully equipped, and at least one cavalry division. We had also to make certain that this force could be mobilised and sent to the place where it might be required as rapidly as any German force could be.[11]

'As rapidly' meant fifteen days, instead of the two months needed at that time to put only 80,000 men into Europe. All Haldane's reforms followed from the need to create this expeditionary force.

Haldane and his advisers decided that the expeditionary force would have to be formed out of the regular troops available in the United Kingdom under Cardwell's two-battalion regimental system, although non-combatant services might be partially manned by the auxiliary forces. Thus they avoided increasing either the size or the cost of the whole regular army or embarking on a fancy new organization such as Arnold-Forster's General Service Army. The new expeditionary force was to be expanded from the far-from-ready field force already stationed at Aldershot under Sir John French (Brodrick's 'First Corps' and Arnold-Forster's 'striking force'). A special Army Order of 1 January 1907 gave details of the new organization.

Re-organization of the two auxiliary forces was a much larger and more ticklish question that involved legislation. The militia had declined from its ancient and proud independence as the 'constitutional' land force of the kingdom. It had become a not always efficient adjunct to the regular army; an avenue to a professional military career for both officers and other ranks. Nor was it any longer filling its nineteenth-century role of a reservoir of mature and partly trained men for the regular army, for the

Militia Reserve had been abolished. It had, however, garrisoned the United Kingdom and some overseas bases in both the Crimean and Boer Wars. The other auxiliary force, the volunteers, was not in much better shape, nor linked to the regular army in one coherent system. As Haldane wrote in a memorandum published in February 1907:

At present the numbers and organisation of the Military Forces in the United Kingdom are based on no scientific standard, and these forces have been raised on no definite plan.[12]

Haldane's answer was to reduce the three echelons of the forces (regulars, militia and volunteers) to two:

... the National Army will, in future, consist of a Field Force and a Territorial or Home Force. The Field Force is to be so completely organised as to be ready in all respects for mobilisation immediately on the outbreak of a great war. In that event the Territorial or Home Force would be mobilised also, but mobilised with a view to its undertaking, in the first instance, systematic training for war. The effect of such training, given a period of at least six months, would be, in the opinion of all military experts, to add very materially to the efficiency of the force. The Territorial Force will, therefore, be one of support and expansion, to be at once embodied when danger threatens, but not likely to be called for till after the expiration of the preliminary period of six months.[13]

Both militia and volunteers were to be abolished in favour of the Territorials. However, men and even units of the volunteers were to be incorporated in the new Territorials. It was hoped that men from the abolished militia would join the new special reserve of the regular army, for which men might volunteer without having first served with the colours. Even during the Great War the special reserve was often referred to as 'the Militia'. It also included a technical reserve, for the lack of technicians to run railways, telegraphs etc. had been sharply felt during the Boer War.

Haldane hoped to make these great changes by agreement with the commanders of the militia and the volunteers. A 'Territorial Force Committee' of some forty-five prominent men was formed under Esher. However, in the face of the bitter opposition of the militia colonels and the militia's political friends, Haldane was forced to fall back on compulsion by legislation. His Territorial Reserve Forces Bill was savagely attacked during its passage through both Houses of Parliament. Critics of Haldane's bill talked of the militia of 1907 as if it were still the proud institution of the eighteenth century. However, Haldane's success in reducing the army estimates by some two million pounds gave him political leverage. The Bill was eventually passed. It contained three main provisions: one, the territorial force was to be administered (but not commanded) by county associations headed by the Lords-Lieutenant; two, the force was to be liable for service anywhere within the United Kingdom but not abroad, and its numbers were to be voted by Parliament; and three, the creation of the new special reserve.

Unlike the old auxiliary forces, the Territorials were to be organized into field divisions, and equipped with all ancillary services such as transport and artillery. The climate of political and public opinion caused the government, however, to reduce Haldane's target of twenty-eight divisions to fourteen, together with fourteen cavalry brigades and corps troops. Many volunteer units were embodied as a whole in the Territorials, while seventy militia battalions amalgamated with regular regimental depots to form part of the new special reserve. The historic rivalry of standing army and militia had finally ended in a merger.

Haldane enjoyed the powerful assistance of royal backing, and in October 1907, Edward VII personally asked a meeting of all Lords-Lieutenant to support the Territorials. On 1 April 1908 the force came officially into being, and that year the first annual fortnight's training camp was held. By the beginning of 1910 the Territorials numbered 276,618 officers and men – 88.5 per cent of establishment. It was a complete vindication of Haldane's hopes.

By 1909 the Haldane reforms were largely completed – new staff methods, new training, new men; an expeditionary force capable of taking the field in Europe within fifteen days, a simple and effective organization of regulars and auxiliaries.

Yet it was powerfully argued that all this was not enough – that compulsory service was essential because the Territorials could not possibly defend the island against the masses of the German army.

Lord Roberts spoke for the National Service League on this topic. Three points need to be noted about the unsuccessful campaign for conscription, or, as its proponents preferred to call it, universal military service, or national service. Firstly, its proponents thought only of conscription for home defence, not for a mass army for deployment in Europe. Secondly, their case rested on the proposition that the navy could not prevent a German invasion – hence their nickname of the 'blue funk' school in contrast to the 'blue water' school of the Royal Navy, which believed that a serious invasion was not possible in the face of the British battle-fleet. Thirdly, and decisively, politicians of both parties were agreed that public opinion would not stomach conscription; exemption from responsibility for his own defence having come to seem an Englishman's constitutional birthright. Conscription in peacetime was never a runner.

After the Haldane reforms, there remained the re-training of the whole army, not only in tactics but in staff work and administration. However, the revolution in British tactics had begun even before the advent of Haldane and Haig, for the old drill-books had been replaced by modern tactical manuals in 1904–5. A foreign military observer had noted as early as 1904:

In their manoeuvres the British infantry showed great skill in the use of ground. Their thin lines of khaki-clad skirmishers were scarcely visible. No detachment was ever seen in close order within three thousand yards. Frontal attacks were entirely avoided ... [14]

With the creation of the General Staff, the Staff College at Camberley acquired a sense of purpose it had never enjoyed before. The remaining traces of the old arid curriculum were swept away in favour of practical training in different staff duties in the field. The war game, complete with full dummy orders and schedules, was introduced. Not since the days of the Commonwealth had the British army been so generally gripped with a sense of professional purpose in peacetime. Even the cavalry learned to fight on foot, with a rifle, and to walk *en route* to spare their horses; they learned that their prime duty was not to go for the enemy bald-headed like old Granby, but to be the distant eyes of the commander-in-chief, and at the same time screen the eyes of the enemy commander-in-chief.

After 1906, the underlying trend of European politics seemed to be towards a general war. In 1907 Britain added an understanding with France's ally Russia to her *Entente* with France. Henceforth Europe was divided between two great armed alliances: the Triple Alliance (Germany, Austria-Hungary, Italy) and the Triple *Entente* (France, Russia, Great Britain). The general staffs polished their plans for war, should diplomacy fail. But what would war be like, in this new era of smokeless powder, the machine-gun, the quick-firing field gun? Of the aeroplane and the airship?

In 1904–5 during the war in Manchuria between Russia and Japan, the armies had gone to ground in trenches behind barbed-wire entanglements because of the killing power of machine-guns and quick-firing artillery, and battles had smouldered on for days and weeks. European staffs drew differing conclusions. The French army continued to believe in the paralysing moral effect of head-long infantry attack under cover of gunfire. The German army increased its unique arm of mobile heavy artillery, and put its faith, tactically and strategically, in finding the enemy's flank and enveloping it. The British army eschewed rigid doctrine, and put its trust in fieldcraft and fast, accurate rifle-fire. But all the general staffs agreed that war, should it come, would be quickly decided and finished. Both the French and the Germans had elaborately planned offensives intended to win the war, in the enemy's territory, in a series of great two- or three-day battles spread over a few weeks. Fascinated by the swift Prussian success against France in 1870, they ignored its dragging aftermath in which hastily-raised French armies, although ill-trained and ill-equipped, were able to keep the Prussian army occupied for months. They also ignored the lessons of the four-year Civil War in America.

It was a Polish banker named Bloch who correctly deduced the results of gearing modern technology and economic power to warfare, and accurately forecast the nature of the war to come. In his book *The War of the Future in its Technical, Economic and Political Relations*, (published in an English translation under the title *Is War Impossible?* in 1899), Bloch wrote:

... instead of war fought out to the bitter end in a series of decisive battles, we shall have as a substitute a long period of continually increasing strain upon the resources of the combatants. ... Everybody will be entrenched in the next war. It will be a great war of entrenchments. The spade will be as indispensable to a soldier as his rifle. ... All wars will of necessity partake of the character of siege operations ... soldiers may fight as they please; the ultimate decision is in the hand of famine ... [15]

He foresaw 'the bankruptcy of nations and the break-up of the whole social organization'.

On 28 June 1914 a chance happening set in irrevocable motion the whole European machinery of alliances and mobilization-plans. The Archduke Francis Ferdinand of Austria and his wife were assassinated in the Bosnian town of Sarajevo. The assassins were Serbs, who enjoyed the blessing of men high in the Serbian government and army. The Austro-Hungarian government saw the murders as an excuse to stop, once and for all, Serbian attempts to stir up sedition in Austria's Slav provinces. Austria sent Serbia an ultimatum giving a choice of submission to Austrian demands or war. The Serb reply being deemed unsatisfactory, Austria declared war and began to mobilize.

However, the Serbs enjoyed a powerful protector in Russia, Austria's long-standing rival for Balkan predominance. Russian plans did not allow for a partial mobilization (against Austria only), but only for complete mobilization (against both Austria and her ally Germany). As soon as Russia announced general mobilization therefore, Germany, whose military plans depended on speed, had no alternative but to mobilize in her turn. And mobilization entailed, according to the Schlieffen Plan, an immediate violation of Belgian territory in order to seize Liége, the gateway to the Belgian plain. For the German strategy for a two-front war against France and Russia was first to throw almost all her strength against France via Belgium, win a decisive victory in six weeks, and then switch to the east to smash the Russians in turn.

Thus an Austrian quarrel with Serbia in the Balkans successively drew in Russia, Germany, France and Belgium, and led to general European war. This was a tragic result of the predominance of the army in the German state, and of over-rigid military planning.

Britain was not involved in this war by any treaty obligation. However, neutrality would have been impossible except at the cost of betrayal of trust. Although it was the Liberal Prime Minister in 1906, Campbell-Bannerman, who had originally authorized staff conversations with France, the decision had never been put to the Cabinet for approval, and under neither Campbell-Bannerman nor Asquith did the British Cabinet ever consider the far-reaching implications of the growing military collaboration with France. While the Liberal government in deference to public opinion refused to entangle Britain in Europe by formal alliances, it ignored the practical political consequences of staff agreements.

In 1910 a fervent admirer of the French army, Sir Henry Wilson, became Director of Military Operations. Collaboration with the French army in the event of war now took specific shape: the British Expeditionary Force (B.E.F.) would fight on the left flank of the French army; it would fight not in any detached and independent role, but as an integral part of the French line, and transportation and concentration plans were made accordingly. The years 1906 to 1914 thus saw the British army committed to close collaboration with the French on a western front.

When in 1914 France called on Britain to honour her moral obligations, the Liberal government was deeply split. There were belated attempts to argue that Britain had neither obligations nor commitments. However, the German invasion of Belgium, hard on the heels of mobilization, provided both a direct threat to the traditional British interest in the independence of the Low Countries and at the same time the emotional pretext needed to swing a volatile public opinion behind war. On 4 August 1914 the British army began to mobilize for its first great European conflict since 1815.

16

The Great War –
a Mass Army
Improvised

ALTHOUGH the war began as a 'cabinet' war, it immediately unleashed popular hatred. All the hostility between different social classes or races within each state was now turned outwards on the enemy. This boded ill, should the hopeful military plans for a quick decision go astray, for mass passions might take the war out of the hands of cabinets.

As a result of the pre-war staff agreements between Britain and France the British Expeditionary Force was committed to the role of close co-operation with the French army. It was to take its place at the extreme left of the five armies in the French line, and act as part of the flankguard to the principal French effort, a headlong offensive into Lorraine. The British mobilization and movement to France was incredibly smooth and well-organized compared with any comparable operation of the past. However, only four instead of six strong divisions were at first sent to France, two being held back to guard against invasion, until eventually despatched in time to take part in the decisive encounters of the 1914 campaign.

The decision to hold the two divisions in England for a time was made by Lord Kitchener, the new Secretary of State for War. In the current national mood nothing seemed more right than to appoint a national hero to take control of the war effort. Nevertheless, at a stroke the government abandoned the hard-won civilian control over grand strategy. Kitchener himself was a man of great ability and insight. He saw at once that Britain must prepare for a war lasting at least three years. However, he was by temperament highly secretive; he worked as a one-man band. His experience had been gained in improvised colonial expeditions, and he had

had neither a share in the army's recent reforms, nor experience of the British political and governmental system. All this, together with his distaste for and lack of knowledge of large-scale staff work and organization, had its dangers for the future.

The British Expeditionary Corps was the best equipped, organized and prepared army that Britain had ever sent abroad at the beginning of a war. Its officers were all professionals, and its rank-and-file all highly trained regulars or regular reservists. Its four (later six) infantry divisions were organized into two corps, to conform with French practice. The corps commanders, Haig (First Corps) and Smith-Dorrien (Second Corps), were men of high reputation. The Commander-in-Chief, Field-Marshal Sir John French, had done well in the Boer War with his energetic defence of Colesberg and his dash to Kimberley. It was Haig's view, however, later borne out by events, that French lacked the capacity for so taxing a command as he now exercised.

The organization of the B.E.F. illustrated the evolution of all armies into ever larger formations. A British infantry division consisted of 18,073 officers and men (slightly larger numbers than in French or German divisions), divided into three brigades each four battalions strong. There were twenty-four machine-guns (two to a battalion, the same allotment as in the French and German armies), and seventy-six guns, of which fifty-four were eighteen-pounder field-pieces, eighteen were 4·5-inch howitzers and four were sixty-pounder heavy guns. In a European army the medium and heavy guns came under corps rather than divisional command. The divisional transport and guns, together with horses for officers, required 5,592 horses. The B.E.F. possessed in addition one cavalry division, consisting of 9,269 officers and men, 9,815 horses, twenty-four thirteen-pounders and twenty-four machine-guns. British cavalry were trained to fight dismounted with the rifle and machine-gun, and to lead, not to ride, their horses on the march. The British cavalry division had four times the number of machine-guns in a German cavalry division. For once, it was the British cavalry who displayed the professional aptitude for reconnaissance and skirmishing, and the European cavalry who thought too much of the charge with sabre or lance.

As well as such older specialist corps as the Army Service Corps and the Royal Army Medical Corps, the B.E.F. possessed one great novelty in the Royal Flying Corps, with its sixty-three aircraft and its function of aerial reconnaissance. For the first time therefore part of a British expeditionary force did not sail to Europe across the Channel; instead 'the squadrons flew to France'.

It had been the assumption of pre-war British strategists that Britain's major role would be naval. While the Royal Navy dealt with the German fleet and blockaded Germany, the Russian and French armies (assisted by the small B.E.F.) would defeat the German and Austrian armies. Here again was the traditional and ever-hopeful view that a great continental enemy might be brought down without Britain herself having to carry much of a military burden. It was an expectation that once again crumbled swiftly when the war plans of all the belligerents broke down in failure.

Germany's plan (the Schlieffen Plan, so called after the Chief of Staff who evolved it in 1905–6) was to concentrate almost her entire field army in the west, smash France, and then turn back to smash the Russians in turn. The essence of the plan was speed: to defeat the French before the sluggish Russians could mobilize and get into the field. The Germans meant to outflank the French frontier defences by swinging wide through the Belgian plain with an enormously strong right wing. This right wing would pivot like a great gate, sweeping the French back into the rear of their own frontier defences. East Prussia, facing the Russians, was left almost denuded of troops. The German deployment in the west consisted of seven armies totalling nearly a million and a half men. Such numbers had never been seen before in history. No one had any experience of handling them in battle.

While the German right wing swung through Belgium towards the French frontier, the French army's own offensive in Lorraine failed with bloody loss. A second French offensive in the Ardennes, aimed at hewing off the German right wing at the joint, also failed. French tactics based on the moral *élan* of attack proved nonsense in the face of machine-guns and artillery. On the other hand, well-trained reserve formations permitted the Germans to deploy in strength all along their front, as well as in overwhelming power on their right.

Meanwhile the B.E.F. was preparing to advance north-east into Belgium alongside the French 5th Army. Orders had already been issued when the British liaison officer with the French hastened to British headquarters to warn that the French were in fact about to retreat. Hastily the British prepared to fight a defensive battle among the houses and ditches and slagheaps of the mining district round Mons.

Von Kluck, commanding the German 1st Army of 320,000 men, the tip of the German swing, had no idea of the whereabouts of the B.E.F. His own intelligence was poor, and the excellent work of Allenby's cavalry division blinded his attempts at reconnaissance. Instead of outflanking the heavily outnumbered B.E.F., von Kluck blundered into a piecemeal frontal attack on one of the two British corps. His dense masses were shot to pieces by accurate and rapid musketry. The German attacks faltered and petered out. This was the Battle of Mons, 23 August 1914, the first battle fought by the British against a European enemy since 1855, and the first fought by the British in western Europe since 1815.

Now the full weight of the German swinging arm was felt all the way from Flanders to Lorraine. Everywhere west of Verdun the French armies were falling back. The B.E.F., on the extreme left of the allied line, was retreating too. The 'Retreat from Mons' was the British share of a fortnight's desperate marching for all the armies, as the Germans pressed on towards Paris and victory. The British rank-and-file proved stauncher in retreat than some members of the British command. While Sir Horace Smith-Dorrien's corps was inflicting a sharp check on Kluck's masses at Le Cateau, Haig, the First Corps commander, at Landrécies displayed momentary signs of being badly rattled. Murray, the Chief of Staff, was dropping with fatigue and overwork. Henry Wilson, his deputy, was ordering the abandonment of equipment to speed the retreat. Sir John French himself, the Commander-in-Chief, having overcome a temptation to shelter his army in the fortress of Maubeuge, finally signalled home that he wanted to remove his army altogether from the allied line and seek repose out of contact with the Germans. The proposal was squashed by Kitchener.

Joffre, the French Commander-in-Chief, became more and more worried about the British command, and the safety of the left flank of all his armies. He felt he must have an army on his left to which he could give orders, not merely requests. He began forming a new French army to the left of the British. It was the germ of the Battle of the Marne. As the German threat to Paris became more menacing Joffre railed troops across from his quiet right flank to his left. Meanwhile he kept the struggling French line together

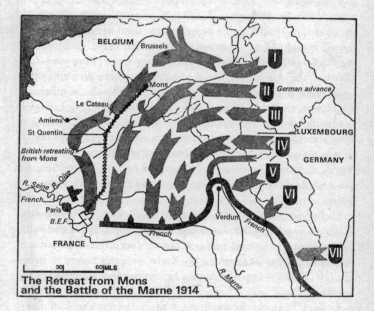

**The Retreat from Mons
and the Battle of the Marne 1914**

during the long retreat by sheer force of personality and will. At Guise the French even counter-attacked, dislocating the German advance for a time.

The Germans too had their troubles. There were not enough men to carry out the Schlieffen plan, and no more could have been kept supplied. Inevitably the German line contracted, forcing them to swing *east* of Paris instead of round the capital to the west. Moltke, the German supreme commander, broke down in health and nerve. Like a team of horses without a driver, the German armies plunged on in growing disorder.

By the first week of September the strategic situation had been reversed: now the allies were outflanking the Germans. Joffre ordered a general counter-offensive. Before battle could really be joined, the German nerve collapsed and their armies beat a retreat. In the Battle of the Marne the B.E.F. played an important but somewhat lethargic part in the allied forward movement.

Paris was saved; France was saved; Germany had failed to win a quick victory. It was now for the allies in their turn to try for a decision. They failed on the Aisne in the second week of September by the margin of one German corps, which came up by forced marches. A stalemate ensued; rudimentary trench lines were dug. Between the Aisne and the sea, however, there was still open country for manoeuvre. Each side tried to outflank the other. As the attempts failed, the line of stalemate – and trenches – extended gradually towards the Channel coast. In October and November 1914 the Allies and the Germans both made final desperate efforts to win a decisive victory. Their attempts collided head-on round Ypres, and failed in bitter touch-and-go fighting. The stalemate reached the dunes of the Belgian coast, and the Western Front was born.

In the east as well there had been no decision, despite partial victories, impressive advances and terrible losses. From the Baltic to the Carpathians, and again on the borders of Serbia, Germans, Russians, Austro-Hungarians and Serbs were still locked in struggle. The brilliant hopes of August lay everywhere trampled in the autumn rains.

Gradually, in every combatant country, the truth sank in that it was going to be a long, grim war. And in the west, it was going to be a war of trenches and artillery, and any new offensive would have to begin by breaking through the enemy front. For the first time in the history of war, the armies had no vulnerable flanks, for one flank rested on the sea, and the other on the Swiss frontier (or more important, Swiss mountains). Manoeuvre was impossible. Brilliant strategic marches were impossible. The armies peered at each other from their unbroken lines of trenches, baffled. What had brought about this situation? It was the enormous increase in European population since the Napoleonic wars, and the power of conscription to tap this increase. For the first time in history there were enough soldiers to hold with sufficient density a battle-line not merely of a few miles, but of 400 miles.

It was clear that in the future France could not carry the military burden almost alone as in 1914; that Britain too would have to create a mass army for the Western Front. So once more in her military history Britain was forced by circumstance to do what she had refused to contemplate before the event; once more she was forced to begin a gigantic task of improvisation – but never before on such a scale. She could not draw on a numerous corps of officers and non-commissioned officers as a nucleus for a mass army, like the Germans; she could only draw on her small professional army, which had already been virtually destroyed by the battles of 1914. 89,000 officers and men had been lost. Otherwise there was only the Territorial force. It was not only trained soldiers that were scarce. Whereas in continental armies clothing, equipment and accommodation had always been provided on a mass scale, and therefore now presented no critical problem, in Britain the scale had been of an army of 200,000, not two million.

In the autumn of 1914 the British set out to create a mass army essentially from scratch from every point of view. How should it be done?

Even now, the Liberal government decided against conscription, so utterly had the ancient English obligation to bear arms in national defence become eclipsed by the later belief that conscription was incompatible with British liberty. Instead, there was a call for volunteers: 'the first hundred thousand', and then as many as could be recruited. Kitchener's personal appeal for men was immortalized in the most famous of all British posters, on which his hooded eyes glared over a pointed finger above the legend: 'Your country needs YOU'.

The call was answered with enthusiasm. Moved by patriotism, by desire for a bit of adventure, by a desire to escape from poverty and unemployment, the crowds queued outside the recruiting offices. By the end of 1914 1,186,337 volunteers had joined up.

In recruiting and organizing his 'New Army', Kitchener made no use of the Territorial army organization and its county associations, for which he had complete contempt and about which he knew little. Instead he was certain that the New Army must be

Recruiting propaganda, 1915. Failure to introduce an orderly system of conscription meant injustice, confusion and increasingly desperate expedients to get volunteers.

formed round the regiments and personnel of the peacetime regular army. No new regiments were raised as in the eighteenth century. Instead, existing two-battalion Cardwell regiments were expanded to thirteen, fourteen, fifteen battalions.

In late 1914 and throughout most of 1915, however, Kitchener's

New Army was an unarmed, ill-housed shambles which its constitution into 'divisions' only mocked. The uncontrolled tide of volunteers entirely swamped a military organization equipped to deal only with a small army. The volunteers lived in improvised tented camps and wore firstly their own clothes, and later an improvised blue uniform. Their weapons consisted of now-obsolete rifles or broomsticks. Their senior officers and non-commissioned officers consisted of Boer War or even pre-Boer War regulars, brought out of retirement. These 'dug-outs' were out of touch with the professional modernization of the army since 1902, and with modern weapons and tactics, modern organization and methods. They were totally ignorant of trench warfare. As products of the Duke of Cambridge's army, they were also too often Colonel Blimps and Sergeant Blimps and Corporal Blimps. The style of command that might have worked with slum-dwellers in the 1890s did not go down well with the citizen volunteers of 1914. The first acquaintance of a cross-section of the nation with military life was not a happy one. And, incalculably inferior though these New Army 'dug-outs' were to the hard core of first-class officers and non-commissioned officers still remaining to the German army, there was nothing like enough of them. One battalion (and it was among the more fortunate) had just three 'trained' officers: a pre-Boer War commanding officer aged sixty-three, a regular subaltern with a badly broken leg and a stone-deaf quartermaster who had retired in 1907.[1] The junior officers and non-commissioned officers were often virtually devoid of any kind of military knowledge or experience. Trained staff-officers to man formation headquarters – essential to the complex mass operations of modern war – were absolutely lacking. In France a tug-of-war began between the trenches and the various headquarters for the handful of good, trained officers available.

While the French continued to carry the main burden of the Western Front, this raw assembly of men had to be made ready to fight the most skilled, best-equipped and organized army in the world. The process of making ready required time. But time, in war, is a scarce commodity.

While Kitchener's New Army was recruited and gradually put

into some kind of shape, the forces of the British empire were gathering. An Indian corps arrived in France; Canadians too. As with the mother country, the empire took time to put forth its strength, but eventually Canada was to contribute four divisions to the war, Australia five divisions and a mounted division, New Zealand one infantry division. Many proved first-class formations, thrustful and intelligent. India's military contribution was second only in size to that of the United Kingdom. Thanks to pre-war agreements on military organization and staff methods, these imperial formations were easily meshed together.

Gradually the B.E.F. in France grew, fed by regulars brought back from colonial garrisons, by territorials, special reservists, and by the first of the New Army formations. On Christmas Day 1914 the B.E.F. was divided into two armies. However, throughout 1915 it remained only a minor part of allied strength in France.

For the Allies the stalemate presented a cruel and inescapable dilemma. Despite the failure of the Schlieffen Plan to win Germany a quick victory, it had nevertheless gained her a vast tract of French territory; it had won her the priceless initiative. No French government or general staff could passively contemplate this German occupation of northern France; the French were inescapably driven to try to turn the Germans out. And this meant frontal offensives against trench systems that were rendered more formidable every month by German thoroughness and ingenuity. The strategic pattern of almost the entire war on the Western Front was thus set: the Germans, squatting on French land, called the tune, and haplessly the Allies had to dance by attacking. In 1915 they were ill-equipped to do so. The French as well as the British had entered the war with little modern heavy artillery. The French were forced to strip their fortresses of their guns, many of them old-fashioned and slow-firing, for field use. Britain and France suffered from appalling shortages of ammunition, because they lacked the modern industries and skills which the Germans were able to convert so swiftly to munition-making. The French and British had to turn to North America for help – costly help. In Britain, the Ordnance Department at the War office, which in peacetime was required to supply small quantities of weapons and munitions under heavy political pressure for caution and economy, was now expected to master-mind national industrial mobilization at breakneck speed and regardless of expense.

When the Ordnance Department failed to produce abundance in a few months, partly because of its habits of caution and red tape, partly because the skills and resources simply did not exist at that time in British industry, it was blamed for incompetence by politi-

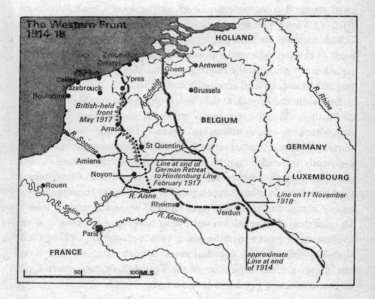

The Western Front 1914-18

HOLLAND

Zeebrugge
Ostend
Calais
Hazebrouck
Boulogne

Ghent
Antwerp

Ypres
Brussels

Scheldt

British-held front May 1917

Arras

BELGIUM

R. Rhine

GERMANY

St Quentin

Amiens

Noyon

Line at end of German Retreat to Hindenburg Line February 1917

LUXEMBOURG

R. Somme

Rouen

R. Oise

R. Aisne

Rheims

Verdun

Line on 11 November 1918

R. Seine

R. Marne

Paris

FRANCE

approximate Line at end of 1914

50   100 MLS

cians like Lloyd George, who, in peacetime, had been hot critics of military expenditure. In the spring of 1915, a great 'shell scandal' blew up, in which high military officers and politicians blamed each other personally for a famine of high-explosive shells arising out of the old-fashionedness of British industry. In June 1915 Lloyd George became head of the new Ministry of Munitions. He was then able to learn at first hand that Britain neither possessed nor could make in sufficient quantity semi-automatic machinery for shell production. The machines had to be bought from America.

Lloyd George also discovered that Britain possessed no chemical industry large and modern enough to make explosives, Britain having depended in peacetime on the German chemical industry. Lloyd George found out that few British firms were equipped to carry out the fine precision work of making fuses.

In fact, the first shells from Lloyd George's own munitions programme did not reach the armies in France until the spring of 1916, and most of the shells fired in the Somme bombardment in 1916 resulted from orders placed by the War Office. When by 1916–17 Lloyd George's undoubted talents had created a great British armaments industry, much of it in new national factories, most of the sophisticated equipment was American. All this illustrated how tightly in the modern age military power was linked to general industrial and economic capability.

But while the French and British struggled to create new industries and build up their heavy artillery, the soldiers had to be committed to vain offensives against German defences that remained almost unscathed by the feeble bombardments, for it was politically impossible not to try to evict the Germans from French soil. The French attacked in Artois, they attacked in Champagne, they attacked over and over again. During 1915, the French lost nearly a million and a half men, killed, wounded and prisoners. Despite this, the French brought their army to a strength of three million men by the end of the year; it was a staggering achievement that Britain, with a population of similar size, was far from matching. Yet the expansion of the French army was carried out at the expense of French war industry.

The B.E.F. launched two offensives of its own in 1915, at Neuve Chapelle and the Aubers Ridge (March) and Loos (September), essentially to prove to the French that their ally was not standing idle. Both suffered from lack of guns and shells. Both revealed the increasingly familiar pattern of allied attacks – any success was achieved in the first rush, after which the fighting 'stuck', and further attacks led only to futile losses against an alerted enemy. At Loos the British used gas (introduced by the Germans at the Second Battle of Ypres in April 1915) for the first time, with mixed results. However, even by the beginning of the year, the difficulty, perhaps impossibility, of breaking the German front had provoked the central strategic argument of the war. As Kitchener put it to Sir John French in January:

I suppose we must now recognise that the French Army cannot make a sufficient break through the German lines to bring about the retreat of the German forces from Northern Belgium.

From this he drew the conclusion:

If that is so, then the German lines in France may be looked on as a fortress that cannot be carried by assault and also cannot be completely invested.

Since a peace on German terms was unthinkable, the alternative to attacking in France was to find somewhere else easier for attacking. In Kitchener's words: ' ... the lines [in France] may be held by an investing force, whilst operations proceed elsewhere'.[2]

In other words, Britain should return to her traditional 'blue water' strategy, and use her command of the sea to land military forces in regions away from the central European battlefields, where they might (it was hoped) fight the enemy at a relative advantage. The prospect of finding an easy and cheap way round to victory proved as seductive in 1915 as it had in the past, and the results of being so seduced were to be just as costly, painful and useless. In 1915 the chosen expedition was to a new locale: the Gallipoli Peninsula, commanding the Dardanelles Straits that led to the Sea of Marmora and to the Bosporus. For Turkey had by now entered the war on the side of Germany and the Central Powers. The strategic objective was Constantinople, capital of the Turkish Empire and the city commanding the links between Europe and Asia, and between the Black Sea and the Mediterranean.

The conception was brilliant and ambitious. The capture of Constantinople might smash one of Germany's allies and challenge German and Austrian predominance in the Balkans – perhaps save hard-fighting Serbia from extinction. It would open a warm-water route to Russia for the war supplies the Russian armies so desperately needed. Nevertheless it did not offer an opportunity of striking at the mass of the German army. And all strategy, to be successful, must be related to the quantity and quality of available resources. Amphibious strokes especially demand meticulous preparation; they demand the highest possible standard of efficiency and organization in fighting troops, supporting services and formation headquarters. The Dardanelles expedition lacked all these essentials. As too often before with British maritime ventures,

all was hasty improvisation. The army commander, Sir Ian Hamilton, had under forty days in which to create an expeditionary force out of the random military bits and pieces to hand in Egypt and elsewhere in the Near (Middle) East: not only that, but build a forward base in Crete. He was given one regular army division, the 29th, which, in the spring of 1915, constituted the world strategic reserve of the British empire. Although composed of excellent regimental soldiers, the 29th Division was neither trained nor experienced as a division, but had been hastily put together from scattered colonial garrisons.

The Gallipoli campaign began on 25 April 1915. Strategic surprise had already been thrown away by abortive attempts to force the Dardanelles by purely naval means. Precarious lodgements were nevertheless won round the tip of the Peninsula, and up its western coast at 'Anzac Cove'. However, the high ground dominating these beachheads remained firmly in Turkish hands. In the eastern Mediterranean as on the Western Front, far-reaching strategic purposes collapsed in tactical failure; the machine-gun, the gun barrage and barbed wire imposed their inevitable paralysis. Nowhere could the allies get more than three miles inland. In August Hamilton tried to break the stalemate by a fresh landing well behind the Turkish front at Suvla Bay. This time there were self-propelled landing barges available. The landing itself was successful against light opposition. But while elderly commanders wasted their opportunity in delay, the Turks swiftly regrouped; the moment passed; the new front too hardened into stalemate. The fighting went on, just as in France. Here there was rock instead of mud; blazing sun instead of rain. It was small advantage, for disease ran high – dysentery, enteric fever, skin sores. And on Gallipoli, far from home, medical services were nothing like so well-organized or well-equipped as in France. In the winter there came severe frostbite. The vision faded into a reality even more unpleasant for the troops than the Western Front. The decision was finally taken to evacuate. The evacuation itself was a masterpiece of staff-work and deception, showing what might have been achieved in the original landings, had it not been for haste, unreadiness and improvisation. On 9 January 1916 the last allied troops were withdrawn. Of 410,000 British empire troops employed, 213,980 were casualties; of 79,000 French troops, 47,000 were lost.

Military criticism focuses on various mistakes and missed opportunities in the conduct of the campaign, but essentially the expedition failed even in its immediate objectives because it was neither large enough, nor well-enough equipped, trained and organized to fulfil the ambitious strategic vision.

Gallipoli was by no means the only reversion to traditional British strategy. Essential protection of the Suez Canal and the Persian Gulf oilfields was inflated into major campaigns against the Turks in Palestine and Mesopotamia. Here, too, hasty improvisation led to early disasters and appalling sufferings and losses among the troops through sickness and the breakdown of medical services. Victory over the Turks required the pumping-in of huge and ill-spared resources. From first to last, some two and a half million British Empire troops fought the Turks, without any commensurate German commitment on the other side. The eventual defeat of Turkey inflicted little damage on German power. It may be doubted whether the Gallipoli expedition would therefore have been really worthwhile even if successful.

In the war against Germany, as in earlier wars against France, British sea-power enabled British expeditions to scoop up enemy colonies. These colonies were valueless to the German war effort. Their conquest gave employment to a million British soldiers during the war. In German East Africa von Lettow-Vorbeck, with some 3,500 Germans and 12,000 Africans, fought until after the Armistice in November 1918, having from first to last drawn in against him 372,950 British Empire troops. Thus, in pursuit of what General Fuller called the 'strategy of evasion' the British employed some three-and-a-quarter million men during the war against only tiny German forces, and conquered nothing that affected Germany's capacity for war.

The argument between the modern proponents of a 'continental' strategy – the 'westerners' – and these of a 'maritime' strategy – the 'easterners' – continued into and through 1917. As in the eighteenth century, it was the politicians – especially Lloyd George and Winston Churchill – who baulked at the cost and difficulty of defeating the enemy's main forces in the field, and looked for the easy way, in Gallipoli, or northern Greece (where a large allied army spent most of the war inactive in what the Germans called the biggest of all internment camps), or Serbia, or, later still, in Italy. Most senior soldiers – in particular, Sir William Robertson, C.I.G.S. after December 1915, and Sir Douglas Haig, Commander-in-Chief of the armies in France from the end of 1915 – believed that the war could be won by defeating the main body of the German armies in France.

The strategic controversy thus developed into a battle between 'the frock-coats and the brass-hats'. There was little mutual understanding and sympathy between generals and politicians. While politicians were ill-informed about strategy and war, soldiers had been trained to avoid political questions and study only their own narrow professional task. A special mistrust between the officer corps and Liberal politicians derived from the Irish crisis of the summer of 1914. The Liberal Home Rule Bill had proposed to place Protestant Ulster under the rule of a predominantly Southern Irish and Catholic parliament in Dublin. The Ulstermen had prepared to resist by force. It had appeared likely that the army would have had to coerce Ulster. However, many officers were in fact Anglo-Irishmen, sympathetic to the Ulster cause. Owing to muddles and misunderstandings, there had been a so-called 'mutiny' at the Curragh army camp in March 1914, when officers had resigned their commissions rather than undertake to coerce Ulster. All this had raised the ghosts of old constitutional quarrels over the role of the army in soceity.

The failures and disappointments of 1915 led to the customary demand for distinguished heads. Kitchener's secretiveness and intensely personal methods as War Secretary were now seen to be productive of confusion and error. In June 1915 he lost his responsibility for munitions production when Lloyd George became the first Minister of Munitions. In December responsibility for advising the government on military matters and strategy was vested in a tough new Chief of the General Staff, Sir William Robertson, a working-class soldier who had risen from the ranks, an outstanding exception to the domination of the army by the upper classes. Kitchener remained War Secretary, a figurehead without much influence, although still the trusted hero of the nation until his death at sea in 1916. In May 1915 the 'shell scandal' and the barren results of the landing on Gallipoli brought down the great Liberal administration that had been in office since 1906; indeed the last Liberal government ever to hold office. Instead a coalition of Liberals, Conservatives and the Labour Party was formed under

Asquith, the Liberal leader. The failure at Gallipoli also cost the job of the man who had most passionately espoused the Dardanelles strategy, Winston Churchill, First Lord of the Admiralty. At the end of 1915, Sir John French, Commander-in-Chief of the armies in France, also became a casualty of failure, and was replaced by Sir Douglas Haig, the First Army Commander.

Haig was to command the British armies in France until he led them to victory over the German army in 1918. He has ever since remained a figure of controversy. In the wave of emotional revulsion in the 1920s and 1930s against the horrors of the war, Haig was made principal scapegoat for the suffering and losses on the Western Front. He had been caricatured as an unfeeling, stupid and ignorant blimp who sent men to futile death in fighting conditions he knew nothing of. In such a continuing climate of emotion and controversy, it is not easy to arrive at a fair critical assessment of Haig's ability and achievement, measured against the problems he faced. Few at the time of his appointment doubted his ability. The vast wartime expansion of the British army had been made possible by staff methods and staff organization designed largely by Haig ten years previously during the Haldane reforms. Haldane himself – a man of first-class intellect and wide education – had complete confidence in Haig's brain and professional knowledge. There is no doubt that Haig had thoroughly studied all that touched his own profession, including the German and other European armies.

Haig was a Lowland Presbyterian Scot, with the appropriate seriousness and sobriety. Few men penetrated his reserved reticence. The literary style of his own private diaries curiously lacks any strong flavour of personality; they display rather a flat conventionality coupled with something approaching self-satisfaction. On the other hand, the drab language expresses a strong and stubborn mind. The diaries also contain shrewd assessments of men and situations, and illustrate Haig's open-mindedness over new weapons and new techniques. Perhaps a fair criticism of him would be that his methods were too permissive. He tended to accede to the advice of his army commanders and specialist advisers, who in fact proved more often wrong than he. Nor could he talk fluently and brilliantly; it was a fatal weakness in dealing with politicians.

No British general before him in history had ever faced such a professional task. He took over command when the British mass army was at last gathering in France, and it was he who had to organize it for battle. In January 1916 it numbered just over a million men, divided into thirty-eight infantry divisions and five cavalry divisions. By midsummer nineteen more divisions swelled its strength. It was then divided into five armies, each much larger than the armies commanded by Marlborough or Wellington. The administrative feat involved in creating and maintaining such a force in the bare downlands of Picardy and the plains of Flanders was enormous.[3] Leaving aside the purely military aspects of the problem, a mass of men as numerous as the population of Birmingham had to be given shelter, water supplies, sanitation, medical services, daily hot food, clothing, workshops of all kinds, building and construction services, off-duty entertainment and recreation, a transport network and a telephone system of immense complication. This gigantic administrative operation was solved with complete success, although the British army began with none of the resources in equipment and in trained and experienced officers that the mass European armies enjoyed.

Bases and communications were the responsibility of the Inspector-General of Communications and the Director of Works. The bases, essential for an army operating out of its own country, were created at Havre, Rouen and Boulogne; each became a small hutted town. Havre specialized in supplies, reinforcements and remounts, while Rouen (in addition) was the base for mechanical transport and ordnance. Boulogne and Rouen handled sick and wounded, Boulogne being the principal port for evacuating wounded. The size of these bases was immense: Rouen, for example, contained nine general hospitals and a reinforcement camp for 40,000. Throughout the French territory behind the British front subsidiary bases and installations sprang up outside the towns: bakeries, veterinary hospitals, engineering workshops, quarries, ammunition depots. Rail and road communications for each army had to be organized and augmented to sustain a great offensive, for every division required two trains of supplies and reinforcements for each day in battle.

Supply and transport was the responsibility of the Army Service Corps, under the Director of Supplies and the Director of Transport. The scope of the supply problem that was solved is illustrated by a few figures. In 1914 3,600,000 pounds of meat were issued monthly; in 1918 67,500,000 pounds. In 1914 4,500,000 pounds of breadstuffs were issued monthly; in 1918 90,000,000. Petrol issued monthly rose in four years from 842,000 gallons to 13,000,000.

Bulk supplies were sent up to advanced supply depots by train. From the advanced supply depots 'section pack' trains (i.e. packed with one day's groceries for one division, each of which had its own 'section' number) went forward to divisional railheads. The lorries of the divisional supply column took the supplies to a 'refilling point', where they were transferred to horse-drawn vehicles for distribution to brigades. From brigade the supplies proceeded by regimental transport and then by ration parties to the men in the line. In addition, mobile field service depots were set up with emergency supplies to safeguard against a breakdown of communications.

Although most supplies were imported into France, some goods, especially forage, were bought locally or further afield on the Continent. These purchases were under the Supplies Special Service Department, perhaps the true heir of the old commissaries. Efficient control over the handling of supply was vested in the Investigation Department, staffed by officers who had been accountants or businessmen.

Army pay and finance was in the hands of the Paymaster-in-Chief, a major-general, and the Army Pay Department. Of the Department's two branches, the command pay office was responsible for all local expenditure by the army (purchase of stores, requisitions and hirings, damage claims), while the clearing house accounted for all money issued to units for payment to the troops, and acted as link with pay offices in the United Kingdom. The command and base cashiers were responsible for safe custody of cash, for its issue, and for making sure there was enough of it to meet demands. The Paymaster-in-Chief acted in close liaison with the Financial Adviser to the Commander-in-Chief (and Local Auditor) appointed in 1915. The Financial Adviser was a civil servant given the rank of brigadier-general, and he was appointed to avoid the waste and muddle over expenditure and accounts that had taken place during the Boer War. He audited all paymaster's accounts, as well as the accounts of store and supply depots and base workshops; and also introduced efficient accounting methods. The Financial Adviser also dealt with money matters involved in transactions with allies. After the war the Public Accounts Committee of the House of Commons praised the system of financial control in the army in France – a remarkable change from the criticisms expressed as recently as the South African War.

Army pay was issued through the field cashiers, who drew it in bulk from the base cashiers. A 'field cashier' was not merely a man, but an office, and there were two to a corps.

The Army Service Corps expanded between 1914 and 1916 more than tenfold. New army and corps heavy-artillery transport units were formed, as well as mobile transport-repair shops and water-tank companies. Whereas in 1914 the B.E.F. had 827 motor-cars and fifteen motor bicycles, in 1918 it had 56,000 trucks and 34,000 motor cycles.

Medical services in the field also enormously expanded and developed between 1914 and 1916. By 1916 there were fifty-eight hospitals in the British Army area, and by August of that year 70,000 beds; seven convalescent depots for other ranks and one convalescent home for officers; twenty-eight ambulance trains. Ancillary medical services included a mobile bacteriological laboratory. There were also twenty hospitals for animals. In France there was none of the avoidable medical horrors of the Crimea – or indeed of Mesopotamia in the current conflict. The number of personnel rose from 200 medical officers, fifty-six quartermasters and 9,000 other ranks to 10,699 officers and 114,939 other ranks; and nursing staff from 516 to over 6,000 (in 1918). Casualty clearing stations were grouped behind the front in twos or threes, and each could cope with up to a thousand cases at a time. They were equipped for operative surgery, and each group enjoyed the advice of two consultant surgeons and one consultant physician. The casualty clearing stations were situated if possible near a railway for easy evacuation of casualties to base hospitals.

Static warfare fought by an immense army led to a corresponding expansion of the ordnance services, which were responsible for supplying all the equipment and installations needed by the army except for aircraft and tanks. Ordnance Corps workshops for repairing artillery became virtual factories. The scale of Ordnance Corps operations is indicated by the following quotation from the official History of the Great War:

... there were issued from Calais alone during the first ten months of 1915, 11,000 prismatic and magnetic compasses, 7,000 watches, 40,000 miles of electric cable, 40,000 electric torches, 3,600,000 yards of flannelette, 1,260,000 yards of rot-proof canvas, 25,000 tents, 1,600,000 waterproof sheets, 12,800 bicycles, 20,000 wheels, 6,000,000 anti-gas helmets, 4,000,000 pairs of horse and wheel shoes, 447,000 Lewis-gun magazines, 2,260,000 bars of soap ... [4]

All ancillary services also underwent colossal expansion. The Army Postal Service, for example, handled more than ten million letters a week. A complete army printing works was created. Welfare for the troops in the field for the first time progressed far beyond the sutler's cart and the local pub. In 1916 the Expeditionary Force Canteen organization was set up, with main depots, and divisional canteens (institutes) which in turn provided canteens on wheels for brigades, and dry canteens for battalions. The new organization eventually became a kind of department store, providing everything from wine to footballs. It even ran cinemas and theatres, for it was a novel feature of welfare in this war that touring companies came out from England to present plays and variety-shows to the troops. The official canteen organization was very greatly supplemented by voluntary canteen and welfare bodies, such as the Y.M.C.A. and the Church Army. The Y.M.C.A. especially, maintained buffets and 'clubs' for other ranks in many towns along the lines of communication and in the bases.

Thus the British army in France by 1916 was the largest, most complicated and most comprehensive single organization ever evolved by the British nation. No peacetime operation of either government or private enterprise could begin to compare with it. No doubt it was often creakingly bureaucratic, irritating and frustrating to the men it tried to serve. Nevertheless it was an outstanding achievement to create this vast organization in less than two years – an organization that in fact coped without breakdown with all the unprecedented demands made upon it. It was the culmination of all the halting progress in the organization of British armies in the field since the days of Elizabeth I. Although the Second World War was to bring new technical changes and developments, the organization of the British army in France in 1916–18 and of its bases and communications was never to be surpassed in scale and comprehensiveness.

*

The new British mass army was to make its début in a grand offensive in mid-1916. Haig faced both a strategic and a tactical dilemma. Strategically he was not a free agent, because the French were still senior partners in the alliance, and it was their country that had to be freed. While Haig would have preferred to attack in Flanders, Joffre, the French commander-in-chief, wanted to attack astride the Somme, since this was the junction point of the two armies. Haig conformed to Joffre's wishes, but neither he nor Joffre ever formulated clear objectives for the offensive, other than to defeat the Germans in battle. Nor was Haig free to choose his own time to attack. The ferocious German offensive against Verdun (opened in February) put appalling strains on the French army. When in May Haig mentioned to Joffre the middle of August as a date for the Somme offensive, Joffre told him that by then the French army would have ceased to exist. Eventually 1 July was fixed for 'Z day' on the Somme. The new British army was therefore not by any means as well trained as Haig wished. He himself wrote in March: 'I have not got an Army in France really, but a collection of divisions untrained for the field.'[5]

At every level, from divisional commanders to subalterns, there were inexperienced or ill-trained officers hastily promoted. The staff, crammed on short courses, could not be compared with the professionals on the German staff. Even 'regular' units belied their promise. One regular battalion commander confided to his diary on 4 June that his men 'are still not PROPERLY TRAINED, although full of courage ... '.[6]

This was the army that had to be launched against the most skilled and experienced army in the world, posted in strong defences that it had taken two years to perfect. The German defences were excavated deep into the chalk of the Somme downlands, and covered by dense belts of barbed wire. Each spur or village was a fortress, each valley a cul-de-sac swept by fire. Was disaster inherent in the situation? Whatever history's answer, Haig had no choice but to attack on 1 July.

The British hope for success lay in the week's preliminary bombardment, which it was believed would destroy the German wire and the defence system behind it. The British command read the wrong lesson from the German bombardment before the attack at Verdun, for although this had been devastating and concentrated, isolated pockets of Frenchmen had survived to prevent a breakthrough by the German infantry. The British bombardment on the Somme was spread over a wider front, and too great a proportion of the artillery was made up of field-guns, not heavies, which British industry had failed to produce in sufficient quantity. The shells produced by hastily expanded industries at home and in North America were not reliable, many bursting in the barrels or failing to explode on impact.

The British command wrongly decided that its half-trained troops were only capable of a deliberate advance in rigid lines, not in small groups making tactical use of the ground. The reserves were to go forward close behind the assaulting troops to avoid the delays in exploitation experienced in earlier battles. This too proved an error.

At 7.30 A.M. on 1 July thirteen British and five French divisions left their trenches and advanced across no-man's-land. It was the 132nd day of the battle of Verdun. The British assault was a failure that incurred losses unprecedented in history for a single day's fighting. At the end of the day the British army had suffered 60,000 casualties—over 19,000 killed—and had won a lodgement in the German defences only in the southern sector. The German defences had not been adequately destroyed, and German machine-gunners emerged from their deep dug-outs before the laden British infantry could cross no-man's-land. The machine-guns cut down the slow-moving British lines like grass. Between the wreckage of the assault troops and formation headquarters there lay a gulf of smashed communications and dead runners.

Yet, with Verdun still under heavy assault, the attack could not be broken off. The Germans had to be gripped in battle. So 1 July was the first of 140 days of continual slogging forward, first here, then there – British, Australians, South Africans, Newfoundlanders. On 11 July the German command was forced to break off its offensive against Verdun. The British slogged on, wrestling in the mud, learning the paradox of modern war – that while it was generally an affair of great organizations, on the battlefield it was a question of small groups of men fumbling in a featureless desert of destruction.

In the autumn of 1916 the Allies – Russians, French and Italians – applied pressure on the Central Powers from every direction, in an attempt to win the war by overwhelming simultaneous attack. The British therefore kept their own offensive going on the Somme. The last stages of the battle, if a familiar experience to Germans and Frenchmen, was something new to the British:

... Whoever it is we are relieving, they have already gone. The trench is empty. In the watery moonlight it appears a very ghostly place. Corpses lie along the parados, rotting in the wet: every now and then a booted foot appears jutting over the trench ... [7]

For this final heave in his offensive, and as part of the allied effort at a decision in 1916, Haig committed a new weapon of war to battle, although it was only available in small quantities. The idea of the 'tank', an armoured and tracked vehicle to roll over wire and machine-guns, had occurred to several different people in 1915, British and French. The British were first to build experimental tanks, and when Haig became Commander-in-Chief at the end of 1915, he pressed for large quantities. However, the promises made to him for delivery of 150 tanks in time for the opening of the Somme battle were not fulfilled, owing to acute production difficulties over engines and track links. Instead, sixty tanks were delivered by late August. Haig decided to use them to spearhead his share in the allies' culminating effort for 1916, for it was the general hope that there might be no 1917 campaign. Haig instructed Rawlinson, the Fourth Army commander, that 'the "tanks" may be used boldly and success pressed in order to demoralise the enemy and, if possible, capture his guns'.[8]

However, on 15 September, the day of the attack, only thirty-two tanks were mechanically fit, and divisional commanders dispersed the tanks along their fronts instead of concentrating them. As a consequence of dispersal and small numbers no decisive success was obtained, but only local advances. The Mark 1 tanks of 1916 were in any case very unreliable and had a battlefield speed of only half a mile an hour.

The allied hopes of overwhelming Germany and her allies in the autumn of 1916 were not fulfilled, although the central powers were very hard pressed. Everywhere the fighting died away, and the Somme offensive was closed down on 18 November.

Had the offensive accomplished anything? Haig and Joffre had certainly failed to break through. The shallow belt of ground won was certainly not worth the immense human cost.* Yet there had been achievements. Verdun had been relieved. For the first time since 1914 another army took over the main burden of the fighting from the French. The German army had been gripped and pounded in battle as never before, month after month. General Ludendorff (who with Field-Marshal Hindenburg took over Germany's war direction in August 1916) recognized that the German army was 'absolutely exhausted'. He wrote that

[We] had to face the danger that 'Somme fighting' would soon break out at various points on our fronts, and that even our troops would not be able to withstand such attacks indefinitely ... [9]

The Somme was the grave of the peacetime-trained German army.

---

*The number of casualties suffered by the three national armies involved is still a matter of controversy. Different countries had different methods of recording losses, and thus comparisons are difficult. The British share has been put as high as 600,000 killed, wounded and missing; and as low as 400,000; as greater and as smaller than the German losses.

Germany, with her smaller population, could afford such losses less than the Allies.

However, the Somme made a lasting and terrible impression on the British national memory. Nothing in their experience of colonial wars had accustomed the British to such immense loss, although in proportion to numbers employed it was in fact at a rate normal for great battles in the past. And for the first time the loss fell not on the professional army, but on civilians in uniform who had volunteered from every section of British society.

*

By the end of 1916 the evolution of technological war was almost complete. The barriers between armies and society had melted. A civilian, for example, ran Haig's railway system. Military requirements, on the other hand, moulded national life. Victorian liberal ideas of *laissez-faire* private enterprise failed to produce efficient war-making. Instead the government and private industry together forged a great national machine for munitions production. New mass-production factories, many 'national', were created with American machines. More and more of national life was controlled and directed by the government.

In 1916 Britain even abandoned the cherished principle of voluntary recruitment in favour of conscription. The voluntary system was pernicious. It produced at first an uncontrolled flood of volunteers that swamped the capacity to train and arm them – volunteers who included many skilled workers essential to war industry – but later dried up. It was also in any case unjust. On 27 January 1916 the Military Service Act was passed, making unmarried men between eighteen and forty-one liable for call-up if not in a reserved occupation. Volunteering had, however, already creamed the national manpower, while war industry itself demanded more and more men. Fewer than 50,000 men were called up between January and July 1916. Henceforth the armed forces and industry were to struggle for dwindling resources of men.

The technical problems of trench warfare continued to baffle the armies of Europe. The tank, in its primitive state and small numbers, offered only promise for the future. In the meantime no infantry could hope to assault successfully until a huge battering engine of artillery had blown a hole in the opposing defences. Gunnery evolved into a complicated science. Targets were determined by aerial reconnaissance, and the fall of shot was corrected by observers in captive balloons. Artillery fired from the map, after allowances for wind and weather. A great preliminary bombardment was orchestrated according to the elaborate schedules of a fire plan. When the infantry began their assault, the guns switched to a creeping barrage—a curtain of fire advancing ahead of the infantry.

Except for sniping, the rifle proved less and less useful in close-range fighting from trench to trench. Bombs (grenades) came back into fashion. Trench mortars provided the infantry with their own short-range artillery, a sphere in which the Germans retained a predominance in numbers to the end of the war. The Germans first used asphyxiating gas at Ypres in April 1915, and the Allies followed suit as quickly as their primitive chemical industries allowed. First released from cylinders, gas was later fired in shells. Though horrible in its outward effects, it was in fact more humane than explosives in terms of death and permanent injury. In the summer of 1917 the Germans introduced mustard gas, a vaporizing liquid that induced huge blisters and burns. Drenching an area with it served to hinder all the movements and operations of the enemy. Thus gas could paralyse a defence without cratering the ground. There was a delay of a year before the Allies were able to produce mustard gas in quantity. The Germans also invented the flame-thrower, an appalling but effective instrument for killing the inhabitants of pill-boxes or dug-outs. In the face of shrapnel and other flying debris, all the armies exchanged their soft or ceremonial headgear for steel helmets. The British army adopted the familiar 'dish' in 1916.

The Great War saw an immense advance in air-power. The British Royal Flying Corps expanded from sixty-three machines in 1914 to 22,000 in 1918. In 1914 the principal role was reconnaissance; and it was a British aircraft which discovered that Kluck was turning east instead of west of Paris. By 1916 the role of the air forces was manifold: tactical support of the ground battle with bombs and machine-gun fire, artillery-spotting, communications, as well as reconnaissance and aerial photography. In the Somme battle, low-flying aircraft had proved an effective means of informing the high command of the whereabouts of leading troops. In 1916 the Allies bombed the Ruhr and the Rhineland, and in 1917 the Germans introduced heavy long-range bombers and attacked London. The moral effects were out of all proportion to the material damage.

Aerial reconnaissance led to a new art, that of camouflage. Roads, gun positions, headquarters were concealed beneath artificial vegetation or painted to merge into the countryside. The British army in France set up its camouflage unit, a 'Special Works Park, R.E.', in 1916.

The machine-gun was queen of the battlefield, cutting battalions down like wheat. In 1915 both the German and British armies raised the number of heavy machine-guns per battalion from two to four. At the end of 1915 the heavy machine-guns were withdrawn from the battalions and concentrated into brigade machine-gun companies with a new regimental title, the Machine Gun Corps. The infantry battalions were issued instead with sixteen Lewis guns. This American-designed weapon was much more portable than the heavy Vickers, with its tripod, water-jacket and ammunition boxes.

The tanks at first formed the 'Heavy Section' of the Machine Gun Corps, but in 1917 became a Tank Corps. On 18 October 1923 this became the Royal Tank Corps.

Yet another new corps was the Women's Army Auxiliary Corps, a sign of modern total war. Although women had joined the army disguised as men in the eighteenth century, this was the first time that the army had welcomed female volunteers; they served as clerks and telephonists.

*

The years 1917 and 1918 were marked by continental strife and suspicion between Haig and Robertson (the C.I.G.S.) on the one hand and Lloyd George, the War Premier, on the other. The gulf between the 'brass hats' and 'the frocks' (frock-coats) was partly personal, partly strategic. Haig and Robertson, having no gifts of flowing speech and winning personality, struck Lloyd George as stiff, obstinate and stupid, while he seemed to them glib, meretricious and ignorant of war. Haig and Robertson continued to believe that the war could only be decided by defeating the main body of the German army, which lay in France. Lloyd George flinched at the cost of going fifteen rounds with such a heavyweight. He favoured action anywhere but on the Western Front: in Italy, where the Italians, with allied artillery support, could do the fighting; in the Balkans; or even in Palestine. This 'eastern' strategy was known as 'knocking away the props', on the curious assumption that Turkey, Austria, and Bulgaria were propping up Germany, rather than the other way round. Lloyd George indeed wanted to sack Haig, but neither his moral courage nor his political position (dependent on Conservative support) enabled him to do this. Instead he intrigued – first early in 1917 with the French to have the British army turned into an army group under complete French control, and secondly in 1918 to set up an allied war council that would give orders to Haig. Neither expedient succeeded in removing Haig's authority over the army or his control over strategy and operations in the field.

The year 1917 was disastrous for the Allies. In March Russia was paralysed by revolution. Although in April America declared war on Germany, at least a year would elapse before an American army could take the field in France. In the meantime unrestricted German submarine warfare appeared certain to cut the Atlantic shipping routes and bring Britain to defeat. In April too a new French Commander-in-Chief, Nivelle, launched an ambitious offensive which he had promised would lead to a swift breakthrough and victory. Instead it led to a costly failure, and morale in the French army and nation plummetted into despair. In May and June widespread mutinies broke out in the French army, and General Petain, who had replaced Nivelle, informed Haig that only limited and delayed French co-operation would now be forthcoming.

Haig's answer to this dismal situation was a British offensive from the Ypres salient aimed at the railway junction of Roulers and ultimately at clearing the Belgian coast. He was certain that the forces of the British Empire could defeat Germany. In any case, to grip the German army in battle was in his view the best way of encouraging the Russians and taking the heat off the French. Lloyd George, on the contrary, believed, like Pétain, that the Allies should sit tight behind their wire and wait for the Americans.

It is hard not to think that Haig was wrong. He relied too much on over-optimistic accounts of German weakness and moral decline fed him by his intelligence department, and perhaps over-estimated the powers of his own army, fine though it now was. The pros and cons of the Flanders offensive were argued out beforehand over months. Eventually Lloyd George simply left the decision whether or not to attack to Haig and Robertson, although it was his consti-tutional right and duty to forbid it if he had strong misgivings. His failure to do so deprives his retrospective attacks on Haig in his *War Memoirs* of any substance. In Lloyd George's own lame words, 'It was decided that I should once more sum up the misgivings which most of us felt and leave the responsibility to Sir William Robertson and Sir Douglas Haig'.[10]

The main offensive was preceded by an attack to secure its southern flank by capturing the Messines ridge. Mounted by the 2nd Army (Sir Herbert Plumer), it was a masterpiece of metic-ulous preparation. On 7 June 1917 nineteen huge mines two years in preparation were exploded under the German lines, and the infantry went in behind a barrage from 2,330 guns and howitzers. By the end of the day the whole ridge was in British hands, and the Germans had lost 24,000 men and sixty-seven guns to British losses of 17,000 killed, wounded, and missing. It was a good omen for the main battle.

This, however, was dogged with ill-fortune. British industry had still failed to produce the mass of tanks* which Haig had hoped would produce a swift breakthrough without a massive prelimin-ary bombardment that broke up the ground. Because Haig was hoping for a rapid advance, he gave command of the battle to Hubert Gough and the 5th Army (Gough being the youngest

*See *The History of the Ministry of Munitions* (H.M.S.O., 1924) for the dismal story of tank production in 1915–18.

army commander and having a reputation for boldness) instead of to Plumer, the expert in set-pieces. However, the 5th Army staff did not enjoy a high reputation among the fighting units. There was a misunderstanding between Haig and Gough about the direction of the principal thrust-line. Although all Augusts in Flanders are wet, that of 1917 was a freak for rainfall. The battle opened in mud on 31 July and went on in mud.

The Third Battle of Ypres (popularly dubbed 'Passchendaele' after the last objective reached) throughout was to offer delusive and fleeting prospects of success that seemed to make further effort worthwhile. After a month of floundering in the mud, Haig handed the battle from Gough over to Plumer. The weather changed; September was fine and dry. Plumer organized three of his set-pieces (Menin Road Ridge, Polygon Wood and Broodseinde) during September and the first week of October. At the Menin Road Ridge there were 1,295 guns, one to every five yards of front, the largest concentration ever achieved by the British army. The rolling barrage in front of the troops was 1,000 yards deep, composed of five separate belts of fire. The infantry occupied the area swept clean by the guns, and then the huge battering engine was laboriously hauled forward and set up for the next advance. At the climax of Broodseinde green fields – the German rear areas – beckoned. Then the rain fell again, and the battlefield dissolved in water. The army of the British Empire struggled on. This last stage of Third Ypres, undertaken by Haig against the general feeling of his army commanders, provided the scenes of nightmare that inspired some of the most memorable of war poetry. Wilfred Owen called the battlefields:

> . . . a sad land (weak with sweats of death)
> Grey, cratered like the moon with hollow woe
> And pitted with great pocks and scabs of
> Plagues.

And Siegfried Sassoon:

> . . . I died in hell
> (They called it Passchendaele) my wound was slight
> And I was hobbling back; and then a shell

Burst slick upon the duck boards; so I fell
Into the bottomless mud, and lost the light.

The offensive must be accounted a complete failure. It did not reach its objectives; it failed to keep Russia in the war; and it failed even to prevent Germany sending its central strategic reserve to help the Austrians win a great victory on the Italian front. So far as can be guessed amid the disputed calculations of relative loss, the German and British armies suffered very great and roughly equal moral and material damage. However, in 1917 – unlike in 1916 – the Germans could better afford the loss, because they could call on forces released from the now almost defunct Russian front.

Eight days after the Third Battle of Ypres was closed down, a novel type of battle opened at Cambrai, in Picardy. At last British industry had produced the tanks, although still in far smaller quantity than hoped for. Without even prior registration of guns on targets, a barrage from 1,000 guns crashed on the forward defences of the Hindenburg Line (a powerful zone of field fortifications) and rolled on. Behind the barrage and under cover of 300 aircraft clanked 378 tanks in co-operation with eight infantry divisions. Major-General Hugh Elles, commanding the Royal Tank Corps, led the centre division in person.

The surprise, aided by fog, was complete. It was a quiet German sector, weak in troops and guns. The tanks crunched over the wire and trenches and advanced in a single day as far as the British army had in months on the Somme and at Ypres, reaching the German rear zone three to four miles behind the front line. However, Cambrai proved a one-day miracle. Sixty-five tanks were lost to German fire, another seventy-one broke down, while forty-three got stuck in ditches. The battle turned into the old familiar confused slogging match, until a swiftly organized and deadly German counter-stroke to a flank wiped out the British gains. It was another bloody draw. Whatever its promise for the future, the tank of 1917 was still too slow, too cumbersome, too vulnerable and too unreliable to achieve sensational strategic advances.

So ended the second year in which the British had relentlessly attacked. Although the Somme and Third Ypres apparently could show nothing but futile loss, in fact they were the equivalent of the appalling exchanges of slaughter between 1800 and 1814 by which the Austrians and the Russians tore the guts of Napoleon's *Grande Armée* – and again of the battles of the Russian front during the Second World War which destroyed the German army under Hitler. History proves that there are no cheap or easy ways to defeat a strong and efficient army.

The British citizen army, as matured by battle, displayed characteristic strengths and weaknesses. It was dogged and resolute but not very dashing. Dash was the speciality of the Canadians and Australians. The British army was good at the rigidly controlled, elaborately organized set-piece attack in which all its commanders believed (including the Australian John Monash, by profession an engineer, whom some commentators have seen as the man who ought to have been Commander-in-Chief in place of Haig). There was therefore a rigidity, an emphasis on hierarchy and strict control from the top which tended to inhibit initiative and swift exploitation in the front line. Nor was this local initiative always evident. By contrast the German system was more flexible, and front-line formations were left to fight their own battles and control their own reserves. German subalterns and non-commissioned officers also seem to have displayed greater tactical cunning and thrustfulness. Even in trench warfare, therefore, the armies remained roughly true to their historical characters.

However, it must always be remembered that the British citizen army in France was only two or three years old; and that even the regular army was only separated by ten years of pre-war reform from colonial warfare and the antique tactics of Omdurman. The German army, on the other hand, had been geared to fighting great European wars for generations.

Despite the disappointments of 1917 Lloyd George still failed to muster the courage to sack Haig, and instead redoubled his attempts to circumvent him. At Lloyd George's suggestion an inter-allied Supreme War Council was set up in early 1918, and Lloyd George attempted to enhance its authority over the national commanders-in-chief. Robertson, the C.I.G.S., resigned rather than accept that Lloyd George would no longer take military advice from him, but from the British representative on the Supreme War Council, General Sir Henry Wilson, whom politicians liked, a glib and charming man, unsound in judgement. Nevertheless Haig and Pétain, the French Commander-in-Chief, resisted attempts to deprive them of either their reserves or their authority.

It was evident by the end of 1917 that 1918 was likely to bring a massive German offensive in the west with troops released from the Russian front. The Germans would attempt to decide the war on the battlefield before the Americans arrived in strength from midsummer onwards. Pétain and Haig each feared that the main German weight would fall on his own army. At urgent French request, since their manpower reserves were now so slender, the British took over fourteen extra miles of line. In January 1918 the fighting strength of the British army in France had fallen by some three per cent from the figure for January 1917, for Haig had been sent 100,000 men as reinforcements instead of the 605,000 he had asked for. Lloyd George and his Cabinet had decided to retain the 607,000 available trained 'A' category men in the United Kingdom, in order to prevent Haig from resuming his own offensive – which indeed had been his intention. At the same time the British army was re-organized into nine-battalion divisions (as had been the German and French armies for some time). The smaller division, with the enhanced firepower of light machine-guns and mortars to compensate for loss of riflemen, was a handier formation. Nevertheless it was dangerous to carry out so radical a re-organization in a citizen army on the eve of an enemy offensive.

The British defence system was based on German manuals and experience; a defence in depth, consisting of a forward zone, a battle zone, and a rear zone, each of mutually supporting posts and barbed wire. Unfortunately time and labour were both too short for the defence to be properly prepared. It was most rudimentary along the sector taken over from the French, occupied by the 5th Army, which also had the longest front. For it was Haig's appreciation that while he could afford to give ground on the Somme, even a short German advance in Flanders could imperil all the communications and installations crowded between the front and the Channel. Nevertheless, there was abundant evidence that the German assault was going to fall on the 5th Army and its neighbour, the 3rd; and the 5th Army had repeatedly informed General Headquarters of its weaknesses.

The German offensive opened on 21 March 1918. It was intended to win the war, and its scale dwarfed the allied offensives of previous years – forty-seven specially trained attack divisions as against eighteen allied divisions at the Somme and Third Ypres. Instead of tanks (which they decided not to build, because of competing demands for steel and engines) the Germans relied on a surprise hurricane bombardment lasting only five hours; gas and high explosive. It aimed not at destruction but dislocation and paralysis. It was completely successful. The German infantry were trained to advance swiftly and deeply, by-passing centres of resistance. These tactics too were successful, especially on the 5th Army front, and were helped by morning fog. By the end of the day the Germans had achieved what had eluded both sides for almost four years – a penetration beyond the enemy's gunline into open country. The 5th Army lost the bulk of its fighting power in its swamped forward zone, and part of the 3rd Army gave way as well.

Nevertheless the Germans made only small and costly progress farther north against denser defences more solidly manned, although here was supposed to be the main axis of their advance. The German plan was thus pulled out of shape more and more in the following week, as Ludendorff, the German commander, sought to exploit the unlooked-for success against the 5th Army. This army, mostly composed of survivors of Third Ypres, fought as well as it could, but disintegrated. Amiens, a vital junction on the railway behind the allied front, and even the Channel coast itself were in danger, as the Germans thrust between the British and French armies, and Haig looked to cover his ports while Pétain looked to cover Paris. At an inter-allied meeting in Doullens, Foch was appointed Supreme Commander to co-ordinate the allied armies and prevent their separation. In fact, he had little effect on the current battle. Gradually the German pressure weakened owing to exhaustion, supply difficulties and allied air attacks, while allied reserves flowed to the point of danger and steadily established a new line of defence.

By the beginning of April the great German offensive had petered out in failure some nine miles short of Amiens. However, it had nearly proved a catastrophe for the Allies – and for want of the troops the government had kept in Britain or in Near Eastern sideshows. Since a scapegoat was needed, Haig was ordered to dismiss Hubert Gough, the luckless and guiltless commander of the 5th Army.

On 9 April Ludendorff struck again, this time in Flanders, though with much smaller forces. A Portuguese division gave way, and the Germans pushed energetically towards Hazebrouck, the rail centre that was the key to Haig's whole position in Flanders. Reserves were scarce, the situation desperate. Haig told his men in an Order of the Day:

… There must be no retirement. With our backs to the wall and believing in the justice of our cause each one must fight on to the end.[11]

They fought on – line regiments, the foot guards – and like their predecessors at Waterloo under the hammer of Napoleon's grand assaults, they prevailed.

At the end of May British troops 'resting' in a quiet French sector were caught in another German offensive, which swept over the Aisne and reached the Marne, only to be stopped by French reserves and the first of the Americans. In early July the French defeated the last of the German strokes, near Rheims. The war paused in the balance. On 18 July the French launched a massive surprise attack with tanks out of the forest of Villers-Cotterêts. The German front broke, to reform only far in the rear. The balance had swung at last and decisively against Germany, and it was right that the gallant French should have been the instrument.

On 8 August Haig launched a second battle of the Somme. Now the reward for the stalemated battles of the past was reaped, for the German army was too short of men, too short of trained and experienced leaders, too shattered in morale to put up the old, resolute and unbreakable defence. The thin German front collapsed under the assault of British, Imperial, American and French troops led by 534 tanks, including the new light 8-m.p.h. 'Whippets'. Although once again the German front was repaired, there now followed a continual succession of allied victories throughout

September and October, first on one sector and then another. It was the British army that played the greatest part in rolling the Germans out of France, and it was Haig's ideas rather than Foch's that moulded allied strategy. In the autumn 1918 offensives the British themselves took 188,700 prisoners, as against 196,070 by the French, Belgians and Americans together, and 2,840 guns as against 3,775 by their three allies. Had Haig been sacked at the end of 1917, his successor would no doubt have received the credit for this achievement, and his achievement contrasted with Haig's 'failures'. In any case, by a curious feat of amnesia, the British nation soon forgot the victories of 1918, while never ceasing to treasure the memories of the Somme and Passchendaele.

Between 27 and 30 September, British and Imperial forces smashed their way through the Hindenburg Line, just as the Cabinet were beginning to worry about another stalemate. The allied victories were a signal to Ludendorff that Germany must make peace. Meanwhile the allied forces based on Salonika had at last achieved a victory; the Bulgarians, deprived of German succour, collapsed and on 29 September signed an armistice. On 5 October the German government asked the American President for an armistice. In October the British and Belgians cleared the Belgian coast. In Palestine the British under Allenby shattered Turkish resistance and pushed on to Aleppo. The Italians defeated the Austrians at Vittorio Veneto. The German fleet mutinied, Germany slid into revolution, and, with her army still falling back slowly, Germany signed the armistice terms on 11 November.

A British regular officer wrote in his diary:

Incidents flash through the memory: the battle of the first four months: the awful winters in waterlogged trenches, cold and miserable: the terrible trench-assaults and shell fire of the next three years: loss of friends, exhaustion and wounds: the stupendous victories of the last few months: our enemies all beaten to their knees.

Thank God! The end of a frightful four years, thirty-four months of them at the front with the infantry, whose company officers, rank and file, together with other front-line units, have suffered bravely, patiently and unselfishly, hardships and perils beyond even the imagination of those, including soldiers, who have not shared them.[12]

It had not been in vain: an enemy more powerful and more dangerous than the France of Louis XIV or Napoleon had been beaten down. Britain's greatest industrial and naval rival lay shattered, rent by civil disruption, indeed revolution. Britain was secure, and herself relatively little damaged. For even her loss of 744,702 dead, immense a figure though it was, was much lower proportionate to population than the German loss, and not much more than half France's losses.

It was the British army's hardest fought and greatest victory.

17
Illusion
and Neglect
1918 – 39

WITHIN a year after the Armistice, the great military machine the British had created was almost entirely dismantled. Conscription was ended. The civilians who had brought all the talents and skills of the nation into the army went back to civilian life – often to chronic unemployment and beggary, for there was no government guarantee that soldiers would be given back their old civilian jobs by their employers. The professional horizon of regular officers shrank again from the complex management of technological war to the life of the regiment, to small wars in hot places and police duties in support of the civil authorities in India and Ireland*, and even in the unhappy industrial areas of Britain. The range of ambition for the young officer shrank equally. The brief union of army and nation after three centuries was already over. Once again the army lay outside the mainstream of the nation's life and thought. It was not merely a return to before 1914, for then the

---

*In 1922, after the British security forces had fought a violent and nasty war of ambush and assassination with Irish terrorists for four years in an attempt to maintain British authority, the British government granted self-government to the southern, or Catholic, Irish. The end of British rule in southern Ireland marked a notable moment in the internal history of the British army. It was in Ireland that the British Crown had first maintained a regular military establishment in peacetime. In the eighteenth century the separate Irish establishment had served to conceal many regiments from the eyes of the House of Commons. Even after the Union Act of 1801 ended the Irish establishment, Irish recruits in great numbers filled out the ranks of the British army until the middle of the century, and even later remained an important element. When the long association of the British army and Ireland, an intimacy of hatred and affection, ended, five famous Irish regiments were disbanded. Yet Catholic Irishmen have continued to enlist in the 'foreign' British army.

army had just been through a wave of reform, and was preparing itself for a major war. In 1919, at the suggestion of the War Secretary, Winston Churchill, the British Cabinet adopted the 'Ten Year Rule' for all defence planning. According to this the services should plan their needs and strategies on the assumption that there would be no major war for ten years. This removed the spur even to theoretical studies. The army was thus put back to the 1890s, a colonial gendarmerie with no major role to play or plan for.

In the 1920s, during the swift regression of the army from a national saviour to a backwater, it was seen how relatively superficial had been the impact of the pre-war reforms and of the war itself on 'the Duke of Cambridge's army' – on the mental climate that derived from the intensely regimental outlook of the British soldier. The old, never really extinguished, conception of soldiering re-asserted itself – a gentleman's occupation that married well with social and sporting life in the countryside – smartness on parade and stiff regimental etiquette and custom. Victory itself also led by the late 1920s to a bristling complacency about existing doctrine and systems. Owing to the small size of the army, there was a bottleneck in promotion, and senior veterans of the Great War succeeded one another at the top of the army, ever older as the years passed. By the middle of the 1930s the average age of the higher commanders was seven years older than in 1914.

The army itself and its leaders were not alone to blame for the stagnation. The government and the electorate could have demanded radical thinking and re-organization, had it been interested. It could have voted money for experimental development. But the nation lost all concern with its defence from 1918 until late in 1938. The very existence of even a comatose army seemed indecent to public opinion in the 1920s and early 1930s, in the prevailing pacifistic climate of belief in disarmament and the League of Nations.

The strong tide of pacifism flowed not only against war itself, which was understandable if unconstructive, but against soldiers. To say that the commanders of the Great War – Haig in the British case – were stupid and callous offered a convenient explanation of the length of the war and its human cost. No one could accept that these were the inevitable results of the collision of two roughly equal coalitions of industrial nations intent on outright victory; nor could public opinion accept that the casualties were not proportionately higher than in earlier great wars. To the British especially, accustomed only to the minute casualties involved in knocking over blacks during the nineteenth century, their 744,702 dead (little more than half the French figure) seemed absolutely monstrous and unthinkable – although the Italians lost 460,000 in only three years of war on one front. Then again, in all Britain's past wars the casualties, though proportionately as heavy as in the Great War, had fallen on two minority social groups. In the Great War the entire nation for the first time had felt the cost of being a great empire. So the Great War losses seemed unthinkable, psychologically requiring an easy explanation, which was found in the alleged incompetence of the generals. The professional soldiers themselves became the scapegoats; the nation's anti-war sentiment became also a strongly anti-armed-forces sentiment, and both were fed by the highly emotional works published by survivors of the trenches in the war-book boom after 1928.

This was not a climate in which the army could easily live a vigorous and creative intellectual life; it was a climate, rather, that, by forcing the army back defensively into an introspective way of life, enhanced the relative power of the traditionalists at the top.

The hard struggle against this traditionalism and complacency and in favour of mechanization and the radical re-casting of strategic and tactical doctrine was led by J. C. Fuller and B. H. Liddell Hart. Although there had been several earlier able British writers on strategy and military history, these two were the first to achieve high international reputations. They studied war not as a narrow subject of battles and tactics, but in the light of philosophy, psychology, sociology and other broad aspects of human society. Their books began to bring the study of war into the mainstream of intellectual life.

Both emerged as prophets of change in the years just after the Great War. Their first attempts at reform were made from inside the army, for the Field Service Regulations of 1924 bore the imprint of Fuller's ideas (though diluted by officialdom), while the Infantry Training Manual of 1922 was much influenced by Liddell Hart. Fuller, the elder of the two, was perhaps more in the forefront during the 1920s. With polemical pungency, not to say violence, he informed the army in books and articles that the day of the horse was over, and that the future lay with the tracked vehicle. The sentiment was not welcome to an officer corps fond of polo and hunting, and the wounding language in which it was sometimes expressed made it the less acceptable. Fuller raised up bitter opposition in his own face. When the army at last held a demonstration of mechanized warfare in November 1926 (the result of Fuller's and Liddell Hart's ceaseless advocacy) Fuller was absent, sent on a mission to India. In 1927 Fuller resigned his commission when he found that an experimental mechanized force that he had just been appointed to command was really just an infantry brigade with some extra vehicles. Although he withdrew his resignation when the C.I.G.S., Field-Marshal Sir George Milne, assured him that the army would in fact be modernized, Fuller was never again given command of the army's small experimental mechanized formations. In 1933 he retired as a major-general. Henceforward his role was that of the outside propagandist, thinker and historian.

According to Fuller's ideas as they had matured by 1933, the linear battlefield of the Great War, manned by vast immobile conscript armies of infantry and artillery, would in the future be replaced by a regional battlefield, in which small, highly-trained mechanized armies would advance and manoeuvre in great depth, pivoting on anti-tank fortresses and supply depots within minefields, and fighting in close collaboration with aircraft. The tank would be the queen of the battlefield, supplying in diverse specialized forms the roles of artillery, cavalry and even infantry. In many ways Fuller predicted the general pattern of the German victories over Poland in 1939 and France in 1940, and even more closely the pattern of the campaign in the Western Desert in 1940–43. However, his own polemical tendency to the extreme and the stubbornness of the opposition to him within the army caused him to exalt the tank above other arms. When the British armoured divisions at last took the field in Africa in 1940–41 they suffered from this over-emphasis on the tank fostered by Fuller and his disciples.

Liddell Hart was less prone than Fuller to proceed to argumentative extremes, and less prone to embody his views on war in ambitious philosophical constructions. Liddell Hart gradually evolved a theory of strategy and tactics, which he called 'the Indirect Approach'. Its foundation was the idea of attacking the enemy where he was weakest, not strongest; where an attack was least, not most, expected. He suggested that the thrustline of such an attack could paralyse the enemy by simultaneously threatening alternative objectives until it was too late for the enemy to move to cover the true objective. Liddell Hart's tactical ideas were developed from the infiltration methods used by the Germans in their great offensive in 1918. He called his system 'the expanding torrent'. Tanks and tracked transport would give the army of the future a capacity to maintain the momentum of an offensive denied to the foot-bound Germans in 1918. The attack would infiltrate rapidly and deeply between the strongpoints of defence, rolling up the flanks of the gap made, pouring deep into open country to disrupt the enemy rear areas – headquarters, supplies and communication. The very speed and depth of this 'expanding torrent' would paralyse a 1914–18-style command and army. Like Fuller, Liddell Hart ceaselessly advocated the transformation of the British army into the completely mechanized *élite* force capable of carrying out such a strategy. Unlike Fuller, Liddell Hart saw this army as combining tanks, mechanized infantry and a tactical air force; it was his conception of an armoured division, and his strategic and tactical ideas that the more influenced the German army in the 1930s when it created the new panzer divisions.

In the struggle for modernization in the British army, Liddell Hart was an even earlier casualty than Fuller; he had to leave the army under pressure in 1924. However, he carried on the battle both through friends and contacts inside the army and by his articles in the *Daily Telegraph* as Britain's only full-time military correspondent. Although he was not so violent a debater as Fuller, nevertheless a frank article exposing the feeble reality behind the War Office's brave announcements of an experimental mechanized force for a time cost him his influence within the War Office, just as the same experimental force cost Fuller his army career. In the late 1920s and early 1930s the question of modernization was therefore sharpened by a personal suspicion of the advocates of change by successive Chiefs of the Imperial General Staff.

Nevertheless the army chiefs had not been totally unwilling to experiment with mechanization. From the 'Experimental Mechanized Force' of 1927 through to manoeuvres in deep and rapid penetration in 1931–4, the British army in fact led the world for a time in experiment with the tank. What stultified these experiments and prevented them leading on to the development of large-scale armoured forces were the draconic limitations of expenditure imposed by successive governments. By a curious irony, it was Winston Churchill who not only originated the fatal 'Ten Year Rule' in 1919, but also, as Chancellor of the Exchequer in 1924–9 (a time of relative national prosperity), out-Gladstoned Gladstone in economies over the armed forces – economies he must have regretted in 1940. And after 1932, the world slump made politicians even more eager to save money on the armed forces.

So, by the mid-1930s the British army was stagnating as an instrument of war while it faithfully carried out its other function of an imperial gendarmerie.

The French army was stagnating even more. It too was ruled by a succession of ever-older generals of the Great War; it too rested on the withering laurels of 1918. Although its conception of a future war took account of tanks and aircraft, it expected they would be used much as in 1918 – as part of a slow-moving engine of fire-power advancing with deliberation on a wide front. Pacifistic sentiment in France too had lowered the prestige of the army, while parsimonious governments had starved it of funds for experiment and development. Because of low pay and lack of opportunity, its officer corps came to contain fewer *noblesse*, more men of the middle class or lower middle class. This did not have the effect, as might be expected, of leading to a more keenly professional outlook, for the underpaid new officers often had the pettifogging caution and love of routine of the low-grade civil servant. At least, however, the French did not entirely dismantle their army, or abolish conscription; and the French army remained until the late 1930s the largest and best-equipped land force in Europe (except for the Red Army).

In Germany the Versailles Treaty had laid an axe on the massive tree that had grown out of the Prussian army of the seventeenth century. The new *Reichswehr* was a force of only 100,000 long-service professionals, and conscription, heavy weapons and an air force were alike forbidden. However, the head of the new *Reichswehr*, Hans von Seeckt, possessed perhaps the most brilliant intellect of any soldier since the elder Moltke, together with an equally brilliant record as a chief of staff in the field. During the 1920s, Seeckt turned the 100,000-man *Reichswehr* into an *élite* force under a handpicked (and mostly aristocratic) officer corps. New theories and techniques of war were evolved and practised; forbidden prototype tanks and aircraft were manufactured abroad and tested in the Soviet Union. However, although Seeckt believed in mobility, he clung to the horse as its basis, rather than the tank and truck. Nevertheless when Adolf Hitler and his Nationalist-Socialist Party came to power in Germany in 1933, they found all the essentials ready for a swift and massive expansion of the German army.

Hitler's own radicalism induced him to give powerful backing to the German army's apostles of mechanization. In 1935 the first three panzer divisions – mechanized formations of all arms – were formed. What Fuller and Liddell Hart and others had been passionately urging on the British army since the early 1920s had come to fruition in Nazi Germany, a state already perceived by some to be a danger to peace. In the same year of 1935 Germany reintroduced conscription and announced that she had an air force; all blatant violations of the Versailles Treaty. The destruction of that Treaty, in any case, had been over and over again declared by Hitler to be his fundamental political aim. In this same year also the French and British – and the League of Nations – failed, owing to lack of military readiness and fear of war, to prevent Fascist Italy conquering Abyssinia.

In 1936 German military re-occupation of the Rhineland (another violation of the Versailles Treaty) in the teeth of a still-powerful French army that was paralysed both by its own lack of a ready striking force and by the feebleness of will of the French and British governments, indicated the growth of Hitler's ambitions and confidence. In 1937, Japan, which in 1931 had been the first power to expose the impotence of the League of Nations by defying its demand to withdraw from Manchuria, began a large-scale conquest of China. Gradually it began to dawn on the British government that to stop ruthless and powerfully armed men, something more than sweet reason and an appeal to their better selves might be needed. In 1937 the British at last began an extensive programme of re-armament. But re-arm for what kind of war? To implement what kind of strategy? For the first time in its history the British Empire faced possible attack by three major powers right across the globe. The Japanese posed a threat to Australia and New Zealand and to Malaya and Borneo; the Italians posed a threat to the Mediterranean and the Suez Canal; the Germans posed a threat to the mother country itself. Although Britain could count on the French in Europe and the Middle East, and might hope for American belligerence if the Japanese attacked in the Far East, the magnitude and dispersal of the danger were unique.

There was also the riddle of air-power. Almost all military thinkers agreed that a future war would almost certainly open with sudden and devastating gas and high-explosive attacks on cities by enemy bombers. These attacks were expected by the air-experts to inflict crippling damage and, worse, bring about a general moral collapse among the civilian population. This immense power of the bomber had been ceaselessly urged by the leaders of the Royal Air Force ever since the Great War. The belief was romantic and optimistic rather than analytical, for in fact the bombers of the day had no such capability; indeed the claims of strategic air-power only really became justified with the dropping of atom bombs in 1945. Nevertheless the claims were widely accepted by politicians in the 1930s.

The belief in the power of the bomber doubly wrecked the British army's chances of adequate re-equipment. Firstly there was (compared with before 1914) a third armed service to take its share of available defence funds. Secondly, the expansion of the bomber force was given priority over re-equipment of the army. This priority was given to the air force partly because it was believed that the bomber could win the next war without the need for painful ground operations; partly because retaliation by British bombers was seen as the only practicable answer to German bombers, which before the invention of radar could not be intercepted. After the invention of radar, however, the Royal Air Force began a vast fighter programme on top of its bomber programme, and the army still remained a bad third behind the air force and the navy in priority of service re-equipment. What was worse, priority within the army's own programme was given to anti-aircraft guns because of the universal misapprehensions about the capability of German bombers. It was felt that until Britain itself had an adequate anti-aircraft defence, it would not be sound to equip and dispatch an expeditionary force overseas, and that public opinion would not sanction such a dispatch.

Since the Royal Air Force was being designed as a bomber and anti-bomber force, there was little room for air co-operation with the army on a battlefield, and 'army co-operation' in the British services meant no more than a handful of slow reconnaissance and artillery-spotting aircraft.

The new German Air Force, the *Luftwaffe*, on the other hand, was designed principally for co-operation with the army. Its medium bombers were intended first to smash enemy air forces on their airfields, and secondly to attack targets in the zone of a ground battle. Its new dive-bombers were intended as flying field-artillery to deliver precise attacks on enemy batteries, strong-points or formations in movement. The Royal Air Force resolutely fought against this kind of role, even after the outbreak of war, with the result that during the critical fighting in France in 1940, British aircraft would be bombing targets many miles behind the German panzer divisions, while the panzers themselves moved unscathed.

The British army therefore entered the period of re-armament after 1937 with totally inadequate funds. Yet its own strategic and tactical thinking was still in the melting-pot. The arguments about mechanization and the future of the tank raged on: arguments clearly linked to the strategic debate. Thus the army had only a rummage-bag of tank prototypes of different specifications when other armies were already receiving quantity deliveries of production models. Even as late as the beginning of 1939 the General Staff could not make up its mind as to what kind of tanks it really wanted. A colonial strategy appeared to mean a light tank, while a Western Front strategy meant a heavy one. Infantry co-operation seemed to need a slow, well-armoured tank; mobile warfare a more lightly-armoured 'cruiser'. This trend towards specialization of types was in marked contrast to Russian and German practice, which preferred standard basic chassis and mechanical designs which could be adapted and developed for different purposes. The key to the British muddle lay in the continued lack of clear decision over strategic and tactical doctrine.

The military prophets like Fuller and Liddell Hart were no less convinced than others that the lesson of the Great War was that Britain should never again commit a mass conscript army to Europe. It was argued that instead Britain should revert to 'blue water' strategy, defending her empire and sea communications, and strangling the enemy by blockade. Until 1938 the expeditionary force was intended for Egypt, not France.

In retrospect it is not easy to see why it followed that, because the British had had to place a large army in France by 1916–17 in order to save the French from collapse, we should not need to do so again. Since the French as a nation were now outnumbered seven to four by the Germans, and since they no longer enjoyed the alliance of Russia, it would have appeared to follow that the French had even more urgent need of a strong British army now than in 1914–18. It is possible that beneath the strategic justifications for refusing to plan for a large British army for Europe, there was an emotional reluctance to face the possibility of another Western Front.

Until 1939, therefore, the re-equipment of the army was based not on rapid expansion, but on making up short-comings in a field force of no more than five regular divisions, and a territorial force of twelve. Within this very limited programme was fought the final battle as to whether the field force should be based on horse transport and cavalry, or on the internal-combustion engine and the tank.

In 1937 Leslie Hore-Belisha became Secretary of State for War, with the personal intention of carrying out reform and modernization. It was a comment on the general state of affairs in the upper reaches of the army that he chose to rely for detailed advice not on the Army Council and the General Staff, but on a private and unofficial adviser. This was Captain Liddell Hart, at that time military correspondent to *The Times* newspaper. Liddell Hart's recommendations, supported by progressive officers inside the War Office, led eventually, against the bitter rearguard opposition of the traditionalists, to the complete mechanization of the British army. In 1939 and even later it was the only totally motorized army in the world. Nevertheless Liddell Hart's position as both an adviser without official responsibilities and a newspaper military correspondent was anomalous, and helped to arouse opposition and suspicion. Although traditionalism and caution were not in the end able to block reforms, they did delay them and dilute them. Britain entered the war with one armoured division in Egypt and two at home, of which one had yet to be equipped.

It was only in the last few months of peace in 1939 that the British government abandoned its belief in a 'limited liability' war, and began to prepare to put a strong army in the field in France. In March, it was announced that the Territorial army would be doubled to twenty-six divisions, which, with the six regular divisions, would give an army of thirty-two divisions. In May 1939 the Compulsory Training Act was passed, by which 'militiamen' (thus reviving an ancient and respectable name) were called up for six months' training.

The British were thus caught by the outbreak of war at the most awkward point in the expansion of an army. Not only was the available field force so small, but the first British panzer divisions were only slowly being formed, with all the teething troubles of organization and equipment. British tactical doctrine for both infantry and tanks was still a kind of half-baked compromise between the German-style ideas advanced by Fuller and Liddell Hart and the orthodox and linear British doctrine of 1917–18 preferred by the die-hards at the head of the army during the 1930s. Thus slowness and rigidity was fatally built into the British army's staff methods and corporate mind on the eve of its fresh expansion, for the German emphasis on speed and the taking of risk was alike repugnant to British doctrine, and, perhaps, to the British temperament.

The British finally evolved the tank and its tactical employment in two separate compartments. There were the so-called 'army tank brigades', which were intended purely for co-operation with infantry and were armed with a heavily armoured 'I' ('infantry') tank that could only move at walking pace. For purely tank warfare there were to be armoured divisions, equipped with fast but lightly armoured 'cruiser' tanks and light tanks. It was a false distinction that later caused much trouble. The evolution of tanks giving a satisfactory balance of armour, gunpower and speed (coupled with reliability) was to baffle the British until 1943. Part of this critical British failure in the Second World War was owing to the lateness of the British programme of modernization; part to indecision and dithering over specifications; part to the sheer technical incompetence of some British engineering firms; part to pre-war Treasury meanness.

The French, for their part, put into the field in 1939 a modernized version of their army of 1918: linear defence and attack, firepower instead of rapid movement, telephones rather than radio, tanks (of which the French had more than the Germans) mostly in small groups in the infantry divisions, and an outnumbered and obsolete air force.

The German army went to war in 1939 after five years of breakneck expansion from the original 100,000 men allowed under the Versailles Treaty. On mobilization it comprised 105 field divisions, including six panzer divisions and ten motorized divisions. The social radicalism of Nazi policy, coupled with the demand for young officers during expansion, swamped the aristocratic officer corps with recruits from all groups in German society and began to demolish the caste ideas of honour and behaviour that had lasted since the days of the Great Elector. In its close comradeship between officers and non-commissioned officers and men and the breakdown of the gulf of status and social class between them, the new German army looked back more to the traditions of the frontline storm troops of the Great War than to traditional Prussian military form. It was an army that (except for the high command) felt itself to be the military arm of a radical and revolutionary creed, and there was a receptiveness to new ideas lacking in the armies of France and Britain. Adolf Hitler, as Führer and Supreme Commander, himself backed new ideas and daring strategy. Although the higher echelons of the German command remained largely in the hands of the old *Junker* officer corps until after 1942, these social traditionalists themselves proved, as they had in the past, technical innovators.

The Germans had seized on the ideas of Fuller and Liddell Hart, experimented with them and developed them. The panzer and motorized divisions formed that small mechanized army of *élite* demanded by the British thinkers. Since German industry, however, had not the capacity to motorize the entire army of over 100 divisions, the eighty-eight infantry divisions remained largely dependent on horse transport, although their equipment in other respects (e.g. anti-tank guns) was more modern and lavish than that of the French or British. A German panzer division of 1939 contained one tank brigade of 400 tanks and one motorized infantry brigade, as well as reconnaissance, engineer, artillery and anti-tank troops. This formation eventually proved too clumsy and too heavy in armour, and in 1942 the panzer division was reorganized as a tank brigade of 200 tanks and two trucked infantry brigades: more flexible and a better balance between the arms.

German armoured and infantry tactics looked for origin to the excellent tactics evolved under Ludendorff's direction in 1917–18. In attack the emphasis was placed on fast infiltration through an enemy defence zone, always following the line of least resistance, in order quickly to bring about a collapse – what Liddell Hart called 'the expanding torrent'. Resisting strongpoints were to be dealt with by follow-up formations. Instead of wide linear pressure against a linear front, the attackers were to go forward as a spear or succession of spears to pierce deeply through. In the case of armoured forces, dive-bombers covered by fighters provided a field artillery of a tactical mobility and range hitherto inconceivable. Close co-ordination between ground troops and tactical air forces and the widespread use of radio for control of the fast-moving battle enabled the German armour to attack sooner, and keep moving faster and deeper, than the British and French believed possible.

The British army entered the war far less ready than in 1914. Behind the B.E.F. of 1914 lay ten years of steady preparation and thought, while behind the B.E.F. of 1939 lay two years of controversial, confused and scrambling modernization. In 1914 Britain had sent the French an expeditionary force of four infantry and one cavalry division within a fortnight of mobilization; in early 1939 Britain told her ally that they could expect four infantry divisions and an armoured division no sooner than thirty-three days after mobilization. In fact the armoured division never arrived. While the B.E.F. of 1914 was outstanding among armies for its fighting power, this was not true of its successor of 1939.

The war itself was begun under the worst strategic circumstances. In 1936, when the French army was strong and the German army weak, the British had not even tried to persuade the French to mobilize and put an end to the illegal German re-militarization of the Rhineland; on the contrary. In 1938, in the Munich crisis, under the spell of bomber-funk and military weakness, the British government had bartered a fine Czech army in exchange for Hitler's promises of goodwill. Now in 1939 the British had elected to fight when the military balance had tipped further in the German favour, for the years 1936–9 had marked the progressive weakening and obsolescence of the French army *vis-à-vis* the German, and the progressive erosion of the French will to fight.

The British were about to pay dearly for their pacifistic illusions; for their refusal to face the hard responsibilities of a great power in an envious and hostile world; and for their squandering of their great victory in 1918.

18
The Cost
of Unreadiness
1939−41

To a superficial view the anatomy of the Second World War
appears very different from that of the Great War. In the Second
World War there was no dominant and static western front, no
stalemate of trench-warfare, but instead several major theatres of
war and fast-moving conquests and retreats. It was a war of
machines and air-power. Whereas the British themselves had been
caught up in the terrible and apparently vain slogging on the
Western Front in the Great War, they were fortunate enough to
escape such battles in the Second World War; a circumstance
reflected in the British army's losses in killed of 144,079 as against
702,410 killed in the Great War. In the Second World War
Germany was brought to defeat after three years of gradual re-
conquest of the territory she had earlier won, while in the Great
War she collapsed suddenly when her armies were still on conquered soil. And finally the Second World War was really two
wars, on opposite sides of the globe, the one against Germany and
Italy, and the other against Japan.

Yet the struggles with Germany in 1914–18 and in 1939–45 were
really two episodes in the same great conflict, and the same fundamental strategic pattern unfolded itself in both.

In 1914 the German answer to the danger of war on two fronts,
against France and Russia, was the Schlieffen plan: smash France
first and then swing back to smash Russia in turn. In 1939 Hitler's
answer was the Soviet–German Treaty, which left him free to beat
France at leisure and with an easy mind. However, still faithful to
the basic premise of the Schlieffen plan, Hitler later turned on
Russia in 1941, with catastrophic results. For in the Second World

War it was the *Eastern* Front which fulfilled the function of the *Western* Front in the Great War. It was here in battles every bit as horrible and costly in human life and suffering as the Somme and Verdun that the German army was bled to death by the Red Army. It is a widespread British illusion that the Second World War was won without 'Western Front' battles because British strategy and generalship were better than in the Great War. In fact it was the German victory in France in 1940, putting an end to the Western Front, that spared the British the experiences of their fathers. Even so, the Western Front had eventually to be re-created in 1944, by the invasion, before Germany could finally be broken. However, by 1944 the strength and fighting efficiency of the German army had been so much worn down by three appalling Russian campaigns that victory in Normandy was easier to achieve than victory in Picardy or Flanders. Thus in the end the Second World War, like the Great War, turned on the defeat of the German army on two extended land fronts. All the rest of the war against Germany and Italy was sideshow.

The sideshows arose, as they had in the Great War, out of the 'strategy of evasion' – the belief in striking anywhere but against the enemy's main forces, in the hope of bringing about his own collapse by the prior collapse of his allies. In the Great War Churchill favoured campaigns against the Turks in the Middle East; in the Second World War against the Italians. In both wars the Balkans exercised a seductive influence on British strategists. However, in the Second World War the extinction of the Western Front in 1940 left the British nowhere to fight but in the Middle East. Step-by-step they led themselves into an enormous imperial effort in the Mediterranean and Middle East. Yet, at Second Alamein, the biggest of the Desert battles, Montgomery engaged some four-and-a-half German divisions, compared with the eighty engaged by Haig during the Battle of the Somme, or the 190 engaged at the time of Alamein by the Russians. Even in Tunisia, when the Americans too were in the field, the opposing Axis forces numbered only some 200,000 men. Later still, in Italy, the German strength never equalled that of the Allies. There is therefore a close parallel between the enormous and unprofitable British investment of resources in peripheral campaigns in the Mediterranean in both the world wars.

However, whereas in the Great War the Mediterranean adventures weakened the Western Front, in the Second World War they weakened the defence of the Far East against Japan. As a consequence of over-great involvement in the Mediterranean and Middle East in 1941–2, Malaya, with all its tin and rubber, and Burma, with its oil, were lost, India threatened and Australia and New Zealand thrown into the protective arms of America.

The British contribution to the Second World War reflected the decline of Britain's relative power. The British *helped* the Russians and Americans to beat Germany, and *helped* the Americans to beat the Japanese; they took the major part only in defeating Italy.

The patterns of warfare itself in the two world wars were also less different than might at first appear. In 1940 the German victory in the west by means of panzer divisions and air-power, by deep, fast penetration, seemed to bear out the pre-war writings of Fuller and Liddell Hart. Here, indeed, was the quick and cheap success offered by these prophets in place of the dismal stalemate of trench warfare. Yet this victory did not win the war; nor did later astonishing German conquests. Despite its dramatic ebbs and flows the Second World War lasted nearly two years longer than the Great War, and was decided likewise by attrition of German manpower and industrial power. Even in the field, after 1942, fearsome slogging matches took the place of panzer breakthroughs, with heavy bombers sometimes supplying the place of Great War heavy artillery. For two months in Normandy in 1944, for example, there was a struggle that may be likened to Passchendaele plus tanks and air-power. It lasted until the German reserves – far more slender than in 1917 – had been drawn in and destroyed, and a breakthrough thus made possible. There are no magic ways to victory against powerful enemies.

*

On the outbreak of war against Germany in 1939, the British empire could put four divisions into the field in France, the equivalent of six infantry divisions and one armoured (forming) in the

Middle East, a field division and a brigade in India, two brigades in Malaya and the usual sprinkling of colonial garrisons. This modest military strength did the world's greatest imperial power little credit. Nor could the army be fast expanded. British industry simply had not the capacity or techniques to sustain a rapid increase of all the armed forces. The British – and the French – as in 1914 and 1915 had to fall back immediately on American resources. However, the Cabinet decided that an army of fifty-five divisions should be formed by September 1941, of which thirty-two were to be British and the rest imperial. In February 1940 this over-ambitious figure was reduced to thirty-six.

In all the circumstances it was hardly extraordinary that the first two years of war were marked by a series of disasters; nevertheless, some of these disasters were by no means inevitable.

The British government declared war at a time of military unreadiness to help a country, Poland, which it was geographically incapable of aiding; a splendid illustration of how not to mesh foreign policy with strategy. Chamberlain's policy of appeasement was continued into the war itself; it was hoped that if the Allies avoided being nasty to the Germans, they in turn would not attack the Allies. While this bloodless stalemate continued, the allied blockade would bring down the rickety German economy; while the Allies sheltered behind the Maginot Line, Board of Trade economists would win the war.

Despite Mr Chamberlain's guarantee, and the British and French declarations of war, Poland fell in eighteen days. The war then hibernated until the spring of 1940. Instead the Russians attacked Finland. With unbelievable and quixotic folly, France and Britain prepared to send an expeditionary force to aid the Finns, thus diverting part of their inadequate strength and risking the addition of the Soviet Union to their enemies. Luckily the Finns lost and made peace before the expedition could be made ready.

In the west Hitler intended to launch a great offensive as soon as the weather was suitable. It had been postponed in November 1939 for this reason and again in January 1940. In the meantime he decided to secure his supplies of Swedish iron-ore through the ice-free Norwegian port of Narvik by occupying Norway and Denmark.

Although the operation was prepared in great haste, the planning and execution reflected high credit on the German armed forces. The keynotes were speed and daring. When it was launched on 9 April 1940, the operation anticipated a modest British plan to mine Norwegian territorial waters used by the iron-ore ships. Despite the fierce resistance of the Norwegians, who were utterly taken by surprise, the Germans swiftly occupied southern Norway and all the major ports and airfields.

The British now decided to offer battle to the Germans in Norway. Although troops allotted to the Finnish expedition were still concentrated in Britain and France, everything else had to be improvised in the usual haste: shipping, air forces, formations, staff headquarters, and expeditionary force headquarters – all had to be thrown together. The result was a compendium of Gallipoli, of Pitt's raids along the French coast and of Drake's failure in Portugal in 1589. Troops were landed at little ports (where some ships could not get in), without supplies or lines of communication, and remote from strategically important areas. The makeshift and ill-equipped formations fought as best they could but were completely outmatched. The *Luftwaffe* ranged freely over all, bombing what moved. On 3 May, the British forces in southern Norway were evacuated. The decision to accept battle in Norway was based on a misconception of the demands of modern war in terms of thorough preparation and adequate equipment; on, therefore, a complete misjudgement of the relative fighting power of the German forces and the makeshift British expedition.

In northern Norway, a separate expedition to capture the port of Narvik itself ran into another traditional difficulty: bad relations between the admiral and the general in the absence of an overall commander. The general was timid; the admiral bursting to go. Only when the general was replaced was Narvik successfully taken and then only to cover the evacuation of allied forces.

Norway was a prime example of one traditional British way of making war. It brought down the Chamberlain government; and the new Prime Minister at the head of the new Coalition government was the man who, as First Lord of the Admiralty, had been most responsible for affairs in Norway: Winston Churchill.

On 10 May 1940 the long-awaited German onslaught fell on Holland and Belgium, and the war really began. Once again the German operations were characterized by a paralysing speed and daring and unorthodoxy; parachute and air-landing troops seized vital airfields or landed on the roofs of great fortresses; bridges were taken undamaged by sheer bluff. The German army and air force advanced with a speed and ferocity that unnerved commanders still (despite Poland and Norway) expecting the deliberate unrolling of a 1914–18 offensive. Holland fell in five days. Meanwhile the roar of guns, the squeal of tank tracks and the terrifying scream of Stuka dive bombers moved on swiftly into Belgium and down towards France.

The allied plan (in fact French, but freely accepted by the British) was based on a belief that the Germans would once more advance through the Belgian plain, with the main weight hitting the allied left. In order to shorten their front and link up with the Belgian army of twenty divisions, the French supreme commander, Gamelin, decided to advance into Belgium and defend the line Antwerp–River Dyle–Namur–River Meuse–Sedan–Maginot Line (which ended at Longuyon). The allied forces comprised more than 130 divisions: twenty-two Belgian, ten British (plus three partly equipped), one Polish and ninety-four French, a heterogeneous collection. Only three were armoured and three were mechanized. Only sixty-seven of the French divisions were field as opposed to fortress troops, and even then mixed in quality. This patchy array was about to be attacked by 134 high-spirited German divisions, of which ten were panzer.

The Germans no longer intended to place their main weight on their right. After having 'fixed' the Allies in the Belgian plain by the swift capture of Liège and an advance towards Brussels, their real offensive would be suddenly unleashed from the Ardennes hills (deemed unsuitable by the French for major operations) to smash the allied centre between Namur and Sedan. Then the panzer divisions would swing to the west and race for the Channel coast, presenting a paralysing alternative threat both to Paris and to the allied armies in Belgium. The risk was colossal – involving an ever longer flank to the south, involving the far outstripping of the infantry divisions slowly following up. The gamble was to beat the French by sheer speed and daring. All worked perfectly; it was one of the most astonishing campaigns in the history of war. In ten days the panzers reached the Channel coast, splitting the allied armies into two sections twenty-five miles apart.

The British army did not play an important role in this battle, as it had in 1914, for this time it did not lie in the track of the main German thrust. The German forces opposite it in the Belgian plain kept up continual frontal pressure to 'fix' the Allies, but no more. It was the French that faced the principal panzer thrust, and the French who quickly collapsed. However, although the British Expeditionary Force did not play a decisive part in the campaign, it saved itself by its skill and fighting qualities. As the German forces swept north past Boulogne and Calais, the British swiftly improvised forces to hold them away from Dunkirk, the last port through which the B.E.F. could escape, while still fighting hard against the Germans in their front. On 27 May the Belgian army capitulated, exposing the northern flank of the British and French in the cut-off northern army group. By a brilliant march at night, the British blocked this flank.

Meanwhile the French command had made hopelessly belated and ineffectual attempts to close the gap in the allied front by ordering simultaneous counter-strokes from north and south. The attempts foundered in the uncertainties of the fast-developing catastrophe. However, the British 1st Army Tank Brigade launched a local counter-stroke at Arras which for a moment stopped and badly shook the 7th Panzer Division – an indication of what might have been the British contribution to the battle, had the British people re-armed earlier. This attack had a disproportionate effect on the German high command, and helped in Hitler's and Rundstedt's decision later to halt the panzers before Dunkirk. Gradually the British and French armies in Belgium fell back on Dunkirk, compressed in a long and narrow sack by overwhelming German forces. At the exposed end of the sack the French 1st Army sacrificed itself in a desperate fight round Lille. Meanwhile Lord Gort, the British Commander-in-Chief, had had to take the difficult decision to abandon hope of fighting his way southwards to the main French armies, and instead make ready for evacuation – if that were possible.

For the allied northern group of armies, comprising the best trained and equipped formations, now faced the near possibility of capitulation in the field. Neither the German command nor the British Admiralty expected that more than a fraction could be evacuated by sea. However, evacuations are easier to improvise than invasions. The Royal Navy, merchant ships and small craft succeeded in bringing back 338,000 allied troops (including 139,000 French) despite violent air attacks by the *Luftwaffe*. On 3 June 'Operation Dynamo' (the evacuation from Dunkirk) was completed. The trained officers and men of the B.E.F., essential nucleus of the new armies to be created, had been saved; but all the B.E.F.'s precious and for a period irreplaceable equipment had been left behind: guns, tanks, trucks.

On 5 June the re-grouped German armies fell upon the now heavily outnumbered French on their new line covering Paris along the Somme and the Aisne. In this second phase of the battle of France only one British division, the 51st (Highland), took part. It was cut off and forced to surrender at St-Valéry-en-Caux. The French army was sliced swiftly into fragments, as the panzers drove west of Paris into Normandy, east of Paris across the rear of the Maginot Line. More British troops were sent to Brittany, only to be evacuated without fighting because of the disintegration of the French army. On 21 June the French signed an armistice with Germany. Hitler stood at the pinnacle of his career.

The fall of France shattered the foundations of the complacent and leisurely British grand strategy – no great ally to shoulder the burden while a mass British army was slowly got ready, no Western Front for any army eventually to fight on; no German bankruptcy but instead the resources of a whole continent for Germany to exploit.

There was a more immediate consideration. What if Hitler could succeed where Philip II, Louis XIV and XV and Napoleon had failed – in throwing an army across the Channel? And in the Middle East, Britain now faced a new enemy – and without French support. Mussolini, true to the Italian tradition of rushing to the aid of the victor, had entered the war on the side of Germany. There was also, though remote as yet, the Japanese menace in the Far East.

Never since the American War of Independence had Britain faced so dangerous a strategic situation so completely isolated.

The current programme for the army called for fifty-five divisions by November 1941. It is hard to see how such a force could have guarded the Middle East against Italy and also, at some stage, landed again in western Europe and taken on a German army of more than 150 divisions. The British hope in the summer of 1940 for eventual victory rested less in reasoned appreciation than in illusion or faith – faith in the ability of the blockade and the heavy bomber to bring about a collapse of German war-making power by the end of 1941; faith that in these circumstances the European peoples would rise in revolt, and that a British expeditionary force would then be enough to administer the *coup de grace*. Had Hitler been a tyrant merely of Napoleon's stamp, peace might have been negotiated in 1940. However, the British government and people decided that whatever the consequences peace could not be made with a pathological criminal. If the war could be kept going, the situation might change in some unforeseeable manner; most hopeful prospect of all, perhaps America could gradually be enticed into belligerency.

In the meantime the British Isles themselves must survive. On 31 May there were only fifteen divisions available for home defence, including one armoured and one Canadian division, but much of the force was immobile and lacking equipment. In size, equipment and mobility the home field force gradually increased during the summer. As a consequence the early military plan against invasion of a largely static defence of the coasts and then inland from a stop-line covering the industrial areas was replaced by the conception of counter-strokes delivered by mobile groups of manoeuvre. Nevertheless in this summer when the British were paying for their trust in international law and the goodwill of other nations, mobility often meant buses and other requisitioned civilian vehicles.

As in previous invasion scares, there was a great boom in the martial spirit. It is fair to say that the British took a keener and more sympathetic interest in things military in 1940 than they had ten or even two years previously. A new volunteer movement arose, in which men over military age were armed and trained for local defence. A master of civil-service English first dubbed them 'Local Defence Volunteers', but the genius of Churchill swiftly re-christened them 'the Home Guard'. Like the volunteers of Kitchener's army, they wore civilian clothes and drilled with broom-sticks; like the volunteers of the 1790s they were sometimes armed with pikes. By 1942, when the danger of invasion had passed away, the Home Guard had developed into a well-equipped and organized auxiliary force.

Tank traps of a feeble kind burgeoned under railway arches and in other narrow defiles. Brick and concrete pill-boxes able to withstand a stone from a boy's catapult were erected in prominent places where they would catch the eye of the advancing panzers. All this improvisation cheered the hearts of the militarily unsophisticated British; but, like the preparation of Elizabethan and Georgian times, it was never tested by the event. The Germans did not come: the Royal Air Force beat the *Luftwaffe* by a narrow margin in the preliminary air battles of the Battle of Britain, and without air superiority the Germans would not risk the crossing.

Despite growing numbers, the home army suffered as much from all the defects of hasty expansion as its predecessor of 1915; and it was the home army that was the central strategic reserve of the empire. General Sir Alan Brooke, the Chief of the Imperial General Staff, wrote:

We still have an amateur army with an average of three pre-war officers per infantry battalion. Shortage of technical equipment would prevent the early formation of new divisions in place of those sent overseas.[1]

Churchill himself was not a cool and patient strategist, but was a man of powerful emotions, and consumed by a strong urge to the offensive. If a serious invasion of western Europe might be impossible for years, then at least there could be raids and landings of the kind familiar for centuries. However, to obviate the inter-service squabbles and muddles that had characterized so many

British seaborne expeditions up to and including Norway, a Combined Operations Command was set up to study and solve the problems of organization, command and special equipment. A special force of assault troops was created for raiding operations, named the 'commandos' after the Boer Commandos of the South African War. They were storm troops equivalent to the grenadiers of the regimental flank companies of the past. A start was made in emulating the German creation of airborne forces. A variety of new regiments and corps was therefore born, just as earlier wars had seen the débuts of fusiliers and hussars and rifle regiments: the Parachute Regiment, the Glider Pilot Regiment, the Special Air Service (all comprising the Army Air Corps), the Reconnaissance Corps. Some (like the Reconnaissance Corps) were new units for old functions and really unnecessary.

In land operations against the Axis powers (Germany and Italy: the Rome–Berlin axis), the British were hampered not merely by their military weakness, but by lack of opportunity, for there was now no common front with the enemy except in Africa. It was a problem similar to that faced by the younger Pitt's successors after Napoleon's victories of 1805–7.

The pre-war order of grand strategic priorities – United Kingdom, Far East, Middle East – was now altered, and the Middle East placed second to the United Kingdom. In Iraq and at the head of the Persian Gulf was the British Empire's principal source of non-dollar oil. The British forces in Egypt protected this oil from Italian attack. From an offensive point of view, the defeat of the Italian forces in Libya would clear the southern coastline of the Mediterranean as far as Tunisia (French) and open the way to an invasion of Europe via Sardinia, Corsica, or Sicily and Italy. It would re-open the Mediterranean and the Suez Canal to traffic between Britain and the Far East. Churchill consequently sought an early opportunity of striking back at the enemy through offensives against the Italians in Africa. By an act of strategic courage 150 of Britain's scarce tanks, together with 100 guns, were dispatched round the Cape to the Middle East.

The Italian Empire in Africa consisted of two widely separated portions. Completely cut off from Italy lay Eritrea and Abyssinia,

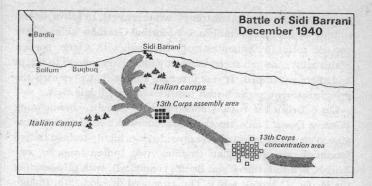

**Battle of Sidi Barrani
December 1940**

Bardia

Sidi Barrani

Sollum   Buqbuq

Italian camps

13th Corps assembly area

Italian camps

13th Corps
concentration area

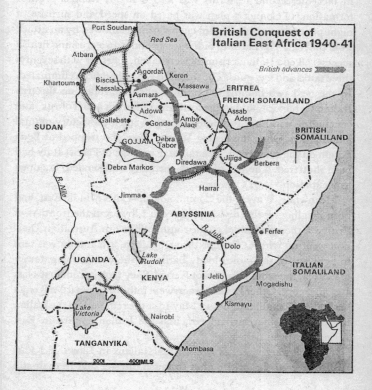

**British Conquest of
Italian East Africa 1940-41**

Port Soudan

Red Sea

British advances

Atbara

Agordat   Keren

Khartoum   Biscia   Massawa   **ERITREA**
Kassala
Asmara   **FRENCH SOMALILAND**
Adowa   Assab
Amba   Aden
Gallabat   Gondar   Alaqi   **BRITISH
SOMALILAND**

SUDAN   **GOJJAM**   Debra
Tabor   Diredawa   Jijiga   Berbera

Debra Markos   Harrar

R. Nile   Jimma

ABYSSINIA

R. Juba   Ferfer
Dolo

UGANDA   Lake
Rudolf   **ITALIAN
SOMALILAND**

KENYA   Jelib
Mogadishu
Lake
Victoria   Kismayu

Nairobi

TANGANYIKA   Mombasa

200   400 MLS

garrisoned by some 200,000 troops: wasting assets. In Libya, linked to Italy by the Mediterranean, lay Marshal Graziani with another 200,000 men. In September 1940 Graziani, with a large portion of this army, had advanced hesitantly some sixty miles into Egypt and there encamped. It was Graziani's force that presented the principal threat to the British positions in the Middle East.

On 9 December 1940, General R.N. O'Connor, commanding Western Desert Force, struck at Graziani with two divisions, some 36,000 men. The infantry were provided by a highly-trained Indian formation, the 4th Indian Division (two Indian brigades, one British, British artillery and British command), with fifty-seven of the heavy 'I' assault tanks. The armoured division (7th, though in fact the second to form) was also a highly-trained pre-war formation. O'Connor's plan was based on speed and surprise: a night penetration of the line of enemy camps followed by an attack from the rear. The battle of Sidi Barrani ended in a crushing British success: 38,000 Italian prisoners were taken, together with seventy-three tanks and 237 guns. The threat to Egypt had been eliminated. In the next two months O'Connor's offensive rolled on through Italian Cyrenaica, taking the fortresses of Bardia and Tobruk, and concluding with that rare military achievement, a victory of total annihilation, when the fleeing Italian army was trapped at Beda Fomm on the coast road. The military prestige of Fascist Italy had been shattered. The rest of Libya, virtually undefended, lay open to occupation.

Meanwhile, Wavell, the Commander-in-Chief Middle East, had been juggling his few divisions between Libya and the frontiers of Eritrea a thousand miles to the south. While 6th Australian Division went on with O'Connor through Libya, 4th Indian was sent to fight one of the most bloody battles of the war at the gateway of Eritrea, the mountain pass of Keren. They took it from first-class Italian troops. Other British forces swept into Abyssinia from Kenya via Italian Somaliland. On 17 May 1941 the remnants of the Italian army in Abyssinia surrendered, and the Italian empire in East Africa had been destroyed.

The sweeping victories against the Italians in Libya and East Africa cheered the British after so much disaster and in their still perilous situation; they re-illuminated failing hopes amid the neutrals, including the United States, that the Axis powers might not win after all. However, they inflicted no damage at all on Germany, whose power, either by occupation or by alliance, now extended from Norway to Bulgaria. The problem still remained of re-creating a front against Germany. In the winter of 1940–41 the British Cabinet came to believe that an opportunity would shortly exist in the Balkans, providing British diplomacy and military aid walked in step.

In December 1940 Mussolini, eager for a glorious conquest of his own, and without informing Hitler, invaded Greece from the Italian possession of Albania. Far from conquering, he was swiftly ejected by the Greeks, who in their turn invaded Albania. The front came to stalemate, but violent fighting throughout the winter confirmed the verdict of British successes: the Italian army was not much good. The Italian action and its failure were both irritating and inconvenient to Hitler, who was already preparing a massive attack on Russia, and who did not want trouble behind his right flank. He decided therefore to mount a German invasion of Greece to crush Greek resistance and turn out the small British ground and air forces present.

The British Cabinet got wind of German preparations in Rumania and Bulgaria. It was Churchill's judgement that a front against the Germans in Europe could be created in Greece if a British expeditionary force took its place in the line beside the Greeks. This might well encourage the Turks and the Yugoslavs to come in as well. It is to be guessed that the Prime Minister, in counting divisions, did not make sufficient allowance for the feeble fighting power of peasant infantry against panzer divisions. But the gamble of sending a British expeditionary force to Greece was concurred in by Wavell, the Commander-in-Chief, Middle East, and by Dill, the C.I.G.S. O'Connor's victorious army, instead of being sent on quickly to complete the conquest of Italian North Africa, was broken up and its best formations sent to Greece.

The course of the Greek campaign showed that British politicians and British generals alike had still appreciated neither the speed and power of a modern German offensive nor the ability of panzer

Britain and Her Army

divisions to operate in all kinds of terrain, nor the decisive impact of air superiority over a battlefield. Ten German divisions fought in Greece, and five of them (including three panzer) against the British Empire force, which consisted only of 1st New Zealand Division, 6th Australian Division and one British armoured brigade. The Royal Air Force flew only eighty aircraft against 800 of the enemy.

The Yugoslavs collapsed in a few days. The Turks stayed neutral. The Greeks, exhausted by long fighting against the Italians, could do little. Although the Australians and New Zealanders fought, as they always do, magnificently, the Greek campaign was France all over again, with panzer spearheads and parachute troops racing the defenders for their ports of embarkation. And, as at Dunkirk, while the navy got most of the men home, all the precious heavy equipment had to be left behind. The Greek adventure led to a disastrous weakening of British strength, still frail enough, that had long repercussions. In May the Germans launched a massive airborne attack on the Greek island of Crete, garrisoned by British imperial forces. It was the most ambitious airborne operation in history to this day. Nevertheless the British resistance was ferocious. Only after a fortnight's savage fighting which virtually broke the German airborne arm was Crete conquered. So narrow was the margin that the guns and tanks lost in Greece might well have secured a German defeat.

Meanwhile a worse disaster had occurred in Libya. Owing to the halt in O'Connor's offensive and the failure to complete the conquest of Libya, Hitler was able to send two German panzer divisions under Lieutenant-General Erwin Rommel to save his ally's colony. A week before the German attack was launched on Greece, Rommel attacked in the Western Desert. The weak, raw and half-trained British forces that had replaced O'Connor's men and their new commander Neame were swiftly outmanoeuvred. Neame and O'Connor himself, sent up to replace Neame, were captured.

Once more Axis forces were on the Egyptian frontier – but Germans now as well as Italians. This was another, and heavy, consequence of the British adventure in Greece. Henceforward, for two years, the campaigns in the Western Desert against Rommel

438

were to dominate British war-making more and more; it is fair to say that the need to beat Rommel and his force of never more than 50,000 Germans became an obsession with the British Prime Minister. The Desert dominated the British press and radio to the disservice of other, less glamorous and indeed more important campaigns fought in the Far East. The Desert War entered into the British folk-memory, a source of legend, endlessly re-written as both history and fiction.

It was a war like no other in history. The arena was a stretch of featureless desert, mostly hard gravel, but with some pockets of soft sand. The only road and the only railways ran along the Mediterranean coast. There were few towns (also on the coast), little population but Arab nomads, little water and no food supplies. The armies fought like land fleets, or like football teams on a bare arena. Food, water, petrol and ammunition had to be ferried forward in great convoys of trucks stretching from horizon to horizon. Tactical features were supplied by slight swells in the desert, or piles of stones or old dried-up wells, or the tombs of long-dead sheiks. There was virtually no limit to free movement by tracked or wheeled vehicles. In the winter there was torrential rain, and mud; in the summer relentless heat and light and dust. It was a healthy environment, free of the clogging presence of civilians. The campaign took on the character of a tournament, not least because of the personality of the German commander, Erwin Rommel.

The Germans brought to North Africa their operational experience in Poland and France, and equipment and tactics evolved and tested since the early 1930s. The British Empire fielded British, New Zealand, South African and Indian troops, all with differing military characters: it was virtually an allied army. None of these diverse troops could match the standard of staff-work, leadership and tactics of the Germans, for all (except the Indians) were composed of hastily-trained civilians plus a small leaven of hastily-promoted professionals. As in 1916, army, corps and divisional commanders and their staffs had never managed large formations in the field. Armoured warfare was an especial mystery. British equipment, especially tanks, was inferior mechanically as well as lacking in quantity until the middle of 1942. And so, as in 1916, the marvel was not that the British made serious mistakes but that they performed as well as they did.

In November 1941 the new 8th Army, under the supreme direction of the new Commander-in-Chief Middle East, Sir Claude Auchinleck, launched its first offensive, code-named *Crusader*. In number of tanks, though not in quality, it enjoyed a considerable superiority over the German-Italian *Panzergruppe Afrika*. The cavalry and yeomanry regiments of the British armoured forces perpetuated their fatal tradition of charging headlong on to enemy guns. There was insufficient co-operation between tanks, guns and infantry. Nevertheless, thanks to larger reserves of men and tanks, the 8th Army gradually wore Rommel down and forced him to withdraw from Cyrenaica – the first British victory over Germans in the war. Auchinleck's offensive came to rest roughly where O'Connor had been halted a year before, at the border of Tripolitania. And again the possibilities of an early advance on Tripoli were marred by the demands of a new campaign elsewhere.

On 7 December 1941, while *Crusader* was still being bitterly fought, the Japanese attacked the United States Fleet at Pearl Harbor, and soon Japanese combined operations developed against the British colonies of Malaya and Borneo as well as against the Dutch East Indies and the American colony of the Philippines. Now the British Empire had to cope with three great theatres of operations at once: the United Kingdom (springboard of an eventual invasion of Europe), the Middle East and the Far East. It had to wage war against two great enemy groups. Whereas since 1940 the Far East had been neglected and starved in favour of the effort in the Middle East, frantic last-minute efforts now had to be made to divert men and equipment from Egypt to Malaya and Burma.

At the end of 1941, the planned date for the completion of the expansion and equipment of the British army, its global deployment was as follows: in the United Kingdom, six armoured divisions and twenty-two infantry; in the Middle East, four armoured divisions and two infantry; in India, one infantry division, and in Malaya another. The British army's total strength in December 1941 was 2,340,000 men. The imbalance between forces allotted to the defence of the Empire – India, Malaya, Burma, Borneo, Australia and New Zealand – and those involved in the Middle East was great. It was emphasized by the additional presence far from home in the Libyan Desert, of the best Indian, New Zealand and Australian forces. Although the ration strength of Middle East Command had risen to over half a million men, the field troops numbered only some 200,000. The rest were swallowed up in what had become a satellite war economy. The countries of the Middle East were too poor and primitive to supply the base of modern war. The British had therefore been forced to create a vast complex of port facilities, communications, assembly and repair plants, stores of all kinds of munitions and equipment, even manufacturing plant. All this had been built up, and was now sustained, by ships from the United Kingdom on the long voyage round Africa.

In any case a modern army, with its sophisticated mechanical and electrical equipment and hungry demand for supplies, inevitably demanded a much higher proportion of its troops in rearward echelons than a 1914–18 army. Whereas for centuries a 'soldier' had been a man with a musket or a sabre or a cannon, he could now be an electrician, a typist-clerk, a telecommunications expert, an accountant, an industrial craftsman. Much of the military profession was being steadily 'civilianized'. This complicated the problem of manpower; the army (and other armed forces) and war industry now competed for similar kinds of trained and skilled personnel.

The new 'civilianized' technological components of the army clashed in temperament and style with the old parade-ground and warrior tradition. The British regular officer, with his rural and gentlemanlike background, did not adjust easily to a 'garage-mechanic's war'. To the end of the war, the British armour (consisting, except for Royal Tank Corps units, of ancient cavalry or yeomanry regiments) was inferior to the infantry and artillery in general battle skill and in maintenance of their equipment. On the other hand, the British artillery, a technical arm for more than two centuries, was considered by German critics to be the most professionally effective of British fighting troops. Unfortunately the

cavalry and the Guards retained their traditional and disproportionate influence in the higher reaches of the army establishment,
to the neglect of tank corps, artillery and infantry officers (especially if those last were from 'unfashionable' regiments). It was the
army's 'gentlemen' that lost the Gazala battle in the Western
Desert in 1942; the 'players' like Auchinleck, Dorman-Smith and
later Montgomery who eventually won. In Burma, too, the credit
for victory was due to a 'player', Slim, of the Indian army.

In the Second World War the British organization for evolving
grand strategy and for linking the military machine to the political
control of the Cabinet differed considerably from that in the Great
War. There was in the first place much closer collaboration between
the three services through the Chiefs-of-Staff Committee which had
been established between the wars. Joint rather than competitive
service advice could thus be offered to the politicians. After 1940
the Chiefs-of-Staff Committee came to deal only with large questions of strategy, while their Deputies dealt with day-to-day matters.
Both committees were served by a Joint Planning Sub-Committee,
composed of the Directors of Plans of the three services, and by a
Joint Intelligence Sub-Committee, which also could report direct
to the Cabinet.

There was no open clash between the brass-hats and the frock-
coats in the Second World War, because the Prime Minister was
also Minister of Defence, and thus himself responsible head of the
combined service machine. The Secretary of State for War, like his
colleagues in the Air Ministry and the Admiralty, dwindled to a
mere departmental head concerned with organization and administration. Cabinet, Minister of Defence and the Chiefs of Staff
Committee were linked and served by the War Cabinet Secretariat.
Thus, instead of the 1916–17 situation, whereby a Chief of the
Imperial General Staff enjoying an independent position at the
head of the army proffered advice to the Prime Minister, the
C.I.G.S. was now merely a senior member of the Prime Minister's
own political household, and exposed to his relentless argument
and pressure through the small hours (Churchill's preferred working day). Instead therefore of formal official confrontations over
questions of strategy, there were interminable intimate arguments

through the cigar-smoke. These wore out Sir John Dill, C.I.G.S. from 1940 to 1941, an able but sensitive man. Alan Brooke, the C.I.G.S. from 1941 until the end of the war, was a capable executive soldier and a tenacious arguer, and possessed of much more stamina than Dill. As Chairman of the Joint Chiefs of Staff, he spoke for all three services on major questions, and in that sense was more strongly placed than the C.I.G.S.s of the Great War, who spoke only for the army and land strategy. Brooke was often able by patience, tact and sheer tenacity to head Churchill off some of his dearly-loved but impracticable projects.

The nearest thing to an open clash between brass-hats and frock-coats in the Second World War lay in the continual exchange of telegrams between London and the commanders-in-chief in the overseas theatres. Prime Ministerial advice often extended to minor tactical matters. The inevitable delays in communications between London and Cairo (and later between London and India) sometimes rendered telegrams from London out of date by the time they arrived, but not less mandatory. Modern communications had stripped theatre commanders of the independent judgement they had enjoyed in the days of Marlborough and Wellington, not with happy results; for whereas Marlborough and Wellington could themselves decide when to attack and when to keep to the defensive, Wavell and Auchinleck were pressed into premature, costly and sometimes disastrous offensives.

Whatever its merits as grand strategy, the colossal British effort in the Middle East was a final and magnificent demonstration of British sea-power. The constant convoys of cargo ships and troop-ships round Africa was only made possible by the domination – narrow at times – over the U-boat by the Royal Navy. Not since the American war had Britain nourished a major campaign so far from home. Yet there was one fundamental difference between the whole British war effort of 1940–41 and that of most previous major conflicts back to those against Louis XIV. It no longer rested on buoyant and rising commercial prosperity – on national wealth that continued to grow even in war. Instead, assets built up in the past were being sold to pay for American equipment. Concentration on war production shattered the British export trade. In 1940 the Treasury had predicted that Britain would exhaust her economic resources by the end of 1941. This in fact came to pass. Only massive American aid under the Lend-Lease Acts enabled the British to go on receiving American war supplies; only American aid masked the wide gap in the British balance of payments. For over two centuries the British had been able to pay poorer nations to fight for them: now they too had become subsidized allies.

19
The Army
and Global War
1941–5

THE American entry into the war after the Japanese air-strikes on Pearl Harbor raised in acute form the age-old problems of co-operation between allies. For while Russia chose to fight her own independent war, Britain wished her relations with America to be as close and as intimate as possible. During the Great War only sketchy machinery for concerting allied strategy and operations had been achieved by 1918, but even then the French and British armies had nevertheless remained independent and distinct national forces under the broad personal guidance of Foch as Supreme Commander. In the Second World War, on the other hand, there quickly evolved close integration of the Americans and the British, extending from heads of government to the organization of forces in the field. At the top, joint grand strategy was hammered out by President Roosevelt and Winston Churchill, advised by the Combined Chiefs of Staff of both nations, in whose name directives were issued to the theatre supreme commanders. Because of this joint Anglo-American direction from above, a general's right of appeal to his own government against an order issued by a 'foreign' supreme commander, as enjoyed in the Great War by Haig and by British Dominion generals in the current war, fell into abeyance. The Anglo-American invasion of French North Africa in November 1942 provided the prototype of allied organization in the field. The supreme commander (over all allied troops, and over air and sea forces) was an American, General Dwight D. Eisenhower, while his deputy was English (General Alexander) and his staff of mixed nationality. In Italy in 1943 the supreme commander was Alexander, with an American deputy and again a mixed staff.

This very close association ended the independent role played by the British army, its commanders and its governments since the time of Marlborough. The British were unable to pursue national strategies of their own, such as that which aimed at reaching Vienna from Italy ahead of the Russians. Nevertheless, international command made for efficient execution of joint enterprises of great complication, such as the seaborne invasions of North Africa, Italy and France. Indeed the invasion of Normandy in 1944 would probably have been impossible without Anglo-American integration. However, it remained true that integration made it difficult for Britain, as the weaker partner, to avoid succumbing to American domination of grand strategy. By contrast, Stalin was careful to retain a completely free hand over Russian policy while extracting from the Western Allies all the aid he could.

The entry of Russia and the United States into the war in 1941 as a result of Axis aggressions justified the British faith in hanging on alone after June 1940. However, it was not until the end of 1942 that the Russians finally forced the German army on to the defensive, and the Americans were able to put an expeditionary force into the field. Meanwhile the catalogue of British catastrophes continued to grow longer, not only in the Middle East, but in the Far East, where the Japanese rolled up the British Empire like an old moth-eaten rug.

Malaya formed the defensive hinterland of Singapore, which had always been intended as the base of a powerful fleet that would bar the Japanese from approaching Australia, New Zealand or India. In late 1941 there were no available ships for this fleet, many having been sunk or disabled off Greece and Crete, and many more being involved in the battle of the Atlantic. Singapore would therefore have to wait for its fleet. It had been decided before the war that the defence of Malaya until the fleet arrived must depend on air-striking forces. In December 1941 only a fraction of the necessary air forces existed. The ground forces had been starved of equipment – especially tanks – in favour of the Middle East. Nor were the Indian and British troops in Malaya in the peak of fighting condition. Few in authority in Malaya took the Japanese seriously enough. British military orthodoxy could not encompass an enemy who advanced on bicycles, carrying them round road-blocks through the undergrowth. Not since the early fights in South Africa in 1899 had a British army been so completely and easily outfought tactically as it was by the Japanese in Malaya. As the Japanese neared Singapore, the British government frantically tried to repair its earlier neglect of Malaya. A British and an Australian division were diverted to the base. Soft and nearly useless after a long voyage packed in troopships, they arrived just in time to surrender with the rest of the garrison of the indefensible island – indefensible because of the presence of the great polyglot civil population of the city of Singapore, who were helpless in the face of air attack and of Japanese capture of the water supplies. On 15 February 1942 Singapore surrendered with 70,000 men – the greatest British surrender and military disaster since Yorktown in 1781.

Burma fell next. Bewildered troops fought as best they could according to the methods they had been taught for a mechanized version of 1914–18 Western Front warfare, but were outmanoeuvred and finally demoralized by the speed of Japanese outflanking movements in difficult country. As against the Germans – or the Boers – the British command systems again proved too slow, rigid and hierarchical. General Harold Alexander led a remnant of troops over the mountains into India after an appallingly difficult, skilful and courageous retreat up through the length of Burma.

Now India, like the Middle East, grew into a satellite war economy, producing many of its own war supplies and munitions. However, all India's military organization and communications had in peacetime been focused on the traditionally threatened north-west frontier with Afghanistan. Road and rail communications with the Burmese frontier were few and primitive. It had never occurred to the Indian authorities that the Japanese could ever pass Singapore and mount a direct threat to India. The Burma front was also starved of supplies and equipment because the attention of the British government and people was fixed on the Allied operations in North Africa and later in Italy. The 14th Army on the India–Burma frontier felt itself forgotten. From 1942 to 1944 the front remained in stalemate, except for two miscarried British offensives in 1943 which proved that the British army and its commanders had still not mastered the arts of fieldcraft and hard-living needed to beat the Japanese, nor perhaps regained their own confidence.

However, the 14th Army fought the most unpleasant campaigns endured by British troops in the Second World War. There was steamy tropical heat and the torrential rains of the monsoon; there were all the horrors of tropical insect and reptile life, including leeches; there was the Japanese soldier himself, ruthless and brave in battle, silent and cunning in jungle stealth. The civilized towns of the Middle East and Italy, with their lavish service clubs and splendid leave camps, found little counterpart in eastern India. Battle casualties were operated upon in rude jungle shelters on operating tables made out of tins hammered flat and nailed down. In terms of discomfort and endurance, the Burma front was the only Second-World-War equivalent of Great-War trench life faced by the British army.

Meanwhile, in the Middle East during 1942, the 8th Army, equipped with the best that British and American war industry

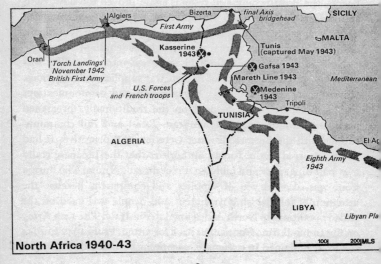

North Africa 1940-43

could supply, continued its tournament with the *Panzerarmee Afrika*, under Rommel. Despite the efforts of the Commander-in-Chief, Sir Claude Auchinleck, to bring the standard of training, staff work and command up to the German level, the 8th Army remained brave but slow and sluggish. Its infantry and its armour still tended to fight separate battles. The armour still tried to win with tanks alone rather than with anti-tank guns used offensively and with lorried infantry. This separation was a joint inheritance from the cavalry tradition of the charge and from the doctrine preached by prophets like Fuller before the war that tanks alone would decide the mobile battles of the future. The British infantry divisions were too large and cumbersome, and too lacking in hitting power for the Desert. The British command therefore tried to create the static situation for which they were intended by building defence systems of 'boxes' – pieces of desert fortified for all-round defence. The Germans, on the other hand, depended hardly at all on infantry divisions, except for Italian troops. They fought their battles with 'groups' – *ad hoc* mixed formations of armour, guns and infantry. Thanks to common doctrine and training, these groups could be

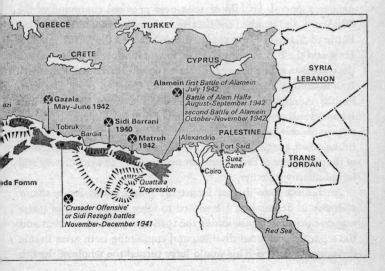

swiftly created out of heterogeneous units in the heat of attack or retreat in a way difficult for the British, with their rigid divisional structure and their multiplicity of ancient regiments, each with its own 'style' of fighting. For even in 1942 a British cavalry or infantry unit retained something of the spirit of the original seventeenth-century or eighteenth-century regiment as a self-regulating institution under its own colonel. British officers, senior and junior, as a whole could not free themselves from the effects of their relative inexperience and their unrealistic peacetime soldiering. Everything in their backgrounds made it hard for them to match the professional zeal and ruthlessness of their enemies.

In the summer of 1942 Rommel won his greatest victory over this British army, during the Gazala battles in Cyrenaica (26 May – 30 June). With 280 German tanks against 850 British tanks he completely outwitted and outmanoeuvred the British command, often by brilliant opportunism, captured the base of Tobruk and 30,000 men, and chased the remnants of the 8th Army, now virtually devoid of armour, into Egypt.

For the first time since Graziani's invasion of 1940, the Nile Delta and all the vast Middle East base seemed in immediate danger. General Auchinleck took over personal command of the 8th Army, and combed the theatre for reinforcements. In the First Battle of Alamein (July 1942) Auchinleck and the 8th Army, like Haig and the B.E.F. in April 1918, fought it out with their backs to the wall. By a subtle policy of directing counter-strokes at Rommel's Italian troops, suggested to him by his Chief of Staff, Dorman-Smith, Auchinleck wrested the initiative from the victorious Rommel and saved Egypt. At the end of July Auchinleck attempted to turn his defensive success into a complete victory, but his attacks broke down, partly because of insufficient strength, partly because of the old failure of British armour and infantry to work closely and harmoniously together.

Auchinleck now began long-term preparations for a major offensive in September. He wished to solve the problem of inter-arm co-operation by abolishing the 1918-style infantry division and the separate armoured division, and combining both arms in one divisional structure. This would have turned the whole of the 8th

Army into a highly mobile tank-infantry force like Rommel's *Afrika Korps*. Before the changes could be made, however, Auchinleck and his senior staff officers were dismissed by the Prime Minister. The sharp division between armour and infantry remained. It was a sign of limited British battle experience, especially in the home forces in the United Kingdom, that the 'expert' now sent out to organize and train the armour in Egypt was a cavalryman who had never commanded an armoured division in action.

At the end of August 1942 Rommel gambled on a last attempt to break through to the Nile, despite shortage of petrol, troops and tanks. In the battle of Alam Halfa, the new 8th Army commander, Montgomery, soundly defeated him in a Wellingtonian battle of strictly defensive and static conception.

On 23 October Montgomery launched the last purely British offensive against Germany in the Second World War. The Second Battle of Alamein took the form of sheer attrition, because for the first time in the desert campaign there were no open flanks. The German defence in depth (barbed wire, minefields) stretched from the Mediterranean Sea to the Quattara Depression. The 8th Army's equipment for the battle reflected the degree to which Britain had now become dependent on American technology: Sherman and Grant tanks formed the backbone of the armoured forces; Dodge, Chevrolet and Ford trucks moved much of the army and its supplies; the self-propelled guns were mostly American, as were the Tomahawk fighters and Mitchell bombers of the air force. The British out-numbered the Germans in tanks by 1,029 to 211 and in men 195,000 to 50,000; and the Germans and Italians together by 195,000 to 105,000. The 8th Army was still heterogeneous: while the armour and two infantry divisions were British, there was an Australian, an Indian, a New Zealand and a South African division, as well as Greek, Polish and Free French troops.

As in the set-piece offensives of 1916–18, hopes of swift progress at Alamein were soon dashed. The initial attack miscarried in the deep German defences, partly because once again the British had failed to solve the problem of combining armour and infantry. The rest of the twelve-day battle was a piecemeal grinding forward. It was the kind of deliberate, dogged, tightly-controlled and slow-moving battle that best suited the doctrine, training and organization of the British imperial forces. At the end of twelve days, when Montgomery still had a few reserves left and Rommel had none, the German front collapsed and the Germans fell back in retreat, although quickly enough to avoid being trapped. There followed 1,500 miles of retreat brilliantly handled by Rommel, while the colossal administrative problems of pursuit were resourcefully solved by the British.

In Britain they rang the bells for Second Alamein. The Prime Minister had wished for a resounding British victory before the British war effort was absorbed into the American alliance, and the resolute Montgomery and his dogged troops had granted the wish. Nevertheless Alamein (even First and Second Alamein taken together) cannot rank with Blenheim or with Waterloo, nor even with Salamanca or Vittoria. Those were triumphs over principal field armies of the great European enemy, while Alamein was a victory over a minor German expeditionary force.

On 8 November 1942, four days after Rommel conceded defeat at Alamein, Anglo-American forces launched the largest opposed amphibious landing so far in history along the coasts of Morocco and Algeria in French North Africa. It was a complete success that owed much to British research and development. For since 1940 the British had at last drawn the right lessons from their failures in Norway and back down the ages. Combined Operations Command had evolved new equipment and techniques for seaborne invasion: combined-headquarters ships, specially adapted landing ships, new kinds of motor-driven barges whose bows dropped on the shore as ramps to permit the rapid disembarkation of assault troops or tanks. The operational lessons learned in French North Africa paved the way for the further seaborne invasions of Sicily and Italy in 1943, and for the largest and most risky invasion of them all – across the English Channel. The problems of such a venture had been harshly illustrated in July 1942 during a large-scale raid on the port of Dieppe. For, despite the new techniques of combined operations, the Dieppe raid proved as crashing a failure as anything launched by the elder Pitt – and proportionately as costly as the disastrous first day of the Battle of the Somme, with twenty per cent casualties, mostly Canadian. The attack went in without the massive preliminary bombing originally intended. The plan for a frontal assault on the hard-core of the German defences was even more rigid and unalterable than the Somme plan in 1916. The main attack was crushed on the beach; only the feint attacks along the coast on both sides of Dieppe made any progress.

Dieppe seemed to prove that a full-scale invasion against a fortified port would be impossible; and yet without a major port an invasion force could not be supplied and built up when ashore. Through 1943 and early 1944 British and American planners wrestled with this and other enormous problems of an opposed landing on a vast scale, while the American army in England steadily increased, and the training of troops went on.

During this long waiting period for the Second Front, for which the Russians in their struggle kept demanding, the Anglo-Americans sought to keep German troops occupied in the Mediterranean. Hitler himself made the disastrous mistake of feeding German troops into Tunisia to oppose the Anglo-American invasion of French North Africa. Eventually these troops were bottled up round Tunis with their backs to the sea by the British 1st Army, the 8th Army and by American and French troops. The final allied onslaught, directed by General Sir Harold Alexander, ended in the surrender of more than 200,000 Germans and Italians in May 1943. This major victory was the climax and conclusion of Britain's long North African campaign, and it opened the way, as had always been hoped, to the invasion of Sicily and Italy.

Although the loss of Sicily caused the downfall of Mussolini and Italy's surrender, the opportunity of a swift occupation of the country was missed. The British had hoped that in the Second World War Italy might prove a running sore to the enemy as Spain had in the Napoleonic wars; a place where a British army could achieve results out of proportion to its size. The hope proved a delusion. German road and rail communications with Germany were rapid and direct, while allied communications ran back by sea to North Africa, and thence via Gibraltar to Britain or America. It was the Allies, not the Germans, who were forced to make the disproportionate investment in the Italian campaign. The long, narrow and mountainous peninsula of Italy proved ideal for protracted defence. While successive German defence systems could only be turned by sea, the requirements of the more important amphibious operations in the Pacific and across the Channel demanded most available landing craft. Both of the two major landings behind the German front (Salerno, 1943, and Anzio, 1944) were blocked into narrow beach-heads by swift German reaction. Despite the skill of the Allied Supreme Commander, Alexander (not least skilful, like Marlborough, at the tactful management of allies), there was no *blitzkrieg* in Italy, but a continual slogging forward against mountain positions and river lines cunningly fortified and resolutely defended. The 8th Army, which had begun its career in swift manoeuvre in the Desert, ended it in position warfare in mountains and mud. There were nine months of some of the bloodiest fighting experienced by the British army and its allies in this war before Rome was captured.

After a brief and hectic period of pursuit, the Allies came up against yet another thoroughly prepared and naturally strong defence position, the Gothic Line. In September 1944 British and American troops carried this line by a succession of bloody frontal assaults. Once more the Germans were able to dig in farther back, and not until the general German collapse in the spring of 1945 did the Allies in Italy finally break through and bring about the disintegration of the German forces. It was the belated culmination of the Mediterranean strategy that had preoccupied British warmaking since 1940. However, American insistence in 1944 on the diversion of resources from Italy to make a landing in the south of France as an adjunct (unnecessary as it turned out) to the Normandy invasion had already wrecked the wider British hopes of striking from Italy into the Balkans. This strategy, on which British politicians and soldiers were equally keen, aimed at reaching Vienna before the Russians by an offensive through the Ljubljana gap in Yugoslavia. Whether – even without the landing in the south of France – allied resources in the Mediterranean would have been adequate to sustain such an ambitious strategy in difficult country must remain very greatly open to doubt. It was the last manifestation of that British fascination with conducting war in the Balkans that had originated with Lloyd George in the Great War.

Instead, the decisive attempt of the western allies to defeat the great European enemy was made in the traditional theatre of war: across the English Channel, in northern France. 'Operation *Overlord*' was intended to be far more than a successful modern version of the Pitts' dismal tip-and-run raids; its purpose was to re-establish the Western Front so that the enemy's main force could be hammered to pieces in battle. Thus, though the Normandy invasion was maritime or 'blue water' strategy in its means of launching, it was then to turn into 'continental' strategy, the commitment of a mass army to a great land campaign. The centuries-old conflict between 'maritime' and 'continental' strategy was thus resolved within the one operation.

The problems of winning a lodgement on a heavily defended coastline roomy enough to permit the deployment of a great army were immense. The scale of the proposed assault landing dwarfed all historical precedents. There were to be five divisions in the first wave, two in the second, all afloat at once in special landing craft. On the first two days of the invasion alone, 20,111 vehicles of all kinds and 176,475 men were to be got ashore. No less immense were the administrative and technical problems of subsequently building up that striking force and all its heavy equipment by cross-Channel transportation at a faster rate than the enemy could concentrate his own forces overland. During the subsequent build-up within the lodgement area the allied army was to be increased to thirty-seven divisions within a few weeks. These gigantic problems were made the more difficult because there would be no major port available. Since the Dieppe raid the Germans had rendered all French Channel ports impregnable to direct assault. The invasion would have to be fed over open beaches, despite the Channel's reputation as one of the most uncertain seas in the world for weather. But British operational research and invention solved all these problems. As a substitute for a major port, two artificial harbours (code name 'Mulberries') were designed and built in sections in Britain and towed across the Channel after D-Day. They comprised outer breakwaters of blockships, inner concrete sectional breakwaters, and floating moles from quays to shore. The 'Mulberries' destroyed the basis of German strategic calculations.

On the British landing sectors specially-adapted tanks whirling flails of chains mowed paths up from the beaches through German minefields and greatly helped the British to achieve a secure lodgement more quickly than their allies. Operations on shore were controlled from fully-equipped headquarters (or command) ships. In every aspect D-Day displayed the results of years of careful thought and manufacture, and of meticulous organization. The contrast with the hasty improvisations of past centuries was complete.

The command structure of the invasion forces represented the final evolution of inter-service and inter-allied collaboration during the Second World War. The Supreme Commander of the Allied Expeditionary Force was an American, General Dwight Eisenhower, and his deputy an Englishman, Air Chief Marshal Sir Arthur Tedder. The Supreme Commander received his directive for the invasion from the Combined British and American Chiefs of Staff, to which he was responsible, although he also enjoyed direct access to each national Chiefs-of-Staff Committee over questions of detail. Eisenhower's own Chief of Staff, General Bedell Smith, was American, and his Deputy Chief of Staff, General Morgan, English. The rest of the staff of Supreme Headquarters Allied Expeditionary Force was international and fully integrated. Under Eisenhower and his Supreme Headquarters were the land, sea and air commanders-in-chief and their headquarters staffs: Admiral Bertram Ramsay (British); Air Chief Marshal Sir Trafford Leigh-Mallory (British); and Field-Marshal Sir Bernard Montgomery (21st Army Group). These headquarters were also international and integrated. Below them came the purely national tactical air forces and sea task-forces.

The command of the land forces presented greater complications. During the establishment of a secure lodgement area and later during the break-out, the land campaign required unified command in the field. Montgomery, as the most experienced allied battlefield commander, was therefore given the temporary post of ground-force commander, as well as his permanent post as Army

Group Commander, 21st Army Group (British and Canadian troops). Later, when the number of American troops began rapidly to exceed the British contribution, and the campaign developed on a wide front, it was intended to create a second, purely American field command, 12th Army Group, whose commander would be Montgomery's equal. Montgomery would then yield overall control of operations to Eisenhower.

The Normandy coast between the Orne River and the Cotentin Peninsula was chosen for the invasion because it was neither so heavily fortified nor so strongly garrisoned as the coast opposite the Straits of Dover, and yet it offered accessible terrain for the lodgement area and for airfields, as well as promise of early capture of a major port, Cherbourg, from the landward side. Successful measures of deception convinced the Germans that the invasion would fall in the Pas-de-Calais, and continued by the threat of a second invasion to fix one German army there until long after the crisis of the Normandy battle.

The invasion was preceded and accompanied by an overwhelming exercise in air-power, which obliterated the *Luftwaffe* and paralysed the German movement on the ground. Road, rail and river communications round the Normandy area were smashed on lines of 'interdiction', successfully isolating the battlefield from swift reinforcement.

The Allies made large-scale use of airborne forces to seize important ground to secure the flanks of the invasion area. Two American airborne divisions and one British were used. It was a tribute to British efficiency that while the Americans were widely scattered, the British 6th Airborne Division was landed tightly in its dropping zone.

On D-Day, 6 June 1944, the Allies achieved complete tactical as well as strategic surprise, for they came ashore in poor weather at high tide under a full moon, a three-fold achievement believed by the Germans to be unlikely or impossible. By nightfall the Allies were solidly ashore, and behind them supplies and reinforcements were pouring in. Despite local setbacks to the Americans on one of their beaches, and the British failure to capture the town of Caen, the German plan to smash the invasion on the beaches, as at

Dieppe, had already failed. D-Day had been the completely successful consummation of the most carefully prepared and complicated operation in the history of war.

Although the problems of cross-Channel supply remained, the military operations now took on the normal form of land warfare, as the British and Americans strove to widen and deepen their lodgement and prepare for a breakthrough into the heart of France; and the Germans struggled to rope the allied invasion off

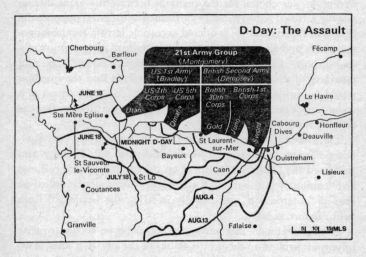

in the excellent defensive country of the *bocage* – full of hedgerows and sunken lanes. In the battle of Normandy the fighting reverted almost completely from *blitzkrieg* to the classical pattern of grim and balanced struggle. The density of German troops (especially panzer divisions) in proportion to extent of front made an early breakthrough impossible. Every attempt by Montgomery to win ground south-eastwards on an axis through the town of Caen was blocked after small initial gains. The attack that eventually won Caen on 8 July and the further offensive ten days later (code-named *Goodwood*) beyond the city closely resembled Plumer's set-pieces in 1917, except that heavy bombers took the place of Plumer's heavy artillery. Massed infantry and tanks moved slowly forward on a narrow front over a carpet of bomb craters. Yet, as in 1917, the bombardment held up the offensive by cratering the battle-field.

Nevertheless, given the strength of the enemy front, there was, as in 1917, no easy way through. Montgomery's massive frontal smashes performed the essential task of attracting the weight of German strength to the British and Canadian sector and of consuming the limited German reserves. His attacks may be compared with Marlborough's on Blenheim village, bloody and vain in themselves, but forcing the enemy to weaken his front elsewhere, at the point where the battle-winning onslaught would eventually be delivered. By the end of July there were six panzer divisions (with 645 tanks) facing the British and Canadians, and only two (with 190 tanks) facing the Americans. Nor had the Germans any more reserves in hand either to patch the front or to use in counter-attack. When the American offensive went in on 25 July, it burst straight through the weak German defences and poured west into Brittany, east along the Loire towards Paris.

In 1944 Montgomery enjoyed advantages denied to Haig in 1917 – a powerful ally; the superiority of strength to enable the attrition battle to be followed by a second, and decisive, blow else-where; an active Russian front; a German opponent already weakened in quality and numbers. For the Anglo-Americans in 1944 were not fighting the German army in its prime. Although the panzer divisions remained good, the infantry was lacking in quantity and often quality. Eisenhower wrote: '... we found opponents inferior, both physically and morally, to those against whom we fought in North Africa.'[1]

By the middle of August 1944 the Germans were fighting to escape from a pocket round Falaise, surrounded by Americans to the south, British and Canadians to the north. The German defence of France had collapsed, and the German soldiers made tracks for the Fatherland at utmost speed. Yet Montgomery's victory in Normandy, though coupled with equally impressive Russian successes in the East, did not, as some expected, lead directly to Germany's fall. The powers of recuperation of the German army were remarkable even in extremity. As the autumn

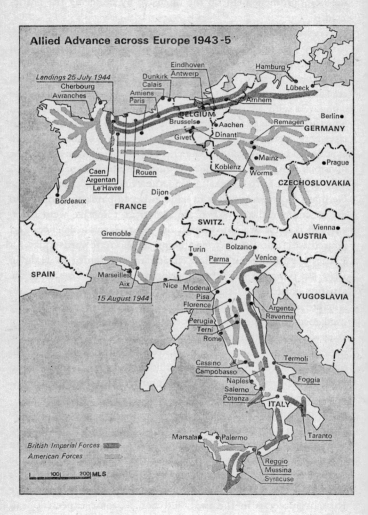

Allied Advance across Europe 1943-5

Landings 25 July 1944
Cherbourg
Avranches
Dunkirk
Calais
Amiens
Paris
Eindhoven
Antwerp
Hamburg
Lübeck
Arnhem
BELGIUM
Brussels
Aachen
Remagen
Berlin •
GERMANY
Dinant
Givet
Caen
Argentan
Le Havre
Rouen
Koblenz
Mainz
Worms
Prague •
CZECHOSLOVAKIA
Bordeaux
Dijon
FRANCE
SWITZ.
Vienna •
AUSTRIA
Grenoble
Turin
Bolzano
Parma
Venice
SPAIN
Marseilles
Aix
Nice
Modena
Pisa
Florence
YUGOSLAVIA
15 August 1944
Argenta
Ravenna
Perugia
Terni
Rome
Cassino
Campobasso
Naples
Salerno
Potenza
Termoli
Foggia
ITALY
Marsala
Palermo
Taranto
British Imperial Forces
American Forces
Reggio
Messina
Syracuse
100| 200| MLS

leaves of 1944 were falling, the Allies lay stalled along the German frontier from Switzerland to Aachen and thence across Holland to the sea.

In September, Montgomery tried to break the stalemate by a narrow and deep offensive across the Dutch river obstacles of the Maas and the two branches of the Rhine, aimed eventually at the Ruhr industrial area. American and British airborne forces were dropped to seize the river crossings, while a powerful ground force drove north along the only road to link up with the airborne troops. It was the riskiest operation ever undertaken by Montgomery, and it narrowly failed. German resistance to the northernmost drop, by the British 1st Airborne Division, was unexpectedly swift and deadly, while the ground troops made slow progress to the rescue against a determined German anti-tank screen which barred the only road that lay above the marshy levels of Holland. The line of operations had been too limited and too obvious.

In December 1944 Hitler gambled on an ambitious counter-offensive intended to split the British and Americans by capturing Antwerp. However, the German army no longer possessed the power and weight of 1940, nor were the British and Americans the static and nerveless French of 1940. After an initial and sensational success against a weak American sector, the German thrust was contained and repulsed.

In the New Year, the Allies went forward again, in a succession of local offensives against stubborn German resistance, until the line of the Rhine had been gained. In the east too the Russians were fighting deeper and deeper inside Germany. At long last the resistance of the German army began quickly to crumble. On 23 March 1945 the British and Canadian troops of 21st Army Group crossed the Rhine north of the Ruhr industrial area, preceded by airborne forces and more colossal air bombardments. The Americans had earlier crossed the Rhine south of the Ruhr. Only now, after six years of war, was the German army reduced to the state of disintegration reached by the French in six weeks. The Ruhr was encircled and its garrisons surrendered; the British raced for Hamburg, the Elbe and the Baltic coast, while the Americans swept eastwards to meet the Russians and southwards through

Bavaria. In the east the Russians took Berlin, a smoking shell, and Nazi Germany foundered under concentric attack. On 2 and 3 May 1945, before the final and complete German unconditional surrender, the British Second Army alone took half a million prisoners. On 5 May Field-Marshal Montgomery took the formal surrender of all German sea, land and air forces in Holland, Denmark and north-west Germany.

It was a moment of British military triumph to place beside the British entry into Cologne in 1918, Marshal Tallard's surrender to Marlborough after Blenheim, or Wellington's entry into Paris after Waterloo. Although the navy and the air force had saved the home island in 1940 and had made the 1944 invasion possible, only the army, together with the armies of great allies as in the past, had been able to defeat the army of the enemy and enter his own territory. In the Second World War, as in all previous great wars touched on in this book, there had proved to be no alternative road to victory.

Japan alone of the Axis powers remained in the field. The war in the Pacific was maritime, not continental. Japan had won her conquests by sea-power and she fed and defended them by sea-power. It was United States sea-power that had been penetrating deeper and deeper through the chains of Japanese-held islands in the Pacific towards the Philippines and Japan herself. The destruction of the Japanese battle-fleet was consummated at the greatest naval battle since Trafalgar, three actions within one great encounter, the battle of Leyte Gulf in the Philippines, in October 1944. The Japanese lost three battleships, four carriers, ten cruisers and nine destroyers, and never put to sea as a fleet again. The defeat of Japan was the most impressive exercise in sea-power since the colonial wars of the eighteenth century, but Britain took little part in it. Even after the defeat of Germany the British Pacific fleet, whose presence was unwillingly accepted by the Americans, constituted only a small task force in a great armada.

The British army itself therefore also took no part in the principal offensives against the heart of Japanese power. Instead, it could, and did, recapture the British colony of Burma in a campaign whose skill and novel techniques showed how completely the army in the east had recovered from the defeats of 1941-2.

The British re-conquest of Burma was preceded by a final Japanese attempt to smash through the British defences in the hills of Assam and invade India. The defeat of this invasion and the subsequent British offensive were the last operations undertaken by the British Indian army that had been created after the Indian Mutiny and re-organized under Roberts and Kitchener before 1914. The Burma campaign saw also the last collaboration in war between this Indian army and the British.

The land forces in India since the Mutiny had consisted of the Indian army (paid for and controlled by the government of India through the Commander-in-Chief in India) and the British army in India. The Indian army consisted of rank-and-file and junior officers voluntarily recruited* from the Indian martial races and from the Gurkhas of the independent state of Nepal, and of British officers. These British officers, however, had never belonged to the British army, but had joined the Indian army at the outset of their careers, on passing out from Sandhurst. Though British, their loyalties were to the Indian army, and to their Indian regiments. Therefore the two British officer-corps (Indian army and British army) were mutually exclusive clubs, each looking with some professional jealousy and distrust on the other. This division of loyalty tended sometimes to make for ill-feeling between the two armies, especially over appointments to higher commands. The Indian army's field formations were not purely Indian even in their rank-and-file, for a third of the troops were normally provided by British army units. In the North African Desert, an Indian division had comprised two Indian brigades to one British. Up on the Burmese frontier a brigade itself might consist of one Indian, one Gurkha and one British battalion.

Under first-class commanders able to rise above professional jealousy, however, this illogical tangle of British and Indian loyalties and organizations had less effect on joint efficiency than might have been expected.

Despite nearly two million men in India under arms, exiguous

---

* Since the 1930s a programme of 'Indianization' had led to progressive replacement of British officers by Indian up to the rank of brigadier.

communications only permitted a field army of six divisions to be maintained in Assam. These divisions formed the 14th Army, under the command of Lieutenant-General (later Field-Marshal Lord) Slim. Slim was an Indian army officer. He was one of the outstanding soldiers of the Second World War, a man of deep humanity, literary gifts and sense of humour. As a commander he combined strategic and tactical insight with the physical and moral courage of the fighting leader; and he inspired the total trust of his British and Indian troops. And they certainly needed inspiration, for this was a campaign lean on the mid-twentieth-century amenities, rich in joys like stinking jungle sores caused by the embedded heads of leeches, malaria and the infestation of wounds by swarming maggots. The claustrophobic atmosphere of the jungle produced its own fears and tension. For the British troops, especially, there was the corroding sense of having been forgotten by the people at home. Slim wrote:

... When I asked a man in his foxhole or sitting beside the track what he was, he would often, instead of answering 'I am a Lancashire Fusilier', or 'an FOO's signaller', or 'the Bren gunner of this section', say, 'I am four and two', or 'Three and ten'. He meant that was the number of years and months he had served in the Far East, and the unspoken question in his eyes was, 'How many more?' I could not answer him .... [2]

The Japanese plan in 1944 was to engulf the British defences in the Assam hills whose keys were the towns of Imphal and Kohima, and seize control of British communications with the interior of India, as a prelude to deeper invasion. The Japanese intended to infiltrate between the British defences, outflank and isolate them and thus bring about their collapse by rapid movement on foot through hill and jungle trails. The Japanese hopes of swift success were dashed by British resistance, by their own errors and by the clogging effects of the 'friction' inescapable in all battles. Nevertheless the British garrisons of Kohima and Imphal were soon closely invested. Had they fallen, the Japanese would have gained control of the scanty road and rail communications that linked the Indian plain and the battlefield. The campaign lasted from March until

July. It was a close-range business of infantry fighting, where some insignificant patch of ground like a district commissioner's tennis court be fought over again and again. It was the nearest thing in the Second World War to the trench-to-trench fighting of the Great War, and here too the survivors fought on among the bodies of the dead. The Japanese displayed their customary qualities of tactical cunning and disregard for death, of a capacity to endure near-starvation and lack of medical care. The battle became a test of sheer fighting endurance – and of ability to supply the forward troops.

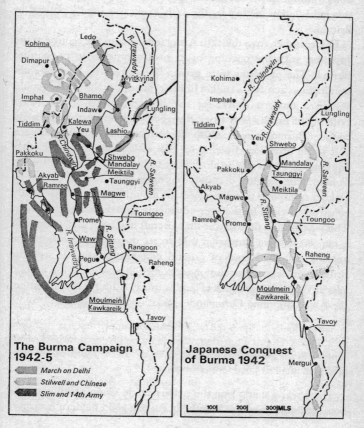

The Burma Campaign 1942-5

- March on Delhi
- Stilwell and Chinese
- Slim and 14th Army

Japanese Conquest of Burma 1942

100 200 300 MLS

While the Royal Air Force cut off the Japanese from all hope of air supply, British Dakotas dropped food, ammunition and medical supplies to British troops isolated on the ground. The Japanese hung on and on despite appalling losses and sufferings. Gradually British relieving troops forced their way up the valleys to re-open ground communications with the forward units. The Japanese grip on Kohima and Imphal was prised open. On 8 July the Japanese commander gave the order to retreat, and a starving and diseased wreck of an army fell back into Burma. Amid the clamour of news from the battle of Normandy just across the English channel, this hard-fought victory by the 14th Army was hardly noticed in Britain.

In December 1944 the 14th Army followed up the repulse of the Japanese with the opening of its own campaign to re-conquer Burma. The problems were great. There were no lines of communications across the Indian frontier into upper Burma that could sustain a modern army; for the Burmese roads and railways system ran northwards from Rangoon. However, a plan to re-conquer Burma from the south after seizing Rangoon from the sea had to be abandoned owing to lack of landing craft and other equipment. There was no alternative to an offensive over the Indian frontier. The problem of supply was again solved by air-power, by Dakota transports trundling over the mountains to airstrips swiftly constructed close to the ever-advancing spearheads of the army. This was the first time in war that aircraft had been used to nourish a major offensive campaign and to set operations free from the ancient umbilical cord of ground communications. It was the British army's most revolutionary contribution during the Second World War to the practice of land warfare. Admiral Mountbatten, the Allied Supreme Commander, South-east Asia, wrote:

... we gradually built up the largest-scale air supply that has ever been seen. It was not just a question of auxiliary supply, because 96% of our supplies to the Fourteenth Army went by air. In the course of this campaign we lifted 615,000 tons of supplies ... [3]

There was a shadow on this achievement. Concentration on the bomber had denied the Royal Air Force a good modern transport aircraft and a large transport fleet. Mountbatten remarks that three-quarters of the 14th Army's supplies were lifted by the United States Air Force and only a quarter by the Royal Air Force. However, half the reinforcements of 315,000 men flown in, and three-quarters of the casualties of 110,000 flown out, were in British aircraft. All this was made possible by ruthless overworking of aircraft and crews to make up for lack of adequate numbers.

The re-conquest of Burma was the most difficult and yet perhaps the most brilliant offensive campaign fought by the British army in the Second World War. In its sustained speed and daring it compares with Wellington's destruction of French power in Spain in 1813. Mountains, tropical forests, rivers that dwarfed the Rhine, swamps, all were traversed in a race to reach Rangoon before the monsoon broke in May. The Japanese themselves, despite their bitter resistance, were outfought in every phase of the fighting. By the skill and dash of its leadership and the mastery of difficult country shown by the troops, the 14th Army under Slim magnificently redeemed the collapses in Malaya and Burma in 1941. No less impressive contributions to victory were made by the engineers who built roads, airfields and bridges to sustain the advance, and the medical services, who reduced the tropical sickness rate from 120 to each battle casualty in 1943 to ten to one in 1945. Its decisive moment was the great victory of Meiktila–Mandalay, in which Slim brilliantly outwitted the Japanese in crossing the massive obstacle of the River Irrawaddy (February–March 1945).

While the main British force drove on towards Rangoon from the north (at one stage covering 300 miles in sixteen days), a task force advanced from the sea to Rangoon, only to find that the Japanese had already evacuated it. By 6 May 1945, the re-conquest of Burma was complete – but the news was again eclipsed at home by the celebration of the surrender of Germany.

A major amphibious operation was now planned for the recapture of Malaya, but before it could be mounted Japan surrendered, beaten by the United States in that maritime struggle which had ended with the elimination of the Japanese fleet, the re-conquest of the Philippines and the occupation of Okinawa. The dropping of the first nuclear bomb, on Hiroshima, on 6 August

1945, was the final, really unnecessary, push to tottering resistance. With, therefore, the first use of a weapon that transformed the character of war by its immense scale of destruction, the last 'conventional' great war of the era of gunpowder came to an end.

*

The organization of the British army in the field in the Second World War was adapted and modernized from the broad principles and structure proven in the Great War.

In 1939 the infantry division consisted of three infantry brigades each of three battalions, some 13,600 men of all ranks, together with artillery, 'cavalry' and engineers. The infantry remained armed with the bolt-action short magazine Lee Enfield rifle, supplemented, however, by fifty light machine-guns, twenty-two anti-tank rifles, two three-inch and twelve two-inch mortars per battalion. The divisional artillery consisted of seventy-two twenty-five-pounder gun-howitzers, an excellent weapon; and forty-eight anti-tank guns. The divisional 'cavalry' in 1939 comprised twenty-eight light tanks and forty-four open tracked Bren-gun carriers.

Corps troops in 1939 consisted of forty-eight field guns, thirty-six medium guns (six-inch howitzers or sixty-pounders) and thirty-six Bofors light anti-aircraft guns, and twenty-six Vickers heavy machine-guns.

By 1945 the light machine-guns in a division had more than doubled to 1,262, while the feeble anti-tank rifle had given way to the 'Piat' (Projector Infantry Anti-tank) of which there were 436 to a division. This weapon, fired from the shoulder, threw an armour-piercing explosive projectile. The anti-tank artillery had been increased to seventy-eight six-pounders and thirty-two seventeen-pounders. The reign of the bolt-action rifle was challenged by the machine-carbine, of which there were 6,525 per division in 1945. Mortars, too, had become a more important weapon – 359 of all calibres in 1945 against 126 in 1939. The infantry division of 1945 was armed against air attack with fifty-four light flak guns. The mechanized 'cavalry' of 1939 had been replaced by a reconnaissance regiment.

There was an immense expansion in armoured forces during the war, from three formations (1st and 7th Armoured Divisions and 1st Army Tank Brigade) in 1939 to twenty-eight armoured brigades by 1945. At the beginning of the war a British armoured division consisted of two armoured brigades, each of three regiments of mixed light and cruiser tanks, and a support group of two motor battalions with field and anti-tank artillery. Later the British followed the German example in halving the number of tanks per division and increasing the strength of trucked infantry, guns and engineers. By 1942 a British armoured division consisted of one armoured brigade (all cruisers), one trucked infantry brigade, one armoured car regiment, artillery and engineers. This was a much more supple and balanced formation than the earlier predominantly tank division. By 1942 the independent armoured brigade, forerunner of the modern brigade group, had made its appearance: three armoured regiments, a motor battalion, artillery and engineers. Such a brigade was placed under command of 1st New Zealand (infantry) Division at Second Alamein and after – the one example of the combination of armour and infantry in one divisional structure advocated by Auchinleck that was carried out by his successors. The expedient was successful, for the intimate co-operation between infantry and armour in the augmented New Zealand Division was in sharp contrast to the misunderstandings and mistrust elsewhere.

The expansion of armoured forces necessitated the creation of three Officer Cadet Training Units, finally combined in one large unit at Sandhurst. The tank schools at Bovington and Lulworth had to be greatly enlarged to supply instructors. In 1941 the post of Commander Royal Armoured Corps Training Establishments was created, and 'promoted' in 1942 to that of Major General Armoured Training. How belated and hasty was this expansion is illustrated by the fact that it was not until June 1940 that an Armoured Fighting Vehicles Directorate was set up in the War Office.

In the supply and support services it was the disasters of Norway and Flanders in 1940 that led to the change-over from the static conceptions of 1914–18. The Royal Corps of Signals, for example, realized that radio was not merely a short-term stand-by in the event of breakdown in landlines but an essential long-term alternative in fast-moving battles. The British, however, were handicapped by late delivery of adequate radio equipment. The 'roo miles radio/telephony' sets ordered in 1940 were not available in quantity and in reliable form until 1944. In overseas theatres of war meagre local telegraph facilities had to be supplemented by a high-speed long-distance radio network; and civilian trunk telephone lines augmented by new trunk cables or radio links. In 1941 the first Director of Signals was appointed in the War Office.

The Corps of Royal Engineers was yet another technical service to grow immensely in importance during the Second World War. In 1941 the office of Engineer-in-Chief was created in the War Office to advise the C.I.G.S. on all matters relating to engineering, whether policy or operations. He was also to be responsible for planning engineering activities, to have executive control (under the Quartermaster-General) of all works services, to advise the General Staff on engineering equipment, organization and training and on the collection and dissemination of engineering intelligence. The Engineer-in-Chief had two deputies to assist him.

In the field the work of the Royal Engineers was immense and astonishingly versatile. They were responsible for constructing airfields, roads, pipelines and all other 'civil' engineering projects, often working in territory only just won from the enemy. In the Middle East a Chief Engineer, Airfields, was appointed, so crucial had become the swift provision of forward airfields. However, the Royal Engineers were hampered in their construction work by shortage of mechanical earth-moving equipment, in which Britain was backward. In the Middle East the bulldozers – insufficient in number – were all American. The Royal Engineers also formed Chemical Warfare Groups and provided an Assault Brigade for D-Day for the demolition of enemy defences. Rail, port and waterway transportation was the responsibility of the Engineers, and in 1939 the first Director of Transportation was appointed in the War Office, followed in 1940 by an Inspector of Transportation Troops and Services. The peak strength of the Corps of Royal Engineers was 280,632 men; smaller than in the Great War but including a higher proportion of officers.

In the case of the R.A.S.C. the successful supply of armies in the foodless and almost waterless desert of North Africa and also in the inaccessible jungles of South-east Asia is itself a proof of the efficiency of its transport services and 'housekeeping'. The R.A.S.C. also created its own merchant marine of fifty assorted vessels.*

Like other support services, the Royal Army Ordnance Corps had to cope with wide variations of environment and with fast-moving campaigns, instead of establishing again the single great static organization of 1914–18. The scale of the R.A.O.C.'s operations is illustrated by some of the figures for the Middle East in October 1942 alone: 40,000 tons of stores received into base ordnance depots, 29,000 tons issued, including 595,000 separate items; 73,000 tons of ammunition received and 68,000 tons issued; nearly 11,000 vehicles received and 6,000 issued; and 94,000 boots repaired. In Italy the R.A.O.C. provided base laundries and bath units, mobile industrial gas units, a clothing factory and a paint factory. In preparation for the Normandy invasion 350 million separate items were packed. In the first two months after D-Day the R.A.O.C. supplied 380,000 tons of ammunition and 190,000 vehicles. The R.A.O.C. reached a peak of 8,000 officers and 130,000 men.

The swift development of sophisticated technology in war was reflected by the creation in October 1942 of the Royal Corps of Electrical and Mechanical Engineers. At the same time a Director of Mechanical Engineering was appointed inside the War Office, with Deputy Directors responsible for Workshop Planning, Organization, Special Projects and Technical (covering all aspects of technological development and design). The new corps was responsible for maintaining and repairing every kind of mechanical and electrical equipment: tanks, wheeled vehicles, artillery, small-arms, fire-control apparatus, searchlights, telecommunications, and so on. The work of R.E.M.E. was divided between a 1st echelon (light aid detachments well forward), 2nd (mobile workshops), 3rd (heavy equipment, semi-mobile), and 4th echelon (base workshops, virtually complete factories).

Compared with 1914–18 the organization of the Royal Army

---

*In 1967 responsibilities for transport previously divided between the R.E. and R.A.S.C. were united in a new Royal Corps of Transport.

Medical Corps was affected both by advances in medicine and surgery and by mobile warfare. In Flanders in 1940 there was little difference from 1918, and casualty clearing stations were often overrun by the enemy because of lack of transport. In 1941 an official report stated that the existing system was too cumbersome and immobile. There were delays in evacuating casualties, who were not benefiting as they ought from modern techniques because surgeons and equipment were too far behind the front. Radical changes followed. The field ambulance unit became highly mobile in order to evacuate casualties promptly. Instead of itself treating wounded, the advanced dressing station gave skilled first aid and sorted out casualties according to wound for treatment in field dressing stations. Of these there were one to an armoured division, two to an infantry division, together with a field surgical unit, which was a fully mobile team comprising a surgeon, an anaesthetist and an operating theatre. Every corps was to have a field surgical unit in addition. Field transfusion units were to be provided on the scale of three per corps and one per army. Each corps was to have a general hospital of 200 beds. The new organization was both vastly more flexible and gave complete medical treatment more swiftly than the old.

Immense strides were made during the Second World War in the co-operation of ground troops and aircraft. Before 1939 'army co-operation' in the British services had meant the provision by the air force of a few slow-flying artillery spotters. According to Royal Air Force doctrine, air-power was something quite apart from a land battle. The R.A.F. was trained and equipped only to bomb far behind the enemy front, not to act like the German dive-bombers as flying artillery, to be called down when needed by the troops on the ground. Thus the R.A.F., despite the bravery of its pilots, played no useful part in the fighting in Flanders in 1940, except in giving fighter cover over Dunkirk, and was not much help in the Desert battles until 1942, preferring to bomb German bases and supply lines rather than the fighting formations. Gradually the R.A.F. consented to join in the army's war, and the 'tactical air force' was born – fighter-bombers and light bombers working through radio links closely with the army in defence and attack.

Intimate air-army co-operation began in Auchinleck's time in the Middle East and was carried further by Montgomery, whose head-quarters were always next door to the Desert Air Force head-quarters. In Normandy in 1944 the allied tactical air forces intervened with immense effect on the battlefield. It was rocket-firing Typhoons of the R.A.F. that helped to smash a major German counter-stroke against the Americans.

The development of airborne forces led to the creation of the army's own 'air forces', the Army Air Corps, responsible at first for troop-carrying gliders and after the war for helicopters and light aircraft.

In provision for the recreation and welfare of the troops the Second World War marked a great advance on 1914–18. Although private charities like the Y.M.C.A. continued to supply their own canteens and rest centres, the Navy, Army and Air Force Institute (N.A.A.F.I.), which had taken the place of the old regimental canteens and institutes, became an immense catering, holidays and entertainment business. Every camp had its N.A.A.F.I.: a club room with bar, hot meals, cigarettes and sweets, toilet requisites on sale, and often a piano. Mobile N.A.A.F.I. shops served outlying units or troops in the field. In large base areas like the Middle East the N.A.A.F.I. provided splendid leave camps, complete with gardens, swimming pools, shops, restaurants, dance-halls and bars. In service clubs in cities like Cairo soldiers enjoyed all the comfort and facilities of a good hotel. It was a long way from the sutler's cart or the 'wet' canteen.

The British soldier of the Second World War himself was less simple in his loyalties and psychology, better educated, than his predecessor in the Great War. He had grown up in the era of radio, the cinema and the popular press. He was not so trusting and obedient as the 'tommy' of 1914–18. Resentment of unemployment and of the general failure of the traditional ruling classes to tackle resolutely the economic, social and political problems facing Britain between the wars had bred a widespread suspicion and cynicism about authority that, if rarely Communist, was at least 'bolshie'. The British army of the Second World War required intelligent management by its leaders. 'Public relations' became a respectable military activity, expressing itself in service and theatre newspapers and the arranged personal confrontation of troops and commanders. The style of leadership altered from the somewhat remote and formal authority of the Commander-in-Chief and his army commanders in France in the Great War to a more personal kind of leadership, more in the tradition of Cromwell or Napoleon or Garnet Wolseley than of Wellington. Commanders like Auchinleck, Alexander, Montgomery, perhaps most of all Slim, became immediate and personal figures to the troops, not merely remote embodiments of command to whom was owed unquestioning respect and obedience.

The men of the Second World War did not show the same qualities of stoical endurance as those of the Great War. Divisions lost their attacking 'edge' more quickly. A lower proportion of casualties than in the Great War was needed to bring a unit to the point of needing relief. This was the price paid for higher effective intelligence and initiative – for social progress. Not even in Burma did the British army endure quite the same degree of hardship and loss as the Japanese, or the Russians and Germans on the Eastern Front.

Yet the fighting personality of British troops remained essentially true to tradition. The British soldier took war and soldiering not seriously but with mocking humour. He was incapable of matching the single-minded German concentration on the job of winning a battle; equally incapable of matching the religious Emperor-worshipping fanaticism of the Japanese. The British army had not known such dedication to winning since the Commonwealth. Instead the British soldier would fight with unflinching doggedness while absolutely necessary and then break off for tea. Just as Wellington could never get his army to follow through victories like Salamanca and Vittoria to the complete destruction of the enemy, so British armies in the Second World War rarely capped a victory with a relentless pursuit. In Normandy, it was the British divisions that carried out the unglamorous slugging that consumed the enemy reserves, as they had at Blenheim and Waterloo; the Americans who made the dashing break-through. It was a just allotment of function according to capability.

*

Thus once again the British armed forces, ignored and neglected in peacetime by the nation, had saved the nation from extinction and had gone on, with the decisive help of great allies, to inflict defeat on the national enemies. It is an irony that many, who as civilians before 1939 must have grudged taxes for the support of the forces and believed hopefully in the League of Nations and appeasement, shared later as conscripts or volunteers in the struggle to bring down Nazi Germany and Japan by force. It was a national disaster that the effort needed to *win* the war was incalculably greater and more costly than that needed to *prevent* war between 1933 and 1939. In 1945, for the first time in history, Britain emerged from war completely exhausted and economically ruined.

Prolonged wars and huge military establishments under Louis XIV had ruined the French *ancien régime*. Britain had always avoided such ruinous involvement, always subordinating her war-making to the interests of national prosperity and growth. She had not hesitated to abandon her allies once a war passed beyond her own real interests into a mere sterile fight to a finish. However, in the two world wars of the twentieth century her politicians had not succeeded in avoiding such a fight to a finish and the colossal military establishments that went with it. Her industry and trade were no longer able to sustain the cost and technical needs of war. The result of having to pursue the war beyond the end of 1941 was the wreck of British prosperity and even solvency, and therefore of independent British power; the end of a cycle of history that had begun with William III's hard fights in the Low Countries and the founding of the Bank of England in the 1690s.

All this was the consequence of the failure of British governments and the British people to live up to their responsibilities as a world power in the 1930s.

V

Full Circle

20

The Army
and the
Retreat from Empire

IN 1945 therefore the British empire was like a magnificent mansion and a noble estate fallen to heirs encumbered with debt and with sadly diminished income. It was hard indeed, in the hour of victory, for statesmen whose entire lives had been shaped by the fact of British greatness to realize that the imperial façade no longer represented power, but weakness and bankruptcy.

Gradually the brutal facts thrust themselves home after 1945. Portions of the imperial estate like India were yielded up. The British, however, like the indigent aristocrats they so resembled, clung on to their old pretensions. Even when almost the entire imperial estate had been dispersed – tenants, 'family' and staff – the British went on pretending that it essentially still existed in the form of a free association or 'Commonwealth'.

The two decades that followed the Second World War constituted therefore a period of painful adjustment, when all the power, wealth and empire won in the two centuries after 1690 finally vanished. It was a major turning-point in British history. And just as the marches of neglected, underpaid red-coats and their thundering volleys had once marked the surge of British expansion, so the soldier in khaki-drill or battledress guarded the hesitant retreat from empire. While the politicians havered, while authority crumbled, the soldier tried to keep order. And when at last the British had gone, from country after country, it was found that the British army was the only British institution to leave a permanent mark – the mark of order and organization amid a carnival of collapsing parliamentary government.

India was the largest single British possession, both in territory and in population; an empire in its own right. Since the late nineteenth century India had come to seem the very foundation of British world power. It was certainly the greatest single factor in the British military system. India had lain at the heart of all British strategic problems and military re-organizations. Indian garrison life and expeditionary warfare in the hills of the north-west frontier had become an essential part of the British soldier's outlook, mystique and tradition. It was India that had made Britain a Far Eastern power; that had created Britain's concern for the Middle East and Mediterranean, and led to her progressive involvement in these areas. India not only swallowed a large part of the British army; it was itself a reservoir of British-officered Indian troops available for use in major conflicts.

When in 1947 the Labour government granted independence to India in the divided form of India and Pakistan, it was therefore a smashing blow at the whole fabric of the British empire. It was more devastating than the loss of the American colonies in 1783, for America had never meant so much, strategically or sentiment-ally, as India. Nevertheless the Labour government's decision was courageous, indeed ruthlessly realistic. The Britain of 1947, propped up by American loans, simply could not afford the cost of holding India by force against Indian hostility. The Mutiny of 1857 too still cast its long shadow.

Ceylon as well became a dominion and Burma an independent country outside the Commonwealth. Thus the whole of the old Indian empire vanished. Only Malaya and Borneo remained of the empire in the Far East, and these two were also scheduled for early independence.

In the communal riots and massacres in India in 1947, the old British Indian army died. It died not without glory; for the discipline of the soldiers, their obedience to their officers and their pride in their regiment survived in a year of frenzied racial and religious killing. For the British troops in India, this was the moment to take leave of a second home – perhaps the army's true home. And although the British were going, and the Indian politi-cians were pleased, the crowds were silent or weeping as the troops marched behind their bands to the dockside.

The far-reaching political and strategic consequences of such a gigantic imperial loss as India were not perceived. The realistic decision to evacuate India stood alone. In Egypt, in Palestine, in Libya, in Aden, in Cyprus, in Malta, the British still guarded the communications of a now-vanished Indian empire: large garrisons, expensive installations; all now without purpose. Whereas the eastern empire itself had been given up, the Labour government, and after 1951 the Conservative government, held on grimly to an imperial lifeline that now led nowhere. Not until 1948 was the expensive garrison withdrawn from Palestine and Jew and Arab left to fight it out. Not until 1946–7 did the British army withdraw its vast base installations from the Nile Delta; only to be re-installed at colossal expense in the Suez Canal Zone, which the British government said could never be abandoned. In the face of Egyptian terrorism, this base too was abandoned in 1954. A new base was then expensively created in Cyprus, despite the lack of a large deep-water port. When Cyprus was abandoned in 1959, yet another new base was created in Kenya, only in its turn to be abandoned when the British left Kenya. All this was in pursuit of a Middle East strategy that only made sense if the British were still a great power in the Indian Ocean. In the 1950s and 1960s British world strategy still followed the basic patterns of the nineteenth century: a chicken that had lost its head – India – but still ran round in circles.

While the British government clung on successively to these pointless military bases, unwelcome to the local peoples, the army had to endure the consequence – terrorism. In Palestine, Egypt, Cyprus, a dreary pattern repeated itself: murder, arson, ambush, cities divided by barbed wire, road-blocks, searches.

The army also bore 'the brunt of governmental tardiness in getting out of African colonies that in the end also it was found too expensive to hold down. Here too the army had to deal with riots and terrorism; had to fight political movements headed by the very politicians to whom eventually the British government handed over power. Between 1947 and 1967, in the twilight of imperial rule, the army was involved in maintaining order at one time or another in Aden, Kenya, the Gold Coast, British Honduras, Singapore, British Guiana, Hong Kong, Nassau, the Cameroons,

Jamaica, Kuwait, Zanzibar, Borneo, Tanganyika, Uganda and Mauritius. The incidental unpleasantness of imperial retreat, like the pains of expansion earlier, fell not on the British at home, but on the army.

However, after 1945 the army's task was not only to cover the slow retreat from empire. As in the past it had to combine the roles of imperial gendarmerie and of a field army ever ready to fight in Europe. Between 1945 and 1948 long-maturing mutual suspicion and distrust between the western powers and Communist Russia broke into the open. In eastern Europe, occupied by the Red Army, all vestiges of parliamentary democracy rapidly vanished in favour of Communist dictatorship. In the west powerful Communist parties exploited the internal weaknesses and hardships of societies emerging from war. And in between lay Germany, now a vast power vacuum in the heart of Europe, the supreme prize to be contended for. The Cold War was under way even as the Second World War spluttered out. In 1945 British troops were involved in clashes with Communist Yugoslavia in the disputed territory of Trieste. In 1946 they supported the Greek government in a war against Communist guerrillas until, in 1947, British poverty forced the Labour government to shed the responsibility to the Americans. Abortive peace conferences sharpened Russian–Western ill-feeling, especially over the future of Germany.

The British forces in Europe therefore found themselves swiftly changing from occupation troops in ex-enemy countries to guardians of the West from possible aggression from the East. Yet by 1948 the massive allied strength of 1945 had been dissipated by demobilization. The problem now was to recreate the military power of the West.

In March 1948 Britain signed the Brussels Treaty with France and the Benelux countries, which created the Western Union organization. It was a watershed in British history, because for the first time Britain consented to commit herself to a military alliance in peacetime that involved her in Europe. She guaranteed in 1948 – as she had refused to do before 1914 or 1939 – to afford any attacked party to the Brussels Treaty 'all the military and other aid and assistance in [her] power'.

A sketchy international command organization, Uniforce, was set up under the chairmanship of Field-Marshal Montgomery, with a French land commander-in-chief, and British air and sea commanders-in-chief. Negotiations were opened, through the medium of Canada, to bring the United States into a larger Western alliance.

The Russians spurred on these developments, firstly by their *coup d'état* in Czechoslovakia in February 1948 and secondly by establishing their land blockade of the Western occupation zones in Berlin in June 1948. The token allied garrisons would have been unable to resist a major assault. Nor were the allied forces in Germany (including the British Army of the Rhine) strong enough to block a Russian invasion of Western Germany. Throughout the Berlin blockade (finally broken by the allied airlift) it was American Strategic Air Command bombers with atom bombs stationed in Britain that deterred the Russians (if they were deterred) from making use of their overwhelming strength on the ground.

Under the stimulus of the Berlin blockade the North Atlantic Treaty was signed in April 1949, involving the United States directly in the defence of Europe (an immense departure in policy for them too). In September 1949 the North Atlantic Treaty Organization, the military machinery of the alliance, began to be created. Belatedly, in September 1951, under the fresh spur of the Communist North Korean invasion of South Korea, Uniforce was replaced by S.H.A.P.E. (Supreme Headquarters Allied Powers Europe) under Eisenhower as Supreme Commander and Montgomery as his deputy. The British Army of the Rhine was henceforth allotted to N.A.T.O. British generals commanded N.A.T.O.'s Northern Army Group in Germany, and also in Norway and Denmark.

In Korea it was the Americans under McArthur who blocked the Communist invasion and then swept them back by a brilliant amphibious stroke deep in their rear at Inchon. However, the British Commonwealth contributed a division to the later bitter fighting that followed the intervention of the Chinese Communists. This division included a brigade from the United Kingdom, which distinguished itself in the retreat from the River Yalu by its skill and discipline. The solidarity of British prisoners, both officers and other ranks, in the face of ruthless and brutal Communist brain-washing also reflected credit on the discipline of the British soldier and on his unquenchable sense of humour.

The Korean War aroused a fresh fear that the Red Army might fall upon western Europe. The N.A.T.O. powers made a luckless decision to create an army of fifty divisions, a target never reached. This intention necessitated re-arming Western Germany. In 1954, after four years of tortuous negotiation, a project to merge the French army, the Benelux forces and the new German forces in a European army, the European Defence Community, was rejected by the French National Assembly. The British government ingeniously saved the situation by suggesting that Western Germany might join an enlarged Western Union, so that German forces could still be tightly corsetted into an international framework. At the same time the British allayed French fears of German military resurgence by promising to maintain a British army of four divisions and a tactical air force on the continent of Europe for as long as a majority of Western Union powers wished. This was yet another watershed in British foreign policy and military strategy.

In the 1950s the British army was stretched to the utmost. As well as Europe and Korea and the traditional role of imperial peace-keeping, there was a full-scale struggle in Malaya against Communist guerrillas, which lasted from 1948 to 1960. It ended with the only victory won by a Western power against practitioners of revolutionary warfare. The British adapted themselves to fighting and living for long periods deep in the jungle on a minimum of supplies. They outwitted and outfought the Communist guerrillas at their own game of jungle tracking, camping and ambush. The Royal Navy blockaded the coasts and cut the guerrillas off from outside help. The Royal Air Force mastered the techniques of accurate air supply and tactical air support to the deep-penetration groups on the ground. At the same time the enemy's ability to live off the local population was destroyed by resettling villagers in model villages under government protection. The ultimate victory of the British forces over the Communists enabled the British to yield their Malayan colony to a democratic and friendly government.

In all the operations that covered the imperial retreat from the Far East, the Middle East and Africa after 1947, the British army displayed not only professional versatility, but its traditional qualities of cool-headedness and good humour. Its techniques of riot control avoided unnecessary shooting and bloodshed. Despite the provocation offered by the murder of comrades, sometimes in cold blood, the British soldier rarely went beyond roughness into the kind of persistent and systematic brutality to which other armies in similar situations resorted.

Meanwhile in Germany the British Army of the Rhine trained and prepared for a major defensive war. What Britain lacked in the 1950s was a powerful strategic reserve ready to serve British *national* policy, and the land, sea and air transport to move such a reserve. This lack was humiliatingly demonstrated to the world by the Suez operations in 1956 – as ripe a political and military fiasco as the British had ever perpetrated in centuries of devotion to half-cock operations of war.

The political purpose of the Anglo-French expedition to Suez was to topple President Nasser of Egypt off his perch, it being believed that he threatened the whole British and French position in North Africa and the Middle East. The ostensible purpose was to separate the Egyptians and the Israelis, already at war. The immediate hope was to re-establish Anglo-French control of the Suez Canal, recently nationalized by Nasser.

In every respect the Suez expeditions compared unfavourably with Sir Garnet Wolseley's expedition to Egypt in 1882, although since 1882 there had been all the valuable lessons in amphibious warfare afforded by Gallipoli, North Africa and D-Day. Wolseley improvised swiftly and well; in 1956 the politicians and the servicemen equally made a hash of it.

The ditherings and uneasy conscience of the British Prime Minister meant that the invasion of Egypt took place after ample advance warning to Egypt and the world, and in circumstances where Britain and France were diplomatically isolated and Egypt could count on the benevolence of the entire world, including both Russia and America; a conjunction that it took diplomatic genius to produce. In any event British finances were so precarious that as soon as the guns fired, there was a run on the pound; and the imminent collapse of sterling brought about the instant collapse of British belligerence. However, the military operations themselves showed British military history repeating itself *yet again* in an appalling muddle of an amphibious invasion – the very kind of operation a maritime power ought to be good at.

In the first place, the Mediterrannean bases to which the British government had clung so expensively and stubbornly – Cyprus and Libya – proved inadequate or unusable. The invasion force had to sail all the way from Gibraltar and Malta, with consequent delays, loss of surprise and complication of control. In the second place the equipment and organization for swiftly assembling and moving a large seaborne force were lacking. The tanks went to the embarkation ports by courtesy of Messrs Pickford, while the loading of ships was not 'tactical', so that gear wanted urgently was packed at the bottom of holds. The aircraft for dropping the parachute troops were obsolete. The British contemplated the modern equipment of their French allies with envy. The confusions and sluggishness of the British operations at Port Said gained nothing by comparison with the faultless speed of Israeli mobilization and the relentless pace of the Israeli conquest of Sinai. There was something awfully familiar about the Suez operation: shades of York's operations in Flanders, of the Crimea, of Gallipoli, of Tudor landings in France or Spain.

The Suez operation was a watershed in British history. Bluntly world pressure (particularly against the pound) at last thrust home the message that Britain was finished as a great independent power. Now the British government began to pack up the rest of the Empire in precipitate haste and look to Europe for the future. Militarily Suez led to a revolution in defence policy. With the Defence White Paper of 1957 the attempt to maintain the large conventional armed forces of a traditional world power (especially in land forces) was abandoned. Instead, the contingency of a crisis between the great powers was to be met by the nuclear (hydrogen bomb) deterrent. This followed an earlier shift in American policy in favour of a predominantly nuclear strategy. Lesser crises, such as civil turmoil in the dwindling empire, were to be met by a conventional strategic reserve stationed in the United Kingdom and flown out swiftly to trouble-spots by an airlift capacity then yet to be created. Garrisons overseas were to be drastically reduced. Since nuclear deterrents, once developed, were cheaper than large conventional forces, the main purpose of the new policy was to cut defence expenditure, particularly on the army. Although the emphasis on strategic mobility through air-power gave an impression of a new look, Duncan Sandys (the then Minister of Defence) was really only treading the same ground as Cardwell and his Victorian predecessors. Sandys's policy eventually achieved some economies because of a special advantage not available to the Victorians – the winding-up of the Empire and of the consequent need to protect it.

The reduction of the role of conventional land forces decided on in 1957 permitted the abolition of conscription in 1960. After 1945 the unsettled state of the world, followed immediately by the beginning of the Cold War, had required larger forces than could be recruited voluntarily. For the first time in British history (except for a few months in 1939) there was National Service in peacetime. By 1957 it was becoming an accepted institution, part of the pattern of British life. Although regular soldiers grew bored with training successive intakes of conscripts, the National Servicemen, especially when they became non-commissioned officers or junior officers, brought all the talents and diversity of the nation into the forces. It was a misfortune therefore that National Service, which had come about so tardily in British history, was again ended. Britain once more became the only European nation without a citizen army. The army went back to its recruiting campaigns, glad in some ways to become once more a small force of highly trained professionals. Once again the army and nation began to drift apart, as the army became a closed 'family', small in numbers.

The new professional army after 1960 presented curious contrasts of change and continuity in comparison with the army before 1939. Professionally it was more serious, more keen, more skilled, than the polo-players of the 1930s – it was master of sophisticated modern weapons and techniques of administration. In its social structure, its way of life and its values, however, the

British army survived the years 1939–60 with surprisingly little
change. The British officer corps was still dominated by 'the
gentleman', although the proportion of public-school men, and in
particular of those from a few leading schools, had fallen greatly
since the beginning of the century. After the Second World War
the Labour government in fact tried to break down the class basis
of the officer corps by opening the Royal Military Academy,
Sandhurst (formed by the amalgamation of the Royal Military
Academy, Woolwich and the Royal Military College, Sandhurst)
to suitable men from the ranks. This reform did not defeat a tradition dating back to the 1660s: 'ranker' officer-cadets proved to be
mostly men from upper- or upper-middle-class backgrounds who
were doing their National Service, whereas pre-war officers of the
so-called 'Y-Cadet' scheme had been true rankers. The way of
life, manners and values of the British officer corps in the 1960s
remained so strongly that of the rural upper class that in ten years
of service a grammar-school boy became indistinguishable from
the son of a land-owner. Alone among the officers of Western
nations, the British officer was still a 'type' recognizably distinct
from the industrial executive. The social gulf – the gulf in status –
between the British officer and his non-commissioned officers and
men equally remained far wider than in European or North
American armies.

After the end of conscription the army therefore again ceased to
reflect the social patterns of the nation, for the urban middle
classes (the executives of industry and commerce) saw little opportunity in a military career. The army returned essentially to its
traditional pattern of a working-class rank-and-file officered by the
upper classes.

Another sign that the British army had survived the social
revolution of the mid twentieth century with its traditions less
damaged than those of other armies lay in the continued power of
regimental loyalties. During the Second World War the regimental
system broke down. It was impossible to solve the problem of drafts
and reinforcements within self-contained regimental compartments. Available men, of no matter what regiment, had to be posted
to battalions that were under strength, of no matter again what

regiment. The separatism of the regiments also made it difficult for the British to emulate the German capacity for meshing heterogeneous units into battle-groups. The practical needs of modern war pointed at only one answer: a Corps of Infantry, like the existing Corps of Royal Artillery, with numbered but not named regiments, a central reservoir of reinforcements, and free transfer of officers and men from unit to unit according to need. This was the German and American system.

Nevertheless after the Second World War passionate sentimental loyalties prevented a Corps of Infantry being formed. Instead all kinds of uneasy expedients were employed in order to try to reconcile flexibility of posting and reinforcement with the independence of the ancient regiments. The task of preserving the regiments was made more difficult by the need to reduce the number of infantry battalions and cavalry regiments, both because of the vastly higher proportion of the army's strength now absorbed in the technical or support services, and because the army's total strength was limited to 185,000 men after the end of conscription. From 1958 to 1961 there were a series of painful marriages between regiments to reduce the number of battalions by half. It is to be wondered whether in the long run it was not more painful for, say, a Royal Scots Fusilier to be joined to a Highland Light Infantryman in a hybrid called the Royal Highland Fusiliers than that both should disappear into a Corps of Infantry – especially when all these new hybrids themselves had to be re-amalgamated later on in the 1960s, when the problems of recruitment and reinforcement became finally insoluble on the basis of 'independent' regiments. Once again the awful fate of a Corps of Infantry was avoided by the formation of 'large regiments' or 'administrative brigades'. A 'large regiment' was formed out of a territorially contiguous group of existing regiments, each of which became a battalion in the new unit. In an 'administrative brigade', the constituent regiments retained their own names and existence. Within the large regiment or administrative brigade there was complete flexibility of posting and reinforcement.

However, even these units soon proved too small for easy contraction or expansion in the number of units, or to allow allotment of manpower on a large scale. Still the ultimate horror of a Corps of Infantry was resisted, and in 1967 the large regiments and administrative brigades themselves began to merge into administrative *divisions*. Traditionalists were happy to note that the new structure of the army very nearly repeated that of Wellington's Peninsular army, with four infantry divisions and a Light Division – plus the original royal guards of 1660. What real regimental tradition, directly carrying forward the histories of individual regiments, continued to live in the eleven or twelve battalion divisions is hard to see. In fact the final result of all the shifts and expedients after 1945 was essentially to produce five corps of infantry instead of a single one. Only the Guards and the Parachute Regiment survived these changes, although the title 'Brigade of Guards' was altered to conform with the new system as 'The Guards Division'.

By virtue of the British talent for the illogical, the 'division' had in fact disappeared as a field formation in 1956, when at last Auchinleck's proposals of 1942 for a brigade-group organization, so scorned at the time, were adopted. The infantry brigade was integrated with armour and given its own artillery. In the 1950s the British forces in Germany, in common with other N.A.T.O. armies, were trained and equipped to fight a tactical nuclear war, tactical nuclear weapons now being relied on to repair Western weakness of numbers. The weapons were all American, and could only be fired by American permission as manifested through electronic devices; an indication of Europe's strategic and technological dependence on the United States.

In the high administration of the army and its political control the two decades after 1945 were also marked by drastic re-organizations. Although during the Second World War Winston Churchill had been Minister of Defence as well as War Premier, this had been a personal office, and there had been no *ministry* of defence. In 1946 the Labour government created a true Ministry of Defence in which were incorporated all the inter-service defence committees and planning staffs set up in the previous thirty years. It was only half a century since this idea had been first mooted. The ministry was manned partly by civil servants, partly by the armed forces.

Its principal task was to allot resources between the three services and to co-ordinate a single defence effort. In 1963 an even more radical reform was made, this time by a Conservative government. Just as during the nineteenth century the separate 'empires' within military administration had been gradually united, a process culminating in the creation of the Army Council in 1904, so now the separate service empires themselves – War Office, Admiralty, Air Ministry – were to become mere departments of a new Ministry of Defence organization. The political heads of the service departments were now to be only Ministers of State, junior to and under the Secretary of State for Defence. The new Defence Council consisted of the Secretary of State for Defence, the Ministers of State for the defence departments, the Chief of Defence Staff (soldiers, sailors and airmen alternating), the Chief of Naval Staff, the Chief Scientific Adviser and the Permanent Under-Secretary of State. Thus the long and glorious history of the Admiralty (under one name or form and another) and the much shorter history of the War Office came to an end.

At the same time the integration of the armed forces and of their supply into one machine was also carried through at a lower level. A Defence Operations Centre and Executive were set up to co-ordinate the operations and operational planning of the services. Separate procurement by each service of clothing, food, fuel and medical stores was replaced by a common procurement organization.

In October 1964 Denis Healey, Defence Secretary in the new Labour government, carried on this radical process of reconstruction and unification. As well as responsibility for his own service, each Minister of Defence was given responsibility for functional questions in particular fields that cut right across service boundaries. This was only a first step, for in November 1967 there was a completely fresh reconstruction which finally altered the fundamental principles on which service administration was organized. Instead of a division of the Ministry of Defence into separate service departments, each still with a wide measure of autonomy, there was to be a division of responsibility according to function.

Two Ministers of Defence were appointed to work under the

Secretary of State for Defence. The Minister of Defence for Equipment was responsible for research, development, production and arms sales – whether for land, sea or air equipment. The Minister of Defence for Administration was responsible for personnel (manpower planning) and logistics (material supply, 'housekeeping'). The residual service departments were now placed under mere Parliamentary Under-Secretaries. All six ministers (including the Secretary of State for Defence) were to be members of the Defence Council.

The new integrated and functional defence organization was an attempt to solve the problem of effective and economical defence by a completely new approach to organization, rather than by a tinkering with the haphazard product of history.

The Labour government also re-organized, or rather virtually destroyed, the army's reserve forces by the Reserve Forces Act of 1966, and by other measures in 1969. Haldane's Territorial Army was reduced first in 1966 to an internal security force, and then in 1969 abolished except for tiny cadres. Apart from Regular Army reservists, the only remaining reserve forces were the Territorial and Army Volunteer Reserve ('the Volunteers') created by the Act of 1966; in 1969 it numbered some 50,000 men, enough to flesh out the army for small wars or emergencies.

In 1968 an Army Strategic Command was created and the bulk of British field forces in the United Kingdom allotted to it.

All this *appeared* to add up to an astonishing revolution in organization. But in many ways the 'new look' had familiar features from the past. The 'Army Strategic Command', despite its helicopters, air transport, sophisticated weapons and modish title, was really the same body of troops always ready for the field that Cardwell, Brodrick, Arnold-Forster and Haldane had tried to create. The British Army of the Rhine, though part of N.A.T.O., was a reincarnation of the Marquis of Granby's troops in Germany during the Seven Years' War, and of other British expeditionary forces back to the time of Elizabeth I. Only the garrisoning of British troops in Europe in peacetime was new.

The really revolutionary transformation was in British national strategy as a whole. In the White Paper of 1968 the Labour

Government announced that what was left of Britain's imperial and global strategic roles would be liquidated by 1971. British forces and British strategy were to be entirely concentrated on Europe. The decision was a belated and unwilling acknowledgement that a cycle of three hundred years of imperial expansion and contraction had come to an end. It was one of the great turning points of British history. Marlborough's and Wellington's victories, the great eighteenth-century sea-fights, mercantile expansion, the industrial revolution, world empire, world power – all of it was past. Britain again stood where she had stood in the reign of Elizabeth I – a second-class, perhaps a third-class, power in terms of relative economic strength, population and warlike capability, living precariously in the face of keen trade rivalry and sandwiched between the superpowers.

For the army, however, the implications of this transformation were immense. It faced what was in terms of its own history a wholly novel situation. For it was itself solely the product of imperial and global needs. Now, by the grace of the unlikely combination of Conservative and Labour policies, Britain was left therefore with an imperial army in a European role. Yet British history, and recent history in particular, made plain that Britain needed for this role not a small, all-regular force, but a large field army formed by the mobilizable trained manpower of the nation.

Indeed, after the Labour Government's re-organizations, the reserves were weaker than they had been for a hundred years – far weaker than in 1914 or 1939, when at least there had stood behind the regulars the fourteen divisions of the Territorials. Even at the cost of totally denuding the United Kingdom of troops, and leaving it therefore without protection against civil disorder or insurrection, the British Army of the Rhine could only be brought up to war establishment; not enlarged. That army was therefore capable of fighting for no more than a week or so before wasting away from want of sleep and reinforcements.

The totally inappropriate (but cheap and politically convenient) choice of an imperial mercenary army without reserves for the defence of Europe was justified by the Labour Government by reference to their faith that prolonged non-nuclear conflict would be impossible in Europe (the Europe of the North Atlantic area stretches from Norway's arctic frontier with Soviet Russia to Turkey's Caucasian frontier with the same power). The Labour Government was certain that major trouble would either be deterred by nuclear weapons, or, if it did occur, go swiftly nuclear. Troops on the ground were wanted only as a plate-glass window, by breaking through which the Russian burglar must announce his presence, thus setting off the nuclear anti-burglar devices.

Here was a novel version of all the ancient heresies by which British governments had for centuries deluded themselves that there was no need to organize in peacetime the kind of armed forces that British involvement in Europe since the days of Elizabeth I had repeatedly shown we needed. If the politicians' gamble, that a prolonged non-nuclear conflict anywhere between the Arctic and the Caucasus (a conflict that might take the form of internal subversion) was impossible, proved as mistaken as the gambles of their predecessors, the British would once again have to create citizen forces from scratch – if they were given the time. No doubt the nation would again blame the army and the generals for lack of initial success against a thoroughly prepared aggressor.

*

In their history, the British solved the problem of reconciling military power with civilian government (and a civilian society) with remarkable success, fundamentally because of their immunity from invasion behind seas commanded by the Royal Navy. On the other hand, the British at times ran close to national catastrophe in their neglect and suspicion of soldiers. May it be that they never run it too close.

REFERENCES

CHAPTER 2

1. Garrett Mattingly, *The Defeat of the Spanish Armada* (1959), p. 265.
2. ibid., p. 242 on Spanish ships and seamanship.
3. ibid., pp. 265–8 for the effects of gunnery.
4. Gladys Scott Thomson, *Lords-Lieutenants in the Sixteenth Century* (1923), p. 46.
5. ibid., p. 73.
6. ibid., p. 88.
7. ibid., p. 90.
8. ibid., p. 69.
9. ibid., p. 87.
10. ibid., p. 104.

CHAPTER 3

1. 'A Right Excellent and Pleasant Dialogue between Mercury and an English Soldier', quoted in Gladys Scott Thomson, *op. cit.*, p. 115.
2. *Henry IV, Part I*, Act IV, Scene II.
3. J. E. Neale, *English Historical Review*, vol. XLV, p. 381.
4. G. C. Cruikshank, *Elizabeth's Army* (1966), p. 142.

CHAPTER 4

1. C. H. Firth, *Cromwell's Army* (1962), pp. 8–9.
2. Quoted in Sir Sibbald Scott, *The British Army, Its Origins, Progress and Equipment* (1868), vol. I, p. 402.
3. Quoted in ibid., p. 403.
4. Dalton, *Life of Sir Edward Cecil*, quoted in Firth, *op. cit.*, p. 2.
5. ibid.
6. Quoted in Firth, *op. cit.*, p. 3.
7. Monro, *His Expedition*, quoted in J. F. C. Fuller, *The Decisive Battles of the Western World* (1963), vol. II, p. 60.
8. S. R. Gardiner, *The Constitutional Documents of the Puritan Revolution* (1906), p. 69.
9. Firth, *op. cit.*, p. 13.
10. ibid.
11. Scott, *op. cit.*, p. 415.
12. ibid., p. 415.

13. ibid., p. 422, note 1.
14. Gardiner, *op. cit.*, p. 209.
15. ibid., p. 227.

CHAPTER 5

1. Quoted in C.H. Firth, *op. cit.*, p. 23.
2. ibid., pp. 24–5.
3. ibid., p. 31.
4. ibid.
5. Speech XI in Thomas Carlyle, *The Letters and Speeches of Oliver Cromwell* (1904), vol. III, pp. 64–5.
6. ibid., vol. I, p. 154.
7. Quoted in Firth, *op. cit.*, p. 142.
8. ibid., p. 138.
9. ibid., p. 144.
10. ibid., p. 294.
11. ibid., p. 60.
12. ibid., pp. 65–6.
13. Quoted in G.M. Trevelyan, *History of England* (1945), p. 145.
14. L.F. Solt, *Saints in Arms: Puritanism and Democracy in Cromwell's Army* (1959).
15. ibid.
16. ibid.

CHAPTER 6

1. J.R. Western, *The English Militia in the Eighteenth Century* (1965), p. 28.
2. Colonel Clifford Walton, *History of the British Standing Army; A.D. 1660 to 1700* (1894), p. 479.
3. David Ogg, *England in the Reigns of James II and William III* (1955), p. 158.
4. Walton, *op. cit.*, pp. 47–8, note 118.
5. 1 Will. & Mar. Sess. 2 Cap. 2, quoted in Sir Charles Grant Robertson, *Select Statutes, Cases and Documents* (1942), p. 131.

CHAPTER 7

1. General Kane, quoted in E.M. Lloyd, *A Review of the History of Infantry* (1908), p. 139.
2. See Major R.E. Scouller, *The Armies of Queen Anne* (1966), Chapter 1, for an excellent analysis of the rise of the Secretary-at-War.
3. Quoted in Colonel Clifford Walton, *op. cit.*, p. 448.
4. ibid., p. 451, note.
5. ibid., p. 453.
6. ibid., p. 671, note.
7. ibid., p. 671.
8. ibid., p. 488.
9. Quoted in Scouller, p. 108.
10. Walton, *op. cit.*, pp. 716–17.
11. ibid., p. 717.
12. Quoted in Scouller, *op. cit.*, p. 165.

13. ibid., p. 154.
14. Private Dean, *A Journal of the Campaign in Flanders*, quoted in Scouller, *op. cit.*, p. 208.
15. Captain Robert Parker, quoted in Scouller, *op. cit.*, p. 224.
16. Scouller, *op. cit.*, p. 224.
17. C. T. Atkinson, *Marlborough and the Rise of the British Army* (1930), p. 217.

CHAPTER 8

1. J. R. Western, *op. cit.*, p. 91.
2. ibid., p. 96.
3. E. M. Lloyd, *op. cit.*, p. 179.
4. ibid., p. 154.
5. ibid., p. 162.
6. J. F. C. Fuller, *op. cit.*, vol. II, p. 206.
7. ibid., p. 210.
8. Lloyd, *op. cit.*, p. 147.
9. ibid.
10. Quoted in Fuller, *op. cit.*, vol. II, p. 201.
11. R. Quarré de Verneuil, *L'Armée en France depuis Charles VII jusqu'à la Révolution (1439–1789)*, (1880), p. 266.
12. Lloyd, *op. cit.*, p. 145.
13. ibid., p. 172.
14. ibid., p. 171.
15. ibid., p. 170.

CHAPTER 9

1. John Fortescue, *A History of the British Army* (1899–1912), vol. II, p. 73.
2. ibid., p. 141.
3. Julian Corbett, *England in the Seven Years' War* (1907), vol. II, p. 173.

CHAPTER 10

1. Sir Reginald Savory, *His Britannic Majesty's Army in Germany During the Seven Years' War* (1966), p. 303.
2. ibid., p. 305.
3. ibid.
4. E. M. Lloyd, *op. cit.*, p. 184.
5. Steven Watson, *The Reign of George III, 1760–1815* (1960), p. 200.
6. J. F. C. Fuller, *op. cit.* (1961), vol. II, p. 297.
7. Admiral Sir Herbert Richmond, *Statesmen and Seapower* (1947), p. 151.
8. Lloyd, *op. cit.*, p. 186.
9. ibid.
10. Richard Glover, *Peninsular Preparation: The Reform of the British Army 1795–1809* (1963), p. 117.
11. Lloyd, *op. cit.*, p. 201.
12. Guibert, *Oeuvres Militaires* (1803), vol. III, p. 212.
13. ibid., p. 250.

CHAPTER 11

1. E. M. Lloyd, *op. cit.*, p. 197.
2. John Fortescue, *A History of the British Army* (1899–1912), vol. IV, Part I, p. 322.
3. Quoted in Hugh Thomas, *The Story of Sandhurst* (1961), p. 20.
4. Richard Glover, *Peninsular Preparation: The Reform of the British Army 1795–1809* (1963), p. 178.
5. ibid., pp. 178–9.
6. ibid., p. 178.
7. ibid., p. 138.
8. J. F. C. Fuller, *Sir John Moore's System of Training* (1925).
9. Quoted in Glover, *op. cit.*, p. 130.
10. ibid., p. 131.
11. ibid., p. 140.
12. ibid., p. 142.
13. ibid., p. 160.
14. Christopher Hibbert, *Corunna* (1961), p. 32.
15. Michael Glover, *Wellington's Peninsular Victories*, p. 23.
16. Michael Glover, *op. cit.*, p. 25.
17. Michael Glover, *op. cit.*, pp. 25–6.
18. Marshall Bugeaud, quoted in Charles Oman, *Wellington's Army* (1912), pp. 91–2.

CHAPTER 12

1. T. H. McGuffie (ed.), *Rank and File* (1964), p. 320.
2. S. G. P. Ward, *Wellington's Headquarters: A Study of the Administrative Problems in the Peninsula 1809–1814* (1957), p. 3, note.
3. Quoted in Sir Robert Biddulph, *Lord Cardwell at the War Office* (1904), p. 40.
4. *Report of the Commission of Enquiry into the Supplies of the British Army in the Crimea* (1855), p. 3.
5. Quoted by Brian Bond, 'Prelude to the Cardwell Reforms', *Journal of the Royal United Service Institution* (1961), p. 233.
6. ibid., p. 235.

CHAPTER 13

1. Sir Robert Biddulph, *Lord Cardwell at the War Office* (1904), p. 162.
2. ibid., p. 116.
3. ibid.
4. Lieutenant-Colonel H. de Wattville, *Lord Roberts* (1938), p. 85.
5. ibid., pp. 107–8.

CHAPTER 14

1. Quoted in E. M. Llyod, *op. cit.*, p. 270.
2. J. F. C. Fuller, *The Conduct of War* (1961), pp. 121–2.
3. ibid., p. 127.
4. Brian Bond, 'The Retirement of the Duke of Cambridge', *Journal of the Royal United Service Institution* (1961), p. 544.

5. Hartington Commission Interim Report.

6. Hartington Commission Report (Cd 5979 of 1890).

7. Fuller, *Decisive Battles*, vol. III, p. 139.

8. Sir Philip Magnus, *Kitchener: Portrait of an Imperialist* (1958). pp. 171–2.

9. *Report of His Majesty's Commissioners on the War in South Africa* (1903), p. 4.

10. ibid., p. 22.

11. ibid., p. 23.

12. ibid., p. 53.

13. ibid., p. 43.

14. ibid., pp. 44–5.

15. ibid., p. 46.

16. ibid., p. 53.

17. Akers-Douglas Committee Report, p. 2.

18. ibid., p. 21.

19. ibid., p. 29.

20. ibid., p. 29.

21. ibid., p. 30.

22. ibid., p. 2.

23. Lord Stanley's Committee Report (1903), p. 11.

CHAPTER 15

1. J. K. Dunlop, *The Development of the British Army 1899–1914* (1938), Appendix A, p. 307.

2. ibid., p. 132.

3. Esher Committee Report (1904), Part 1, p. 1.

4. Dunlop, *op. cit.*, p. 215.

5. ibid., p. 180.

6. Esher Committee Report, Part I, p. 25.

7. ibid.

8. ibid., p. 9.

9. Dunlop, *op. cit.*, p. 324.

10. ibid., p. 248.

11. ibid., p. 243.

12. ibid., p. 279.

13. ibid.

14. ibid., p. 226.

15. I. S. Bloch, *Is War Impossible?* (1899), quoted in Fuller, *The Conduct of War*, p. 130.

CHAPTER 16

1. See Sir James Edmonds, *History of the Great War: Military Operations, France and Belgium Winter 1914–15* (1922–47), Chapter III for recruitment and munitions crisis.

2. ibid., p. 61.

3. ibid., *Sir Douglas Haig's Command to the 1st July*, Chapters IV, V and VI for the expansion and organization of the B.E.F. and all its services.

4. ibid., 1916 vol., pp. 116–17.

5. Robert Blake (ed.), *The Private Papers of Sir Douglas Haig* (1952), p. 137.
6. John Terraine (ed.), *General Jack's Diary* (1964), p. 138.
7. Quoted in A. H. Farrar-Hockley, *The Somme* (1964), p. 500.
8. John Terraine, *Douglas Haig: the Educated Soldier* (1963), p. 224.
9. Ludendorff, *My War Memoirs, 1914–1918* (1919), vol. I.
10. David Lloyd George, *War Memoirs* (n.d.), vol. II, p. 1293.
11. Edmonds, *op. cit.*, *March-April: Continuation of the German Offensives*, Appendix 10, p. 512.
12. John Terraine (ed.), *General Jack's Diary*, p. 297.

CHAPTER 18

1. J. R. M. Butler, *History of the Second World War: Grand Strategy* (1957), vol. II, pp. 293–4.

CHAPTER 19

1. *Report by the Supreme Commander to the Combined Chiefs of Staff on the Operations in Europe of the Allied Expeditionary Force* (1946), p. 38.
2. Field-Marshal Sir William Slim (now Lord Slim), *Defeat into Victory* (1956), p. 521.
3. Admiral the Viscount Mountbatten (now Admiral of the Fleet Earl Mountbatten of Burma) 'The Strategy of the South-East Asia Campaign', *Journal of the Royal United Service Institution*, November 1946, p. 481.

BIBLIOGRAPHY

André, L., *Michel le Tellier et Louvois*, 2nd edn (Paris: Felix Alcan, 1943).

Andrzejewski, Stanislaw, *Military Organization and Society* (London: Routledge & Kegan Paul, 1957).

Anon, *The Indian Army: A Sketch of its History and Organization* (Oxford: Clarendon Press, 1907).

   The Story of the RASC 1939–1945 (London: Bell, 1955).

Atkinson, C. T., *Marlborough and the Rise of the British Army* (London: Putnam, 1930).

Baring Pemberton, W., *Battles of the Crimean War* (London: Batsford, 1962).

Barker, A.J., *The March on Delhi* (London: Faber & Faber, 1963).

   Suez: The Seven-Day War (London: Faber & Faber, 1964).

Barnett, Correlli, *The Desert Generals* (London: William Kimber, 1960).

   'The Education of Military Elites', *Journal of Contemporary History*, vol. 2, No. 3, p. 15. Reprinted in Rupert Wilkinson (ed.), *Governing Elites* (New York: O.U.P.).

Beller, E.A., 'The Military Expedition of Sir Charles Morgan to Germany 1627–9', *English Historical Review*, vol. 43, 1928.

Biddulph, Sir Robert, *Lord Cardwell at the War Office* (London: John Murray, 1904).

Blake, Robert (ed.), *The Private Papers of Sir Douglas Haig 1914–1919* (London Eyre & Spottisoode, 1952).

Bond, Brian, 'Prelude to the Cardwell Reforms', *Journal of the Royal United Service Institution*, 1961, p. 233.

   'The Retirement of the Duke of Cambridge', *Journal of the Royal United Service Institution*, 1961, p. 544.

   (ed.), *Victorian Military Campaigns* (London: Hutchinson, 1967).

Bonham-Carter, Victor, *Soldier True: The Life and Times of Field-Marshal Sir William Robertson 1860–1933* (London: Muller, 1963).

Boynton, Lindsay, 'Billeting: the example of the Isle of Wight', *English Historical Review*, vol. 74, 1959.

   The Elizabethan Militia 1558–1638 (London: Routledge & Kegan Paul, 1967).

   'Martial Law and the Petition of Right', *English Historical Review*, vol. 79, 1964.

Bryant, Sir Arthur, *The Turn of the Tide* (London: Collins, 1957).

Burne, A. H., *The Noble Duke of York* (London: Staples Press, 1949).

    and Young, P., *The Great Civil War* (London: Eyre & Spottiswoode, 1959).

Butler, J.R.M., *History of the Second World War: Grand Strategy* (London: H.M.S.O., 1957).

Carlyle, Thomas, *The Letters and Speeches of Oliver Cromwell* (London: Metheun, 1904), volume cited.

Carsten, F.L., *Princes and Parliaments in Germany* (Oxford: O.U.P., 1900).

Castellan, Georges, *Histoire de l'Armée* (Paris: Presses Universitaires de France, 1948).

Clark, Sir George, *War and Society in the Seventeenth Century* (Cambridge: C.U.P., 1958).

Connell, John, *Auchinleck* (London: Cassell, 1959).

    Wavell: Soldier and Scholar (London: Collins, 1964).

Contamine, Henri, *La Revanche, 1871–1914* (Paris: Berger-Levrault, 1957).

Cooper, J.P., 'Differences between English and Continental Governments in the Early Seventeenth Century' in Bromley and Kossman (eds), *Britain and the Netherlands* (London: Chatto & Windus, 1960).

Corbett, Julian, *England in the Seven Years' War* (London: Longmans Green, 1918).

Craig, Gordon, *The Politics of the Prussian Army 1640–1945* (New York: O.U.P., 1964).

Crew, F.A.E. (ed.), *United Kingdom Medical Series, History of the Second World War*, 'Army Medical Services (Administration)', vol. 1 (London: H.M.S.O., 1953).

Cruikshank, C.G., *Elizabeth's Army*, 2nd edn (Oxford: Clarendon Press, 1966).

Davies, Godfrey, 'The Army of the Eastern Association 1644–45', *English Historical Review*, vol. 46, 1931, pp. 88–96

    'The Parliamentary Army under the Earl of Essex', *English Historical Review*, vol. 49, 1934, pp. 32–54.

    The Restoration of Charles II (Oxford: O.U.P., 1955).

Demeter, Karl, *The German Officer Corps in Society and State 1650–1945* (London: Weidenfeld & Nicolson, 1965).

de Gaulle, Charles, *La France et Son Armée* (Paris: Berger-Levrault, 1945).

de la Gorce, Paul-Marie, *La République et Son Armée* (Paris: Fayard, 1963).

de Verneuil, R. Quarré, *L'Armée en France depuis Charles VII jusqu'a la Révolution (1439–1789)* (Paris: Librairie militaire de J. Dumaine, 1880).

Dunlop, J.K., *The Development of the British Army 1899–1914* (London: Metheun, 1938).

Earle, Edward Meade (ed.), *Makers of Modern Strategy* (Princeton, N.J.: Princeton University Press, 1966).

Edmonds, Sir J.E., *History of the Great War: Military Operations, France and Belgium*, 14 vols (London: Macmillan, 1922–47), volumes cited.

Elton, G.R., *England Under the Tudors* (London: Metheun, 1965).

Ensor, R.C.K., *England 1870–1914* (Oxford: Clarendon Press, 1966).

Farrar-Hockley, A.H., *The Somme* (London: Batsford, 1964).

Fernyhough, Brigadier A.H., and Major H.E.D. Harris, *History of the RASC 1920–1945* (Royal Army Ordnance Corps, n.d.).

Firth, C.H., *Cromwell's Army* (London: Metheun, 1962).

Bibliography

Fortescue, John, *A History of the British Army*, 7 vols (London: Macmillan, 1899–1912), volumes cited.

Fuller, J.F.C., *The Conduct of War* (London: Eyre & Spottiswoode, 1961).
   The Decisive Battles of the Western World, 3 vols (London: Eyre & Spottiswoode, 1963), volumes cited.
   Sir John Moore's System of Training (London: Hutchinson, 1925).

Gardiner, S.R., *The Constitutional Documents of the Puritan Revolution* (Oxford: Clarendon Press, 1906).

Girardet, Raoul, *La Société Militaire dans la France Contemporaine* (Paris: Plon, 1953).

Glover, Michael, *Wellington's Peninsular Victories* (London: B.T. Batsford, 1963).

Glover, Richard, *Peninsular Preparation: The Reform of the British Army 1795–1809* (Cambridge: C.U.P., 1963).

Godwin-Austen, A.R., *The Staff and the Staff College* (London: Constable, 1927).

Gordon, Donald C., *The Dominion Partnership in Imperial Defence 1870–1914* (Baltimore, Md: Johns Hopkins University Press, 1965).

Guedalla, Philip, *The Duke* (London: Hodder & Stoughton, 1946).

Guibert, *Oeuvres Militaires* (Paris: 1803).

Hay, George Jackson, *The Constitutional Force: an epitomized History of the Militia* (London: United Services Gazette, n.d.).

Hibbert, Christopher, *Corunna* (London: Batsford, 1961).
   The Destruction of Lord Raglan (London: Longmans, 1961).

Howard, Michael, *The Franco-Prussian War* (London: Rupert Hart-Davis, 1963).
   (ed.), *Soldiers and Government* (London: Eyre & Spottiswoode, 1957).

H.M.S.O., *Report of the Royal Commissioners Appointed to Enquire Into the Civil and Professional Administration of the Naval and Military Departments and the Relation of those Departments to Each Other and to the Treasury*, 1890 (Hartington Commission).
   Report of His Majesty's Commissioners on the War in South Africa, 1902.
   Report of the Committee appointed to Consider the Education and Training of the the Officers of the Army, 1902.
   Report of the Committee Appointed by the Secretary of State for War to Enquire into the Nature of Expenses Incurred by Officers of the Army and to Suggest Measures for Bringing Commissions within reach of Men of Moderate Means, 1903 (Lord Stanley's Committee).
   Report of the Commission of Enquiry into the Supplies of the British Army in the Crimea, 1855.
   Report of the War Office (Reconstitution) Committee (Esher Committee) Parts I, II and III, 1904.

Janowitz, Morris, *The Professional Soldier: A Social and Political Portrait* (London: Collier-Macmillan, 1964).

Jarvis, Rupert C., 'Army Transport and the English Constitution; with special reference to the Jacobite Risings', *Journal of Transport History*, vol. 11, No. 2, 1955.

Joslen, H.F., *Orders of Battle, Volume 2: United Kingdom and Colonial Formations and Units in the Second World War* (London: H.M.S.O., 1960).

Kitchen, Martin, *The German Officer Corps 1890–1914* (Oxford: Clarendon Press, 1968).

Lehmann, Joseph H., *All Sir Garnet – A Life of Field Marshal-Lord Wolseley* (London: Jonathan Cape, 1964).

Lewis, Michael, *The History of the British Navy* (London: Allen & Unwin, 1959).

Liddell Hart, B. H., *The Real War 1914–18* (New York: Little, Brown, 1930).
 Memoirs, 2 vols (London: Cassell, 1965–6).
 The Tanks, 2 vols (London: Cassell, 1959).

Lloyd, E. M., *A Review of the History of Infantry* (London: Longmans, 1908).

Lloyd George, David, *War Memoirs*, 2 vols (London: Odhams, n.d.).

Ludendorff, F. W. E., *My War Memoirs, 1914–1918* (London: Hutchinson, 1919).

Luvaas, Jay, *The Education of an Army: British Military Thought 1815–1940* (London: Cassell, 1965).

McGuffie, T. H., (ed.) *Rank and File* (London: Hutchinson, 1964).

MacMunn, A. C., *The Armies of India* (London: Adams & Charles Black, 1911).

Magnus, Sir Philip, *Kitchener: Portrait of an Imperialist* (London: John Murray, 1958).

Mattingly, Garrett, *The Defeat of the Spanish Armada* (London: Jonathan Cape, 1959).

Millis, Walter, *Armies and Men* (London: Jonathan Cape, 1958).

Montgomery of Alamein, Field-Marshal the Viscount, *Memoirs* (London: Collins, 1958).

Nalder, Major-General R. H. F., *The Royal Corps of Signals* (Royal Signals Institution, 1958).

Neale, H. E., 'Elizabeth and the Netherlands 1586–7', *English Historical Review*, vol. xlv, 1930.

Nef, John U., *War and Human Progress* (London: Routledge & Kegan Paul, 1950).

Ogg, David, *England in the Reigns of James II and William III* (Oxford: Clarendon Press, 1955).

Oman, Charles, *A History of War in the Sixteenth Century* (London: Methuen, 1937).
 Wellington's Army (London: Arnold, 1912).

Pakenham-Walsh, Major-General R. P., *The History of Royal Engineers*, vol. 8 (Chatham: Institution of Royal Engineers, 1958).

Peterson, Harold L., *The Book of the Gun* (London: Paul Hamlyn, 1966).

Phillips, Thomas R. (ed.), *Roots of Strategy* (London: The Bodley Head, 1943).

Portway, Donald, *Science and Mechanization in Land Warfare* (Cambridge: Heffer, 1938).

Rhodes-Wood, Major E. H., *A War History of the Royal Pioneer Corps 1939–1945* (Aldershot: Gale & Polden, 1960).

Richmond, Admiral Sir Herbert, *Statesman and Seapower* (Oxford: Clarendon Press, 1947).

Roberts, M., *The Military Revolution* (Belfast: Belfast University Press, 1956).

Robertson, Sir Charles Grant, *Select Statutes, Cases and Documents* (London: Methuen, 1942).

Rosinski, Herbert, *The German Army* (London: Pall Mall Press, 1966).

Savory, Sir Reginald, *His Britannic Majesty's Army in Germany During the Seven Years' War* (Oxford: Clarendon Press, 1966).

Bibliography

Scott, Sir Sibbald, *The British Army, Its Origins, Progress and Equipment*, 3 vols (London: Cassell, Petter, Galpin, 1868).

Scouller, Major R. E., *The Armies of Queen Anne* (Oxford: Clarendon Press, 1966).

Singh, Brigadier Rajendra, *History of the Indian Army* (Delhi: Sardar Attar Singh Army Educational Stores, 1963).

Slim, Field-Marshal Sir William, *Defeat into Victory* (London: Cassell, 1956).

Smyth, Sir John, *Sandhurst: The History of the Royal Military Academy, Woolwich, the Royal Military College, Sandhurst, and the Royal Military Academy, Sandhurst, 1741–1961* (London: Weidenfeld & Nicolson, 1961).

Solt, L. F., *Saints in Arms: Puritanism and Democracy in Cromwell's Army* (Oxford: O.U.P., 1959).

Terraine, John, *Douglas Haig: the Educated Soldier* (London: Hutchinson, 1963).
    (ed.) *General Jack's Diary* (London: Eyre & Spottiswoode, 1964).

Thomas, Hugh, *The Story of Sandhurst* (London: Hutchinson, 1961).

Thomson, Gladys Scott, *Lords Lieutenants in the Sixteenth Century* (London: Longmans, 1923).

Trevelyan, G. M., *History of England* (London: Longmans, 1945).

Walton, Colonel Clifford, *History of the British Standing Army, A.D. 1660 to 1700* (London: Harrison, 1894).

Ward, S. G. P., *Wellington's Headquarters: A Study of the Administrative Problems in the Peninsula 1809–1814* (Oxford: O.U.P., 1957).

Watson, Steven, *The Reign of George III, 1760–1815* (Oxford: O.U.P., 1960).

Watteville, Lieutenant-Colonel H. de, *Lord Roberts* (Glasgow: Blackie, 1938).

Western, J. R., *The English Militia in the Eighteenth Century* (London: Routledge & Kegan Paul, 1965).

Whitworth, Rex, *Field-Marshal Lord Ligonier: A Story of the British Army 1702–1770* (Oxford: Clarendon Press, 1958).

Woodward, Sir Llewellyn, *The Age of Reform 1815–1870* (Oxford: Clarendon Press, 1962.)

Woolrych, Austin, *Battles of the English Civil War* (London: Pan, 1961).

Young, Lieutenant-Colonel F. W., *The Story of the Staff College* (Camberley: The Staff College, 1958).

INDEX

Aachen, 461

Abercromby, General James, 202, 203, 204

Abercromby, Sir Ralph, 249

Aboukir, battle of (1801), 249

Aboukir Bay, 247

Abyssinia, 315, 414, 434, 436

Acadia (Nova Scotia), 194

Addington, Henry, 250

Addiscombe, 276

Aden, 292, 481

Adjutant-General, office of, 240, 242, 260, 336, 360

Admiralty, 133, 198, 222, 334, 442, 491

Afghanistan, 275, 277, 283, 316, 317, 447

Africa, 413, 434–6, 481, 485
    See also East Africa, etc.

Afrika Korps, 451

Aghrim, battle of (1691), 150

Agincourt, battle of, 3, 5, 12

Air Ministry, 442, 491

Airborne Division (British)
    1st, 461
    6th, 457

Aisne, River, 376, 407, 431

Aix-la-Chapelle, Peace of (1748), 195

Akers-Douglas Committee, 343, 344

Alam Halfa, battle of (1942), 451

Alamein,
    Auchinleck's victory at First Battle of, 450
    Montgomery's victory at Second Battle of, 451–2, 469

Albania, 437

Albany, 220, 221

Albemarle, Duke of (George Monck), 64, 104, 105, 109, 110, 111, 115, 133
    pacifies Highlands, 104
    restores Charles II, 109–10

Albert, Archduke, 54, 55

Albuera, battle of (1811), 242

Aldershot, 314, 356, 358, 364

Aleppo, 408

Alexander, General Sir Harold (later Field-Marshal Earl Alexander of Tunis), 445, 447, 453, 454, 474
    courageous retreat of from Burma, 447
    victory of at Tunis, 453
    dogged campaign of in Italy, 454

Alexandria, 321

Algeria, 290, 452

Aliwal, battle of (1846), 277

Alleghenies, 195

Allenby, General Edmund (later Viscount), 374, 408

Alma, battle of (1854), 290

Almanza, battle of (1708), 148

Alsace, 155

Alva, Duke of, 101

Amherst, General Jeffrey (later Lord), 177, 186, 202, 204, 206, 207, 210, 214, 218, 237, 239
    given command of Louisbourg expedition, 202
    Commander-in-Chief, America, 206
    organizer and tactician, 206
    takes Montreal, 210

Amiens, 406
    Peace of (1802), 250, 251

Anhalt-Dessau, Prince Leopold of, 157

Anne, Queen, 122, 125, 135, 144, 147, 148, 165, 172, 175, 196, 238

Anton, James, 242

Antwerp, 53, 298, 429

Anzio, 454

Arabi Pasha, 321, 322

Arabia, 275

Arabs, 304

Arctic, 494

Ardennes, 373, 429

Ardres, Peace of (1546), 15

Armada, Spanish (1588), 28, 29, 30, 31, 35, 52

Armoured Divisions (British)
    1st, 469
    7th, 436, 469

507

Index

MORE ABOUT PENGUINS
AND PELICANS

Penguinews, which appears every month, contains details of all the new books issued by Penguins as they are published. From time to time it is supplemented by *Penguins in Print*, which is a complete list of all available books published by Penguins. (There are well over four thousand of these.)

A specimen copy of *Penguinews* will be sent to you free on request. For a year's issues (including the complete lists) please send 30p if you live in the United Kingdom, or 60p if you live elsewhere. Just write to Dept EP, Penguin Books Ltd, Harmondsworth, Middlesex, enclosing a cheque or postal order, and your name will be added to the mailing list.

Note: *Penguinews and Penguins in Print* are not available in the U.S.A. or Canada

WEAPONS AND TACTICS

Tom Wintringham and J. N. Blashford-Snell

Tom Wintringham's ideas (formulated during the Spanish Civil War) for training the Home Guard in street-fighting and guerrilla tactics certainly influenced Orde Wingate and helped to shape the army's Battle Schools.

In *Weapons and Tactics* this semi-legendary soldier, recommending theory as the soul of practice, provided a popular history of the development of warfare on land, with its alternating phases of armoured and unarmoured dominance. His account of sword, bow, halberd and pike, of arquebus, musket, bombard, cannon and rifle, of phalanx, legion, regiment and division makes an intriguing and logical tale of the development of fighting from Alexander the Great to Montgomery and of the effects of social and scientific advances on war.

But all that, we uneasily feel, belongs to the past. Hence John Blashford-Snell (himself something of a legend as soldier and explorer) has brought Wintringham's study up to the present. And the second half of this Pelican introduces the frightening possibilities, the blessed limitations and the latest thinking in this age of 'ABC' – atomic, biological and chemical warfare.

PELICAN BIOGRAPHIES

GOD'S ENGLISHMAN
Oliver Cromwell and the English Revolution

Christopher Hill

Cromwell told the Barebones Parliament that 'indeed there are histories that do give you narratives' but went on to declare that what mattered was those things wherein the life and power of them lay.

This is not conventional biography, but a number of brilliant interpretative essays, analysing the forces which Cromwell helped to create, and which created him.

'Undoubtedly this is the most intelligent summation we have on Cromwell, and it is written with the grace and power we have come to expect from Dr Hill' – J. P. Kenyon in the *Observer*.

'A humane and imaginative book by a historian writing at the peak of his powers, coping from long experience with the difficulties of a hectic age – Ivan Roots in the *Daily Telegraph*.

'*God's Englishman* is a very fine book' – J. H. Plumb in the *Guardian*.

PELICAN BIOGRAPHIES

NAPOLEON

Vincent Cronin

'As an explanation of the past in personal terms, this is probably the best life of Napoleon we have. . . . It was high time that a skilful writer came to grips with this classical figure of the great man, and it is satisfactory to see how Mr Cronin has seized the opportunity to write an excellent book' – *Economist*.

'Mr Cronin is not only very calm and cool, he is lucid, writes plainly and well, and organizes his huge amount of raw material capably. . . . A book of great interest' – Nigel Dennis in the *Sunday Telegraph*.

'His book must be pressed upon the general reader: it is so lively and so well-written. . . . Like his study of Louis XIV, this book (which has been carefully produced) is absorbing throughout' – Raymond Mortimer in the *Sunday Times*.

'To present Napoleon plausibly as the classical hero of his own imagining takes nerve, originality, prodigious powers of research and a true historical imagination. Vincent Cronin displays all these qualities' – Michael Foot in the *Evening Standard*.

NOT FOR SALE IN THE U.S.A.

BRITAIN IN THE CENTURY OF TOTAL WAR
War, Peace and Social Change 1900–1967

Arthur Marwick

Can war be regarded as a positive instrument of social progress? Does the stagnation and disenchantment of recent years call for the stimulus of a 'moral equivalent to war'? In examining the social history of Britain between the years 1900 and 1967, Arthur Marwick discusses the major factors which have contributed to our modern technological society, and explains the four 'modes' in which the two World Wars have shaken the traditional 'gradualness' of British history. He goes on to consider the interplay between Britain's declining world role and her domestic consciousness, weaving the major changes in morals, fashion and the arts into his overall pattern.

'A valuable and constructive analysis which brings sense into recent British history' – *Listener*.

'A fascinating and, in parts, highly controversial work, which is at the same time an admirable synthesis of the present state of historical knowledge' – *Spectator*.

THE CONTINENTAL COMMITMENT:
The Dilemma of British Defence Policy
in the Era of Two World Wars

Michael Howard

'Mr Howard has taken the threads of imperial defence, home defence and power, traced them through two world wars of this century, and eventually woven them into a tapestry which depicts the gradual shift of British defence policy from the high noon of Empire to the continental commitment . . . the result is infinitely more rewarding than ambitious undertakings by less perceptive observers of the military scene' – Alun Chalfont in the *Sunday Times*.

'Essential background reading. This is a deeply instructive book, short, learned and easy to read, because Mr Howard is a model of the teaching writer: mild, clear, just and explicit in his values' – Elizabeth Young in the *Listener*.

'Admirable . . . he presents the broad lines of British policy with the sure grasp of a first-rate military historian' – A. J. P. Taylor in the *Observer*.

TOTAL WAR:

Causes and Courses of the Second World War

Peter Calvocoressi and Guy Wint

Total War was designed by its authors to show a rising generation why the Second World War happened and how it went. In this bold feat of compression they give us much stress and space to political, social and moral forces (not to mention intelligence and other activities 'behind the lines') as to the ensuing clashes of arms.

Here is a sample of what critics have said of the book:

'The best single-volume history in English of the struggle' – *Economist*.

'Can hardly be regarded as less than the best one-volume history of the Second World War so far' – *The Times Educational Supplement*.

'In generally short, vigorous sentences they survey with marked objectivity the political, military, economic and personal factors leading up to and operating during hostilities' – *New Statesman*.

'They have written what must rank as the best historical work on (the war) published to date' – *Financial Times*.

NOT FOR SALE IN THE U.S.A.